11th Workshop on Argument Mining (ArgMining 2024)

Bangkok, Thailand
15 August 2024

ISBN: 979-8-3313-0156-9

Printed from e-media with permission by:

Curran Associates, Inc.
57 Morehouse Lane
Red Hook, NY 12571

Some format issues inherent in the e-media version may also appear in this print version.

Printed with permission by Curran Associates, Inc. (2025)

For permission requests, please contact the Association for Computational Linguistics at the address below.

Association for Computational Linguistics
209 N. Eighth Street
Stroudsburg, Pennsylvania 18360

Phone: 1-570-476-8006
Fax: 1-570-476-0860

acl@aclweb.org

Additional copies of this publication are available from:

Curran Associates, Inc.
57 Morehouse Lane
Red Hook, NY 12571 USA
Phone: 845-758-0400
Fax: 845-758-2633
Email: curran@proceedings.com
Web: www.proceedings.com

ArgMining 2024

The 11th Workshop on Argument Mining

Proceedings of the Workshop

August 15, 2024

Introduction

Argument Mining ("argumentation mining") is an emerging research area within computational linguistics. It initially focused on automatically identifying and classifying argument elements across various text genres. In the recent years, the field has expanded to explore argument quality and synthesis on multiple levels. This growth has led to the development of practical applications such as argument-focused search and debating technologies, exemplified by IBM Project Debater. The increasing interest in computational argumentation has resulted in the organization of several tutorials at major NLP conferences, providing a wealth of knowledge and insights to the community.

While basic tasks such as argument element segmentation and classification are maturing, many current and emerging tasks in diverse genres and topics still need to be solved amidst global polarization and the emergence of large language models.

The ArgMining community is constantly growing, as demonstrated by the increasing number of submissions on argument mining being accepted at top-level international conferences in NLP and AI. This year's 11th edition of the workshop allowed the submission of long, short, and demo papers for the main workshop track. Also, ArgMining2024 hosted two shared tasks as part of the workshop: The Perspective Argument Retrieval Shared Task and DialAM-2024: The First Shared Task on Dialogical Argument Mining. We had 28 valid paper submissions; 16 were for the main workshop (13 long, 3 short), and 12 were for the two shared tasks (5 short and 1 overview long paper for each). The submissions came from institutions in 11 countries. For the main workshop, we accepted 6 long papers and 1 short paper (44% acceptance rate compared to 41% for last year's ArgMining 2023). All accepted papers are included in the proceedings.

The one-day workshop had a hybrid format. Yufang Hou from IBM Research Europe presented a keynote on "Reconstructing Fallacies in Misrepresented Science and Argument Mining in the Wild". Also, following the steps of the previous ArgMining workshops, we hosted a panel of distinguished researchers: Joonsuk Park (University of Richmond), Iryna Gurevych (Technical University of Darmstadt), Daniel Hershcovich (University of Copenhagen), Lucie Flek (University of Bonn), and Johannes Kiesel (Bauhaus-Universität, Weimar). The panel was moderated by Henning Wachsmuth (Leibniz Universität Hannover) on the topic "The Human in Computational Argumentation", covering personalization, subjectivity, and perspectivism.

We thank our Program Committee members for their continuous support and helpful input. Also, we thank IBM for sponsoring the Best Paper award and the members of our Best Paper Selection Committee: Benno Stein (Bauhaus-Universität, Weimar), Gabriella Lapesa (GESIS and Heinrich-Heine University Dusseldorf), and Eduardo Blanco (University of Arizona). The awards are announced on the official workshop website: https://argmining-org.github.io/2024/index.html.

We would like to also thank everyone who showed interest and submitted a paper this year, all of the authors for their contributions, and all the attendees of the workshop for their support and participation.

Yamen Ajjour, Roy Bar-Haim, Roxanne El Baff, Zhexiong Liu, and Gabriella Skitalinskaya
(ArgMining 2024 Co-Chairs)

Organizing Committee

Organizing Committee

Yamen Ajjour, Leibniz Universität Hannover
Roy Bar-Haim, IBM Research AI
Roxanne El Baff, German Aerospace Center and Bauhaus-Universität, Weimar
Zhexiong Liu, University of Pittsburgh
Gabriella Skitalinskaya, Leibniz Universität Hannover

Program Committee

Program Committee

Rodrigo Agerri, University of the Basque Country
Tariq Alhindi, Noetica AI
Emily Allaway, Columbia University
Laura Alonso Alemany, Universidad Nacional de Córdoba
Milad Alshomary, Columbia University
Özkan Aslan, Afyon Kocatepe University
Marie Bexte, Fernuniversität Gesamthochschule Hagen
Miriam Butt, Universität Konstanz
Elena Cabrio, Université Côte d'Azur
Chung-Chi Chen, AIST, National Institute of Advanced Industrial Science and Technology
Elena Chistova, Federal Research Center Computer Science and Control, RAS
Greta Damo, Université Côte d'Azur
Johannes Daxenberger, summetix GmbH
Neele Falk, University of Stuttgart
Jia Guo, National University of Singapore
Shohreh Haddadan, Moffitt Cancer Research center
Annette Hautli-Janisz, Universität Passau
Philipp Heinisch, Universität Bielefeld
Daniel Hershcovich, University of Copenhagen
Andrea Horbach, Universität Hildesheim
Xinyu Hua, Bloomberg
Omid Kashefi, Educational Testing Service
Khalid Al Khatib, University of Groningen
Christopher Klamm, Universität Mannheim
John Lawrence, University of Dundee
Boyang Liu, University of Manchester
Ziqian Luo, Oracle
Joonsuk Park, University of Richmond
Simon Parsons, University of Lincoln
Olesya Razuvayevskaya, University of Sheffield
Chris Reed, University of Dundee
Myrthe Reuver, Vrije Universiteit Amsterdam
Julia Romberg, GESIS Leibniz Institute for the Social Sciences
Allen G Roush, Oracle
Ramon Ruiz-Dolz, University of Dundee
Florian Ruosch, University of Zurich
Sougata Saha, Mohamed bin Zayed University of Artificial Intelligence
Patrick Saint-Dizier, CNRS
Robin Schaefer, Universität Potsdam
Jodi Schneider, University of Illinois, Urbana Champaign
Lutz Schröder, Friedrich-Alexander Universität Erlangen-Nürnberg
Arushi Sharma, University of Pittsburgh
Manfred Stede, Universität Potsdam
Aswathy Velutharambath, University of Stuttgart
Henning Wachsmuth, Leibniz Universität Hannover
Vern R. Walker, Hofstra University

Ruifeng Xu, Harbin Institute of Technology
Xiutian Zhao, University of Edinburgh
Yang Zhong, University of Pittsburgh
Timon Ziegenbein, Leibniz Universität Hannover

Shared Task Organizers

Ramon Ruiz-Dolz, University of Dundee
John Lawrence, University of Dundee
Ella Schad, University of Dundee
Chris Reed, University of Dundee
Neele Falk, University of Stuttgart
Andreas Waldis, TU Darmstadt and Lucerne University of Applied Science and Arts
Gabriella Lapesa, GESIS and Heinrich-Heine University Düsseldorf
Iryna Gurevych, University of Darmstadt

Best Paper Committee

Benno Stein, Bauhaus-Universität, Weimar
Gabriella Lapesa, GESIS and Heinrich-Heine University Düsseldorf
Eduardo Blanco, University of Arizona

Keynote Talk

Reconstructing Fallacies in Misrepresented Science and Argument Mining in the Wild

Yufang Hou
IBM Research Europe - Ireland

Abstract: In this talk, Yufang Hou will discuss their recent work on applying and investigating language model (LM)-based argument mining technologies in real-world scenarios, including fact-checking misinformation that misrepresents scientific publications and tackling traditional argument mining tasks in various out-of-distribution (OOD) scenarios. First, she will discuss their work on reconstructing and grounding fallacies in misrepresented science, in which health-related misinformation claims often falsely cite a credible biomedical publication as evidence. The speaker will present a new argumentation theoretical model for fallacious reasoning, together with a new dataset for real-world misinformation detection that misrepresents biomedical publications. In the second part of the talk, she will discuss their findings on LMs' capabilities for three OOD scenarios (topic shift, domain shift, and language shift) across eleven argument mining tasks.

Bio: Yufang Hou is a research scientist at IBM Research Ireland. She is also a visiting professor and co-supervisor at UKP Lab - TU Darmstadt. Her research interests include referential discourse modelling, argument mining, and scholarly document processing. Yufang received WoC Technical Innovation in Industry Award in 2020. She has served in numerous roles for ACL conferences, recently as a Senior Area Chair for EMNLP 22/23/24, and NAACL 24. She co-organized the 8th workshop on Argument Mining, the first workshop on Argumentation Knowledge Graphs, Key Point Analysis Shared Task 2021, and Dagstuhl Seminar 22432 on "Towards a Unified Model of Scholarly Argumentation".

Panel

The Human in Computational Argumentation

Computational argumentation aims to develop methods for extracting, analyzing, and generating human arguments. This field holds significant promise for applications ranging from automated debate systems to advanced decision-support tools. Central to these advancements are language models, which are trained to simulate human language processing. However, a critical issue with language models is their tendency to inherit and propagate social and stereotypical biases present in their training data. Moreover, these models typically learn from aggregated absolute labels, which do not accurately reflect the nuanced spectrum or distribution of truth in argumentation. Additionally, computational argumentation tasks, such as assessing the persuasiveness of arguments, are inherently subjective and heavily influenced by the author and audience.

This panel session will discuss the role of the human in computational argumentation, exploring ways of creating more representative, fair, and effective computational models of argumentation that better capture the complexities of human discourse. The discussion will focus on two strategies of capturing human context, views, and preferences: perspectivism and personalization. While personalization aims at integrating information about the speaker and target audience (e.g., values and culture) in training or instructing language models, perspectivism aims at ensuring that the views captured by models are representative of the relevant social groups. The panel will look at the consequences, opportunities, and challenges of adapting perspectivism and personalization in computational argumentation.

Table of Contents

Program

Thursday, August 15, 2024

09:00 - 09:10 *Opening Remarks*

09:10 - 10:30 *Session 1*

Multi-Task Learning Improves Performance in Deep Argument Mining Models
Amirhossein Farzam, Shashank Shekhar, Isaac D. Mehlhaff and Marco Morucci

Computational Modelling of Undercuts in Real-world Arguments
Yuxiao Ye and Simone Teufel

Detecting Scientific Fraud Using Argument Mining
Gabriel Freedman and Francesca Toni

Exploiting Dialogue Acts and Context to Identify Argumentative Relations in Online Debates
Stefano Mezza, Wayne Wobcke and Alan Blair

ARIES: A General Benchmark for Argument Relation Identification
Debela Gemechu, Ramon Ruiz-Dolz and Chris Reed

10:30 - 11:00 *Coffee Break*

11:00 - 12:30 *Panel Session*

12:30 - 14:00 *Lunch Break*

14:00 - 14:30 *The Perspective Argument Retrieval Shared Task*

14:30 - 15:00 *DialAM-2024: The First Shared Task on Dialogical Argument Mining*

15:00 - 15:30 *Session 2*

MAMKit: A Comprehensive Multimodal Argument Mining Toolkit
Eleonora Mancini, Federico Ruggeri, Stefano Colamonaco, Andrea Zecca, Samuele Marro and Paolo Torroni

Thursday, August 15, 2024 (continued)

	DeepCT-enhanced Lexical Argument Retrieval Alexander Bondarenko, Maik Fröbe, Danik Hollatz, Jan Heinrich Merker and Matthias Hagen
15:30 - 16:00	*Coffee Break*
16:00 - 17:00	*Keynote Speech*
17:00 - 17:40	*Poster Session (Shared Task Papers + Main Workshop Papers)*
17:40 - 17:55	*Closing Remarks + Best Paper Award*

ARIES: A General Benchmark for Argument Relation Identification

Debela Gemechu, Ramon Ruiz-Dolz and Chris Reed
Centre for Argument Technology (ARG-tech)
University of Dundee
Dundee DD1 4HN, United Kingdom

Abstract

Measuring advances in argument mining is one of the main challenges in the area. Different theories of argument, heterogeneous annotations, and a varied set of argumentation domains make it difficult to contextualise and understand the results reported in different work from a general perspective. In this paper, we present ARIES, a general benchmark for Argument Relation Identification aimed at providing a standard evaluation for argument mining research. We evaluated three different architectures for Argument Relation Identification on ARIES: sequence and token modelling, and sequence-to-sequence alignment, together with the three main Transformer-based model architectures: encoder-only, decoder-only, and encoder-decoder. Furthermore, the benchmark consists of eight different argument mining datasets, covering the most common argumentation domains, and standardised with the same annotation structures. This paper provides a first comprehensive and comparative set of results in argument mining across a broad range of configurations to compare with, both advancing the state-of-the-art, and establishing a standard way to measure future advances in the area. Across varied task setups and architectures, our experiments reveal consistent challenges in cross-dataset evaluation, with notably poor results. Given the models' struggle to acquire transferable skills, the task remains challenging, opening avenues for future research.

1 Introduction

Argument mining was originally defined as the task of automatically identifying argument structures from unstructured natural language inputs (Mochales and Moens, 2011). Although argument mining research has been split into several subtasks in the literature such as segmentation, argument classification and argument relation identification (Lippi and Torroni, 2016; Lawrence and Reed, 2020) it is the latter that represents the main challenge in argument mining due to its complexity. Argument Relation Identification (ARI) starts from the point where all the relevant argument sequences have been segmented, and its main objective is to identify argumentative relations between them building complete argumentative structures. Therefore, it is the ARI subtask that provides us with the argument structures from unstructured natural language. In addition, while outstanding results have been reported in the previous stages, results on ARI are more limited, representing one of the most difficult tasks in natural language processing due to its implicitness, the lack of data, and the lack of solid baselines with which to compare.

One of the main challenges in the area of argument mining, however, has always been to compare advances in different contexts, understanding these contexts as different annotation theories or argumentative domains. Therefore, previous work reports different findings and advances, but it does that without providing a general picture of them and a comprehensive understanding of their findings for the argument mining community as a whole. A lack of a consistent cross-domain benchmark, as it has been done in many other areas of natural language processing (see GLUE (Wang et al., 2018), Superglue (Wang et al., 2019), TweetEval (Barbieri et al., 2020), or Superb (Yang et al., 2021) among others), hinders our advances as a research community. Although previous effort has been put in this direction, none of these previous work considers state-of-the-art NLP algorithms considering multiple language modelling approaches, and typically focused on specific tasks or domains (Cocarascu et al., 2020; Ruosch et al., 2022). Providing relevant results in the good direction, but limited in terms of generalisability. Therefore, the definition of a general benchmark for state-of-the-art argument mining is something that remains unaddressed. This limitation, taking the success of the GLUE benchmark for natural language under-

Proceedings of the 11th Workshop on Argument Mining, pages 1–14
August 15, 2024 ©2024 Association for Computational Linguistics

standing tasks (Wang et al., 2018) into account, motivates the development of an argument mining-specific benchmark to comprehensively evaluate and measure the advances done in the area.

In this paper, we present the Argument Relation Identification Evaluation Strategy (ARIES), a robust, cross-dataset benchmark for evaluating existing and future contributions to the ARI task. ARIES represents the first and most extensive benchmark to evaluate ARI systems, thus providing a robust framework for comparative evaluation of argument mining systems. Our main contribution is the formal definition of ARIES, including eight different corpora, three different natural language modelling approaches, and three different model architectures. Furthermore, we carried out extensive experimentation, implementing the previous natural language modelling approaches and model architectures with different pre-trained language models. From our results, we do not only advance the state-of-the-art in ARI, but also identify a concerning limitation of the generalisation capabilities of argument mining systems. This way, ARIES provides an ideal base on which to compare, propose, and implement argument mining systems addressing the ARI task.

2 Related Work

The latest advances in natural language processing have been reflected in argument mining and especially in ARI research, the most challenging part of it. These natural language processing advances have been gradually integrated into argument mining systems with (in order) the use of LSTM networks (Cocarascu and Toni, 2017), the Transformer architecture (Ruiz-Dolz et al., 2021a), contrastive learning (Shi et al., 2022), generative language models (Bao et al., 2022), end-to-end architectures (Morio et al., 2022), or the most recent large language models (LLMs) (Gorur et al., 2024). All these advances, however, are difficult to compare and contextualise due to a lack of a standardised set of evaluation baselines.

Some effort has been put with previous research on the definition of benchmarks for argument mining. Initially proposed in (Cabrio and Villata, 2014), the authors define NoDE, a natural language argument benchmark consisting of three datasets and 792 related proposition pairs. In this early benchmark, the authors pointed out the needs of standardising the evaluation of argument mining systems. Following this direction, Cocarascu et al. (2020) extended the previous benchmark with a total of ten datasets containing 35,918 related proposition pairs. Both benchmarks exclusively focused on the classification of argument relations, a subset of the ARI task in which the relation is assumed to be known, limiting their applicability in more general situations. Recently in (Ruosch et al., 2022), the authors address this limitation by proposing a benchmark for argument mining (BAM), in which all the argument mining subtasks are brought into consideration together. The BAM framework, however, is proposed as a pipeline-like method combining different previously existing argument mining systems to cover the complete argument mining process (Ruosch et al., 2023), rather than a thorough analysis of state-of-the-art NLP modelling techniques and architectures. Furthermore, its current version only contains argumentative information in scientific documents, making it a valuable resource for this domain but limiting its generalisability to other application domains.

3 Benchmark

The main contribution of this paper is the definition of ARIES, a state-of-the-art benchmark for argument relation identification in datasets of different domain and nature, which can be used as a reference to advance and to relativise the real impact of new findings in this area. Furthermore, ARIES also reflects on a wide variety of model architectures, providing more insight on the capabilities of state-of-the-art algorithms. This section provides an in-depth presentation of all the variables taken into account in the proposed ARIES benchmark.

3.1 Data

In order to develop a robust, challenging and wide-ranging assessment, we include eight different datasets as part of ARIES. These eight datasets were selected mostly based on two criteria. First, we selected the most representative datasets on the area of argument mining. This way, ARIES can be used as reference, not only for future contributions, but also for these ones already existing. Second, our selection was determined by our goal of creating a sufficiently heterogeneous dataset in terms of domain to be able to measure the robustness of state-of-the art systems. Therefore, ARIES consists of eight different argumentation domains. The eight datasets included into ARIES are: MTC (Peldszus and Stede, 2015), AAEC (Stab and Gurevych,

Dataset	Domain	Inferences	Conflicts	Neutral	Total
MTC	Structured Argumentation	272	108	713	1,093
AAEC	Essay	4,841	497	10,676	16,014
CDCP	Financial	694	82	1,552	2,328
ACSP	Scientific	8,069	697	17,532	26,298
AMP	Online	2,111*	-	5,929	8,040
AbstRCT	Medical	2,290	344	4,581	7,215
US2016	Political	2,765	866	7,262	10,893
QT30	Question Answering	2,714	545	6,518	9,777
Total	-	23,756	3,139	54,763	81,658

Table 1: Summary of the ARI datasets included in the ARIES benchmark. We use * to indicate that AMP involves only binary labels, indicating whether a relation is present or not.

2017), CDCP (Park and Cardie, 2018), ACSP (Lauscher et al., 2018), AMP (AMPERSAND) (Chakrabarty et al., 2019), AbstRCT (Mayer et al., 2020), US2016 (Visser et al., 2020), and QT30 (Hautli-Janisz et al., 2022). A summary of the most relevant features of these eight corpora is depicted in Table 1.

3.2 Task

The ARIES benchmark evaluates the ARI task. ARI consists of the identification of existing argumentative relations between two or more Argumentative Discourse Units (ADUs). This way, this task takes an unstructured set of ADUs as its input and outputs complete structured arguments, making it the cornerstone of argument mining. For practicalities, within the ARIES framework, we define the ARI task as a three-class classification problem, considering the Inference, Conflict, and Neutral classes of argumentative relations. The inference relation represents an argumentative support, the conflict relation represents an argumentative attack, and the neutral class indicates that there exists no argumentative relation between a set of ADUs. Some models distinguish a fourth category of rephrase because it has become increasingly clear in linguistic work (Koszowy et al., 2022) that this is relation is a key driver of argumentation. It is, however, far from ubiquitous in argument mining research, and so is not adopted in the current ARIES framework.

It is also important to emphasise that the ARIES benchmark goes one step further compared to the Argument Relation Classification (ARC) task, which only considers attacks and supports. While ARC can be framed as a sentiment analysis problem with positive and negative sentiments, and it is based on the assumption that the existing argument relations are all known, ARI does not make such assumption, and therefore modelling the underlying (and sometimes implicit) argumentative features of ADUs is essential if we want an algorithm to succeed on this task.

3.3 Models

We consider three different natural language modelling approaches in the ARIES benchmark: sequence classification (see Figure 1a), token classification (see Figure 1b), and sequence-to-sequence alignment (see Figure 1c). Complementing these modelling approaches, we have also included three different model architectures in our benchmark: encoder only, decoder only, and encoder-decoder. This way, we cover the majority of the existing approaches for argument mining in the literature.

3.3.1 Sequence Classification

First, our benchmark reports results when addressing ARI as a sequence (pair) classification task. This way, our sequence classification benchmark models the conditional probability of the most likely relation class (i.e., $\hat{s}$) for a given pair of ADUs as depicted in Equation 1.

$$\hat{s} = \arg\max_{s \in S} P(s|x_1^N, y_1^M) \quad (1)$$

where S stands for the complete set of possible argumentative relations (i.e., Inference, Conflict, or Neutral), x_1^N represents the first ADU of length N, and y_1^M is the second ADU of length M. With this framing, the two ADU inputs are treated as a whole sequence of text, modelling natural language at a higher level and looking for sequence features that can be helpful to determine whether a pair of propositions is related with an inference, a conflict, or presents no relation between them. This is one of the most widely researched approaches when it comes to the identification of argument relations (Cocarascu and Toni, 2017; Ruiz-Dolz et al., 2021a; Shi et al., 2022; Kikteva et al., 2023; Gorur et al., 2024).

The loss ($\mathcal{L}_{\text{class}}$) for the argument relation classification task is computed using the standard cross-entropy loss based on the predicted logits and true labels for the argument relation type.

$$\mathcal{L}_{\text{class}} = -\frac{1}{B}\sum_{i=1}^{B} \log(\text{softmax}(r_i^{pred})) \cdot r_i^{true} \quad (2)$$

where r_i^{true} represents the true label of the argument relation type for the i-th sample and r_i^{pred}

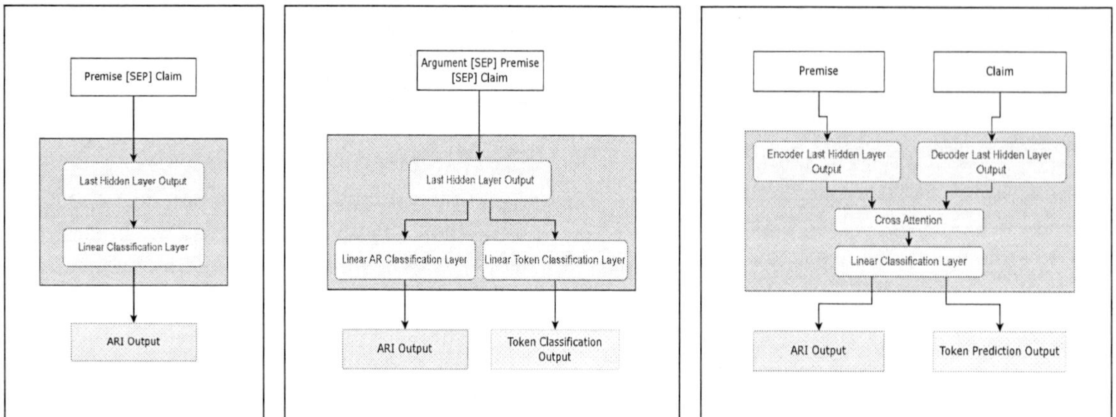

(a) Sequence classification. (b) Token classification. (c) Sequence-to-sequence alignment.

Figure 1: The architecture for the three tasks: (a) sequence classification, (b) token classification, and (c) sequence-to-sequence alignment. In this paper, we evaluate only the ARI output (highlighted in light blue), while the token classification and token prediction outputs (highlighted in light yellow) serve as auxiliary tasks and are not evaluated.

denotes the predicted logits of the argument relation type for the i-th sample.

3.3.2 Token Classification

Second, we also benchmark ARI as a token classification task, aiming to predict the span of conclusions given a premise or vice versa, while simultaneously predicting the argument relation between the premise and conclusion in a multi-task setup. Inspired by Eger et al. (2017), who modeled argument mining as a token classification task, jointly addressing component identification and relation identification, assigning each token a label indicating the category of the component and the argument relation type, our work acknowledges their finding of sub-optimal coupling between the two tasks and advocates for treating them separately while modelling them jointly. Consequently, we adopt a multi-task setting that independently models both tasks. The multi-task learning setup encompasses two primary objectives: span prediction and argument relation identification.

For the span prediction sub-task, given an argument (i.e., the complete structure resulting from the concatenation of the premises and conclusion), we model the boundaries of the conclusion within the argument given the premises and vice-versa (See Appendix A.2 for more details regarding the input format). Our token classification approach, therefore, first models the conditional probability of the most likely span boundaries (i.e., $\hat{t}$) as depicted in Equation 3.

$$\hat{t} = \arg\max_{t \in T} P(t | n_1, ..., n_{i-1}, n_i) \tag{3}$$

where T represents the set of possible token labels (i.e., beginning (B), inside (I), or outside (O)), and n_i represents each token at a given position i, followed by the previously observed tokens in the complete argument sequence. This approach treats tokens in a more independent way than in sequence classification, allowing to look for lower level features, where each token is assigned a specific label. The loss ($\mathcal{L}_s$) for the span prediction sub-task is computed using the standard cross-entropy loss based on the predicted and true labels for each token in the argument.

$$\mathcal{L}_{span} = -\frac{1}{N} \sum_{i=1}^{N} \sum_{j=1}^{C} Y_{p,ij}^{true} \cdot \log(Y_{p,ij}^{pred}) \tag{4}$$

where N represents the total number of tokens in the argument, C is the set of token labels, $Y_{p,ij}^{true}$ denotes the ground truth probability of token i belonging to class j, and $Y_{p,ij}^{pred}$ is the predicted probability of token i belonging to class j.

The second step in the token classification approach is the identification of argumentative relations. This second task involves predicting the argument relation between the premise and conclusion in a similar way as described in Equation 1. It takes both the premise and conclusion resulting from the previous span detection sub-task as inputs and predicts the argument relation. Since the primary focus is on ARI, the span detection serves as an auxiliary task. The loss from the token classification approach results from adding the previously defined span prediction loss $\mathcal{L}_{span}$ to the sequence classification loss $\mathcal{L}_{class}$ (see Equation 2), resulting in the overall loss ($\mathcal{L}_{total}$) as defined in Equation 5.

$$\mathcal{L}_{total} = \mathcal{L}_{span} + \mathcal{L}_{class} \tag{5}$$

3.3.3 Sequence-to-sequence Alignment

Finally, the third approach included in the ARIES benchmark corresponds to a sequence-to-sequence alignment modelling of the relation between argument proposition pairs. In this last approach, we address ARI in a similar way as machine translation is done, where the model is trained to predict a complete sequence related to the input (Stahlberg, 2020). Therefore, we consider the argument premise as the input and provide the argument claim as the expected output, modelling this way the semantic connections between both propositions resulting in the argumentative relation between premise and claim as depicted in Equation 6.

$$\hat{c}_1^N = \arg\max_{c_1^N} P(c_1^N | p_1^M) \tag{6}$$

Where c_1^N stands for the output claim sequence of length N, and p_1^M for the input premise sequence of length M. The sequence-to-sequence alignment approach is divided into two steps. First, we do the sequence-to-sequence modelling according to Equation 6 attempting to improve the embedding representation of our argumentative inputs (i.e., premise-claim pairs). Second, we leverage the embedding of the premise-claim representations to train a classifier that predicts our three relation classes in a similar way as described in Equation 1. Although less researched in the literature, sequence-to-sequence approaches have also been recently investigated in the area of argument mining thus making them an important addition to our global benchmark (Kawarada et al., 2024).

The loss ($\mathcal{L}_{\text{seq}}$) for the sequence-to-sequence alignment approach is computed using the standard cross-entropy loss based on the predicted logits and true labels for each token in the conclusion sequence.

$$\mathcal{L}_{\text{seq}} = -\frac{1}{B}\sum_{i=1}^{B}\sum_{j=1}^{N}\log(\text{softmax}(c_{ij}^{pred}))\cdot c_{ij}^{true} \tag{7}$$

Where B indicates the batch size, N is the length of the conclusion sequence, c_{ij}^{true} denotes the true label of the j-th token in the i-th sample, c_{ij}^{pred} represents the predicted logits of the j-th token in the i-th sample, and softmax$(\cdot)$ represents the output of the softmax function.

The loss ($\mathcal{L}_{\text{class}}$) for argument relation classification is computed using the same loss function as in the sequence classification approach defined in Equation 2. The overall loss ($\mathcal{L}$) is the sum of both losses:

$$\mathcal{L} = \mathcal{L}_{\text{seq}} + \mathcal{L}_{\text{class}} \tag{8}$$

This hybrid approach, combining sequence-to-sequence modelling with ARI, allows us to capture the relationship between the premise and conclusion while effectively predicting argument relation types.

3.3.4 Model Architectures

In addition to the three natural language modelling approaches, we have also included the three main model architectures in state-of-the-art natural language processing. This way, we consider encoder-only (Devlin et al., 2019), decoder-only (Brown et al., 2020), and encoder-decoder (Vaswani et al., 2017) architectures. For the first two natural language modelling approaches (i.e., sequence and token classification), the ARIES benchmark considers the three possible architectures. However, for the sequence-to-sequence alignment approach, we can only rely on the encoder-decoder architecture, given its nature requiring both encoder and decoder (see Appendix A.2 for more details).

4 Experiments

4.1 Experimental Setup

We use Adam optimisation (Kingma and Ba, 2014) to minimise the loss function, using a learning rate of 2×10^{-5} and categorical cross-entropy loss and a batch size of 16 (more details on the experimental setup is provided in Appendix A). The dataset is randomly partitioned, with 70%, 10%, and 20% allocation for training, validation, and testing respectively, ensuring uniformity throughout the dataset. Refer to Table 1 for the breakdown of argument relations. All our results represent the average of three runs using different random seeds. Precision, recall, and F1-score are computed, and macro-averaged F1-scores are reported for the test dataset. The code used

Task	Architecture	Model	Eval	Dataset							
				MTC	AAEC	CDCP	ACSP	AMP	AbstRCT	US2016	QT30
SeqCls	**ED**	**RoBERTa**	ID	63	75	**72**	82	**84***	**84**	76	83
			CD	35	47	40	**50**	51*	40	48	45
	DD	**DialoGPT**	ID	66	**78**	**72**	**84**	**84***	82	**79**	**85**
			CD	40	**48**	41	49	**52***	39	**49**	**49**
	ED-DD	**T5**	ID	65	74	71	83	80*	80	74	84
			CD	37	37	36	38	40*	37	38	39
TokCls	**ED**	**RoBERTa**	ID	61	76	68	80	-	81	73	82
			CD	33	42	31	37	-	33	37	35
	DD	**DialoGPT**	ID	63	77	70	82	-	80	75	82
			CD	34	42	33	39	-	35	38	37
	ED-DD	**T5**	ID	62	73	65	81	-	78	71	80
			CD	33	35	34	36	-	33	35	33
SeqAln	**ED-DD**	**T5**	ID	**68**	75	70	81	78*	83	76	83
			CD	**41**	42	**42**	42	46*	**41**	43	41

Table 2: In-dataset (ID) and cross-dataset (CD) macro-averaged F1-score results. We use * to denote that the evaluation results reported on the AMP represent binary predictions.

in our experiments can be publicly accessed at `https://github.com/debelatesfaye/ArgumentMining24-ARIES-Benchmark`.

4.2 Evaluation Setup

In-Dataset Evaluation. In the in-dataset (ID) evaluation, each model configuration is trained and evaluated on the same dataset, enabling us to assess the performance of models within the same domain. Each of the three task setups: sequence classification (SeqCls), token classification (TokCls), and sequence-to-sequence alignment (SeqAln), are trained and evaluated across the datasets. The three task setups are evaluated on eight datasets, with the exception of TokCls, which is evaluated on all datasets except AMP. This exception arises because AMP solely focuses on the pair of propositions, while TokCls requires the entire argument in addition to the pair of propositions. Within SeqCls and TokCls, the three transformer architectures—Encoder only (ED), Decoder only (DD), and Encoder-Decoder (ED-DD)—are evaluated. However, considering the specific requirements of the SeqAlg task and its architectural demands, only the ED-DD configuration is evaluated. This provides three architecture variants for the SeqCls task: ED-based SeqCls, DD-based SeqCls, and ED-DD-based SeqCls, each of which undergoes training and evaluation across eight datasets, providing a total of 24 configurations, respectively. The TokCls task encompasses 21 configurations across the seven datasets, whereas the Seq-Alg task is limited to the ED-DD configuration across eight datasets, totaling eight configurations.

Cross-Dataset Evaluation. The cross-dataset (CD) evaluation setup involves training each model on one dataset and subsequently evaluating its performance on each of the remaining seven datasets, providing insights into their generalisation and domain adaptability. Accordingly, for both the SeqCls and TokCls tasks, the three transformer architectures are trained on eight and seven training datasets, respectively, resulting in a total of 45 models (24 for SeqCls and 21 for TokCls tasks). Subsequently, each model is evaluated on the remaining datasets not used for training, resulting in an evaluation matrix encompassing a total of 294 configurations (3 architectures * 8 training datasets * 7 evaluation datasets for SeqCls and 3 architectures * 7 training datasets * 6 evaluation datasets for TokCls). Conversely, the Seq-Alg task, involves training the ED-DD configuration across the eight training datasets and evaluated on the remaining 7 dataset not used for training, resulting in an evaluation matrix encompassing 56 configurations (1 architecture * 8 training datasets * 7 evaluation datasets).

4.3 Results

Table 2 illustrates the macro F1-scores achieved in both ID and CD evaluation scenarios. In the ID evaluation configuration, the F1-scores are determined from models trained and evaluated on the same dataset. Conversely, in the CD evaluation setup, each model undergoes training on one dataset, and evaluated on the remaining datasets. The average F1-scores of each model trained on one dataset and evaluated on the remaining is reported in Table 2. The comprehensive CD evaluation results can be found in Tables 4 and 5, located in the Appendix.

As can be seen from Table 2, in the ID evaluation, an average F1-score of 76.1% was achieved across the three tasks and architectures. Conversely, in the CD evaluation, the average F1-score was notably lower at 42.7%. To facilitate a direct comparison among the three task setups, we calculate the average performance across the entire dataset, excluding AMP, as TokCls does not undergo evaluation on this specific dataset. Accordingly, the sequence-classification setup attains an average F1-score of 77.5%, 40.2% across all architectures in both ID and CD evaluations, respectively, while token-classification models achieve an average F1-score of 74.3%, 35.5%. Sequence-to-sequence alignment task achieves comparable performance with sequence classification task with an average F1-score of 76.8% and 40.4% on ID and CD setups, respectively. It is noteworthy that the average F1-score of the ED-DD architecture for sequence classification and token classification is 34.7% in CD evaluations. This represents a 5.7% improvement in the task performance in the CD evaluation setup. This observed gain underscores the task's effectiveness, especially when compared to the lower performance achieved by the same underlying model (T5) in the other two task setups, highlighting its ability to learn transferable features across domains. This phenomenon could be attributed to the inherent nature of the task setup, which presents challenging learning scenarios, potentially combating shortcut learning and encouraging the model to learn more generalised representations. Moreover, it might also suggests the task allowing to learn the alignment of the premise and conclusion based on the outputs of the encoder and decoder.

Sequence classification models exhibited faster convergence during training compared to token classification and sequence-to-sequence alignment counterparts, indicating their ability to learn and adapt more efficiently to the task at hand. The slower convergence observed in token classification and sequence-to-sequence alignment setups could be attributed to the complexity of the tasks, requiring the model to learn token-level relationships to predict argument relations.

Across all dataset and task combinations, ED (RoBERTa) configurations demonstrate an average F1-score of 75.4%, 38.4% in ID and CD evaluation settings, respectively. In contrast, DD configurations achieve an F1-score of 76.8%, 39% in the ID and CD evaluation settings, respectively. Configurations using DialoGPT exhibit a 1.4% improvement over RoBERTa across datasets and tasks in ID evaluation. DialoGPT's superior performance could be attributed to its pre-training strategy and dataset, which specifically target dialogical datasets extracted from Reddit comment chains. As DialoGPT is exclusively pre-trained on dialogical data, configuration utilising the model could leverage the argument-relevant features encoded during its pre-training stage. This advantage might enable DialoGPT based configurations to outperform configurations based on models pre-trained on generic datasets. The specificity of DialoGPT's pre-training strategy likely helps capture the subtleties of argumentation and discourse, thereby enhancing performance in ARI tasks.

Moreover, the performance variations among the transformers architectures can be indicative of the relevance of the underlying pre-training objectives and architectures to ARI. Notably, the next sentence prediction objective, crafted for classification tasks involving sequence pairs, aligns with ARI, as the task involves pairs of propositions. However, RoBERTa, which does not involve the next sentence prediction objective, demonstrates competitive performance in ARI tasks (Ruiz-Dolz et al., 2021a), suggesting the absence of this objective does not hinder the model's ability to capture argument relations. Similarly, the ED-DD architectures is relevant to ARI since it allows learning the alignment of pair of sequences (the pair of propositions in ARI). Our result shows that the architecture attains competitive performance only in the sequence-to-sequence alignment task setup. This can be evidenced by the performance improvement of T5 on sequence-to-sequence alignment task over both sequence-classification and token-classification tasks.

These findings highlight the critical significance of tailoring task setups, architectures, and evaluation methodologies to suit the unique intricacies of ARI tasks.

5 Discussion

To contextualise the results reported in the ARIES benchmark, providing a better understanding of their impact in the argument mining community, we compared the best model architecture observed in ARIES with the best performing and most recent identified previous work addressing ARI in each of the datasets individually. Works by Morio et al.

(2022), Ruosch et al. (2022), Chakrabarty et al. (2019), Ruiz-Dolz et al. (2021a), and Kikteva et al. (2023) represent the best possible reference with which to compare ARIES, given the similarity in the way that the ARI task is approached. The resulting comparison is depicted in Table 3.

As it can be observed, ARIES represents a significant jump in performance compared to previous works. Our benchmark consistently outperforms the previously reported results in the most similar instances of the ARI task considering the same eight selected datasets. The direct comparison, however, is difficult to do due to the high variability in which different authors address the task and interpret argumentative concepts. For example, Morio et al. (2022) does it with an end-to-end model, and although we selected the reported results assuming an oracle system for ADU segmentation, the proposed models are not entirely focused on ARI, considering other aspects of argument mining such as component classification. Other works such as (Ruiz-Dolz et al., 2021a) and (Kikteva et al., 2023) consider an additional relation for ARI, the rephrase between two argument propositions. Thus making the ARI a four-class classification problem instead of considering the three classes included in ARIES. Therefore, this comparison needs to be understood as a motivation and a starting point towards a more consistent and unified way of evaluating argument mining systems rather than a direct comparison between works. While worse results in a simpler version of the task should be taken as concerning, worse results in a more complex version of it do not need to mean that the system is worse. With our benchmark, we expect that future contributions in argument mining can be better contextualised and evaluated, moving forward together as a community rather than reporting specific results for heterogeneous setups that are difficult to compare and understand from a broader viewpoint.

Furthermore, we clearly observed how in the CD evaluation of the different natural language modelling approaches and architectures, the performance consistently dropped to the point of being close to the majority baseline. Thus limiting the usability of the resulting models in different domains than the ones included during training. Although some work has investigated cross-domain and cross-language argument mining (Al Khatib et al., 2016; Eger et al., 2018), this issue has never been systematically explored in-depth, leaving the door open to a new challenging direction: robustness in argument mining (Ruiz-Dolz et al., 2024). Considering the relevance of language and domain in natural language argumentation, developing robust systems is a main issue if we want to be able to effectively deploy them in real-world scenarios. For this purpose, ARIES represents a valuable resource, allowing not only to compare between different datasets, but also to measure the cross-dataset robustness of the developed argument mining systems.

Finally, we would also like to mention that recently, Gorur et al. (2024) conducted a thorough study comparing the performance of generative LLMs (i.e., decoder-based architectures) for ARC. Although some of the reported results might seem higher than the ones included in the ARIES benchmark, as noted in the beginning of this paper, relation classification assumes that the relation has already been identified and classifies it as an attack or a support, significantly simplifying the task. Therefore, we excluded these results from our comparison, being a significantly different task highly dependant on a previous step. Instead, ARI represents a completely independent task embedding the main purposes of argument mining (i.e., identifying argument structures from unstructured natural language inputs).

6 Conclusion

In this paper we presented ARIES, a global benchmark for the identification of natural language arguments. ARIES represents an effort to ease the understanding of argument mining contributions and their impact to the community. We achieve this by providing solid results comparing the three main modelling approaches in NLP (i.e., sequence and token classification, and sequence-to-sequence alignment) combined with the three main model architectures (i.e., encoder, decoder, and encoder-decoder). Our benchmark goes all over eight different corpora, presenting new state-of-the-art results for the ARI task, and setting a new reference for research in argument mining. Furthermore, we pointed out the limitations of domain-specific argument mining systems, showing poor results in cross-dataset evaluation. This limitation raises the question of how useful argument extraction systems can be when deployed in the wild, given their limited generalisability, highlighting the need to investigate the robustness of argument mining systems.

	MTC		AAEC		CDCP		ACSP		AMP		AbstRCT		US2016		QT30	
	(1)	ARIES	(1)	ARIES	(1)	ARIES	(2)	ARIES	(3)	ARIES	(1)	ARIES	(4)	ARIES	(5)	ARIES
F1-score	47	**71**	56	**78**	21	**72**	32	**84**	40	**84**	51	**84**	70*	**79**	56*	**85**

Table 3: Comparison of the ARIES benchmark with the previous reported results for ARI in terms of macro-averaged F1-scores. We use * to indicate that the ARI results included rephrase as an additional relation type. For readability purposes we have represented the references in the table as follows (1): (Morio et al., 2022), (2): (Ruosch et al., 2022), (3): (Chakrabarty et al., 2019), (4): (Ruiz-Dolz et al., 2021a), (5): (Kikteva et al., 2023).

As future work, we foresee expanding the ARIES benchmark to more languages than English. Although argument mining has been mostly researched in English, corpora in Catalan (Ruiz-Dolz et al., 2021b), Spanish (Cantador et al., 2020), Japanese (Kimura et al., 2022), or Chinese (Wu et al., 2023) among others have been annotated and publicly released in the recent years. Increasing the language richness in argument mining research can be beneficial, not only for implementing more robust models, but also to help us investigating the differences between relevant natural language argument features underlying different languages.

Acknowledgements

This research is supported in part by: the Swiss National Science Foundation under grant 10001FM_200857; the Volkswagen Foundation under grant 98 543; and the Office of the Director of National Intelligence (ODNI), Intelligence Advanced Research Projects Activity (IARPA), via Contract 2022-22072200004. The views and conclusions contained herein are those of the authors and should not be interpreted as necessarily representing the official policies, either expressed or implied, of ODNI, IARPA, or the U.S. Government. The U.S. Government is authorized to reproduce and distribute reprints for governmental purposes notwithstanding any copyright annotation therein.

References

Khalid Al Khatib, Henning Wachsmuth, Matthias Hagen, Jonas Köhler, and Benno Stein. 2016. Cross-domain mining of argumentative text through distant supervision. In *Proceedings of the 2016 conference of the north american chapter of the association for computational linguistics: human language technologies*, pages 1395–1404.

Jianzhu Bao, Yuhang He, Yang Sun, Bin Liang, Jiachen Du, Bing Qin, Min Yang, and Ruifeng Xu. 2022. A generative model for end-to-end argument mining with reconstructed positional encoding and constrained pointer mechanism. In *Proceedings of the 2022 Conference on Empirical Methods in Natural Language Processing*, pages 10437–10449.

Francesco Barbieri, Jose Camacho-Collados, Luis Espinosa Anke, and Leonardo Neves. 2020. Tweeteval: Unified benchmark and comparative evaluation for tweet classification. In *Findings of the Association for Computational Linguistics: EMNLP 2020*, pages 1644–1650.

Tom Brown, Benjamin Mann, Nick Ryder, Melanie Subbiah, Jared D Kaplan, Prafulla Dhariwal, Arvind Neelakantan, Pranav Shyam, Girish Sastry, Amanda Askell, et al. 2020. Language models are few-shot learners. *Advances in neural information processing systems*, 33:1877–1901.

Elena Cabrio and Serena Villata. 2014. Node: A benchmark of natural language arguments. In *Computational Models of Argument*, pages 449–450. IOS Press.

Iván Cantador, María E Cortés-Cediel, and Miriam Fernández. 2020. Exploiting open data to analyze discussion and controversy in online citizen participation. *Information Processing & Management*, 57(5):102301.

Tuhin Chakrabarty, Christopher Hidey, Smaranda Muresan, Kathleen Mckeown, and Alyssa Hwang. 2019. Ampersand: Argument mining for persuasive online discussions. In *Proceedings of the 2019 Conference on Empirical Methods in Natural Language Processing and the 9th International Joint Conference on Natural Language Processing (EMNLP-IJCNLP)*, pages 2933–2943.

Oana Cocarascu, Elena Cabrio, Serena Villata, and Francesca Toni. 2020. Dataset independent baselines for relation prediction in argument mining. In *COMMA 2020-8th International Conference on Computational Models of Argument*, volume 326, pages 45–52.

Oana Cocarascu and Francesca Toni. 2017. Identifying attack and support argumentative relations using deep learning. In *Proceedings of the 2017 Conference on Empirical Methods in Natural Language Processing*, pages 1374–1379.

Jacob Devlin, Ming-Wei Chang, Kenton Lee, and Kristina Toutanova. 2019. BERT: Pre-training of deep bidirectional transformers for language understanding. In *Proceedings of the 2019 Conference of the North American Chapter of the Association for*

Computational Linguistics: Human Language Technologies, Volume 1 (Long and Short Papers), pages 4171–4186.

Steffen Eger, Johannes Daxenberger, and Iryna Gurevych. 2017. Neural end-to-end learning for computational argumentation mining. *arXiv preprint arXiv:1704.06104*.

Steffen Eger, Johannes Daxenberger, Christian Stab, and Iryna Gurevych. 2018. Cross-lingual argumentation mining: Machine translation (and a bit of projection) is all you need! In *Proceedings of the 27th International Conference on Computational Linguistics*, pages 831–844.

Deniz Gorur, Antonio Rago, and Francesca Toni. 2024. Can large language models perform relation-based argument mining? *arXiv preprint arXiv:2402.11243*.

Annette Hautli-Janisz, Zlata Kikteva, Wassiliki Siskou, Kamila Gorska, Ray Becker, and Chris Reed. 2022. Qt30: A corpus of argument and conflict in broadcast debate. In *Proceedings of the 13th Language Resources and Evaluation Conference*, pages 3291–3300. European Language Resources Association (ELRA).

Masayuki Kawarada, Tsutomu Hirao, Wataru Uchida, and Masaaki Nagata. 2024. Argument mining as a text-to-text generation task. In *Proceedings of the 18th Conference of the European Chapter of the Association for Computational Linguistics (Volume 1: Long Papers)*, pages 2002–2014.

Zlata Kikteva, Alexander Trautsch, Patrick Katzer, Mirko Oest, Steffen Herbold, and Annette Hautli. 2023. On the impact of reconstruction and context for argument prediction in natural debate. In *Proceedings of the 10th Workshop on Argument Mining*, pages 100–106.

Yasutomo Kimura, Hokuto Ototake, and Minoru Sasaki. 2022. Budget argument mining dataset using japanese minutes from the national diet and local assemblies. In *Proceedings of the Thirteenth Language Resources and Evaluation Conference*, pages 6131–6138.

Diederik P Kingma and Jimmy Ba. 2014. Adam: A method for stochastic optimization. *arXiv preprint arXiv:1412.6980*.

Marcin Koszowy, Steve Oswald, Katarzyna Budzynska, Barbara Konat, and Pascal Gygax. 2022. A pragmatic account of rephrase in argumentation: linguistic and cognitive evidence. *Informal Logic*, 42(1):49–82.

Anne Lauscher, Goran Glavaš, and Simone Paolo Ponzetto. 2018. An argument-annotated corpus of scientific publications. In *Proceedings of the 5th Workshop on Argument Mining*, pages 40–46.

John Lawrence and Chris Reed. 2020. Argument mining: A survey. *Computational Linguistics*, 45(4):765–818.

Marco Lippi and Paolo Torroni. 2016. Argumentation mining: State of the art and emerging trends. *ACM Transactions on Internet Technology (TOIT)*, 16(2):1–25.

Yinhan Liu, Myle Ott, Naman Goyal, Jingfei Du, Mandar Joshi, Danqi Chen, Omer Levy, Mike Lewis, Luke Zettlemoyer, and Veselin Stoyanov. 2019. Roberta: A robustly optimized bert pretraining approach. *arXiv preprint arXiv:1907.11692*.

Tobias Mayer, Elena Cabrio, and Serena Villata. 2020. Transformer-based argument mining for healthcare applications. In *ECAI 2020*, pages 2108–2115. IOS Press.

Raquel Mochales and Marie-Francine Moens. 2011. Argumentation mining. *Artificial intelligence and law*, 19:1–22.

Gaku Morio, Hiroaki Ozaki, Terufumi Morishita, and Kohsuke Yanai. 2022. End-to-end argument mining with cross-corpora multi-task learning. *Transactions of the Association for Computational Linguistics*, 10:639–658.

Joonsuk Park and Claire Cardie. 2018. A corpus of erulemaking user comments for measuring evaluability of arguments. In *Proceedings of the Eleventh International Conference on Language Resources and Evaluation (LREC 2018)*.

Andreas Peldszus and Manfred Stede. 2015. An annotated corpus of argumentative microtexts. In *Argumentation and Reasoned Action: Proceedings of the 1st European Conference on Argumentation, Lisbon*, volume 2, pages 801–815.

Colin Raffel, Noam Shazeer, Adam Roberts, Katherine Lee, Sharan Narang, Michael Matena, Yanqi Zhou, Wei Li, and Peter J Liu. 2020. Exploring the limits of transfer learning with a unified text-to-text transformer. *Journal of machine learning research*, 21(140):1–67.

Ramon Ruiz-Dolz, Jose Alemany, Stella M Heras Barberá, and Ana García-Fornes. 2021a. Transformer-based models for automatic identification of argument relations: A cross-domain evaluation. *IEEE Intelligent Systems*, 36(6):62–70.

Ramon Ruiz-Dolz, Chr-Jr Chiu, Chung-Chi Chen, Noriko Kando, and Hsin-Hsi Chen. 2024. Learning strategies for robust argument mining: An analysis of variations in language and domain. In *Proceedings of the 2024 Joint International Conference on Computational Linguistics, Language Resources and Evaluation (LREC-COLING 2024)*, pages 10286–10292.

Ramon Ruiz-Dolz, Montserrat Nofre, Mariona Taulé, Stella Heras, and Ana García-Fornes. 2021b. Vivesdebate: A new annotated multilingual corpus of argumentation in a debate tournament. *Applied Sciences*, 11(15):7160.

Florian Ruosch, Cristina Sarasua, and Abraham Bernstein. 2022. Bam: Benchmarking argument mining on scientific documents. CEUR Workshop Proceedings.

Florian Ruosch, Cristina Sarasua, and Abraham Bernstein. 2023. Dream: Deployment of recombination and ensembles in argument mining. In *Proceedings of the Conference on Empirical Methods in Natural Language Processing*, pages 5277–5290. Association for Computational Linguistics.

Lida Shi, Fausto Giunchiglia, Rui Song, Daqian Shi, Tongtong Liu, Xiaolei Diao, and Hao Xu. 2022. A simple contrastive learning framework for interactive argument pair identification via argument-context extraction. In *Proceedings of the 2022 Conference on Empirical Methods in Natural Language Processing*, pages 10027–10039.

Christian Stab and Iryna Gurevych. 2017. Parsing argumentation structures in persuasive essays. *Computational Linguistics*, 43(3):619–659.

Felix Stahlberg. 2020. Neural machine translation: A review. *Journal of Artificial Intelligence Research*, 69:343–418.

Ashish Vaswani, Noam Shazeer, Niki Parmar, Jakob Uszkoreit, Llion Jones, Aidan N Gomez, Łukasz Kaiser, and Illia Polosukhin. 2017. Attention is all you need. *Advances in neural information processing systems*, 30.

Jacky Visser, Barbara Konat, Rory Duthie, Marcin Koszowy, Katarzyna Budzynska, and Chris Reed. 2020. Argumentation in the 2016 us presidential elections: annotated corpora of television debates and social media reaction. *Language Resources and Evaluation*, 54(1):123–154.

Alex Wang, Yada Pruksachatkun, Nikita Nangia, Amanpreet Singh, Julian Michael, Felix Hill, Omer Levy, and Samuel Bowman. 2019. Superglue: A stickier benchmark for general-purpose language understanding systems. *Advances in neural information processing systems*, 32.

Alex Wang, Amanpreet Singh, Julian Michael, Felix Hill, Omer Levy, and Samuel Bowman. 2018. Glue: A multi-task benchmark and analysis platform for natural language understanding. In *Proceedings of the 2018 EMNLP Workshop BlackboxNLP: Analyzing and Interpreting Neural Networks for NLP*, pages 353–355.

Hongyi Wu, Xinshu Shen, Man Lan, Shaoguang Mao, Xiaopeng Bai, and Yuanbin Wu. 2023. A multi-task dataset for assessing discourse coherence in chinese essays: Structure, theme, and logic analysis. In *The 2023 Conference on Empirical Methods in Natural Language Processing*.

Shu Wen Yang, Po Han Chi, Yung Sung Chuang, Cheng I Jeff Lai, Kushal Lakhotia, Yist Y Lin, Andy T Liu, Jiatong Shi, Xuankai Chang, Guan Ting Lin, et al. 2021. Superb: Speech processing universal performance benchmark. In *22nd Annual Conference of the International Speech Communication Association, INTERSPEECH 2021*, pages 3161–3165. International Speech Communication Association.

Yizhe Zhang, Siqi Sun, Michel Galley, Yen-Chun Chen, Chris Brockett, Xiang Gao, Jianfeng Gao, Jingjing Liu, and William B Dolan. 2020. Dialogpt: Large-scale generative pre-training for conversational response generation. In *Proceedings of the 58th Annual Meeting of the Association for Computational Linguistics: System Demonstrations*, pages 270–278.

A Experiment Setup

A.1 Training Procedure

Hyper-parameters: We employ Adam optimisation (Kingma and Ba, 2014) to minimise the cost function, using a learning rate of 2×10^{-5} and categorical cross-entropy loss and a batch size of 16.

Gradient Clipping: To prevent exploding gradients during training, we applied gradient clipping. We used a maximum gradient norm (`max_grad_norm`) parameter to determine the threshold for gradient clipping.

Warm-up and Learning Rate Schedule: We employed a linear warm-up strategy for the learning rate. The number of warm-up steps was set to 10% of the total training steps. Following the warm-up phase, the learning rate schedule was determined by a lambda function. This function linearly increases the learning rate during the warm-up phase and decreases it linearly thereafter.

A.1.1 Input Setup

For the sequence classification task, we combine the premise and conclusion using a special token `[SEP]`. In the sequence-alignment task, the encoder receives the premise while the decoder processes the conclusion separately. The token-classification task is provided with the entire argument along with one of the propositions (say the premise). To ensure consistency across architectures, the maximum input length is set to 512. In the sequence-to-sequence alignment task, where inputs are provided separately to the encoder and decoder, we set the maximum input size to 256 for both components to enable direct comparison. For the token-classification configuration, if the input length exceeds 512, we extract a span of the argument relevant to the premise and conclusion. Initially, we measure the size of one proposition (the premise) and if the combined size of the argument and premise is less than 512, we use the entirety of both. Otherwise, we use the following heuristic to extract the relevant part of the argument: extract a span of argument involving both the premise and conclusion if the size of the span and the premise is less than 512. If not, expand the span in the direction of the conclusion until the size constraint is met and append the conclusion to the argument span.

A.2 Model Configurations

To facilitate direct comparisons between architectures and configurations, we ensure comparable model sizes across all setups. Specifically, we employ RoBERTa-large (Liu et al., 2019) (355 million parameters) for the ED, DialoGPT-medium (Zhang et al., 2020) (345 million parameters) for the DD, and T5-base (Raffel et al., 2020) (220 million parameters) for the ED-DD configuration.

A.3 Sequence-to-sequence Alignment Task

For the sequence-to-sequence alignment task, we try two configurations. First, we leverage the `T5ForConditionalGeneration`[1] implementation, fine-tuned to generate conclusions given premises. We also concatenate the final hidden state of the encoder with that of the decoder which is then fed into a linear layer to predict the argument relation between the premise and conclusion. In an alternative approach, we employ the `T5ForSequenceClassification`[2] implementation, where the model is fine-tuned in the identification of argument relations, without the added complexity of conclusion generation given a premise. Across the configurations, the premise is provided as input to the encoder, while the conclusion serves as the input to the decoder. Our experiment reveals that T5ForConditionalGeneration configuration provides better result and all the experimental results on the SeqAln task is reported based on this configuration.

A.4 Sequence Classification Task

For the ED architecture, we utilise the final output of the HuggingFace implementation of RoBERTaForSequenceClassification[3]. Similarly, DD architecture, we leverage the final output of the HuggingFace implementation of DialoGPTForSequenceClassification [4]. For the ED-DD, we use the final output of the decoder based on the HuggingFace implementation of T5ForSequenceClassification[5]. Across the sequence classification task, the input to the respective models is the concatenation of the premise and conclusion.

[1]https://huggingface.co/docs/transformers/en/model_doc/t5#transformers.T5ForConditionalGeneration

[2]https://huggingface.co/docs/transformers/en/model_doc/t5#transformers.T5ForSequenceClassification

[3]https://huggingface.co/docs/transformers/en/model_doc/RoBERTa#transformers.RoBERTaForSequenceClassification

[4]https://huggingface.co/docs/transformers/en/model_doc/dialogpt

[5]https://huggingface.co/docs/transformers/en/model_doc/t5#transformers.T5ForSequenceClassification

Model	Train Data	AAEC	ACSP	ABstRACT	US2016	QT30	CDCP	MTC	AMP
DialogPT	AAEC	-	0.402	0.473	0.462	0.410	0.454	0.465	0.573*
	CDCP	0.365	0.390	0.432	0.425	0.390	-	0.312	0.564*
	ACSP	0.413	-	0.425	0.413	0.434	0.336	0.467	0.562*
	QT30	0.470	0.479	0.472	0.479	-	0.480	0.467	0.553*
	ABstRACT	0.281	0.342	-	0.365	0.340	0.400	0.435	0.610*
	MTC	0.363	0.291	0.434	0.356	0.316	0.381	-	0.631*
	US2016	0.461	0.430	0.424	-	0.463	0.471	0.461	0.563*
	AMP	0.532*	0.551*	0.523*	0.574*	0.621*	0.465*	0.346*	-
RoBERTa	AAEC	-	0.390	0.459	0.399	0.446	0.454	0.535	0.561*
	CDCP	0.322	0.312	0.411	0.403	0.373	-	0.379	0.562*
	ACSP	0.479	-	0.489	0.520	0.560	0.379	0.504*	0.542*
	QT30	0.388	0.370	0.491	0.501	-	0.405	0.479	0.523*
	ABstRACT	0.332	0.358	-	0.345	0.362	0.475	0.491	0.586*
	MTC	0.309	0.302	0.319	0.361	0.331	0.284	-	0.542*
	US2016	0.399	0.426	0.512	-	0.456	0.420	0.420	0.571*
	AMP	0.512*	0.551*	0.502*	0.566*	0.614*	0.479*	0.348*	-
T5	AAEC	-	0.306	0.342	0.395	0.339	0.355	0.390	0.491*
	CDCP	0.356	0.362	0.363	0.355	0.368	-	0.261	0.501*
	ACSP	0.304	-	0.378	0.336	0.339	0.305	0.444	0.456*
	QT30	0.351	0.322	0.344	0.359	-	0.349	0.419	0.541*
	ABstRACT	0.342	0.305	-	0.320	0.333	0.376	0.376	0.511*
	MTC	0.319	0.312	0.346	0.351	0.359	0.315	-	0.529*
	US2016	0.345	0.328	0.364	-	0.389	0.399	0.355	0.473*
	AMP	0.486*	0.462*	0.396*	0.421*	0.441*	0.365*	0.245*	-

Table 4: CD evaluation performance of each model architecture on the SeqCls task setup. We use * to denote that the evaluation results reported on the AMP represent binary predictions.

Model	Train Data	AAEC	ACSP	ABstRACT	US2016	QT30	CDCP	MTC
DialogPT	AAEC	-	0.312	0.40	0.441	0.467	461	0.479
	CDCP	0.277	0.285	0.355	0.376	0.335	-	0.335
	ACSP	0.368	-	0.418	0.427	0.414	0.319	0.366
	QT30	0.346	0.358	0.268	0.500	-	0.479	0.267
	ABstRACT	0.334	0.311	-	0.377	0.320	0.322	0.423
	MTC	0.347	0.297	0.397	0.423	0.322	0.274	-
	US2016	0.389	0.378	0.287	-	0.519	0.400	0.279
RoBERTa	AAEC	-	0.294	0.447	0.440	0.433	0.442	0.450
	CDCP	0.267	0.265	0.334	0.341	0.307	-	0.323
	ACSP	0.349	-	0.411	0.411	0.407	0.300	0.337
	QT30	0.328	0.316	0.256	0.509	-	0.237	0.238
	ABstRACT	0.290	0.297	-	0.354	0.319	0.291	0.404
	MTC	0.335	0.264	0.380	0.417	0.336	0.286	-
	US2016	0.311	0.307	0.230	-	0.359	0.246	0.246
T5	AAEC	-	0.269	0.365	0.365	0.342	366	0.365
	CDCP	267	0.279	0.352	0.361	0.307	-	0.342
	ACSP	0.332	-	0.411	0.401	0.413	0.281	0.332
	QT30	0.321	0.298	0.241	0.486	-	0.423	0.237
	ABstRACT	0.265	0.282	-	0.361	0.324	0.318	0.413
	MTC	0.323	0.264	0.380	0.421	0.336	0.286	-
	US2016	0.333	0.317	0.251	-	0.522	0.398	0.266

Table 5: CD evaluation performance of each model architecture on the TokCls task setup.

Detecting Scientific Fraud Using Argument Mining

Gabriel Freedman, Francesca Toni
Imperial College London, UK
{g.freedman22,f.toni}@imperial.ac.uk

Abstract

A proliferation of fraudulent scientific research in recent years has precipitated a greater interest in more effective methods of detection. There are many varieties of academic fraud, but a particularly challenging type to detect is the use of paper mills and the faking of peer-review. To the best of our knowledge, there have so far been no attempts to automate this process. The complexity of this issue precludes the use of heuristic methods, like pattern-matching techniques, which are employed for other types of fraud. Our proposed method in this paper uses techniques from the Computational Argumentation literature (i.e. argument mining and argument quality evaluation). Our central hypothesis stems from the assumption that articles that have not been subject to the proper level of scrutiny will contain poorly formed and reasoned arguments, relative to legitimately published papers. We use a variety of corpora to test this approach, including a collection of abstracts taken from retracted papers. We show significant improvement compared to a number of baselines, suggesting that this approach merits further investigation.

1 Introduction

The growing problem of fraudulent academic research poses a threat to scientific progress. Research is an iterative process, where arguments presented in previous papers are used as the basis of subsequent work. Researchers do not necessarily have the time or resources available to verify that all the claims that have been made in previous publications are well-formulated, or valid. Instead they tend to rely on the scrutiny imposed during the publication process to offer reasonable guarantees about the legitimacy of the content.

However, these guarantees have been undermined by revelations about the extent of malpractice taking place in many scientific publications (Cookson, 2023; Economist, 2023). As an indication of the scale of the problem, there have been estimates that over a fifth of new medical publications are implicated in some form of fraudulent activity (Sabel et al., 2023). Prevalent types of fraud include: plagiarism, data manipulation and circumvention of a legitimate peer-review process.

Relatively simple methods can help detect some of these forms of fraud, such as pattern matching in the case of plagiarism (Butler, 2018). However, where the peer-review process is compromised, or the services of paper mills are employed, these techniques are not effective. In these cases, researchers have had some success detecting characteristic patterns (van Noorden, 2021; Else and van Noorden, 2021) - but this is not a universal panacea as it is simple for authors to make slight stylistic alterations to avoid these methods of detection. The consensus of the research community investigating these matters is that there are a large number of such articles that have not yet been retracted from the journals they are published in, and this number is on the rise (Sabel and Seifert, 2021).

The hypothesis underlying this research is that papers published by illicit means (specifically those that have been produced by paper mills, or have not undergone peer-review) will be based on substandard reasoning. This could take the form of fallacious arguments. Alternatively, arguments may be based on spurious premises, or lack any relevant and novel insights. We believe this is a legitimate supposition due to the nature of scientific inquiry: the fundamental aim of scientific research is to construct valid and interesting arguments from a sound empirical or theoretical basis.

Anecdotal evidence supporting this hypothesis is presented in Table 1. Both arguments address the efficacy of social distancing as a method to combat the spread of COVID-19. However, the argument given in the retracted article is very weak. The claim: 'Social distancing measures ought to be followed by everyone to minimize the spread of COVID-19', is perfectly reasonable. The premises

Retracted	Not retracted
Social distancing measures ought to be followed by everyone to minimize the spread of COVID-19. Eventually, maintaining social distance will become a habit in the future. Owing to that, our proposed system gives an accurate output of 90% at detecting people with a one-meter distance between them in public areas, which also provides indications in green and red bounding boxes around people.	After three COVID-19 waves, the growing number of new infections still reminds us of the importance of taking precautionary measures. SD and wearing masks have been proven to be efficient nonpharmaceutical intervention measures (Özbek, Syed, & Öksüz, 2021). They are low-cost, convenient, and non-invasive to slow the spread of COVID-19 and flatten the curves of infection (Srivastava, Zhao, Manay, & Chen, 2021).

Table 1: Comparable arguments for social distancing presented in a retracted article (Pooranam et al., 2021), and non-retracted article (Himeur et al., 2022).

that follow, however, are very loosely connected to the claim, and the argument in its entirety is both unconvincing and hard to follow. On the other hand, the argument in the non-retracted article is much more effective. The premises are directly addressing the points raised in the claim, and they back up their assertions with verifiable evidence in the form of citations.

In order to empirically test this hypothesis, we adopt techniques from the Computational Argumentation literature. Specifically, we build on past research in the fields of **argument mining** (Lawrence and Reed, 2020) and **argument quality evaluation** (Toledo et al., 2019). Models trained for these purposes are able to extract arguments from a passage of text and evaluate the quality of such arguments respectively. When done sequentially, this amounts to a way of assessing the reasoning present in a piece of text.

We use a number of pre-existing corpora both to train and test the various models we develop. These include datasets that have been compiled especially for scientific argument mining: SciARK (Fergadis et al., 2021) for training and AbstRCT (Mayer et al., 2020) for testing. Also, we use a dataset that contains human evaluated arguments for training our argument quality evaluation model: the Grammarly Argument Quality Corpus (GAQCorpus) (Lauscher et al., 2020).

In order to collect a sufficient sample of retracted articles to evaluate the performance of the complete system, we use the Retraction Watch database (Marcus and Oransky, 2023). The metadata included therein allows us to specify the subset of retracted articles that we are interested in detecting.

Our initial results indicate that implementing this strategy leads to a considerable improvement in detecting fraudulent articles, compared with a number of baselines. This suggests that the developed method has theoretical validity and merits further investigation.

2 Related Work

2.1 Scientific Fraud Detection

As awareness grows about the existing and potential problems caused by academic fraud (Bolland et al., 2022; Fanelli et al., 2022; Kim et al., 2019; Garmendia et al., 2019), researchers have begun to take steps to tackle the problem. There is generally still an emphasis put on human-centered interventions. Such proposals include introducing more stringent criteria for publications to choose their referees (Mavrogenis and Scarlat, 2023), improving the quality of oversight and guidance offered by regulatory bodies (Candal-Pedreira et al., 2021), and producing effective guidelines to help both academics and journals cooperate to avoid any fraudulent activity (Wager et al., 2017).

Due to the scale of the problem, some researchers have recognised that it is necessary to at least partially automate the discovery process. There have been varying degrees of automation suggested. Zhao et al. (2021) propose a method to improve the selection of referees. They compare a vector embedding of the paper under review with embedded representations of a number of potential referees' previous papers to more accurately determine who has the most relevant expertise.

Other approaches focus on using information about the authors of the papers or the publication venue itself. Abalkina has proposed using the archives (Abalkina, 2021a) and the metadata (Abalkina, 2021b) of papers that have appeared in compromised journals in order to detect other publication venues that may have also been compromised. Similarly Chakraborty et al. (2021) focus on analysing irregular citation patterns to find self-referencing networks of fraudulent papers.

Some authors have attempted to propose solutions that rely more fully on computational methods. Haunschild and Bornmann (2021) investigate the possibility of using scepticism expressed on social media as a metric to determine possible fraudulent activity. Furthermore, Kinney et al. (2021) use measures of text overlap to detect plagiarism and Horton et al. (2020) attempt to use statistical methods to uncover patterns in manipulated data. However, these latter two approaches are not applicable to all types of academic fraud, and would not necessarily work for faked peer-reviews or papers produced by paper mills.

We aim to advance the current state of this research by developing and implementing a system that can make fully automated predictions about whether a paper has bypassed a legitimate peer-review, or equivalently has been produced by a paper mill. We were not able to find any comparable research in the literature, suggesting that our work constitutes a novel research program.

2.2 Argument Mining

Argument mining (Lawrence and Reed, 2020) is an important task in Computational Argumentation. It is the automatic extraction of arguments contained within text. Once these arguments have been identified, it is possible to create formal representations which deliver a greater flexibility and ability to reason (Peldszus and Stede, 2013).

The task is a very challenging aspect of natural language processing, and has not yet been solved with a high level of accuracy. The heterogeneity of argument types and structure make reliable and consistent representations hard to achieve. However, since the advent of the transformer architecture (Vaswani et al., 2017) and the consequent improvement in language modelling capabilities (Devlin et al., 2019; Brown et al., 2020), advances have also been made in the field of argument mining. The ability to fine-tune pre-trained large language models (LLMs) on task-specific datasets has made the integration of argument mining into practical applications a possibility.

There are roughly three subtasks that make up the argument mining task: the detection of individual argumentative entities (e.g. premises and claims), intra-argument relations (how premises and claims in arguments relate) and inter-argument relations (how different arguments relate).

There are a number of specifically curated datasets for each of these tasks. Stab and Gurevych (Stab and Gurevych, 2016) demonstrate the feasibility of developing guidelines that lead to a high inter-annotator agreement, producing a corpus of over four hundred annotated persuasive essays. There are also a number of datasets with a particular focus on the scientific domain. These include SciARG (Accuosto et al., 2021), SCiARK (Fergadis et al., 2021) and AbstRCT (Mayer et al., 2020).

Modelling the distribution of entities (claims and premises), and modelling the relationships between these entities are often separated into distinct tasks. For example, Cocarascu et al. (2020) develop a set of domain-agnostic models that can be applied to the relation prediction task. Ruiz-Dolz et al. (2020) attempt to solve a similar task, focusing on comparing the performance of different transformer-based architectures.

Similarly to our work, Fergadis et al. (2021) develop a variety of models that specifically address the entity identification subtask. Furthermore, Mayer et al. (2020) and Accuosto et al. (2021) both develop two types of model, one for the entity identification task and one for the relation prediction task. Thorburn and Kruger (2022), on the other hand, test different optimisation techniques with a GPT-like model, to attempt to create a more adaptable and versatile approach to different argument mining subtasks.

2.3 Argument Quality Evaluation

Evaluating the quality of arguments is a relatively unexplored aspect of Computational Argumentation. Wachsmuth et al. (2017) set out a broad framework that can be used to help define argument quality.

There have been a number of practical efforts to compile such a dataset. Initial efforts used a pairwise comparison between arguments (Habernal and Gurevych, 2016; Simpson and Gurevych, 2018). This is the most straightforward approach for annotators but is limited in its applicability to multiple arguments in different domains.

As a part of the IBM *Project Debater*, this approach was refined (Toledo et al., 2019; Gretz et al., 2019). In order to produce arguments with continuous numerical quality representations, questions with binary answers were asked about each argument. Numerous annotators were asked to consider the same arguments. Various methods of taking a weighted average are then explored, providing a continuous quality for each argument between 0 and 1. Joshi et al. (2023) have recently compiled a similar dataset, but they include 'argument-analysis pairs', which provide additional rationale behind

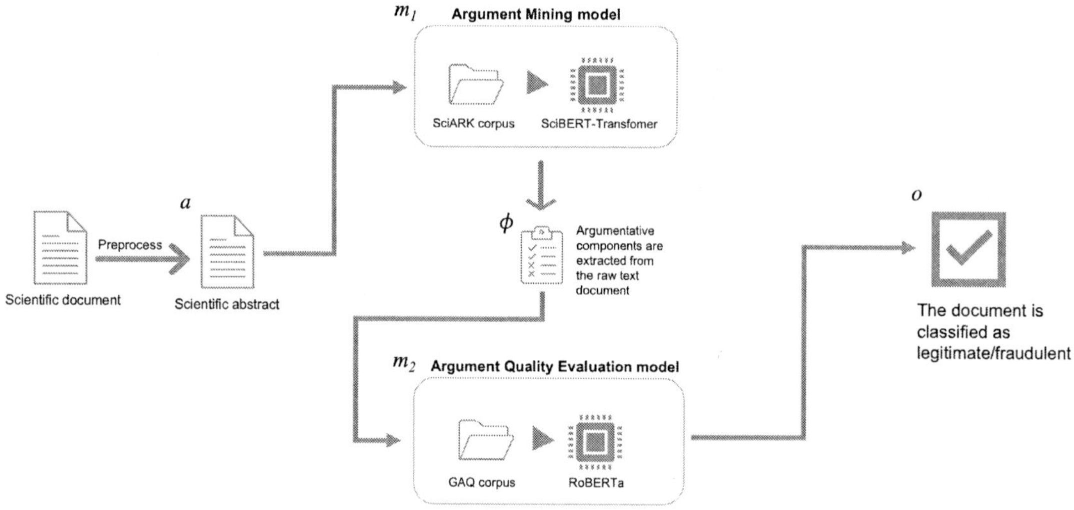

Figure 1: An overview of our proposed system architecture.

why the argument is effective.

Lauscher et al. (2020) take a more direct approach to producing continuous quality ratings. They take the average of three annotators' ratings, on a scale of one to five, over three different measures of quality. This allows for a more descriptive and fine-grained interpretation of different aspects of argument quality. We leverage this innovation by using state-of-the-art natural language processing techniques to develop an effective model for argument quality prediction.

3 Methodology

The goal of this research is to test the hypothesis that evaluating the quality of a scientific article's reasoning can be an effective way of determining whether it was produced fraudulently. In practice, this amounts to extracting and then evaluating arguments that are indicative of the overall level of reasoning present in the article. We achieve this by training two models separately.

An important feature of our framework is that we only analyse the abstracts of papers. We have two primary motivations for this decision. Firstly, it provides an effective way to minimise artefacts in our data. Research papers are generally heterogeneous in format, containing inconsistently structured sections. Abstracts, however, are fairly consistent in form, and from an argumentative perspective, usually contain the principle argument motivating the rest of the paper.

The second reason is that if we are able to demonstrate that the abstract alone is sufficient, then this offers practical advantages. Only considering a minimal subset of the entire text reduces both the theoretical and computational burden. This latter consideration is especially pertinent when considering that deploying such a system would be most advantageous in situations which require processing high volumes of inputs.

We describe our proposed fraud prediction framework with the following formalisation.

Let $a = \{s_1, s_2, ..., s_n\}$ represent a paper abstract consisting of a list of n sentences. We define a model m_1 such that:

$$m_1 : s_i \mapsto c_j \tag{1}$$

where $c_j \in \{none, evidence, claim\}$ is the category to which the sentence s_i is mapped.

The list of categorisations $c = \{c_1, c_2, ..., c_n\}$ along with the original abstract a is then transformed using a transformation function ϕ:

$$\phi : (a, \{c_1, c_2, ..., c_n\}) \mapsto t \tag{2}$$

where t is the transformed representation of the abstract a, amounting to a single string.

The transformed abstract is then input to another model m_2:

$$m_2 : t \mapsto v \tag{3}$$

where $v \in [1, 5]$ is a real-valued output.

The final status o of the abstract is determined by comparing the output v to a threshold $T = 3$:

$$o = \begin{cases} \text{legitimate}, & \text{if } v > T \\ \text{fraudulent}, & \text{if } v \leq T \end{cases} \quad (4)$$

Both models in our system architecture (see Figure 1), are realised based on fine-tuned foundation models (Bommasani et al., 2021), using data from a number of different sources. In Section 3.1 we describe the data we use for fine-tuning and testing our individual models, as well as testing our system in its entirety. Sections 3.2 and 3.3 provide descriptions of the Argument Mining (AM) model (m_1) and Argument Quality Evaluation (AQE) model (m_2) respectively. Finally in Section 3.4, we outline the entire system as presented in Figure 1.

3.1 Data

There is a relatively limited amount of annotated data focused on the tasks comprising argument mining, especially those that are relevant to scientific domains. Likewise, there have been even fewer datasets compiled for the purpose of training argument quality evaluation models. However, there is a sufficient amount of data available to support the training and testing of the models required to realise our system.

The SciARK (Fergadis et al., 2021) dataset consists of 1,000 annotated scientific abstracts (containing 12,374 annotated sentences in total), across a range of different domains (each domain corresponding to a UN Sustainable Development Goal (Biermann et al., 2017)). For each abstract, every sentence has been annotated with one of three labels: *evidence* (equivalent to premise), *claim* and *neither*. This dataset is used to train the AM model.

We use the AbstRCT dataset (Mayer et al., 2020) for evaluating the performance both of our AM model, and our fraud prediction system in its entirety. The dataset consists of 669 abstracts, and is annotated in the same way as the SciARK dataset, with each sentence being labelled either *evidence*, *claim* or *neither*. The abstracts are taken from publications in prestigious peer-reviewed medical journals. The rigorous and scientific form of argumentation contained in these samples makes them well-suited for testing the capabilities of the AM model we developed. Furthermore, the quality of the journals chosen by the compilers provides us with a sufficient level of confidence that none of the samples contained within the dataset were produced using fraudulent means. Therefore, it is also suitable to be used as the representative sample of *legitimate abstracts* that we use to evaluate our complete fraud prediction system.

For fine-tuning our AQE model we take 1,104 samples from GAQCorpus, compiled by (Lauscher et al., 2020). This dataset makes use of arguments taken from various internet forums. Annotators were recruited to give each argument a score on a scale between one and five, for each of three metrics: *cogency*, *effectiveness* and *reasonableness*. Despite the subjectivity inherent in human judgements, taking the average of multiple annotators' scores for each sample reduces the amount of noise present in the data.

In order to compile a sufficient corpus of *fraudulent abstracts*, for evaluating the performance of our system, we collected 420 relevant papers from the Retraction Watch database (Marcus and Oransky, 2023). The database currently contains tens of thousands of retracted articles from a wide variety of different journals. However, there are numerous reasons cited for each retraction, with the majority having to do with fake data or plagiarism.

For the sake of this study we are only interested in the subset of papers that have been published either by means of a paper mill, or by faking the peer-review. Furthermore, we restrict the papers we collect to the medical domain, in order to match the domain of those contained in the AbstRCT dataset, which constitute our test set of *legitimate abstracts*. We do this so our results are not influenced by features that are irrelevant to the focus of our study - namely the subject of the papers.

3.2 Argument Mining model

The AM model we developed is influenced by the architecture in (Fergadis et al., 2021). The model consists of three components: a *Sentence Encoder*, *Context Encoder* and a *Fully Connected Layer*.

The Sentence Encoder is a SciBERT model (Beltagy et al., 2019) - a BERT-like LLM, which has been trained specifically to improve performance on scientific texts. For each sentence in the input text, a `[CLS]` token is outputted, representing a sentence vector $s \in \mathbb{R}^{728}$. These tokens are used as input to the Context Encoder, providing a representation of the entire abstract during the production of the embedding for each sentence.

The Context Encoder provides a detailed representation of the specific sentence being considered. The best performing implementation from (Fergadis et al., 2021) uses a BiLSTM (Graves and Schmidhuber, 2005), taking as input both the sentence vectors before and after the current sentence. The dense layer simply takes the embedded representation and returns an output of one of three categories: *evidence*, *claim* or *null*.

We augment this model by replacing the BiLSTM Context Encoder with a transformer, better suited for handling long-range dependencies, which is particularly useful in the context of a scientific abstract where all concepts mentioned are often relevant throughout the entire passage.

Due to the nature of the setting we forego inter-argument and intra-argument relation prediction. This is because all our samples are scientific abstracts. These are relatively short passages, and also, in theory, should only be presenting the one principle argument being introduced in the paper. This means that simply identifying the argumentative entities is sufficient, as we assume that each sample contains at most one claim (possibly spanning multiple sentences), and potentially multiple premises supporting that claim.

3.3 Argument Quality Evaluation model

Once the arguments have been extracted from the raw text, the AQE model is used to evaluate the quality of the arguments. The models that achieved the best validation scores on the training data were all fine-tuned versions of BERT. The best performing model was a RoBERTA model (Liu et al., 2019), trained on roughly 1,100 samples contained within the GAQCorpus (Lauscher et al., 2020).

Before using the data for fine-tuning, we preprocess it to make the arguments more closely aligned to the arguments found in scientific literature. The original dataset spans three different domains: *debate* forums, *answer* forums and *review* forums. We exclude the data taken from the *review* forum from our training data, as these samples are the least argumentative and most subjective in terms of content. There is also a binary feature included in the data that determines whether the annotators deemed the sample argumentative or not - we remove all samples where there is not a unanimous agreement that the sample is argumentative.

Furthermore, we make slight modifications to the remaining samples in our training set to increase syntactical similarity with the scientific arguments. Rhetorical questions are frequently used in the forum data, which is not found in any scientific content. There is also use of very short sentences (five words or less), which is practically non-existent in scientific writing. Therefore, we remove any sentences that fit into either of these categories, as well as converting any extraneous punctuation (e.g. exclamation marks) into full stops. An example of the preprocessing is presented in Table 5.

Instead of using an average of the three metrics which are contained within the GAQCorpus, we only make use of the *cogency* rating. This is due to the relevance of cogency to scientific argumentation, and the relative irrelevance of the other two metrics (*reasonableness* and *effectiveness*) within the context of scientific literature. To illustrate this, the definition for *cogency* used by Lauscher et al. (2020) to guide the annotators was: '[cogency] relates to the logical aspects of [argument quality], for instance, whether an argument's premises are acceptable (local acceptability) or whether they can be seen as relevant for the conclusion (local relevance)'.

3.4 Full Argumentation-Based System

The final system in its entirety takes the output from the argument identification model and uses it to perform a transformation of the input text data. The transformation is a linearisation (Stede and Sauermann, 2008) of the extracted argumentative components, so that a string can be used as input to the AQE model, reflecting the training data. This string consists of the claim sentence(s) followed by the premises. This is chosen as it most closely resembles the format of the arguments in the non-scientific training corpus (GAQCorpus).

In order to make the final classification into 'legitimate' or 'fraudulent', it is necessary to establish a threshold (T) which the quality score can be compared to. There are five quality classes in total. In order to create a system that is less likely to return false positives (classify fraudulent articles as legitimate), we only consider an argument as legitimate if it is in the highest two classes of quality. If it is in the bottom three classes of quality we classify the sample as fraudulent.

Our decision to choose a threshold weighted towards the classification of samples as fraudulent was done with the practical purpose of the finished system in mind, as well empirical validation. Relative to false negatives (classifying fraudulent documents as legitimate), false positives (flagging legitimate documents as fraudulent) are less detrimental to a system which is built to assist in the detection of academic fraud.

4 Results and Discussion

In Section 4.1 we present a comparison of our novel AM model with two existing alternatives. Then, we outline the performance on the overall fraud prediction task of three novel baselines (Section 4.2) and the full argumentation-based model (Section 4.3).

4.1 Scientific Argument Mining

In order to evaluate our AM model, described in Section 3.2, we use two of the best performing models developed by Fergadis et al. (2021) as baselines. All three models are trained on the SciARK dataset and tested on the AbstRCT dataset.

The results in Table 2 show that the overall F_1 score was best when using our novel *scibert-transformer*. As previously mentioned, we infer that the transformer's capability to efficiently handle long-range dependencies - compared to the BiLSTM used in the second best model - is advantageous for this task.

4.2 Baselines for Fraudulent Paper Detection

So that we could provide insightful benchmarks and ablations for the fraudulent paper detection task in its entirety, we compared our argumentative approach with five baselines. This was necessary due to the novelty of our research, and the consequent absence of existing systems in the literature that performed a comparable function. Three of these benchmark utilise BERT-style modes, mirroring our main method. The other two use autoregresssive LLMs, Mistral (Mistral-7B-Instruct-v0.2) (Jiang et al., 2023) and Mixtral (Mixtral-8x7B-Instruct-v0.1) (Jiang et al., 2024).

Our first model, *SciBERT direct inference*, was designed to infer legitimacy directly. Instead of training the model to determine the quality of the reasoning in a sample as an intermediary step, we trained it with legitimate and fraudulent samples directly. For our fraudulent training samples, we collected a separate training set of 556 fraudulent samples from the Retraction Watch database. These samples were taken from a diverse range of domains, in order to reflect the diversity of domains present in the SciARK corpus which we used for our training set of legitimate samples. Thus we limited the possibility that the performance of the model was influenced by subject matter, and instead learnt the 'legitimacy' and 'fraudulence' features present in the respective samples.

We tested various base LLMs and identified that fine-tuning a SciBERT model resulted in the best performance. However, its performance was still lacking. We propose that a significant reason for this was the limited number of negative samples contained in our dataset, which restricted the model's ability to capture a comprehensive representation of the sample space.

The second baseline we investigated, *full text quality*, simply skipped the argument identification stage, and used the original, unmodified abstracts as input to the AQE model. Similarly, for our third baseline we first summarised the abstracts using a LLM, Mixtral, as a form of feature extraction, and once again used that as input to the AQE model.

The summarisation technique produced better results than using the full text. However, it was still relatively ineffective compared to the full argumentation-based approach. Both the summary and the argumentative content of a piece of text are comparable features, but our belief is that the argumentation-based approach provides a more faithful representation of the quality of reasoning in a passage of text.

For our fourth and fifth baselines we leveraged the task-agnostic, general capabilities of state-of-the-art LLMs. For both the Mistral and Mixtral models, we use zero-shot chain-of-thought (COT) (Wei et al., 2022; Zhang and Parkes, 2023) prompting. The full prompt can be seen in Appendix C. All outputs were generated with greedy sampling (equivalent to setting temperature to 0). As can be observed in Table 3, the Mixtral model performed the best out of all the baselines. This is especially notable in light of the zero-shot setting in which the experiments were conducted. This introduces the prospect that the use of even larger LLMs could present further gains in performance. This conjecture also applies to the use of larger LLMs as the components of our argumentative system.

4.3 Full Argumentation-Based Model for Fraudulent Paper Detection

The proposed method demonstrates a considerable improvement over the baselines, as illustrated by Tables 3 and 4. By comparing these results to the five distinct baselines we developed, we highlight that both the AM and AQE components contributed to the improved performance of the system.

The favourable comparison with the *direct in-*

Model	Evidence			Claim			Average
	P	R	F_1	P	R	F_1	F_1
SciBERT-Only	0.778	**0.728**	**0.752**	**0.808**	0.359	0.497	0.625
SciBERT-Bilstm	0.815	0.688	0.747	0.874	0.458	0.601	0.674
SciBERT-Transformer	**0.878**	0.57	0.693	0.858	**0.557**	**0.675**	**0.684**

Table 2: Performance metrics for the Argument Mining models described in Section 3.2. We compare our novel *Scibert-Transformer* model with the previous models introduced in Fergadis et al. (2021). All models are trained on the SciARK corpus and evaluated on the AbstRCT corpus (Mayer et al., 2020).

Model	Accuracy	Precision	Recall	F_1
SciBERT Direct Inference	0.543	1	0.109	0.197
Full Text Quality	0.461	1	0.012	0.024
Summary Quality	0.463	0.676	0.23	0.343
Mistral COT	0.622	0.021	1	0.041
Mixtral COT	0.637	0.429	0.537	0.476
Argumentation-Based Model	0.761	0.708	0.648	**0.677**

Table 3: Performance metrics for the baseline models described in Section 4.2 and our novel methodology *Argumentation-Based Model*.

	Predicted Fraudulent	**Predicted Legitimate**
Actual Fraudulent	272	148
Actual Legitimate	112	557

Table 4: Argumentation-Based Model's performance on 1,089 legitimate and fraudulent abstracts.

ference model validates that the development of a more intricate approach is appropriate and worthwhile. Likewise, the comparisons with the *full text quality* and *summary quality* models, give credence to the hypothesis that the evaluation of arguments, rather than full texts or summaries, is beneficial to the system's overall performance.

As well as performing better, relative to directly training a model on legitimate and fraudulent samples, the methodology developed for evaluating argument quality provides a more flexible and generalisable approach. This is due to the noise inherently present in a training set that consists solely of scientific abstracts. There is no clear way to disentangle useful properties of the data - namely, legitimacy of the article - from noisy properties such as subject matter and syntactical idiosyncrasies. This would not present such a significant obstacle if the available data for training were large and diverse enough, but as this is far from being the case it must be taken into consideration.

We also gain valuable insights by comparing the results of the fully argumentative model with the two baselines that provide different inputs to the AQE model. We observe that using the arguments contained within the abstracts as representative features is more effective than using the full text, or using summaries as a feature. There are a number of possible explanations for this finding. One plausible suggestion is that mining the arguments contained within a scientific abstract is a good way of extracting a representation of the reasoning contained therein, and, furthermore, the quality of this reasoning is indicative of the article's legitimacy. This would confirm our initial hypothesis.

Another factor to consider is the architecture of the AQE model we have developed. The training data that we used from the GAQCorpus (Lauscher et al., 2020) is composed of samples that have been evaluated for their argumentative quality. The metric we choose to consider (*cogency*), is something that is relevant to argumentation, but not so much for summaries.

4.4 Qualitative Error Analysis

In this section we provide examples and analysis of mined arguments that were falsely classified by the AQE model as legitimate and fraudulent respectively.

Incorrectly classified as legitimate

> Compared to GES-1 cells, the expressions of miR-214, -catenin and survivin in MKN-28 cells were upregulated, along with downregulation of GSK-3 expression. After the transfection of miR-214 inhibitor and/or pSicoR-GSK-3, GSK-3 expression was induced in MKN-28 cells while -catenin and survivin expressions were inhibited, along with the increase of cell apoptosis.

Incorrectly classified as fraudulent

> At 6 months after the end of RT, global HRQOL was higher in the TPF arm than in the PF arm, but the low compliance does not allow to draw definitive conclusions. Swallowing and coughing problems decreased more in the TPF arm than in the PF arm at the end of cycle 2, but to a limited extent.

Both examples demonstrate the complexity of the task. The first example, which is taken from a fraudulent abstract, almost entirely consists of technical terminology. While the data used to train SciBERT consists of scientific text, medical literature contains a large amount of domain-specific language, which is sometimes exclusively used by the community working on the specific problem. Besides this, the content of the argument also seems to be sound. This is inevitable due to the scale of papers produced fraudulently, so must be taken into consideration in the context of our solution. It is essential that any fully-fledged system takes into account other factors that may indicate fraudulence, such as the presence of irregular images or data. In this case argument quality may be considered as one out of many features.

For the second example, taken from a legitimate abstract, one might note some unorthodox grammatical constructions as reasons for the fraudulent classification. For example, 'the low compliance does not allow to draw definitive conclusions' contains a slight grammatical error ('allow *one* to draw' would be a more sound construction). While this is entirely reasonable to expect in a legitimate manuscript, it may lead to a fraudulent classification as it is less commonly found in legitimate papers compared to those produced by a paper mill.

It is important to note that the above are human interpretations of the data, and may not be faithful to the true underlying processes carried out by the model. Future work could be undertaken to apply established methods from the explainable AI literature. Furthermore, there are a diverse range of incorrect classified samples, with the examples chosen being representative of one type. The reasons for these errors is likely to vary across inputs.

5 Conclusion and Future Work

The aim of this study was to determine whether it is possible to automate the detection of fraudulently produced scientific publications. To achieve this, we introduced and implemented a novel framework, building upon existing architectures from the argument mining literature.

We developed state-of-the-art methods in the fields of scientific argument mining and argument quality evaluation. By using both models in conjunction, we created a method for evaluating the quality of reasoning in scientific articles.

We compared this approach to three baselines, observing favourable comparisons in each case. By using a variety of baselines we were able to demonstrate that both the argument mining and quality evaluation components positively contributed to the overall performance of the system.

Although the initial results were promising, there are a number of potential developments that would merit further exploration. For instance, the quality evaluation component would benefit from being trained on arguments that have been taken directly from scientific papers. Furthermore, introducing methods to assess the quality of the individual premises and claims, in addition to the overall argument, could benefit performance.

As mentioned previously, there are various advantages to restricting our inputs to abstracts. However, analysing entire articles also has benefits. State-of-the-art LLMs have made this plausible. An evident direction for future work would be the utilisation of larger, more sophisticated language models, while keeping in mind the trade-off between performance and computational cost.

Finally, widening the range of modalities that are included in the analysis would lead to a more comprehensive system. It is standard practice in scientific articles to include arguments that consist of more than just textual components. Images, graphs, citations and tabular data are all commonly incorporated as sources of evidence. An ideal system would be able to assess the quality and relevance of all these forms of data with respect to the arguments contained within an article.

Limitations

The system has not yet been sufficiently scrutinised to confidently assert that it could be effectively deployed in a real-world setting. Due to the sensitivity of the domain, it is important that the system undergoes extensive testing and is validated by individuals with expertise in fraudulent article detection, before it can be effectively and safely deployed.

Due to the inefficiency of the existing human-centric process of detecting fraudulent articles, there is a relatively small dataset of retracted articles to use for evaluation. Therefore some caution should be exercised in making assumptions about the totality of articles that have been published using illegitimate means, as there may be bias present in the subset of articles that have already been detected.

Ethics Statement

Academic Fraud is an important and sensitive issue and any attempts to automate its detection must be approached with some degree of caution. It is essential that any such tool is used in conjunction with human experts, and is not used in isolation to make decisions.

Acknowledgements

This research was partially supported by ERC under the EU's Horizon 2020 research and innovation programme (grant agreement No. 101020934), by J.P. Morgan and the Royal Academy of Engineering under the Research Chairs and Senior Research Fellowships scheme and by UKRI through the CDT in Safe and Trusted Artificial Intelligence (Grant No. EP/S023356/1) and through the INDICATE project (Grant No. EP/Y017749/1). We thank Retraction Watch and Grammarly for providing access to their respective datasets.

References

Anna Abalkina. 2021a. Detecting a network of hijacked journals by its archive. *Scientometrics*, 126:7123 – 7148.

Anna Abalkina. 2021b. Publication and collaboration anomalies in academic papers originating from a paper mill: evidence from a russia-based paper mill.

Pablo Accuosto, Mariana L. Neves, and Horacio Saggion. 2021. Argumentation mining in scientific literature: From computational linguistics to biomedicine. In *BIR@ECIR*.

Iz Beltagy, Kyle Lo, and Arman Cohan. 2019. Scibert: A pretrained language model for scientific text. In *Conference on Empirical Methods in Natural Language Processing*.

Frank Biermann, Norichika Kanie, and Rakhyun E. Kim. 2017. Global governance by goal-setting: the novel approach of the un sustainable development goals. *Current Opinion in Environmental Sustainability*, 26:26–31.

Mark J. Bolland, Andrew Grey, and Alison Avenell. 2022. Citation of retracted publications: A challenging problem. *Accountability in Research*, 29(1):18–25. PMID: 33557605.

Rishi Bommasani, Drew A. Hudson, Ehsan Adeli, Russ Altman, Simran Arora, Sydney von Arx, Michael S. Bernstein, Jeannette Bohg, Antoine Bosselut, Emma Brunskill, Erik Brynjolfsson, S. Buch, Dallas Card, Rodrigo Castellon, Niladri S. Chatterji, Annie S. Chen, Kathleen A. Creel, Jared Davis, Dora Demszky, Chris Donahue, Moussa Doumbouya, Esin Durmus, Stefano Ermon, John Etchemendy, Kawin Ethayarajh, Li Fei-Fei, Chelsea Finn, Trevor Gale, Lauren E. Gillespie, Karan Goel, Noah D. Goodman, Shelby Grossman, Neel Guha, Tatsunori Hashimoto, Peter Henderson, John Hewitt, Daniel E. Ho, Jenny Hong, Kyle Hsu, Jing Huang, Thomas F. Icard, Saahil Jain, Dan Jurafsky, Pratyusha Kalluri, Siddharth Karamcheti, Geoff Keeling, Fereshte Khani, O. Khattab, Pang Wei Koh, Mark S. Krass, Ranjay Krishna, Rohith Kuditipudi, Ananya Kumar, Faisal Ladhak, Mina Lee, Tony Lee, Jure Leskovec, Isabelle Levent, Xiang Lisa Li, Xuechen Li, Tengyu Ma, Ali Malik, Christopher D. Manning, Suvir Mirchandani, Eric Mitchell, Zanele Munyikwa, Suraj Nair, Avanika Narayan, Deepak Narayanan, Benjamin Newman, Allen Nie, Juan Carlos Niebles, Hamed Nilforoshan, J. F. Nyarko, Giray Ogut, Laurel J. Orr, Isabel Papadimitriou, Joon Sung Park, Chris Piech, Eva Portelance, Christopher Potts, Aditi Raghunathan, Robert Reich, Hongyu Ren, Frieda Rong, Yusuf H. Roohani, Camilo Ruiz, Jack Ryan, Christopher R'e, Dorsa Sadigh, Shiori Sagawa, Keshav Santhanam, Andy Shih, Krishna Parasuram Srinivasan, Alex Tamkin, Rohan Taori, Armin W. Thomas, Florian Tramèr, Rose E. Wang, William Wang, Bohan Wu, Jiajun Wu, Yuhuai Wu, Sang Michael Xie, Michihiro Yasunaga, Jiaxuan You, Matei A. Zaharia, Michael Zhang, Tianyi Zhang, Xikun Zhang, Yuhui Zhang, Lucia Zheng, Kaitlyn Zhou, and Percy Liang. 2021. On the opportunities and risks of foundation models. *ArXiv*, abs/2108.07258.

Tom B. Brown, Benjamin Mann, Nick Ryder, Melanie Subbiah, Jared Kaplan, Prafulla Dhariwal, Arvind Neelakantan, Pranav Shyam, Girish Sastry, Amanda Askell, Sandhini Agarwal, Ariel Herbert-Voss, Gretchen Krueger, T. J. Henighan, Rewon Child, Aditya Ramesh, Daniel M. Ziegler, Jeff Wu, Clemens Winter, Christopher Hesse, Mark Chen, Eric Sigler, Mateusz Litwin, Scott Gray, Benjamin Chess, Jack Clark, Christopher Berner, Sam McCandlish, Alec

Radford, Ilya Sutskever, and Dario Amodei. 2020. Language models are few-shot learners. *NIPS*.

Declan Butler. 2018. Researchers have finally created a tool to spot duplicated images across thousands of papers. *Nature*, 555:18–18.

Cristina Candal-Pedreira, Alberto Ruano-Raviña, and Mónica Pérez-Ríos. 2021. Should the european union have an office of research integrity? *European journal of internal medicine*.

Joyita Chakraborty, Dinesh K. Pradhan, and Subrata Nandi. 2021. On the identification and analysis of citation pattern irregularities among journals. *Expert Systems*, 38(4):e12561.

Oana Cocarascu, Elena Cabrio, Serena Villata, and Francesca Toni. 2020. Dataset independent baselines for relation prediction in argument mining. In *Comma*.

Clive Cookson. 2023. Study reveals scale of 'science scam' in academic publishing. *The Financial Times*.

Jacob Devlin, Ming-Wei Chang, Kenton Lee, and Kristina Toutanova. 2019. Bert: Pre-training of deep bidirectional transformers for language understanding. *ArXiv*, abs/1810.04805.

The Economist. 2023. There is a worrying amount of fraud in medical research. *The Economist*.

Holly Else and Richard van Noorden. 2021. The fight against fake-paper factories that churn out sham science. *Nature*, 591:516 – 519.

Daniele Fanelli, Julie Wong, and David Moher. 2022. What difference might retractions make? an estimate of the potential epistemic cost of retractions on meta-analyses. *Accountability in Research*, 29(7):442–459. PMID: 34196235.

Aris Fergadis, Dimitris Pappas, Antonia Karamolegkou, and Haris Papageorgiou. 2021. Argumentation mining in scientific literature for sustainable development. In *Proceedings of the 8th Workshop on Argument Mining*, pages 100–111, Punta Cana, Dominican Republic. Association for Computational Linguistics.

Craig A Garmendia, Liliana Nassar Gorra, Ana Lucia Rodriguez, Mary Jo Trepka, Emir Veledar, and Purnima Madhivanan. 2019. Evaluation of the inclusion of studies identified by the fda as having falsified data in the results of meta-analyses: the example of the apixaban trials. *JAMA Internal Medicine*, 179(4):582–584.

Alex Graves and Jürgen Schmidhuber. 2005. Framewise phoneme classification with bidirectional lstm and other neural network architectures. *Neural networks : the official journal of the International Neural Network Society*, 18 5-6:602–10.

Shai Gretz, Roni Friedman, Edo Cohen-Karlik, Assaf Toledo, Dan Lahav, Ranit Aharonov, and Noam Slonim. 2019. A large-scale dataset for argument quality ranking: Construction and analysis. In *AAAI Conference on Artificial Intelligence*.

Ivan Habernal and Iryna Gurevych. 2016. Which argument is more convincing? analyzing and predicting convincingness of web arguments using bidirectional lstm. In *Annual Meeting of the Association for Computational Linguistics*.

Robin Haunschild and Lutz Bornmann. 2021. Can tweets be used to detect problems early with scientific papers? a case study of three retracted covid-19/sars-cov-2 papers. *Scientometrics*, 126:5181 – 5199.

Yassine Himeur, Somaya Ali Al-Maadeed, Noor Almadeed, Khalid Abualsaud, Amr Mohamed, Tamer M. S. Khattab, and Omar Elharrouss. 2022. Deep visual social distancing monitoring to combat covid-19: A comprehensive survey. *Sustainable Cities and Society*, 85:104064 – 104064.

Joanne Horton, Dhanya Krishna Kumar, and Anthony Wood. 2020. Detecting academic fraud using benford law: The case of professor james hunton. *Research Policy*, 49(8):104084.

Albert Q. Jiang, Alexandre Sablayrolles, Arthur Mensch, Chris Bamford, Devendra Singh Chaplot, Diego de las Casas, Florian Bressand, Gianna Lengyel, Guillaume Lample, Lucile Saulnier, Lélio Renard Lavaud, Marie-Anne Lachaux, Pierre Stock, Teven Le Scao, Thibaut Lavril, Thomas Wang, Timothée Lacroix, and William El Sayed. 2023. Mistral 7b.

Albert Q. Jiang, Alexandre Sablayrolles, Antoine Roux, Arthur Mensch, Blanche Savary, Chris Bamford, Devendra Singh Chaplot, Diego de las Casas, Emma Bou Hanna, Florian Bressand, Gianna Lengyel, Guillaume Bour, Guillaume Lample, Lélio Renard Lavaud, Lucile Saulnier, Marie-Anne Lachaux, Pierre Stock, Sandeep Subramanian, Sophia Yang, Szymon Antoniak, Teven Le Scao, Théophile Gervet, Thibaut Lavril, Thomas Wang, Timothée Lacroix, and William El Sayed. 2024. Mixtral of experts.

Omkar Joshi, Priya Pitre, and Yashodhara V. Haribhakta. 2023. Arganalysis35k : A large-scale dataset for argument quality analysis. In *Annual Meeting of the Association for Computational Linguistics*.

Soo Young Kim, Hyun Jung Yi, Hye-Min Cho, and Sun Huh. 2019. How many retracted articles indexed in koreamed were cited 1 year after retraction notification. *Science Editing*.

Nick Kinney, Araba Wubah, Miguel Roig, and Harold R. Garner. 2021. Estimating the prevalence of text overlap in biomedical conference abstracts. *Research Integrity and Peer Review*, 6.

Anne Lauscher, Lily Ng, Courtney Napoles, and Joel Tetreault. 2020. Rhetoric, logic, and dialectic: Advancing theory-based argument quality assessment in natural language processing. In *Proceedings of the 28th International Conference on Computational Linguistics*, pages 4563–4574, Barcelona, Spain (Online). International Committee on Computational Linguistics.

John Lawrence and Chris Reed. 2020. Argument mining: A survey. *Computational Linguistics*, Just Accepted:1–55.

Yinhan Liu, Myle Ott, Naman Goyal, Jingfei Du, Mandar Joshi, Danqi Chen, Omer Levy, Mike Lewis, Luke Zettlemoyer, and Veselin Stoyanov. 2019. Roberta: A robustly optimized bert pretraining approach. *ArXiv*, abs/1907.11692.

Adam Marcus and Ivan Oransky. 2023. The retraction watch database. *New York: The Center for Scientific Integrity*.

Andreas F. Mavrogenis and Marius M. Scarlat. 2023. Quality peer review is mandatory for scientific journals: ethical constraints, computers, and progress of communication with the reviewers of international orthopaedics. *International Orthopaedics*, 47:605–609.

Tobias Mayer, Elena Cabrio, and Serena Villata. 2020. Transformer-based argument mining for healthcare applications. In *ECAI 2020 - 24th European Conference on Artificial Intelligence*, volume 325 of *Frontiers in Artificial Intelligence and Applications*, pages 2108–2115. IOS Press.

Andreas Peldszus and Manfred Stede. 2013. From argument diagrams to argumentation mining in texts: A survey. *Int. J. Cogn. Informatics Nat. Intell.*, 7:1–31.

N. Pooranam, Priya P N Sushma, Sai Sruthi, and Dhanya K Sri. 2021. A safety measuring tool to maintain social distancing on covid-19 using deep learning approach. *Journal of Physics: Conference Series*, 1916.

Ramon Ruiz-Dolz, José Alemany, Stella Heras Barberá, and Ana García-Fornes. 2020. Transformer-based models for automatic identification of argument relations: A cross-domain evaluation. *IEEE Intelligent Systems*, 36:62–70.

BA Sabel, E Knaack, G Gigerenzer, and M Bilc. 2023. Fake publications in biomedical science: Redflagging method indicates mass production.

Bernhard A. Sabel and Roland Seifert. 2021. How criminal science publishing gangs damage the genesis of knowledge and technology—a call to action to restore trust. *Naunyn-Schmiedeberg's Archives of Pharmacology*, 394:2147 – 2151.

Edwin Simpson and Iryna Gurevych. 2018. Finding convincing arguments using scalable bayesian preference learning. *Transactions of the Association for Computational Linguistics*, 6:357–371.

Christian Stab and Iryna Gurevych. 2016. Parsing argumentation structures in persuasive essays. *Computational Linguistics*, 43:619–659.

Manfred Stede and Antje Sauermann. 2008. Linearization of arguments in commentary text.

Luke Thorburn and Ariel Kruger. 2022. Optimizing language models for argumentative reasoning. In *ArgML@COMMA*.

Assaf Toledo, Shai Gretz, Edo Cohen-Karlik, Roni Friedman, Elad Venezian, Dan Lahav, Michal Jacovi, Ranit Aharonov, and Noam Slonim. 2019. Automatic argument quality assessment - new datasets and methods. In *Conference on Empirical Methods in Natural Language Processing*.

Richard van Noorden. 2021. Hundreds of gibberish papers still lurk in the scientific literature. *Nature*, 594:160 – 161.

Ashish Vaswani, Noam M. Shazeer, Niki Parmar, Jakob Uszkoreit, Llion Jones, Aidan N. Gomez, Lukasz Kaiser, and Illia Polosukhin. 2017. Attention is all you need. In *NIPS*.

Henning Wachsmuth, Nona Naderi, Yufang Hou, Yonatan Bilu, Vinodkumar Prabhakaran, Tim Alberdingk Thijm, Graeme Hirst, and Benno Stein. 2017. Computational argumentation quality assessment in natural language. In *Proceedings of the 15th Conference of the European Chapter of the Association for Computational Linguistics: Volume 1, Long Papers*, pages 176–187, Valencia, Spain. Association for Computational Linguistics.

Elizabeth Wager, Sabine Kleinert, Michele Garfinkel, Volker Bahr, Ksenija Badarić, Michael J. G. Farthing, Chris Graf, Zoë Hammatt, Lyn Horn, Susan King, Debra Parrish, Bernd Pulverer, Paul Taylor, and Gerrit van Meer. 2017. Cooperation & liaison between universities & editors (clue): recommendations on best practice. *Research Integrity and Peer Review*, 6.

Jason Wei, Xuezhi Wang, Dale Schuurmans, Maarten Bosma, Brian Ichter, Fei Xia, Ed H. Chi, Quoc V. Le, and Denny Zhou. 2022. Chain-of-thought prompting elicits reasoning in large language models. In *NeurIPS 2022*.

Hugh Zhang and David C. Parkes. 2023. Chain-of-thought reasoning is a policy improvement operator. *CoRR*, abs/2309.08589.

Yue Zhao, Ajay Anand, and Gaurav Sharma. 2021. Reviewer recommendations using document vector embeddings and a publisher database: Implementation and evaluation. *IEEE Access*, 10:21798–21811.

A Hardware Configuration

All models presented in this paper were trained on a computing cluster containing the following GPUs:

- Nvidia Tesla A30 with 24GB RAM
- Nvidia Tesla T4 with 16GB RAM
- Nvidia GeForce GTX Titan Xp with 12GB RAM

B Code and Data

The following repository contains all relevant code and data: https://github.com/GIFRN/Scientific-Fraud-Detection/tree/main.

We also present a detailed breakdown, including hyperparameters, of the AQE model that we use for all experiments. This is because we include the trained model already in the repository, where as for the AM modle we include the training script and training data. Hyperparameters were optimised by means of extensive grid search.

B.1 Argument Quality Evaluation model

The same architecture is used for the results reported in Tables 3 and 4, and for both of the 'Quality' models in Table 3.

Input dimensions
Max token length: 512

RoBERTa Model
Number of training epochs: 5
Number of folds: 5
Dropout rate: 0.2
Batch size: 8

AdamW Optimizer
Learning Rate: 1×10^{-5}
Weight Decay: 1×10^{-2}

C Prompt

The following is the prompt used for both the Mistral and Mixtral baselines described in Section 4.2:

```
"Please return whether the following
scientific abstract is fraudulent or
legitimate. A fraudulent abstract
is one that has been produced
by a paper mill or has not
undergone a proper peer review process.
Please think through your answer
step by step before returning
your final answer.
Present your final answer as
'STATUS: Legitimate'
if the abstract is legitimate or
'STATUS: Fraudulent'
if the abstract
is fraudulent.\nAbstract: " + abstract
```

D Argument Quality Evaluation Preprocessing

In Table 5 we show two examples of samples taken from the GAQCorpus, used for training the AQE model. We show the samples before and after preprocessing, and include the rating.

Original Text	**Preprocessed Text**	**Cogency Rating**
Wow, that's tough. Is your assignment to argue that retribution is socially cohesive, or did you come up with this yourself? This is what I can think of: Retributive justice is based on the idea that criminals should be punished for undermining social "harmony" or "balance." Therefore, we can't dole out retributive punishment before we first have a definition of what is social harmony or balance. Social harmony and balance can be defined through laws, custom, or religion. The PROCESS of defining social harmony and balance is socailly cohesive because, to some extent, we must generally agree on what the definition of social order is. In other words, the PROCESS of accepting and agreeing on laws/customs/religion is socially cohesive. The rehabilitation theory of punishment is probably the most socially cohesive because it is based on rehabiliting the criminal so that he can successfully reenter society.	This is what I can think of: Retributive justice is based on the idea that criminals should be punished for undermining social "harmony" or "balance. " Therefore, we can't dole out retributive punishment before we first have a definition of what is social harmony or balance. Social harmony and balance can be defined through laws, custom, or religion. The PROCESS of defining social harmony and balance is socailly cohesive because, to some extent, we must generally agree on what the definition of social order is. In other words, the PROCESS of accepting and agreeing on laws/customs/religion is socially cohesive. The rehabilitation theory of punishment is probably the most socially cohesive because it is based on rehabiliting the criminal so that he can successfully reenter society.	4
Am I reading this right? A pot head is waging war on a meth head?! I never thought this sort of reasoning would make it farther than the 'idea' having moment during a toking. You got more tar in your head than you do brains. And yes, Meth addicts DO need jail time. Every one of them made a clear and concious decision to pick up that hot rail, needle or pipe to smoke crystal when they started and the time it took to become 'uncontrolably' addicted, so they accepted the risks. Besides, MOST users sell, they keep cutting some out every time it exchanges hands, so lock 'em up!! And I can't belive someone is trying to defend the 'poor' addicts. What and idiot you are Cripple play!!!	I never thought this sort of reasoning would make it farther than the 'idea' having moment during a toking. You got more tar in your head than you do brains. And yes, Meth addicts DO need jail time. Every one of them made a clear and concious decision to pick up that hot rail, needle or pipe to smoke crystal when they started and the time it took to become 'uncontrolably' addicted, so they accepted the risks. Besides, MOST users sell, they keep cutting some out every time it exchanges hands, so lock 'em up. And I can't belive someone is trying to defend the 'poor' addicts. What and idiot you are Cripple play.	2

Table 5: Illustrative examples from the GAQCorpus, before and after preprocessing

DeepCT-enhanced Lexical Argument Retrieval

Alexander Bondarenko
Leipzig University and
Friedrich-Schiller-Universität Jena

Maik Fröbe
Friedrich-Schiller-Universität Jena

Danik Hollatz
Martin-Luther-Universität Halle-Wittenberg

Jan Heinrich Merker
Friedrich-Schiller-Universität Jena

Matthias Hagen
Friedrich-Schiller-Universität Jena

Abstract

The recent Touché lab's argument retrieval task focuses on controversial topics like 'Should bottled water be banned?' and asks to retrieve relevant pro/con arguments. Interestingly, the most effective systems submitted to that task still are based on lexical retrieval models like BM25. In other domains, neural retrievers that capture semantics are more effective than lexical baselines. To add more "semantics" to argument retrieval, we propose to combine lexical models with DeepCT-based document term weights. Our evaluation shows that our approach is more effective than all the systems submitted to the Touché lab while being on par with modern neural re-rankers that themselves are computationally more expensive.

1 Introduction

Lexical retrieval models like BM25 (Robertson et al., 1994) or DirichletLM (Zhai and Lafferty, 2001) are the basis of many of the early argument retrieval approaches (Chernodub et al., 2019; Potthast et al., 2019; Stab et al., 2018; Wachsmuth et al., 2017) and also were the most common choice of many participants of the Touché lab's shared task on argument retrieval for controversial questions (Bondarenko et al., 2020, 2021). A few neural rankers like K-NRM (Xiong et al., 2017) and CEDR (MacAvaney et al., 2019) were used by the task participants but showed to be less effective than the task's official DirichletLM-based baseline. Interestingly, also newer neural retrieval models like ColBERTv2 (Santhanam et al., 2022) and LaPraDoR (Xu et al., 2022) are less effective than BM25 on the Touché subset of the BEIR benchmark for zero-shot retrieval (Thakur et al., 2021).

In this paper, we propose to improve the effectiveness of lexical argument retrieval models by adding a semantic document expansion step that uses term weights calculated by DeepCT (Dai and Callan, 2020b). For term weighting, DeepCT utilizes contextualized word representations generated by BERT (Devlin et al., 2019) and is then fine-tuned to predict whether a document term is likely to appear in "relevant" queries. At the inference step, a fine-tuned model is applied to every document in the retrieval collection independently from the test queries. Hence, an advantage of DeepCT is that the inference can be done offline before indexing the corpus. Another advantage is that DeepCT does not necessarily require relevance judgments either for training or for inference making DeepCT beneficial for retrieval tasks in specialized domains that have no or little training data.

For our experiments, we use the lexical retrieval models BM25 and DirichletLM and their combination with the query expansion model RM3 (Abdul-Jaleel et al., 2004). We test these models on the Touché 2020 and 2021 test collections consisting of 49 and 50 test queries on controversial topics respectively, the args.me corpus (Ajjour et al., 2019) as a document collection (about 400,000 documents, i.e., English arguments crawled from online debate portals), and 6,000 graded relevance judgments (not relevant, relevant, and highly relevant) from Touché. Additionally, we expand the documents in the retrieval corpus based on the term weights predicted by fine-tuned DeepCT models. To fine-tune the DeepCT models (originally trained on the MS MARCO dataset (Nguyen et al., 2016)) specifically for the argument retrieval task, we make use of the args.me structured documents, consisting of the argument premises, the conclusion, and the main debate topic. We use either the conclusions or the debate topics combined with the conclusions as ground truth terms in the reference field of DeepCT. Afterwards, we apply the fine-tuned DeepCT model to the whole args.me corpus and expand the document's premises by repeating terms based on the learned DeepCT term weights.

We compare our approaches with the following

Proceedings of the 11th Workshop on Argument Mining, pages 29–35
August 15, 2024 ©2024 Association for Computational Linguistics

baselines: (1) the most effective Touché systems (that use BM25 and DirchletLM combined with query and document processing) and (2) BM25 combined with neural re-rankers: (a) a contextualized late interaction model ColBERT (Khattab and Zaharia, 2020), (b) pointwise cross-encoders monoBERT (Nogueira and Cho, 2019) and monoT5 (Nogueira et al., 2020), and (c) a zero-shot listwise re-ranker LiT5 (Tamber et al., 2023).

To evaluate the retrieval effectiveness, we use nDCG@5 (Järvelin and Kekäläinen, 2002), the official evaluation measure of the Touché task. To account for missing relevance judgments (up to 60%; see Table 2), we measure nDCG@5 after removing unjudged documents from ranked results as proposed by Sakai (2007) and use the bpref measure (Buckley and Voorhees, 2004) which is robust to missing relevance judgments.

The evaluation results show that our DeepCT-enhanced lexical argument retrieval approach is more effective than all the systems submitted to the Touché task while being on par with modern neural re-rankers that are more computationally expensive. Our findings thus may indicate the potential of combining lexical models with semantic document expansion for specialized retrieval tasks like argument retrieval, where little or no training data (in terms of relevance judgments) is available.[1]

2 Related Work

Retrieving relevant arguments from the Web is essential to support discussions on controversial topics like 'Should bottled water be banned?' (Ajjour et al., 2019). Until now, lexical retrieval models like BM25 (Robertson et al., 1994) and DirichletLM (Zhai and Lafferty, 2001) have been the most effective retrievers for this task (Potthast et al., 2019). For instance, argument search engines args.me (Wachsmuth et al., 2017), ArgumenText (Stab et al., 2018), and TARGER (Chernodub et al., 2019), all use BM25 for initial retrieval. However, even though neural retrievers like ColBERTv2 (Santhanam et al., 2022), LaPraDoR (Xu et al., 2022), or COCO-DR (Yu et al., 2022) have led to effectiveness improvements in many domain-specific retrieval tasks as evaluated in the BEIR benchmark (Thakur et al., 2021), for argument retrieval (e.g., the Touché subset of BEIR), lexical retrievers still outperform neural models.

Studying argument retrieval approaches was also carried out as part of the Touché lab's shared tasks on argument retrieval for controversial questions (Bondarenko et al., 2020, 2021). Most of the participant's approaches used lexical retrieval models (i.e., BM25 and DirichletLM) for initial document retrieval combined with various query processing and reformulation techniques. The initial document candidates were further re-ranked based on the estimated document argumentativeness (i.e., the presence of conclusions and premises) and argument quality. Several tested neural rankers, like K-NRM (Xiong et al., 2017) and CEDR (MacAvaney et al., 2019) were less effective (measured with nDCG@5) than the lexical models.

Lexical retrieval models (that rely on an exact match between the query and document terms), conversely, may suffer from "ignoring" the semantic similarity between the query and document terms. Hence, we propose to combine lexical retrievers (that are effective for argument retrieval) with document expansion based on estimated semantic term importance (term weights) predicted by DeepCT (Dai and Callan, 2020b,a). The DeepCT model exploits the BERT (Devlin et al., 2019) fine-tuning paradigm by fine-tuning a pre-trained BERT model to predict the importance of words in documents w.r.t. reference terms (e.g., query terms). Fine-tuning aims to minimize the mean square error between the predicted term weights and the ground truth term weights. The ground truth labels can be generated using documents only, relevance labels, or pseudo-relevance feedback. In our work, we use the documents-only approach which does not require manual relevance labels for fine-tuning DeepCT (cf. Section 3 for more details). The fine-tuned DeepCT is then applied to the documents and predicts the document term importance scores. Finally, the documents are modified by repeating terms proportionally to predicted weights ($w * 100$, where term weights $w \in [0, 1]$), thus boosting the term frequency of the repeated terms in the inverted index. Thus, lexical retrieval models that rely on the term frequency as a relevance signal can benefit from repeated "relevant" document terms. It has been shown that combining DeepCT with lexical models improves the effectiveness of ad hoc retrieval (Dai and Callan, 2020b,a) on general-domain document collections, e.g., MS MARCO (Nguyen et al., 2016) or Wikipedia articles (Dietz et al., 2017). Thus, we aim to test a combination of lexical re-

[1]Code and data are at https://github.com/webis-de/argmining24-deepct-lexical-argument-retrieval/

trieval models with semantic document expansion for the argument retrieval task.

For the evaluation of argument retrieval approaches, several datasets (Abbott et al., 2016; Hidey et al., 2017; Ajjour et al., 2019) and the Touché test collections (Bondarenko et al., 2020, 2021) emerged. By far the largest and hence one of the most frequently used document collections, the args.me corpus, contains about 400,000 arguments crawled from online debates on controversial topics (Ajjour et al., 2019). The Touché shared tasks on argument retrieval for controversial questions also used the args.me corpus. Additionally, the task organizers created and published manual relevance judgments and runs (ranked results) submitted by the task participants. Our experiments use the Touché data from the years 2020 and 2021.

3 Data and Approach

Data. In this work, we use the datasets from the Touché 2020 and 2021 tasks on controversial argument retrieval (Bondarenko et al., 2020, 2021). The task was to retrieve and rank relevant argumentative documents for queries addressing socially important (and often controversial) topics like 'Should bottled water be banned?'. The document collection was the args.me corpus (Ajjour et al., 2019) containing about 400,000 arguments crawled from different online debate portals. Each document is structured and contains a debate topic field (e.g., 'Pollution'), an argument conclusion (e.g., 'Plastic bottles should be banned'), and a main content containing several premises (i.e., reasons, opinions, or evidence that support or attack the conclusion). We access all the data inside the PyTerrier framework (Macdonald and Tonellotto, 2020) via `ir_datasets` (MacAvaney et al., 2021), including queries, document collection, and available document-level manual relevance judgments (the participants' systems are available at the Touché task website `https://touche.webis.de`).

DeepCT-based term weighting. Our pilot experiments using the original DeepCT model pretrained on the MS MARCO dataset showed that the retrieval effectiveness of lexical models degrades (cf. DirichletLM + DeepCT achieves nDCG@5 of 0.59 vs. 0.83 that DirichletLM achieves on the unmodified args.me corpus). This is likely due to the document domain change (general domain vs. argument retrieval). We thus opt for fine-tuning DeepCT for the argument retrieval task on the args.me corpus. To create training samples for fine-tuning, we use a content-based weak-supervision strategy proposed by Dai and Callan (2020a) that determines the target important terms by utilizing the document's structure (i.e., different fields like debate topic, conclusion, and premises in our case). Since the Touché queries are used for testing, as a reference field for fine-tuning, we use either an argument's conclusion field of the args.me document or a concatenation of a debate topic and conclusion.

Table 1: Example of a training sample to fine-tune DeepCT created using the conclusion 'Banning bottled water would reduce waste and protect the environment' as a reference field. The important terms identified by DeepCT at the inference step are in bold; superscripts indicate the number of times each term is repeated in the document (term weights predicted by DeepCT (from 0 to 1) multiplied by 100).

Passage:	Plastic **water**$^{(48)}$ **bottles**$^{(23)}$ were the third most commonly collected **waste**$^{(34)}$ during the Ocean Conservancy's International Coastal Cleanup behind cigarette butts and plastic food wrappers. By 2050, estimates suggest there will be more plastic **waste**$^{(14)}$ by weight in the oceans than fish. [...] A nation-wide **ban**$^{(27)}$ on **bottled**$^{(21)}$ **water**$^{(17)}$ would lead to an estimated 68 billion fewer plastic **water**$^{(14)}$ **bottles**$^{(19)}$ being manufactured, purchased, used, and discarded.
Reference:	water: 1.0, bottles: 1.0, waste: 1.0, ban: 1.0, bottled: 1.0.

Following the original DeepCT fine-tuning strategy (Dai and Callan, 2020b), we split the premises of the args.me documents into passages of 500 tokens to comply with the DeepCT input limit of 512 tokens. To identify the reference field's ground truth terms, we remove stop words using NLTK (Bird, 2006) from passages, conclusions, and debate topics. Afterwards, we apply stemming using the NLTK's Porter stemmer (Porter, 1980). The reference field's ground truth terms are selected as follows: If there is a stem of a word from a passage and this stem also appears in the stemmed conclusion (or debate topic + conclusion), the original form of the word is added to the reference field. The target term weights are assigned 1.0 (see Table 1 for an example).

To fine-tune DeepCT, we use three variants of the args.me corpus: (1) all documents in the corpus; and to analyze the effect of possible train-test leakage: (2) judged documents from the Touché 2020 and 2021 tasks are removed, and (3) top-50 documents from all systems submitted to Touché 2020

Table 2: Retrieval effectiveness of the best data transformation technique to fine-tune DeepCT (as per nDCG@5) per retrieval model (BM25, DirichletLM (DLM), and their combinations with RM3; model parameters tuned, see Column 'PT') on the Touché 2020 and 2021 datasets: (1) all args.me documents, (2) judged documents are removed, and (3) top-50 documents are removed. Document fields used as the reference field for DeepCT: debate topic and conclusion (TC), or conclusion only (C). Both retrieval models without DeepCT doc. term weighting, best Touché systems, and neural baselines from TIREx are reported for comparison. The nDCG@5 scores are evaluated after removing unjudged documents (cf. the ratio of retrieved documents with relevance judgments, 'judged@5'). The bpref score is robust to unjudged documents. Underlines denote the best system per metric; bold indicates significant equivalence to the best system within ± 0.1 (two one-sided t-tests, $p < 0.05$, Bonferroni correction).

	Retrieval model	PT	Data transf.	nDCG@5	bpref	judged@5
Touché 2020	DeepCT + DLM + RM3	✓	(1), C	**0.88**	0.71	0.45
	BM25 + monoT5	×	n/a	**0.87**	**0.81**	0.41
	DeepCT + BM25 + RM3	✓	(2), TC	**0.87**	**0.77**	0.46
	BM25 + RM3	✓	n/a	**0.87**	0.71	0.43
	BM25 + LiT5	×	n/a	0.86	0.51	0.39
	BM25 + monoBERT	×	n/a	0.85	**0.79**	0.41
	DeepCT + BM25	✓	(2), TC	0.84	0.71	0.47
	BM25 + ColBERT	×	n/a	0.83	**0.77**	0.42
	Best Touché	×	n/a	0.83	0.70	1.00
	DeepCT + DLM	✓	(2), TC	0.82	0.68	0.47
	DLM + RM3	✓	n/a	0.82	0.58	0.51
	BM25	✓	n/a	0.80	0.64	0.44
	DLM	✓	n/a	0.78	0.57	0.56
Touché 2021	BM25 + monoT5	×	n/a	**0.77**	**0.80**	0.70
	DeepCT + BM25	✓	(3), TC	0.74	0.74	0.78
	DeepCT + BM25 + RM3	✓	(2), TC	0.74	0.74	0.70
	Best Touché	×	n/a	0.74	0.73	1.00
	DeepCT + DLM	✓	(1), TC	0.74	0.72	0.79
	BM25 + monoBERT	×	n/a	0.73	**0.77**	0.69
	BM25 + LiT5	×	n/a	0.73	0.59	0.79
	DeepCT + DLM + RM3	✓	(1), TC	0.70	0.73	0.72
	BM25 + RM3	✓	n/a	0.70	0.65	0.82
	BM25 + ColBERT	×	n/a	0.69	**0.75**	0.63
	BM25	✓	n/a	0.67	0.62	0.95
	DLM	✓	n/a	0.67	0.62	0.94
	DLM + RM3	✓	n/a	0.64	0.56	0.75

and 2021 are removed from args.me. After expanding the passages using the fine-tuned DeepCT models, the passages are concatenated back into complete documents. The original args.me corpus is then modified with the three differently fine-tuned DeepCT models, resulting in three corpus variants.

Retrieval models. For every variant of the modified corpus, we test the effectiveness of BM25 and DirichletLM and their combination with the query expansion model RM3. We select the model's parameters using grid search and two-fold cross-validation (each fold is either the Touché 2020 or 2021 relevance judgments) implemented in PyTerrier (Macdonald and Tonellotto, 2020).

4 Evaluation

We compare our approaches (lexical retrieval models with DeepCT-based corpus transformations) with the most effective systems at Touché 2020 (49 queries, and 2,298 relevance judgments) and 2021 (50 queries, and 3,711 judgments) as well as with four strong neural retrieval baselines implemented in TIREx (Fröbe et al., 2023).

Due to the high portion of missing judgments for systems not in the Touché's original pool (cf. column 'judged@5' in Table 2), we measure nDCG@5 (Järvelin and Kekäläinen, 2002), the official evaluation measure of the Touché task, after removing unjudged documents as proposed by Sakai (2007). In our evaluation, we also include the bpref measure (Buckley and Voorhees, 2004) that is invariant to missing judgments. While removing unjudged documents and using bpref have been accepted in IR evaluation, filling in missing judgments by manual annotation can provide more robust evaluation results in future work. We use the effectiveness measures implemented in `ir_measures` (MacAvaney et al., 2022).

At Touché 2020, the most effective system (highest nDCG@5 and highest bpref; cf. Table 2) was the official Touché task baseline that used Lucene's (Bialecki et al., 2012) DirichletLM implementation without any query or document processing (all the participants' systems were less effective). In 2021, the most effective participants' systems were the following: (1) Lucene's BM25, stop word removal, and boolean `OR` query (highest nDCG@5), and (2) Lucene's DirichletLM, stop word removal, and stemming using the Krovetz stemmer (Krovetz, 1993) (highest bpref).

We complement the best systems at Touché (which are all based on lexical retrieval) with four neural re-rankers: (1) ColBERT (Khattab and Zaharia, 2020), a contextualized late interaction model that uses BERT (Devlin et al., 2019), (2–3) monoBERT (Nogueira and Cho, 2019) and monoT5 (Nogueira et al., 2020), two pointwise cross-encoder models based on BERT and T5 (Raffel et al., 2020), and (4) LiT5 (Tamber et al., 2023), a zero-shot listwise re-ranker using T5. All four models were used in a re-ranking setting using TIREx (Fröbe et al., 2023), to re-rank the top-1000 documents retrieved by BM25.

Results. With respect to both nDCG@5 and bpref, our approach of using DeepCT for semantic document term weighting improves over the Touché best systems when using the BM25 retrieval model. When using DirichletLM, the DeepCT term weighting does not outperform the participants' systems on the Touché 2021 data. We also find that the best neural baseline, monoT5 as a re-ranker, is also more effective than the best Touché systems of 2021, while the other neural re-rankers fall back behind. Our most effective DeepCT-based approach does not outperform monoT5; yet, it is on par with monoT5 for Touché 2020 data (significantly equivalent to the best system within a ± 0.1 band, see Table 2) and not far off on the 2021 data. The promising effectiveness indicates the potential of combining lexical models with semantic document term weighting for argument retrieval tasks. In contrast to neural models, however, DeepCT is applied at index time and does not require model inference at query time. As we also showed, fine-tuning DeepCT does not require manual relevance judgments. Thus, our approach can have beneficial properties for deployment in low-resource environments which is common for specialized tasks like argument retrieval.

Furthermore, in at least half of the retrieval scenarios, fine-tuning DeepCT on the args.me documents after removing the judged ones, results in the highest evaluation scores. Thus, we do not observe strong evidence of the train-test leakage influence on the retrieval results. Moreover, combining an argument conclusion with a debate topic for fine-tuning DeepCT often benefits the retrieval effectiveness of lexical models.

5 Conclusion

In this paper, we proposed to combine lexical retrieval models with semantic document expansion for argument retrieval. Specifically, to calculate the term weights, we fine-tuned DeepCT on the args.me corpus. The main advantages of DeepCT are that the calculation of term weights can be done in an offline fashion before document indexing and that its training does not require manual relevance judgments. This is especially important in the specialized domains (e.g., argument retrieval), where no or little training data is available. Furthermore, at query time only lexical retrieval models are used on the expanded documents that require less computational resources than neural models.

Our evaluation results showed that adding some "semantics" to strong lexical argument retrieval approaches improves the overall effectiveness over the lexical retrieval alone. Additionally, we showed that our approach is on par with modern neural rerankers, which themselves can be more computationally expensive. However, we also indicated that for a more robust conclusion, further experiments should be conducted, where the missing relevance judgments are filled.

Another potentially interesting future direction can be to include the argument mining step in the document expansion process, for instance, using only argumentative parts (conclusions and premises) of documents for fine-tuning DeepCT.

Acknowledgments

This work was partially supported by the DFG (German Research Foundation) through the project "ACQuA 2.0: Answering Comparative Questions with Arguments" (project 376430233) as part of the priority program "RATIO: Robust Argumentation Machines" (SPP 1999) and by the Stiftung für Innovation in der Hochschullehre under the "freiraum 2022" call (FRFMM-58/2022).

References

Rob Abbott, Brian Ecker, Pranav Anand, and Marilyn A. Walker. 2016. Internet argument corpus 2.0: An SQL schema for dialogic social media and the corpora to go with it. In *Proceedings of LREC 2016*, pages 4445–4452, Paris. ELRA.

Nasreen Abdul-Jaleel, James Allan, W. Bruce Croft, Fernando Diaz, Leah S. Larkey, Xiaoyan Li, Mark D. Smucker, and Courtney Wade. 2004. UMass at TREC 2004: Novelty and HARD. In *Proceedings of TREC 2004*, volume 500-261 of *NIST Special Publication*, Gaithersburg. NIST.

Yamen Ajjour, Henning Wachsmuth, Johannes Kiesel, Martin Potthast, Matthias Hagen, and Benno Stein. 2019. Data acquisition for argument search: The args.me corpus. In *Proceedings of KI 2019*, volume 11793 of *LNCS*, pages 48–59, Berlin. Springer.

Andrzej Bialecki, Robert Muir, and Grant Ingersoll. 2012. Apache Lucene 4. In *Proceedings of OSIR@SIGIR 2012*, pages 17–24, Otago. University of Otago.

Steven Bird. 2006. NLTK: The natural language toolkit. In *Proceedings of ACL 2006*, pages 69–72, Kerrville. ACL.

Alexander Bondarenko, Maik Fröbe, Meriem Beloucif, Lukas Gienapp, Yamen Ajjour, Alexander Panchenko, Chris Biemann, Benno Stein, Henning Wachsmuth, Martin Potthast, and Matthias Hagen. 2020. Overview of Touché 2020: Argument retrieval. In *Proceedings of CLEF 2020*, volume 12260 of *LNCS*, pages 384–395, Berlin. Springer.

Alexander Bondarenko, Lukas Gienapp, Maik Fröbe, Meriem Beloucif, Yamen Ajjour, Alexander Panchenko, Chris Biemann, Benno Stein, Henning Wachsmuth, Martin Potthast, and Matthias Hagen. 2021. Overview of Touché 2021: Argument retrieval. In *Proceedings of CLEF 2021*, volume 12880 of *LNCS*, pages 450–467, Berlin. Springer.

Chris Buckley and Ellen M. Voorhees. 2004. Retrieval evaluation with incomplete information. In *Proceedings of SIGIR 2004*, pages 25–32, New York. ACM.

Artem N. Chernodub, Oleksiy Oliynyk, Philipp Heidenreich, Alexander Bondarenko, Matthias Hagen, Chris Biemann, and Alexander Panchenko. 2019. TARGER: Neural argument mining at your fingertips. In *Proceedings of ACL 2019*, pages 195–200, Kerrville. ACL.

Zhuyun Dai and Jamie Callan. 2020a. Context-aware document term weighting for ad-hoc search. In *Proceedings of WWW 2020*, pages 1897–1907, Geneva. IW3C2.

Zhuyun Dai and Jamie Callan. 2020b. Context-aware term weighting for first stage passage retrieval. In *Proceedings of SIGIR 2020*, pages 1533–1536, New York. ACM.

Jacob Devlin, Ming-Wei Chang, Kenton Lee, and Kristina Toutanova. 2019. BERT: Pre-training of deep bidirectional transformers for language understanding. In *Proceedings of NAACL-HLT 2019*, pages 4171–4186, Kerrville. ACL.

Laura Dietz, Manisha Verma, Filip Radlinski, and Nick Craswell. 2017. TREC complex answer retrieval overview. In *Proceedings of TREC 2017*, volume 500-324 of *NIST Special Publication*, Gaithersburg. NIST.

Maik Fröbe, Jan Heinrich Reimer, Sean MacAvaney, Niklas Deckers, Simon Reich, Janek Bevendorff, Benno Stein, Matthias Hagen, and Martin Potthast. 2023. The information retrieval experiment platform. In *Proceedings of SIGIR 2023*, pages 2826–2836, New York. ACM.

Christopher Hidey, Elena Musi, Alyssa Hwang, Smaranda Muresan, and Kathy McKeown. 2017. Analyzing the semantic types of claims and premises in an online persuasive forum. In *Proceedings of ArgMining@EMNLP 2017*, pages 11–21, Kerrville. ACL.

Kalervo Järvelin and Jaana Kekäläinen. 2002. Cumulated gain-based evaluation of IR techniques. *ACM Trans. Inf. Syst.*, 20(4):422–446.

Omar Khattab and Matei Zaharia. 2020. ColBERT: Efficient and effective passage search via contextualized late interaction over BERT. In *Proceedings of SIGIR 2020*, pages 39–48, New York. ACM.

Robert Krovetz. 1993. Viewing morphology as an inference process. In *Proceedings of SIGIR 1993*, pages 191–202, New York. ACM.

Sean MacAvaney, Craig Macdonald, and Iadh Ounis. 2022. Streamlining evaluation with ir-measures. In *Proceedings of ECIR 2022*, volume 13186, pages 305–310, Berlin. Springer.

Sean MacAvaney, Andrew Yates, Arman Cohan, and Nazli Goharian. 2019. CEDR: Contextualized embeddings for document ranking. In *Proceedings of SIGIR 2019*, pages 1101–1104, New York. ACM.

Sean MacAvaney, Andrew Yates, Sergey Feldman, Doug Downey, Arman Cohan, and Nazli Goharian. 2021. Simplified data wrangling with ir_datasets. In *Proceedings of SIGIR 2021*, pages 2429–2436, New York. ACM.

Craig Macdonald and Nicola Tonellotto. 2020. Declarative experimentation in information retrieval using PyTerrier. In *Proceedings of ICTIR 2020*, pages 161–168, New York. ACM.

Tri Nguyen, Mir Rosenberg, Xia Song, Jianfeng Gao, Saurabh Tiwary, Rangan Majumder, and Li Deng. 2016. MS MARCO: A human generated MAchine Reading COmprehension dataset. In *Proceedings of CoCo@NIPS 2016*, volume 1773 of *CEUR Workshop Proceedings*, online. CEUR-WS.org.

Rodrigo Frassetto Nogueira and Kyunghyun Cho. 2019. Passage re-ranking with BERT. arXiv 1901.04085.

Rodrigo Frassetto Nogueira, Zhiying Jiang, Ronak Pradeep, and Jimmy Lin. 2020. Document ranking with a pretrained sequence-to-sequence model. In *Findings of EMNLP 2020*, pages 708–718, Kerrville. ACL.

Martin F. Porter. 1980. An algorithm for suffix stripping. *Program*, 14(3):130–137.

Martin Potthast, Lukas Gienapp, Florian Euchner, Nick Heilenkötter, Nico Weidmann, Henning Wachsmuth, Benno Stein, and Matthias Hagen. 2019. Argument search: Assessing argument relevance. In *Proceedings of SIGIR 2019*, pages 1117–1120, New York. ACM.

Colin Raffel, Noam Shazeer, Adam Roberts, Katherine Lee, Sharan Narang, Michael Matena, Yanqi Zhou, Wei Li, and Peter J. Liu. 2020. Exploring the limits of transfer learning with a unified text-to-text transformer. *J. Mach. Learn. Res.*, 21:140:1–140:67.

Stephen E. Robertson, Steve Walker, Susan Jones, Micheline Hancock-Beaulieu, and Mike Gatford. 1994. Okapi at TREC-3. In *Proceedings of TREC 1994*, volume 500-225 of *NIST Special Publication*, pages 109–126, Gaithersburg. NIST.

Tetsuya Sakai. 2007. Alternatives to bpref. In *Proceedings of SIGIR 2007*, pages 71–78, New York. ACM.

Keshav Santhanam, Omar Khattab, Jon Saad-Falcon, Christopher Potts, and Matei Zaharia. 2022. ColBERTv2: Effective and efficient retrieval via lightweight late interaction. In *Proceedings of NAACL 2022*, pages 3715–3734, Kerrville. ACL.

Christian Stab, Johannes Daxenberger, Chris Stahlhut, Tristan Miller, Benjamin Schiller, Christopher Tauchmann, Steffen Eger, and Iryna Gurevych. 2018. ArgumenText: Searching for arguments in heterogeneous sources. In *Proceedings of NAACL-HLT 2018*, pages 21–25, Kerrville. ACL.

Manveer Singh Tamber, Ronak Pradeep, and Jimmy Lin. 2023. Scaling down, LiTting up: Efficient zero-shot listwise reranking with seq2seq encoder-decoder models. arXiv 2312.16098.

Nandan Thakur, Nils Reimers, Andreas Rücklé, Abhishek Srivastava, and Iryna Gurevych. 2021. BEIR: A heterogeneous benchmark for zero-shot evaluation of information retrieval models. In *Proceedings of NeurIPS Datasets and Benchmarks 2021*, online. Proceedings.org.

Henning Wachsmuth, Martin Potthast, Khalid Al Khatib, Yamen Ajjour, Jana Puschmann, Jiani Qu, Jonas Dorsch, Viorel Morari, Janek Bevendorff, and Benno Stein. 2017. Building an argument search engine for the Web. In *Proceedings of ArgMining@EMNLP 2017*, pages 49–59, Kerrville. ACL.

Chenyan Xiong, Zhuyun Dai, Jamie Callan, Zhiyuan Liu, and Russell Power. 2017. End-to-end neural ad-hoc ranking with kernel pooling. In *Proceedings of SIGIR 2017*, pages 55–64, New York. ACM.

Canwen Xu, Daya Guo, Nan Duan, and Julian J. McAuley. 2022. LaPraDoR: Unsupervised pretrained dense retriever for zero-shot text retrieval. In *Findings of ACL 2022*, pages 3557–3569, Kerrville. ACL.

Yue Yu, Chenyan Xiong, Si Sun, Chao Zhang, and Arnold Overwijk. 2022. COCO-DR: Combating distribution shifts in zero-shot dense retrieval with contrastive and distributionally robust learning. arXiv 2210.15212.

ChengXiang Zhai and John D. Lafferty. 2001. A study of smoothing methods for language models applied to ad hoc information retrieval. In *Proceedings of SIGIR 2001*, pages 334–342, New York. ACM.

Exploiting Dialogue Acts and Context to Identify Argumentative Relations in Online Debates

Stefano Mezza, Wayne Wobcke and Alan Blair
School of Computer Science and Engineering
UNSW Sydney, NSW 2052 Australia
{s.mezza|w.wobcke|a.blair}@unsw.edu.au

Abstract

Argumentative Relation Classification is the task of determining the relationship between two contributions in the context of an argumentative dialogue. Existing models in the literature rely on a combination of lexical features and pre-trained language models to tackle this task; while this approach is somewhat effective, it fails to take into account the importance of pragmatic features such as the illocutionary force of the argument or the structure of previous utterances in the discussion; relying solely on lexical features also produces models that over-fit their initial training set and do not scale to unseen domains. In this work, we introduce ArguNet, a new model for Argumentative Relation Classification which relies on a combination of Dialogue Acts and Dialogue Context to improve the representation of argument structures in opinionated dialogues. We show that our model achieves state-of-the-art results on the Kialo benchmark test set, and provide evidence of its robustness in an open-domain scenario.

1 Introduction

Argumentative Dialogues are discussions between two or more parties involving an opinionated topic, i.e. any topic which may divide the interlocutors into a number of conflicting opinions. These discussions are usually different from ordinary conversations, in that the speakers' goal is usually to convince their interlocutors of their own point of view by defending their own stance and attacking their opponents' arguments. Figure 1 shows an example of a debate from the Kialo online debate platform. A key aspect in the study of Argumentative Dialogues is identifying the relationship between an argument step in the discussion and preceding argument steps introduced by other speakers; this task is commonly referred to as *Argumentative Relation Classification* (Stab and Gurevych, 2014), or sometimes *Argument Polarity Prediction* (Cayrol and Lagasquie-Schiex, 2005) when it only involves a binary classification between two possible relations. In this work, we will use the term **Argumentative Relation Classification**, to avoid any confusion with similar tasks such as *Sentiment Analysis* or *Stance Classification*.

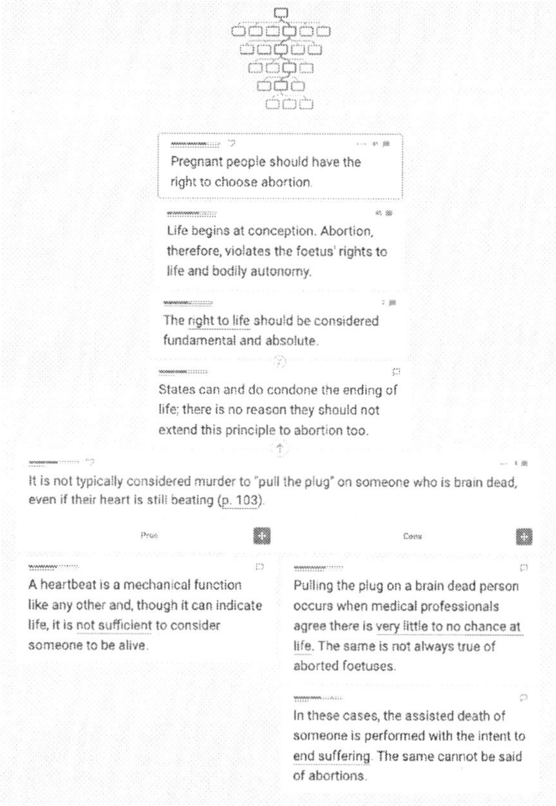

Figure 1: An example of a debate from the Kialo online debate platform. Green nodes agree with the original thesis (in blue), while red nodes disagree with it. Nodes are annotated with the *argumentative move* that they perform on their parent node in the graph (i.e. *Support* or *Attack*). Users annotate their own stance towards the thesis, as well as their argumentative move towards the node they are responding to.

Existing works in the literature that aim to

Proceedings of the 11th Workshop on Argument Mining, pages 36–45
August 15, 2024 ©2024 Association for Computational Linguistics

solve this task usually rely on either hand-crafted syntactic and lexical features (Stab and Gurevych, 2014; Lenz et al., 2020), pre-trained language models (Agarwal et al., 2022; Ruiz-Dolz et al., 2021) or both (Cocarascu et al., 2020). While these models are becoming increasingly accurate, there are some shortcomings in their approach. First, they often ignore any non-lexical aspect of the dialogue, which hinders their capability to correctly understand the conversation. Second, they have limited understanding of the surrounding context of the argument contributions, and struggle to take long-term dependencies into account. Finally, they are often tested in a domain-specific scenario in which the system learns to predict relations between argument contributions that belong in the same dataset it was trained on; this makes it hard to correctly assess their capability to adapt to unseen conversations, which is crucial for practical applications such as the development of Automated Dialogue Agents.

In this work, we explore the hypothesis that contextual information and pragmatic features (such as Dialogue Act Tags) can be highly beneficial in increasing the accuracy of Argumentative Relation Classification models. We also aim at analysing how much existing models can generalise to entirely unseen topics of discussion, and how these features can help a model become less dependent on its training domain. There is evidence in the literature that Dialogue Act Tags may be used as a feature to improve a model's understanding of the argumentative structure of a debate (Petukhova et al., 2016; Budzynska et al., 2014). There is also evidence that contextual information is highly beneficial for Argument Mining tasks and, more specifically, to increase the accuracy of Argumentative Relation Classification models (Agarwal et al., 2022).

We build on this existing evidence and introduce **ArguNet**, a novel approach to Argumentative Relation Classification that relies on on a combination of Dialogue Acts and a specialised encoding of the previous nodes in the debate. ArguNet uses ISO 24617-2 Dialogue Acts (DAs) annotated with the DASHNet architecture (Mezza et al., 2022) to enrich the input utterances with additional syntactic and pragmatic information. BERT (Devlin et al., 2018) is used to encode the enriched input utterances into dense sentence embeddings, with the addition of Utterance Manipulation Strategies from Whang et al. (2021) to further increase the effectiveness of the contextual embeddings from BERT. Our approach is trained and tested on data from the Kialo online debate platform, a high-quality, publicly-available source of conversations annotated with argumentative relations. We use the same Kialo scrape introduced by Agarwal et al. (2022); however, instead of shuffling the argument contributions and dividing them in a training and test split, we split at the debate level, so that contributions from the same debate will not appear in different splits. This is done to test the hypothesis that existing models identify lexical information in the training debates and are able to use this information when tested on argument contributions from the same debates. We also sampled an additional, smaller collection of Kialo debates called *KialoAbortion* that involve discussions on reproductive rights, which we use to further test our hypothesis that Argumentative Relation Classification is highly sensitive to the topic of the classified debates.

In our experimental section, we provide evidence that the ArguNet architecture achieves state-of-the-art results on the Kialo dataset; we also provide evidence that our model outperforms existing models in the literature when tested on debates from the *KialoAbortion* test set, which shows how ArguNet can generalise to unseen domains better than existing architectures.

2 Related Work

The formal study of argumentative discussions is known in the literature as *Argumentation Theory* (van Eemeren et al., 1996). Walton (2009) divides argumentative study into four separate tasks: *identification*, which involves identifying Argumentative Dialogue Units (ADUs) in a dialogue and inserting them into a pre-determined *argumentation scheme*; *analysis*, which deals with identifying premises and conclusion of each argument; *evaluation*, which involves assessing an argument's quality and persuasive power; and *invention*, which involves the creation of novel arguments for the debate. In this work we will focus on the task of *identification* of pre-constructed ADUs in an argumentation scheme.

The identification of a logical structure for

reasoning goes back to the seminal works by Pollock (1987) and (Nute, 1988), which introduced *Defeasible Logic*, a formalism in which *conclusions* are supported by *premises* that may no longer be justified when additional premises are introduced. Dung (1995) introduced an abstract theory of *Acceptability of Arguments* in which arguments are seen as a set of logical statements, and each argument can be *accepted* or *defeated* depending on whether it clashes with other arguments. Prakken (2010) elaborated on this theory and presented a framework for structured arguments in which arguments can be supported with premises that justify their validity, and other arguments can attack the speaker's viewpoint by either attacking the argument directly, or one of its premises. Cabrio and Villata (2012) combine textual entailment and argumentation graph into a unified framework that aims at automatically detecting accepted and defeated arguments based on the entailment between them. Lenz et al. (2020) adopted this scheme in their study on Argumentative Relation Classification on the Kialo corpus, and defined *Default Inference* and *Default Conflict* relations between arguments that support and attack each other respectively. The scheme was adopted by Fabbri et al. (2021), who use Natural Language Inference models to directly compute Argumentative Relations. This approach, however, does not distinguish between the semantic problem of determining logical relations between argument steps and the pragmatic problem of determining dialogue moves in a sequence of contributions.

Rosenfeld and Kraus (2016) introduced a graph-like scheme for argumentative moves in a debate called the *Bipolar Argumentation Graph* (BAG), in which claims are represented as nodes in a weighted graph, and can be supported by other claims or *premises* that can either *Support* or *Attack* each other. As the Kialo dataset uses a graph-like structure that resembles a BAG, we will sometimes use their terminology in this work, particularly when referring to the argumentative moves between argument nodes.

Various models have been proposed in the literature for the annotation of argumentation schemes. One of the earliest examples of a formal approach to Argumentative Relation Classification is Cabrio and Villata (2012), which proposes an approach based on Textual Entailment. Naderi and Hirst (2016) uses a combination of Skip-Thought Vectors and Cosine Similarity to predict argumentative relations in parliamentary debates; their work is one of the earliest that takes advantage of pre-trained word embeddings for this task. Cocarascu and Toni (2017) propose a neural architecture based on LSTM cells to annotate a multi-topic corpus which included debates on movies, technology and politics; they formulate the problem as a three-way classification problem between the classes *Attack*, *Support* and *Neither*. Cocarascu et al. (2020) proposed a set of strong baselines for argumentative relation prediction in a dataset-independent setting, which included an attention-based model and an autoencoder. Their emphasis on dataset-independent classification is highly relevant to our work; however, they do not analyse the difference between in-domain and out-of-domain accuracy for their model and they do not provide details on how they split their data when separating training and test sets.

Recently, Agarwal et al. (2022) proposed GraphNLI, a graph-based neural architecture that uses graph walking techniques to obtain contextual information, which is then encoded with RoBERTa embeddings (Liu et al., 2019). Their model was a source of inspiration for our work, as it shares our reliance on context encoding for Argumentative Relations Classification; however, their approach does not use pragmatic features like Dialogue Acts, and it also uses weighted averaging for embeddings rather than relying on a structured approach for context encoding, which we argue is less effective when trying to capture contextual information.

The idea of adopting Dialogue Acts (DAs) as input features for Argument Mining systems has been investigated before in the literature. Fouqueré and Quatrini (2013) proposed a unified framework for argumentative analysis and inference which used DAs as part of the argumentation scheme, and used it to annotate a discussion from Prakken (2008). Budzynska et al. (2014) introduced Inference Anchoring Theory (IAT), a framework designed to model arguments via a combination of argumentative moves and the DAs associated with them. Both works utilised DA schemes that are difficult to adopt due to the scarcity of annotated data. Petukhova et al. (2016) use ISO 24617-2 DAs as part of a model designed to understand the ar-

Dimension	Communicative Function
Task	PropQuestion, SetQuestion, ChoiceQuestion, Inform, Agree, Disagree, Answer, Directive, Commissive
Social	Greeting, Goodbye, Thanking, AcceptThanking, Apology, AcceptApology
Feedback	AlloFeedback

Table 1: The DASHNet tagging scheme. Tags, also known as *Communicative Functions*, are grouped in *Semantic Dimensions* which represent different aspects of utterance functions

gumentative behaviour of participants in a debate in order to predict its outcome. This is the official standard taxonomy for DA tagging, and includes domain-independent tags across various semantic dimensions that cover different aspects of the conversation (e.g. *Social Obligations*, *Feedbacks* etc.) While their study provides useful insights on how DAs can be used to model argumentative discussions, it is limited by the use of outdated ML methods for the task and was tested on a limited number of debates. In our work, we adopt ISO 24617-2 DAs due to their flexible, multi-dimensional and domain-independent taxonomy; we rely on our previous DASHNet model from Mezza et al. (2022) which achieved state-of-the-art accuracy on various benchmark test sets for DA tagging. Table 1 illustrates the DASHNet tagging scheme.

3 Methodology

3.1 Task Definition

A debate D comprises of a set of *Argument Contributions* $D = \{A_0, , ..., A_N\}$ arranged as *nodes* in a tree structure, with contribution A_0 being the root of the tree and representing the *Thesis* (or *Topic*) of the debate, and with each contribution A_j comprising one or more sentences connected to the thesis node A_0 via a sequence of nodes $A_{j-1}, ..., A_0$, which we will refer to as the *Context* of the argument. Finally, each contribution A_j is connected to its predecessor A_{j-1} with an *Argumentative Move* $M_j \in \{Support, Attack\}$. We define **Argumentative Relation Classification** as the task of automatically identifying the argumentative move M_j characterising the relation between A_j and A_{j-1}.

3.2 Data

For this study, we chose to work with data from the Kialo online debate platform [1]. We have decided to use Kialo because it is a highly-curated platform with moderated debates and a vote system for posts, which minimizes the amount of noise, ad hominem attacks and other irrelevant information in the debate. Moreover, as the dataset is moderated, it is free of indentifiable information about individuals or offensive content. Finally, there is extensive research on many aspects of the Kialo corpus, such as the argument specificity and stance of the participants (Durmus et al., 2019) and the argumentative relevance of its conversations (Guo and Singh, 2023). Kialo debates are organised in a weighted graph-like structure: nodes in the graph represent individual, fully-formed arguments from a single participant in the debate and are called *Contributions*. Contributions are linked together with weighted edges, with the weights representing the *Argumentative Relation* between the two contributions linked by the edge. Every debate graph forms a tree-like structure, with the thesis being debated as the root node of the tree; dialogues have multiple participants, and the participants construct the tree structure collectively.

We use a scrape of Kialo introduced in Agarwal et al. (2022), which we refer to as *KialoDataset*, which is a complete scrape of the website as of January 2020. We also collected a newer scrape of the website, which we refer to as *KialoAbortion*, focusing on a specific topic; we choose *Reproductive Rights* as this is a very popular and polarising debate topic at the time of writing. We made sure that no debates from the *KialoAbortion* corpus appear in the *KialoDataset* corpus, so that the former could be used in domain studies without the risk of data leakage. The *KialoDataset* corpus contains a total of 1,470 debates and 311,238 contributions, of which 1,051 debates (231,945 contributions) are used for training, 278 debates (53,699 contributions) for testing, and the remaining ones for validation. The *KialoAbortion* corpus is significantly smaller, with a total of 40 debates (10,584 contributions), of which 27 debates (8,970 contributions) are used for training, and the remaining ones for testing. Experiments in the literature sometimes split the debates without preserving their integrity; this *Single Contribution* splitting strategy produces

[1] https://www.kialo.com/

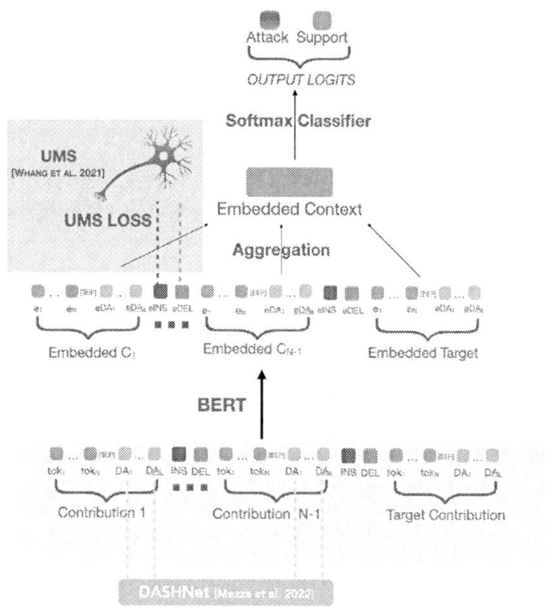

Figure 2: The ArguNet architecture.

splits which may contain argument contributions from the same debates. In contrast to that approach, we adopt a *Whole Debate* splitting strategy and split our data at the debate level, meaning that each split contains whole debates and contributions from the same debate do not appear in different splits.

3.3 Model

In this section we will outline the details of the **ArguNet** model for *Argumentative Relation Classification*. Figure 2 provides an overview of the model's architecture. ArguNet is a transformer-based architecture with a few enhancements designed to increase its accuracy when dealing with argumentative data. It uses BERT (Devlin et al., 2018) to produce dense embeddings of each token in the input arguments. In order to increase the model's ability to correctly understand each argument's underlying meaning, we enhanced the input of ArguNet with ISO 24617-2 Dialogue Act (DA) Tags extracted with the DASHNet architecture (Mezza et al., 2022). We chose the DASHNet classifier because of its multidimensional and open-domain nature, which suits our use case very well; moreover, the model uses data from the Internet Argument Corpus (Abbott et al., 2016; Walker et al., 2012), which is similar in nature and scope to the Kialo data.

ArguNet also uses Utterance Manipulation Strategies (UMS) from Whang et al. (2021) to obtain a better encoding of the context of the arguments to classify: special "[INS]" and "[DEL]" tokens are randomly inserted in the input and the corresponding utterance is either removed (in the case of "[DEL]") or erroneously inserted in the wrong spot (in the case of "[INS]"). The network has separate loss functions that control its learning of the correct UMS tags; this is combined with the classification loss from the final Softmax classifier, and the losses are averaged together to produce the final loss of the network. We added UMS to this model due to the high relevance of the order of debate turns in understanding argumentative moves; previous work acknowledged this, but leveraged context in ways that do not take into account the exact order of the utterances, such as weighted sum of embedded turns (Agarwal et al., 2022). The order of previous contributions is especially relevant to our architecture as it relies on context-aware DAs (Mezza et al., 2022); as we show in Section 4.4, UMS and DAs function especially well when combined.

Our input is an argument contribution $A_N = T_1, ..., T_M$, where T_i is the i-th token of the contribution, together with its context $C_{A_N} = A_{N-1} ... A_{N-k}$, where k is the context window size of our model. We keep the window size at 5, following evidence in the literature that this is the optimal amount of context for an Argumentative Relation Classification model (Agarwal et al., 2022). We also only utilise argument contributions that directly preceded the target contribution in the debate, as opposed to alternative branches in the graph or future arguments in the discussion; this is done to make our model suitable for a real-life application in which future arguments may not be available for the analysis.

Our data is pre-annotated with the DASHNet architecture to obtain a DA-enriched argument contribution $\tilde{A_N} = T_1, ..., T_M, [SEP], DA_1, ..., DA_H$. Each contribution in the context is also annotated with its DA tags. Figure 3 shows an example of an argument contribution annotated with DASHNet Dialogue Acts; note that DASHNet tags provide structural information about single utterances in the contribution, which we argue are highly beneficial to understand Argumentative Moves in a debate. As DASHNet operates on individual utterances, a contribution may have multiple DA tags

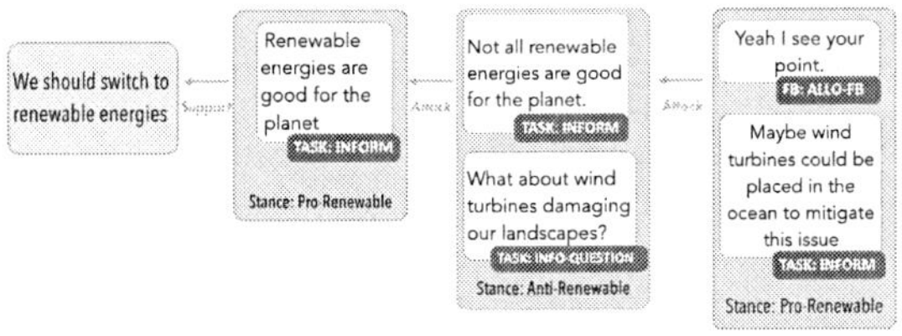

Figure 3: An example of an argument snippet annotated with Dialogue Acts. Note that DAs are annotated for each individual utterance in the contribution, and DAs might belong to different semantic dimensions (in this example, DAs from the *Task* and *Feedback* dimensions are shown)

associated with it. The input is then reshaped to utilize Utterance Manipulation Strategies, similarly to the UMS-ResSel model introduced in (Whang et al., 2021). We only utilize *Insertion* and *Deletion* strategies, as we found in our experiments that the *Search* strategies did not impact the accuracy of the resulting model when the other two strategies were present. For the insertion strategies, a target argument contribution in the context is randomly removed from its original position and placed at the end of the context window. Special [INS] tokens are placed before each contribution in the context to encode whether the target contribution should be placed in that position. Target values for the [INS] tokens are 1 for the position in which the target argument contribution originally belonged, and 0 for all other tokens. For the deletion strategies, a random outlier contribution from a different context window is randomly placed in a random place in the context. Special [DEL] tokens are placed before each argument contribution in the context to encode whether that contribution is the outlier argument or not.

The input is concatenated with its UMS-enhanced context and they are all passed to the BERT model, which produces embeddings for each token in the input (including the DA tags and the UMS tokens). A binary cross-entropy loss function is applied to the UMS tokens to determine whether the network correctly guessed the positions of the argument contributions in the context. The tokens are then stacked together to produce a dense input representation which is then fed to a Softmax Classifier similar to the one used in Sentence-BERT (Reimers and Gurevych, 2019). The final loss of the model is the sum of the classification loss and the UMS losses.

4 Experiments and Results

In this section, we illustrate the results of our experimental study. We ran three sets of experiments for this study: the first one was aimed at assessing ArguNet's accuracy when trying to determine the Argumentative Relation between two argument contributions, and compare it to existing methods in the literature, the second one was aimed at measuring the impact of each feature of the model via an ablation study, while the third one aimed at measuring how much our model and existing models rely on domain-specific lexical information in order to produce their prediction. We replicated the following models from the literature:

- **Majority Baseline:** this is just the frequency of the most prevalent argumentative move in the dataset. Both of our datasets are reasonably balanced: *KialoDataset* is comprised of 56.2% *Attack* relations and 43.8% *Support relations*, while *KialoAbortion* contains 54.8% *Attack* relations and 45.2% *Support* relations.

- **ReCAP:** this is a model trained and tested on the Kialo corpus, originally introduced in (Lenz et al., 2020) as part of a larger study on argument mining pipelines to transform textual arguments into argument graphs. The authors trained various machine learning models to predict the relation type between Kialo posts. We report results for their XG Boosting model, which is the most accurate based on our replication study.

- **BERT-Base:** this is the result of fine-tuning the BERT model on the Kialo dataset, using a single argument contribution as the context window ($k = 1$). A softmax classifier is applied to the output BERT embeddings. We chose BERT as a baseline language model since it is the foundational input embedding architecture for both ArguNet and GraphNLI.

- **GraphNLI:** this is the GraphNLI model as presented in (Agarwal et al., 2022). We used the code released by the authors, with the best-performing setting reported by the authors (weighted sum average for aggregation and *Weighted root-seeking path* with a context length of 5). As described in Section 3.2, we altered the training and test splits of the Kialo dataset to keep debates intact, rather than shuffling and splitting the argument contributions;

while we were able to replicate the authors' results with their settings, our results when evaluating this model are different from the ones they reported.

- **ArguNet:** our model (see Section 3.3).

For the ablation study, we implemented the following variations of the ArguNet model:

- **Without UMS:** this is a variation of the ArguNet model that removes the UMS from Whang et al. (2021). The DASHNet annotation is still maintained.
- **Without DA:** this is a variation of the ArguNet model that removes the DASHNet DAs. The UMS strategies are still maintained in the network.
- **Without DA and UMS**: this version of the model removes both the UMS strategies and the DASHNet annotations, leaving just the BERT embedding layer and the final Softmax Classifier.

All of the variants implemented for the ablation study maintain a context window of $k = 5$.

4.1 Implementation Details

We trained our models on Google Colab, using an NVIDIA A100 GPU with the "High RAM" setting. Training of our models took a total of roughly 400 GPU Hours, which includes all the re-trainings we had to do for our various experiments. We trained the UMS and ArguNet models for 20 epochs, but implemented early stopping with a patience of 3 (most models finished training between epochs 8 and 12). We use a Dropout rate of 0.8 for the final classification layer, a learning rate of 3e-05 and AdamW optimiser with epsilon value of 1e-8. We used BERT with 12 hidden layers, and an embedding dimension of 768, with a Dropout rate for its attention layer of 0.1. We validated all of these hyperparameters using the validation set of the *KialoDataset*. We used the "BERT base uncased" version of the BERT model from Hugging Face for any experiment involving BERT embeddings, and truncated contributions longer than 100 tokens to 100 tokens to fit the model's maximum input length of 512 (this was not generally an issue, as the average length of Kialo contributions in our data is 60 tokens. Since we had standardised training, test and validation splits for our experiments, we did not use cross-validation in our evaluation.

4.2 Argumentative Relation Classification

We trained various models from the literature on the combined train splits of the *KialoDataset* and *KialoAbortion* datasets, and compared their results to the ones obtained by the ArguNet model. We used accuracy as a metric and tested on both the *KialoDataset* and *KialoAbortion* test sets separately. All the models were trained and tested on the same data, and were trained with the *Whole Debate* splitting strategy (i.e. contributions from the same debate are kept in the same split) which produced some differences between the results we obtained and the ones reported by the authors of the respective papers. Table 2 shows the results:

Model	**Accuracy (KialoDataset)**	**Accuracy (KialoAbortion)**
Majority Baseline	54.7%	54.5%
ReCAP (Lenz et al., 2020)	66.8 %	64.1%
BERT-Base (Devlin et al., 2018)	79.2%	74.4%
GraphNLI (Agarwal et al., 2022)	79.9%	78.9%
ArguNet	**82.1%**	**81.6%**

Table 2: Argumentative Relation Classification results for our novel models, ArguNet and GraphNLI-DA, compared with other models in the literature. We replicated all models for this work.

The results show that ArguNet achieves state-of-the-art accuracy on the *KialoDataset* and *KialoAbortion* test sets. We can see that models based on BERT embeddings outperform the ReCAP model which is based on shallow machine learning methods. The GraphNLI model shows a significant decrease in accuracy on the *KialoDataset* with respect to the original result reported by the authors (82.87%): this was expected, as that result was obtained with the *Single Contribution* splitting strategy, meaning that the model would have seen other contributions from the test set during training. The model still outperforms the BERT baseline on both test sets. ArguNet shows a significant boost in accuracy over GraphNLI, which validates empirically the validity of its input encoding and context understanding strategies.

4.3 In-domain vs Out-of-domain accuracy

One of the main hypotheses that led to the design of the ArguNet architecture is that existing models in the literature largely rely on lexical information from their training corpora, which makes them less accurate when annotating debates on entirely unseen topics. In order to test this hypothesis, we compared the results of our implemented models when trained with and without the *KialoAbortion* training data. We used accuracy on the *KialoAbortion* benchmark test set as a metric. Table 3 shows the results of this study.

Model	OOD training	In-domain training	difference (%)
ReCAP (Lenz et al., 2020)	62.3 %	64.1%	1.8%
BERT-Base (Devlin et al., 2018)	72.3%	74.4%	2.1%
GraphNLI (Agarwal et al., 2022)	78.8%	79.9%	1.1%
ArguNet	**80.9%**	**81.6%**	**0.7%**

Table 3: Difference in accuracy between our implemented models when trained with/without in-domain data. All models were tested on *KialoAbortion*.

Results indicate that ArguNet outperforms existing approaches in the literature on both the in-domain and out-of-domain data, while also showing the lowest accuracy loss when trained without in-domain data. In general, models that utilise contextual information and other non-lexical features seem to be less prone to accuracy loss when trained without in-domain data: ReCAP and BERT-Base show significant accuracy losses (1.8% and 2.1% respectively) when trained without in-domain data, whereas GraphNLI and ArguNet exhibit much lower accuracy losses when in-domain training data is removed. This appears to validate our hypothesis that models that rely mainly on lexical features are more prone to committing annotation errors on OOD data when compared to models that adopt a more sophisticated encoding of the input.

4.4 Ablation Study

We trained various alterations of the original ArguNet architecture by removing some of its features, in order to measure their impact on the overall accuracy of the model. All variations were tested on the same test sets used in the Argumentative Relation Classification experiments. Table 4 shows the results of this study.

Model	Accuracy (KialoDataset)	Accuracy (KialoAbortion)
Without DA and UMS	79.7%	78.5%
Without DA	80.7%	80.0%
Without UMS	80.3%	79.6%
ArguNet	**82.1%**	**81.6%**

Table 4: Ablation study for the ArguNet model.

The results confirm our hypothesis that an unstructured encoding of the context is less effective than a specialised encoding, as the model trained without UMS shows a decrease in accuracy on both the *KialoDataset* and *KialoAbortion* corpora, with a 1.8% and 1.0% difference respectively. The DA feature also appears to be highly beneficial to the classification, with the "Without DA" model being significantly outperformed by the full ArguNet architecture on both the *KialoAbortion* dataset (1.4% increase) and the *KialoDataset* (1.6% increase). This follows our hypothesis that Dialogue Act Tags provide an input signal that correlates with Argumentative Relation types. The DASHNet model uses data from the Internet Argument Corpus V2 (IAC) (Abbott et al., 2016; Walker et al., 2012) ; as this corpus contains argumentative discussions that are similar in scope and style to those found in Kialo, this may also have helped the classification.

5 Conclusions

In this work, we introduced ArguNet, a neural model for the classification of Argumentative Relations between argument contributions in online debates. We showed how it achieves state-of-the-art results when tested on the Kialo dataset of online debates, and provided evidence that its defining features, namely the use of Dialogue Acts and well-structured encoding of the context of the conversation, are highly beneficial for the task at hand. Finally, we showed how its architecture is more robust to out-of-domain classification when compared to existing approaches in the literature, and provided a comparison between in-domain and out-of-domain performance for all of our baselines.

References

Rob Abbott, Brian Ecker, Pranav Anand, and Marilyn Walker. 2016. Internet Argument Corpus 2.0: An SQL Schema for Dialogic Social Media and the Corpora to Go with It. In *Proceedings of the Tenth International Conference on Language Resources and Evaluation (LREC'16)*, pages 4445–4452.

Vibhor Agarwal, Sagar Joglekar, Anthony P Young, and Nishanth Sastry. 2022. GraphNLI: A Graph-based Natural Language Inference Model for Polarity Prediction in Online Debates. In *Proceedings of the ACM Web Conference 2022*, pages 2729–2737.

Katarzyna Budzynska, Mathilde Janier, Chris Reed, Patrick Saint-Dizier, Manfred Stede, and Olena Yakorska. 2014. A Model for Processing Illocutionary Structures and Argumentation in Debates. In *Proceedings of the 9th International Conference on Language Resources and Evaluation (LREC 2014)*, pages 917–924.

Elena Cabrio and Serena Villata. 2012. Combining Textual Entailment and Argumentation Theory for supporting Online Debates Interactions. In *Proceedings of the 50th Annual Meeting of the Association for Computational Linguistics (Volume 2: Short Papers)*, pages 208–212.

Claudette Cayrol and Marie-Christine Lagasquie-Schiex. 2005. On the Acceptability of Arguments in Bipolar Argumentation Frameworks. In *Proceedings of the European Conference on Symbolic and Quantitative Approaches to Reasoning and Uncertainty*, pages 378–389.

Oana Cocarascu, Elena Cabrio, Serena Villata, and Francesca Toni. 2020. Dataset Independent Baselines for Relation Prediction in Argument Mining. In *Proceedings of the 8th International Conference on Computational Models of Argument*, pages 45–52.

Oana Cocarascu and Francesca Toni. 2017. Identifying Attack and Support Argumentative Relations using Deep Learning. In *Proceedings of the 2017 Conference on Empirical Methods in Natural Language Processing (EMNLP)*, pages 1374–1379.

Jacob Devlin, Ming-Wei Chang, Kenton Lee, and Kristina Toutanova. 2018. BERT: Pre-training of Deep Bidirectional Transformers for Language Understanding. *arXiv preprint arXiv:1810.04805*.

Phan Minh Dung. 1995. On the Acceptability of Arguments and its Fundamental Role in Nonmonotonic Reasoning, Logic Programming and N-Person Games. *Artificial Intelligence*, 77:321–357.

Esin Durmus, Faisal Ladhak, and Claire Cardie. 2019. Determining relative argument specificity and stance for complex argumentative structures. *arXiv preprint arXiv:1906.11313*.

Alexander Richard Fabbri, Faiaz Rahman, Imad Rizvi, Borui Wang, Haoran Li, Yashar Mehdad, and Dragomir Radev. 2021. ConvoSumm: Conversation Summarization Benchmark and Improved Abstractive Summarization with Argument Mining. In *Proceedings of the 59th Annual Meeting of the Association for Computational Linguistics and the 11th International Joint Conference on Natural Language Processing (Volume 1: Long Papers)*, pages 6866–6880.

Christophe Fouqueré and Myriam Quatrini. 2013. Argumentation and Inference: A Unified Approach. *Baltic International Yearbook of Cognition, Logic and Communication*, 8(1):4.

Zhen Guo and Munindar P Singh. 2023. Representing and determining argumentative relevance in online discussions: A general approach. In *Proceedings of the International AAAI Conference on Web and Social Media*, volume 17, pages 292–302.

Mirko Lenz, Premtim Sahitaj, Sean Kallenberg, Christopher Coors, Lorik Dumani, Ralf Schenkel, and Ralph Bergmann. 2020. Towards an Argument Mining Pipeline Transforming Texts to Argument Graphs. In *Computational Models of Argument*, pages 263–270. IOS Press.

Yinhan Liu, Myle Ott, Naman Goyal, Jingfei Du, Mandar Joshi, Danqi Chen, Omer Levy, Mike Lewis, Luke Zettlemoyer, and Veselin Stoyanov. 2019. RoBERTa: A Robustly Optimized BERT Pretraining Approach. *arXiv preprint arXiv:1907.11692*.

Stefano Mezza, Wayne Wobcke, and Alan Blair. 2022. A Multi-Dimensional, Cross-Domain and Hierarchy-Aware Neural Architecture for ISO-Standard Dialogue Act Tagging. In *Proceedings of the 29th International Conference on Computational Linguistics*, pages 542–552.

Nona Naderi and Graeme Hirst. 2016. Argumentation mining in parliamentary discourse. In *Principles and Practice of Multi-Agent Systems*, pages 16–25, Cham. Springer.

Donald Nute. 1988. Defeasible reasoning and decision support systems. *Decision support systems*, 4(1):97–110.

Volha Petukhova, Andrei Malchanau, and Harry Bunt. 2016. Modelling argumentative behaviour in parliamentary debates: Data collection, analysis and test case. In *Principles and Practice of Multi-Agent Systems*, pages 26–46, Cham. Springer.

John L Pollock. 1987. Defeasible reasoning. *Cognitive science*, 11(4):481–518.

Henry Prakken. 2008. A Formal Model of Adjudication Dialogues. *Artificial Intelligence and Law*, 16:305–328.

Henry Prakken. 2010. An Abstract Framework for Argumentation with Structured Arguments. *Argument & Computation*, 1(2):93–124.

Nils Reimers and Iryna Gurevych. 2019. Sentence-bert: Sentence embeddings using siamese bert-networks. In *Proceedings of the 2019 Conference on Empirical Methods in Natural Language Processing and the 9th International Joint Conference on Natural Language Processing (EMNLP-IJCNLP)*, pages 3982–3992.

Ariel Rosenfeld and Sarit Kraus. 2016. Strategical Argumentative Agent for Human Persuasion. In *Proceedings of the 22nd European Conference on Artificial Intelligence*, pages 320–328.

Ramon Ruiz-Dolz, Jose Alemany, Stella M Heras Barberá, and Ana García-Fornes. 2021. Transformer-based models for automatic identification of argument relations: A cross-domain evaluation. *IEEE Intelligent Systems*, 36(6):62–70.

Christian Stab and Iryna Gurevych. 2014. Identifying Argumentative Discourse Structures in Persuasive Essays. In *Proceedings of the 2014 Conference on Empirical Methods in Natural Language Processing (EMNLP)*, pages 46–56.

Frans H van Eemeren, Rob Grootendorst, A Francisca Snoeck Henkemans, J Anthony Blair, Ralph H Johnson, Erik CW Krabbe, Christian Plantin, Douglas N Walton, Charles A Willard, John Woods, et al. 1996. Fundamentals of Argumentation Theory: A Handbook of Historical Backgrounds and Contemporary Developments.

Marilyn Walker, Jean E Fox Tree, Pranav Anand, Rob Abbott, and Joseph King. 2012. A Corpus for Research on Deliberation and Debate. In *Proceedings of the Eighth International Conference on Language Resources and Evaluation (LREC'12)*, pages 812–817.

Douglas Walton. 2009. *Argumentation Theory: A Very Short Introduction*, pages 1–22. Springer, Boston, MA.

Taesun Whang, Dongyub Lee, Dongsuk Oh, Chanhee Lee, Kijong Han, Dong-hun Lee, and Saebyeok Lee. 2021. Do Response Selection Models Really Know What's Next? Utterance Manipulation Strategies for Multi-Turn Response Selection. In *Proceedings of the AAAI Conference on Artificial Intelligence, 35*, pages 14041–14049.

Multi-Task Learning Improves Performance in Deep Argument Mining Models

Amirhossein Farzam
Duke University
a.farzam@duke.edu

Shashank Shekar
New York University
shashank.shekhar@nyu.edu

Isaac D. Mehlhaff
Texas A&M University
imehlhaff@tamu.edu

Marco Morucci
New York University
marco.morucci@nyu.edu

Abstract

The successful analysis of argumentative techniques in user-generated text is central to many downstream tasks such as political and market analysis. Recent argument mining tools use state-of-the-art deep learning methods to extract and annotate argumentative techniques from various online text corpora, but each task is treated as separate and different bespoke models are fine-tuned for each dataset. We show that different argument mining tasks share common semantic and logical structure by implementing a multi-task approach to argument mining that meets or exceeds performance from existing methods for the same problems. Our model builds a shared representation of the input and exploits similarities between tasks in order to further boost performance via parameter-sharing. Our results are important for argument mining as they show that different tasks share substantial similarities and suggest a holistic approach to the extraction of argumentative techniques from text.

1 Introduction

Text content generated by online users is a fundamental source of information for understanding the ideas, feelings, and behavior of large populations of interest for social scientists. Within these texts, it is important to be able to recognize ideas and worldviews expressed by individuals on a large scale. To this end, argument mining (AM) has emerged in recent years as a sub-field of natural language processing (NLP) focusing on creating language models capable of detecting and classifying argumentative strategies in online texts.

Within AM, several different sub-tasks have been proposed. For example, Misra and Walker (2013) focus on identifying agreement and disagreement in online texts, Oraby et al. (2017) propose a method to distinguish factual from emotional argumentation techniques, Lawrence et al. (2017) detect the presence of certain rhetorical figures in arguments, and Wachsmuth et al. (2017a,b) produce measures of argument quality. These are only some examples of the many distinct classification tasks that have been identified in AM, not to mention a wide range of work on span identification (e.g. Morio et al., 2022). In this paper, we suggest that all these AM sub-tasks share substantial similarity and use this idea to formulate a model that achieves high accuracy in several of these problems.

More specifically, existing work in AM treats many of the classification tasks within the field as separate problems and focuses on fine-tuning bespoke models for each task (e.g. Abbott et al., 2011; Stab and Gurevych, 2014, 2017; Sheng et al., 2020). While this approach has been demonstrated to work in many settings, it fails to take advantage of the substantial similarities between AM tasks.

In this paper we propose to take advantage of the similarities across AM tasks by constructing a multi-task model (Caruana, 1997; Zhang et al., 2014; Zhao et al., 2018; Liu et al., 2015), that is trained on all tasks at once and builds a shared latent representation of the inputs for each task, and uses this representation to make more accurate predictions for each individual task. Our models also provide evidence that AM sub-tasks do indeed share substantial conceptual overlap (Schulz et al., 2018); the latent representations of different tasks output by our model depicted in Figure 1 clearly depict clusters of individual tasks as well as substantial overlap between these clusters in representation space, indicating that the same latent features are informative for multiple tasks.

The model we propose achieves performance similar to or greater than existing models on all tasks for which we had information on previous metrics, and it also surpasses individual-task models fine-tuned on similar architectures for these tasks. In addition, our models allow for substantial

Proceedings of the 11th Workshop on Argument Mining, pages 46–58
August 15, 2024 ©2024 Association for Computational Linguistics

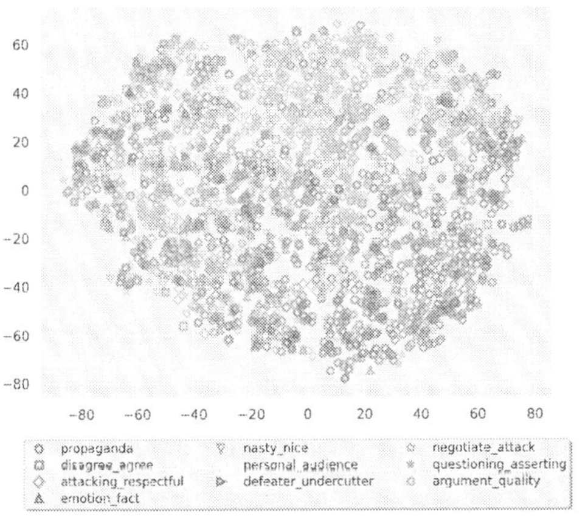

Figure 1: t-SNE projection of the BERT embedding included as the first layer in our model. Points are color-coded according to their task.

computational gains over individual-task models as they permit training inference for many outputs at once, instead of training and evaluating an individual model for each desired task.

Overall, our results have the important implication for AM as a field that further research and model-building should not only focus on taking advantage of the structure of the specific task of interest (e.g. Jin et al., 2022), but also on incorporating information from similar tasks into the model for better performance.

2 Related Work

We build on an active research agenda in argument mining (AM)—the automated extraction of argumentative structure, reasoning, and features from text (Habernal and Gurevych, 2017). Cabrio and Villata (2018) identify two stages in AM: identifying arguments within documents and classifying those arguments on their characteristics, such as supporting, attacking, or background information. Our work is situated in the second stage, involving the identification of features or typologies of arguments.

Much computational work in AM has investigated argumentation in online interactions (Abbott et al., 2011; Rosenthal and McKeown, 2015; Swanson et al., 2015), due in part to the vast amounts of available data and the ease of collecting it. But some scholars have used news articles to construct corpora of propaganda and fact-checking (e.g., Da San Martino et al., 2019; Rashkin et al., 2017). Still others have leveraged monologues like persuasive essays or legal decisions (Stab and Gurevych, 2014; Walker et al., 2019). We incorporate all three types of data into our models to further show that tasks with different data-generating processes and textual characteristics nevertheless exhibit common semantic structure.

There is evidence that many natural language tasks share a common core (Radford et al., 2019), and models trained on one task tend to also perform well on others. Halder et al. (2020) demonstrate that multi-task approaches benefit model performance in several natural language tasks such as topic detection and sentiment analysis. Multi-task approaches have been more rare within AM, but two existing works suggest the framework may offer benefits to these unique tasks.

Schulz et al. (2018) apply multi-task learning to token-level tagging for AM tasks. They consider six datasets each with different token annotations and train a recurrent model to learn all of them at once, providing initial evidence that gains in model performance can be attained via multi-task learning in AM. Similar results are echoed in Schiller et al., who focus on stance detection instead. Morio et al. (2022) present an end-to-end multi-task architecture for identifying argument components in unstructured text. Our task differs from theirs in two ways: First, Morio et al.'s model is especially focused on span identification and relation classification, wherein the model links, for example, premise to claim. Our primary objective in this paper would more accurately be described as component classification. Second, the component classification part of their model is focused on more traditional AM tasks like classifying texts as claims for or against. We focus instead on argument characteristics that are more complex or subjective and, in some cases, can be understood as being nested within overarching concepts.

Cheng et al. (2020) propose a model trained simultaneously on two tasks: argument identification within texts and argument-rebuttal pair matching across texts. Again, our approach is focused on argument classification, not span identification, and we aim to classify argument *types*. Moreover, our use of multi-task learning differs slightly. Whereas Cheng et al. train a model to perform two complementary but quite distinct tasks, we show that a single model can perform multiple argument classification tasks simultaneously. Accordingly, our proposed architecture differs from both Morio et al. and Cheng et al.

A prevalent model architecture for multi-task learning within computer vision involves segregating the network into shared and task-specific components. This conventional structure, termed a "shared trunk" (Crawshaw, 2020), typically comprises a universal feature extractor, constructed of convolutional layers that are employed by all tasks, and a distinct output branch for each task (Zhang et al., 2014; Dai et al., 2016; Zhao et al., 2018; Liu et al., 2019). Further enhancements on this shared trunk template have been made by (Zhao et al., 2018) and (Liu et al., 2019), who incorporated task-specific modules into the original framework.

This template is not confined to computer vision but is also prevalent in multi-task learning models in NLP. Traditional feed-forward architectures, using the shared trunk template in combination with task-specific modules, have been utilized for multi-task NLP by a variety of researchers (Collobert and Weston, 2008; Collobert et al., 2011; Liu et al., 2015, 2016). These architectures bear a structural resemblance to their counterparts in computer vision, featuring a shared, global feature extractor followed by task-specific output branches. However, in the context of NLP, the features in question are text representations.

3 Data

We draw on three benchmark corpora to create a dataset with a diverse number of argument characteristics. We take eight tasks from the Internet Argument Corpus (IAC), a collection of posts extracted from several online debate and discussion fora (Abbott et al., 2016; Walker et al., 2012). Each post is annotated on a variety of characteristics, such as whether the post expresses disagreement or uses an emotion- or fact-based argument, with a value in $[-5, 5]$ on each characteristic. Some researchers have dichotomized these data by removing observations around the midpoint Oraby et al. (2015). This practice is not appropriate in the multi-task setting, however, as it would remove too much information that the model could use to build shared representations across tasks. Instead, we dichotomize the data by simply cutting on the scale midpoint.

A wide array of studies have used the IAC to construct unique tasks (Galitsky et al., 2018; Hartmann et al., 2019; Misra et al., 2016) and train single-task models (Lukin et al., 2017; Misra and Walker, 2013; Oraby et al., 2016). Three tasks have received notable attention: the classification of disagreement Abbott et al. (2011); Wang and Cardie (2014), emotional or factual arguments Oraby et al. (2015), and nasty or nice tone Lukin and Walker (2013).

The second benchmark corpus we draw on is IBM-Rank-30k, a corpus of crowd-sourced arguments Gretz et al. (2020). Two quality scoring functions then translated binary annotations into a continuous value of argument quality in $[0, 1]$. We use scores produced by the authors' weighted average scoring function because it accounts for coder reliability, leading to less noisy annotations. As with the IAC labels, we dichotomize the data by cutting on the scale midpoint.

The final corpus is introduced by Da San Martino et al. (2019), who collect articles from both propagandistic and non-propagandistic news sources and annotate sentences within each article that contain one or more of eighteen different propaganda techniques, such as loaded language or causal oversimplification. We extract all sentences from each article, including those that are annotated as containing no propaganda techniques. Data from all three corpora are combined to create our final dataset. We use 80% of the data for training and set aside 10% each for validation and test sets.

Finally, to help guard against overfitting, we conduct four types of data augmentation on the training set (Shorten et al., 2021). In back-translation, we translate the text into a different language, then translate it back to the original language. We choose German as the target language for its high lexical similarity to English. In contextual word embedding, we randomly choose thirty percent of tokens, feed the surrounding words to BERT (Devlin et al., 2018), and substitute the predicted word in for the original. In synonym augmentation, we randomly choose thirty percent of tokens and substitute the most similar word from the WordNet lexical database (Fellbaum, 1998). Finally, in random cropping, we randomly delete thirty percent of tokens. Table 1 shows the total number of observations in the training set as well as the class balance for each task.

4 Methodology

Our methodology is based on a multi-task learning approach which leverages the shared information across tasks corresponding to different sources of data, leading to improved performance on each task. The model architecture and the loss function are the two key components of our methodology.

Task	Training N	Balance
Propaganda	61,909	63/37
Disagree/Agree	66,684	21/79
Emotion/Fact	76,403	41/59
Attacking/Respectful	65,998	66/34
Nasty/Nice	65,829	73/27
Personal/Audience	24,749	25/75
Defeater/Undercutter	24,357	38/62
Negotiate/Attack	26,604	44/56
Questioning/Asserting	29,791	66/34
Argument Quality	96,036	6/94

Table 1: Size and class balance of training data.

Additionally, we make use of several standard training and optimization techniques, described in this section, in order to improve performance.

4.1 Model Architecture

Our model architecture shares a key similarity to network templates comprising a shared trunk feeding task-specific modules, common to multi-task learning architectures proposed in previous works (e.g. Zhao et al., 2018; Liu et al., 2015). Morio et al. (2022) also use an architecture with corpus-specific branches, but this portion of their architecture is only used in pre-training; they then fine-tune the model on each corpus individually. Our model is fully multi-task, thus showing the benefit of a multi-branch architecture that needs no fine-tuning.

This architecture aims to utilize shared information across tasks through the shared trunk while learning distinct task features through the task-specific modules. Following the same principle, we use a network with double-branching in layers following the shared trunk, in order to make use of commonalities across different types of tasks as well as more fine-grained information about each individual task.

We therefore use a feed-forward neural network with four sequential sets of layers: a base text embedding model shared across all tasks, followed by a shared encoder, which is followed by a double branching structure feeding two sets of task-specific modules. The main results we report use small BERT as the base embedding model (Devlin et al., 2018), but any base model can be used, and we report results across five such models below.

The base embedding model is followed by three dense layers, each followed by dropout. These layers help in learning features that are shared across tasks. The architecture then branches out to learn task-type and task-specific features. In particular, the architecture consists of four sets of layers, described below, and visualized in Figure 2. Each dense layer in the network uses a ReLU activation, with the exception of the final activation layer, which is a sigmoid for binary classification.

- **Shared embedding layers:** We use a BERT model (Devlin et al., 2018) to obtain an embedding of the text input. In order to keep the model size small and training practical, we use small BERT (Turc et al., 2019), which outputs a 128-dimensional embedding. The embedding model, shared across all tasks, is fine-tuned through our training.

- **Shared encoding layers:** In addition to the base embedding model, all tasks share an encoder, consisting of two sequential dense layers each followed by a dropout layer. This helps learn a shared representation, used by all tasks, while allowing for sparsity and reducing the problem to learning our target features.

- **Task-type Layers:** The first branching in the network architecture follows the shared layers aiming to learn coarse-grained task-specific features which are expected to share logical structures across tasks within each type. This is particularly suitable for multi-task learning on data consisting of a mixture of datasets, where the number of labels exceeds the number of sources in the mixture. Given such input data, in the first step towards learning the shared representation, the task-type layers learn dataset-specific features, while still utilizing commonalities between individual tasks sharing a dataset. For each task-type branch, we use two sequential dense layers each followed by dropout. Since we have three sets of target labels each corresponding to their own dataset, we use three main branches.

- **Task-specific Layers:** Each main branch further branches out into individual task layers. These layers aim to learn more fine-grained features from the representations produced through the main branches, and output a vector representation for each task. Each task-specific branch contains two sequential dense and dropout layers, which feed a sigmoid activation layer for predicting labels. The number of these sub-branches equals the number of individual features in the combined dataset. In the branch corresponding to propaganda techniques, we additionally use a maximum pooling layer to reduce the eighteen individual propaganda technique labels to a single binary propaganda classification, predicting whether a propaganda technique is used.

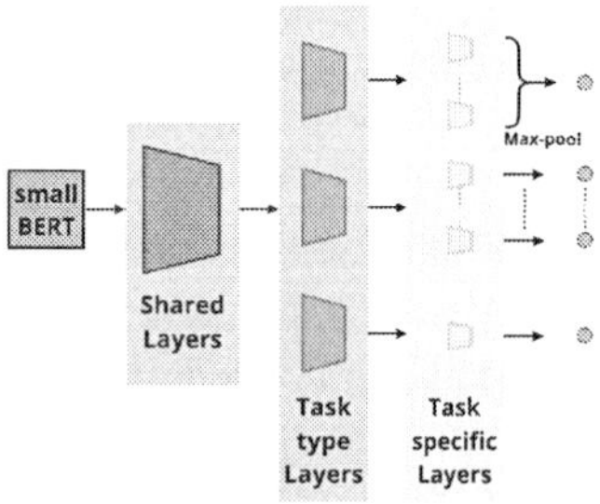

Figure 2: Model architecture.

The full architecture is illustrated in Figure 2. Using this architecture, we obtain a vector representation of the size of the fine-grained features described in the dataset. Note that this need not be the same as the size of the target output. It is not in this case, as we apply max-pooling to eighteen entries of the output corresponding to propaganda techniques in order to obtain a binary label. The network outputs a real-valued 10-dimensional vector which is then mapped to a binary vector of size 10 using individual thresholds for each label. For the results produced in the main text of this paper, we use a model with 32536 trainable parameters in addition to the parameters in small BERT.[1]

4.2 Loss Function

The loss function plays a crucial role in our multi-task learning approach, which relies on a mixed corpora corresponding to different task types. The custom loss function is designed to handle the data size imbalance across task types, in addition to class imbalance. This helps the model capture the contribution of each prediction to the overall loss, while task types are randomly shuffled in the input data. Considering this, given predicted labels $\hat{y}$ and true labels y, the total loss $\mathcal{L}$ used in our gradient descent optimization is:

$$\mathcal{L}\left(\hat{y}|y\right) = \sum_k \nu_k \mathcal{L}(\hat{y}|y, \mathcal{D}_k),$$

where D_k denotes the set of data point indices corresponding to task-type k, and $\nu_k \sim 1/|D_k|$ are the task-type weights. The loss for each task type k, which accounts for the class imbalance across output labels, is:

$$\mathcal{L}(\hat{y}|y, \mathcal{D}_k) \sim \frac{1}{|T_k|} \sum_{j \in D_k} \sum_{t \in T_k} \sum_{c \in C_t} w_t^c \, l(\hat{y}_j | y_j = c),$$

where $l(.)$ is the loss function, T_k denotes the set of tasks within task type k, and $\mathcal{C}_t$ is the corresponding set of classes. The class weights w_t^c, which are proportional to the inverse of the enrichment of class c in task t within dataset k, counter the impact of class imbalance. We use the binary cross-entropy loss for the loss function l throughout our computations. In the implementation, the loss computation is vectorized using masked matrices to filter entries by task.

4.3 Model Training

For training the parameters in our model, we take advantage of an array of optimization and training enhancement techniques. We use an AdamW optimizer (Loshchilov and Hutter, 2017) for the stochastic gradient descent with an initial learning rate of 0.0003. To help avoid overfitting, we employ a weight decay rate of 0.01 and 40% dropout. We use 5% of data for warmup, a batch size of 256, and stop training after two epochs without a decrease in loss. We also incorporate threshold tuning, maximizing true positive rate while minimizing false positive rate, for optimal mapping of the sigmoid layer's output to binary labels. All training hyperparameters are tuned through a standard grid search over 72 sets of hyperparameters and selected based on validation F1 score.

5 Empirical Results

We evaluate our multi-task model's performance in terms of prediction metrics, computational efficiency, and comparison against existing metrics on the target labels. We also offer evidence that the tasks we combine do indeed share important similarities by presenting text embeddings and intermediate layer representations, in Figure 1 and Figure 3. We show that our model performs favorably in comparison to previously published models (Table 2), while being substantially more computationally efficient than single-task counterparts (Figure 4).

[1] Including bias terms, there are $64 \times 32 + 32$ learnable parameters in the shared layer, $32 \times 32 + 32$ between the shared layer and each of the task-type branches, $32 \times 16 + 16$ in each task-type branch, $16 \times 16 + 16$ between each task-type branch and each task-specific branch, and $16 \times 8 + 8$ in each task-specific branch.

5.1 Commonalities Across Tasks

Our model was trained on three different corpora, described in section 3, which we argue possess important semantic similarities. To provide evidence of our ten tasks existing within a common representation space, we present t-SNE projections (Van der Maaten and Hinton, 2008) of the input text embeddings corresponding to each label at three different locations within the neural network. Figure 1, discussed in section 1, shows the t-SNE projection from the output of the BERT model we use as our base encoder. Points are color-coded according to their task. If our text data carried mutually exclusive information applicable only to the particular task for which it was labeled, we would see distinct clusters of representations in Figure 1.

There is some minor evidence of clustering, particularly with respect to the propaganda and argument quality tasks, but even those tasks have observations spanning the entire representation space, and they clearly mix with other task representations. This suggests the fine-tuned BERT model is learning representations that reflect similar semantic and logical structures across tasks. We also highlight that the clustering behavior within tasks observable in the figure shows that our model's embeddings are not completely discarding task-specific structure. Rather, our model learns task-specific representations, and those representations exist within a common space with other task-specific representations, thus further lending evidence to the theory behind our approach.

This pattern is preserved throughout the layers of our model. Figure 3 presents similar t-SNE projections of two other intermediate layers: a shared layer (before any model branching occurs) and the final task-specific layer before the sigmoid activation (after the double-branching). Following the BERT model, each successive layer in the neural network gradually becomes more task-specific, and encodes information that is more relevant to distinguishing among tasks and among labels within tasks. It is notable, then, that we observe similar levels of clustering in the t-SNE projections regardless of model layer. Propaganda and argument quality tasks appear to inhabit more discernible regions of the representation space, but their clusters are neither well-defined nor tightly constrained.

We take this consistent pattern as evidence that AM tasks share a common semantic space. Enabling a model to learn these fine-grained similarities and differences between tasks and across task types is therefore likely to improve performance relative to models that rely solely on shared features or no sharing at all. We test this conjecture in the next section.

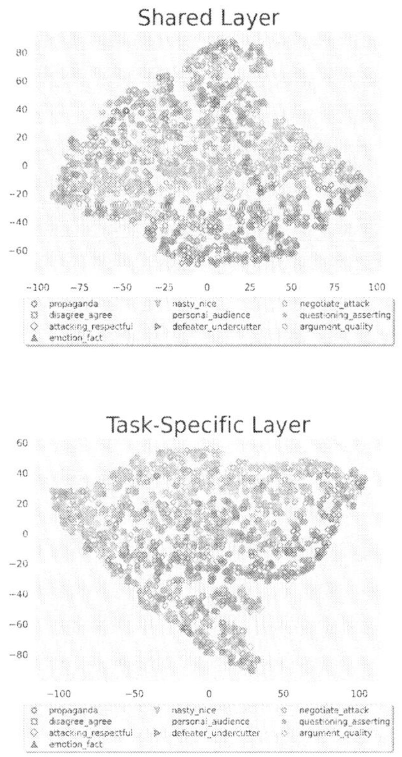

Figure 3: t-SNE projections of representations from the shared layers (top) and the task-specific layers (bottom).

5.2 Performance Evaluation

We evaluate the performance of our model primarily in terms of weighted F1 scores, which account for the class imbalances noted in Table 1. Our proposed method represents a significant departure from common approaches to argument classification, so we want to be sure our model is performing favorably relative to other models.In comparison with previous metrics (Table 2), our model shows superior performance in predicting all of the tasks for which we had previous information available. This indicates that effectively leveraging shared features improves performance across multiple tasks.

Table 3 shows a comparison of the predictive performance (as measured by the class-weighted F1-score) between baselines, single-task, and multi-task versions of the same model. The baseline metrics represent random guessing and the unigram metrics are produced by a naive Bayes classifier. As may be expected, baselines underperform all

Task	Citation	Metric	Previous	New	Absolute Gain	Relative Gain
Propaganda	Da San Martino et al. (2019)	F1	60.98	61.74	0.76	1.25
Disagree/Agree	Wang and Cardie (2014)	F1	63.57	71.38	7.81	12.29
Disagree/Agree	Abbott et al. (2011)	Acc.	68.20	70.73	2.53	3.71
Emotion/Fact	Oraby et al. (2015)	F1	46.20	63.93	17.73	38.38
Nasty/Nice	Lukin and Walker (2013)	F1	69.00	73.69	4.69	6.80

Table 2: Comparison to previously published metrics.

deep-network-based approaches.

Morio et al.'s (2022) multi-task model outperforms their single-task benchmarks about 80% of the time, and we see similar results here. Our multi-task model outperforms single-task models based on the same encoder architecture in six of our nine tasks. Ablating some layers brings that number up to seven. Again, we take this as evidence that our multi-task model is capable of exploiting the common structure between tasks in order to improve predictions. In Table 6 in the Appendix, we show that this performance gain is not merely due to adding additional trainable parameters; multi-task models of various sizes perform comparably.

We further investigated the impact of changing the base encoding model from small BERT to small ELECTRA (Clark et al., 2020) and base ALBERT (Lan et al., 2019), as well as freezing all BERT layers to prevent the pre-trained weights from being fine-tuned. In addition, we examined the effect of removing the base encoder entirely and using embeddings from two decoder-only architectures—Llama 2 (Touvron et al., 2023) and GPT-3 (Brown et al., 2020)—as input to the model. Table 4 shows a comparison of performance across these different variants of our multi-task model. All models have the architecture described in Section 4, however, the base encoder differs each time. Generally, multi-task models trained on different encoders or embeddings seem to display similar performance, indicating that the gain in performance due to the adoption of our framework is not necessarily due to the specific architecture of the encoder chosen. This is further demonstrated by the comparison of performance for each model variant across individual tasks, which is offered in Table 5 of the Appendix.

5.3 Ablation Study

We executed an ablation study to dissect the contributions of each component of our proposed multi-task architecture to its performance. To this end, we omit each of the shared, task-type, and task-specific layers to obtain the ablated neural networks. The results of this ablation analysis are detailed in Table 3, which compares the performances of the full multi-task model ('Multi-Task') against the counterparts with the shared ('Multi-Task-s'), task-type ('Multi-Task-p'), and task-specific ('Multi-Task-t') layers removed.

Removing any part of the model leads to a decline in task performance for a majority of tasks. Ablating the task-specific layers ('Multi-Task-t') causes the most extreme performance drops, with decreases of up to 39.99 F_1 points compared to the full model. This points to the significance of the task-specific branches for learning fine-grained representations. No ablated model surpasses the complete multi-task architecture on more than 2 tasks, suggesting that each element of the model structure enables gains in generalization. The results in Table 3 further show that ablation of the task-type and task-specific layers could lead to marginal improvement on two tasks at the cost of significant decline in performance on a few other tasks. This suggests that while the ablated model could better fit a minority of the tasks, different components of the full model facilitate simultaneous learning of *all* tasks toward consistently strong performance. Moreover, the model with shared layers ablated does not surpass the full model on any task, reinforcing the importance of the shared representations contained in those layers. Overall, these findings affirm the hierarchical design of our multi-task learning framework, where each layer contributes uniquely to the model's overall success.

5.4 Computational Efficiency

A key consideration, particularly when adding more trainable parameters as our model does, is whether the performance gain comes at the cost of more costly computation. We evaluate the peak GPU RAM usage and time to train our multi-task model and compare them to the same metrics from training the full set of single-task models. We conduct this evaluation by randomly sampling 5%,

Task	Baseline	Unigrams	Single-Task	Multi-Task	Multi-Task-s	Multi-Task-p	Multi-Task-t
Propaganda	55.47	38.46	**63.07**	61.74	23.21	47.35	21.75
Disagree/Agree	47.29	7.49	71.15	**71.38**	44.88	52.68	65.17
Emotion/Fact	45.80	21.91	**68.11**	63.93	59.78	62.10	64.00
Attacking/Respectful	56.47	51.16	67.46	**68.07**	55.42	56.20	53.37
Nasty/Nice	59.35	61.03	66.90	**73.69**	55.54	53.16	50.01
Personal/Audience	39.90	9.23	63.25	**65.69**	61.13	58.54	58.67
Defeater/Undercutter	53.4	45.21	45.97	55.65	50.23	**56.13**	41.68
Negotiate/Attack	36.93	55.31	64.76	**64.81**	62.13	61.33	61.68
Questioning/Asserting	50.57	57.47	59.61	**63.23**	55.36	62.71	60.75
Argument Quality	76.54	0.76	80.93	79.17	75.91	79.52	**84.14**

Table 3: Weighted F1 scores comparing baselines, single-task, and multi-task models, as well as multi-task model with ablated layers. Baseline metrics are produced by random guessing and unigram metrics by a naive Bayes classifier. The single-task and multi-task models fine-tune a small-BERT encoder as their embedding layer. "Multi-Task-s/p/t" refer to the multi-task model without the shared/task type/task-specific layers.

Model	Prec.	Rec.	F1
	Baselines		
Baseline	62.26	52.43	52.17
Unigrams	33.65	44.55	34.80
	Multi-Task Models		
BERT	**69.37**	**65.76**	**66.73**
BERT (frozen)	57.54	45.98	43.64
ELECTRA	69.19	63.98	65.16
ALBERT	58.65	63.10	58.34
Llama 2	64.55	55.57	56.72
GPT 3	64.56	62.13	60.23

Table 4: Class-weighted metrics, averaged across tasks, for various base encoders and embedding models.

10%, 20%, and 40% of the training data to assess how computational load increases with data size. All models for this analysis were trained on one NVIDIA A100 GPU for one epoch. Figure 4 displays the results.

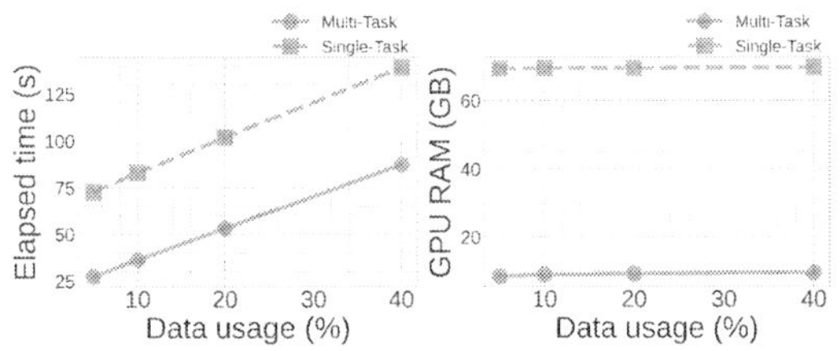

Figure 4: Computational efficiency of the multi-task model (green) compared against the single-task model (blue) in terms of elapsed training time (left) and peak GPU RAM usage (right) as the data usage increases. Both models were run on one NVIDIA A100 GPU for one epoch.

Our multi-task model achieves better performance using substantially lower computational resources overall, proving the branched task-specific modules in our model architecture to be an effective, yet practical, strategy for learning fine-grained features for label prediction. Comparing our model's performance with single-task classification on individual tasks (Table 3), we observe that it achieves comparable performance while decreasing the computation time by at least 31%.

Put together, these observations indicate that this multi-task learning approach simultaneously has a performance and computational efficiency advantage over single-task models. Computational efficiency plots for different multi-task model sizes are included in the Appendix for comparison.

6 Conclusion

Natural language tasks share substantial semantic and structural similarities, and deep learning models have been shown to be able to take advantage of these similarities in order to achieve better performance (Radford et al., 2019). In this paper, we further extend this result to the field of argument mining. We show that AM tasks do indeed share a substantial amount of features, and that these shared features can be used to boost model performance across previously unrelated tasks. We combine three data sources and propose models that outperform existing models on several of these tasks. Our models are also more computationally efficient and have better overall predictive accuracy than single-task models with comparable architectures. Aside from the practical usefulness of our models, our results are important for argument mining as a field, as they suggest that further research and model building should focus on exploiting commonalities between different tasks to boost performance.

In future work, we propose to extend our analysis to several other AM tasks that share commonalities with those studied here (e.g. Jin et al., 2022), as well as other language tasks such as topic modeling. We also propose devising improved model architectures for our multi-task setting. In particular, we propose to take advantage of frameworks such as contrastive learning (e.g. Chen et al., 2020) to encode known similarities between tasks within the representations learned by the model.

7 Limitations

As with all proposed models, ours carries important limitations. Although we show in the Appendix that the choice of base encoder does not have a drastic effect on performance, we suspect that the performance of our models is largely dependent on the ability to fine-tune a base encoder. Indeed, baseline models using unigram features performed quite poorly. Fine-tuning large base encoders—not to mention training one from scratch—can be computationally expensive. However, transfer learning may be able to help. Common semantic and logical structures across tasks point to opportunities for using transfer learning or pre-trained models from warm start to re-train on new tasks.

Multi-task models also depend on data quality and sufficient semantic overlap across tasks. This is especially challenging in AM, as argument annotation is often highly subjective (e.g. Walker et al., 2012), which can lead to noisy training data. Combining one low-quality dataset with other higher-quality ones may have a detrimental effect on model performance, as the model is unable to learn a shared representation space from noisy annotations, thus degrading performance on all tasks.

References

Rob Abbott, Brian Ecker, Pranav Anand, and Marilyn A. Walker. 2016. Internet Argument Corpus 2.0: An SQL Schema for Dialogic Social Media and the Corpora to Go With It. In *Proceedings of the Tenth International Conference on Language Resources and Evaluation*, pages 4445–4452, Portorož, Slovenia.

Rob Abbott, Marilyn Walker, Pranav Anand, Jean E. Fox Tree, Robeson Bowmani, and Joseph King. 2011. How Can You Say Such Things?!? Recognizing Disagreement in Informal Political Argument. In *Proceedings of the Workshop on Language in Social Media*, pages 2–11, Portland, OR. Association for Computational Linguistics.

Tom B. Brown, Benjamin Mann, Nick Ryder, Melanie Subbiah, Jared Kaplan, Prafulla Dhariwal, Arvind Neelakantan, Pranav Shyam, Girish Sastry, Amanda Askell, Sandhini Agarwal, Ariel Herbert-Voss, Gretchen Krueger, Tom Henighan, Rewon Child, Aditya Ramesh, Daniel M. Ziegler, Jeffrey Wu, Clemens Winter, Christopher Hesse, Mark Chen, Eric Sigler, Mateusz Litwin, Scott Gray, Benjamin Chess, Jack Clark, Christopher Berner, Sam McCandlish, Alec Radford, Ilya Sutskever, and Dario Amodei. 2020. Language Models are Few-Shot Learners.

Elena Cabrio and Serena Villata. 2018. Five Years of Argument Mining: A Data-Driven Analysis. In *Proceedings of the Twenty-Seventh International Joint Conference on Artificial Intelligence*, pages 5427–5433, Stockholm. International Joint Conferences on Artificial Intelligence Organization.

Rich Caruana. 1997. Multitask learning. *Machine learning*, 28:41–75.

Ting Chen, Simon Kornblith, Mohammad Norouzi, and Geoffrey Hinton. 2020. A simple framework for contrastive learning of visual representations. In *International conference on machine learning*, pages 1597–1607. PMLR.

Liying Cheng, Lidong Bing, Qian Yu, Wei Lu, and Luo Si. 2020. Ape: Argument pair extraction from peer review and rebuttal via multi-task learning. In *Proceedings of the 2020 Conference on Empirical Methods in Natural Language Processing (EMNLP)*, pages 7000–7011.

Kevin Clark, Minh-Thang Luong, Quoc V Le, and Christopher D Manning. 2020. Electra: Pre-training text encoders as discriminators rather than generators. *arXiv preprint arXiv:2003.10555*.

Ronan Collobert and Jason Weston. 2008. A unified architecture for natural language processing: Deep neural networks with multitask learning. In *Proceedings of the 25th international conference on Machine learning*, pages 160–167.

Ronan Collobert, Jason Weston, Léon Bottou, Michael Karlen, Koray Kavukcuoglu, and Pavel Kuksa. 2011. Natural language processing (almost) from scratch. *Journal of machine learning research*, 12(ARTICLE):2493–2537.

Michael Crawshaw. 2020. Multi-task learning with deep neural networks: A survey. *arXiv preprint arXiv:2009.09796*.

Giovanni Da San Martino, Seunghak Yu, Alberto Barrón-Cedeno, Rostislav Petrov, and Preslav Nakov. 2019. Fine-grained analysis of propaganda in news article. In *Proceedings of the 2019 conference on empirical methods in natural language processing and the 9th international joint conference on natural language processing (EMNLP-IJCNLP)*, pages 5636–5646.

Jifeng Dai, Kaiming He, and Jian Sun. 2016. Instance-aware semantic segmentation via multi-task network cascades. In *Proceedings of the IEEE conference on computer vision and pattern recognition*, pages 3150–3158.

Jacob Devlin, Ming-Wei Chang, Kenton Lee, and Kristina Toutanova. 2018. Bert: Pre-training of deep bidirectional transformers for language understanding. *arXiv preprint arXiv:1810.04805*.

Christiane Fellbaum, editor. 1998. *WordNet: An Electronic Lexical Database*. The MIT Press, Cambridge, MA.

Boris Galitsky, Dmitry Ilvovsky, and Dina Pisarevskaya. 2018. Argumentation in Text: Discourse Structure Matters. In *19th International Conference on Computational Linguistics and Intelligent Text Processing*, Hanoi.

Shai Gretz, Roni Friedman, Edo Cohen-Karlik, Assaf Toledo, Dan Lahav, Ranit Aharonov, and Noam Slonim. 2020. A Large-Scale Dataset for Argument Quality Ranking: Construction and Analysis. *Proceedings of the AAAI Conference on Artificial Intelligence*, 34(5):7805–7813.

Ivan Habernal and Iryna Gurevych. 2017. Argumentation Mining in User-Generated Web Discourse. *Computational Linguistics*, 43(1):125–179.

Kishaloy Halder, Alan Akbik, Josip Krapac, and Roland Vollgraf. 2020. Task-aware representation of sentences for generic text classification. In *Proceedings of the 28th International Conference on Computational Linguistics*, pages 3202–3213.

Mareike Hartmann, Tallulah Jansen, Isabelle Augenstein, and Anders Søgaard. 2019. Issue Framing in Online Discussion Fora. In *2019 Annual Conference of the North American Chapter of the Association for Computational Linguistics: Human Language Technologies*, arXiv:1904.03969, Minneapolis, MN. Association for Computational Linguistics.

Zhijing Jin, Abhinav Lalwani, Tejas Vaidhya, Xiaoyu Shen, Yiwen Ding, Zhiheng Lyu, Mrinmaya Sachan, Rada Mihalcea, and Bernhard Schölkopf. 2022. Logical fallacy detection. *arXiv preprint arXiv:2202.13758*.

Zhenzhong Lan, Mingda Chen, Sebastian Goodman, Kevin Gimpel, Piyush Sharma, and Radu Soricut. 2019. Albert: A lite bert for self-supervised learning of language representations. *arXiv preprint arXiv:1909.11942*.

John Lawrence, Jacky Visser, and Chris Reed. 2017. Harnessing rhetorical figures for argument mining. *Argument & Computation*, 8(3):289–310.

Pengfei Liu, Xipeng Qiu, and Xuanjing Huang. 2016. Recurrent neural network for text classification with multi-task learning. *arXiv preprint arXiv:1605.05101*.

Shikun Liu, Edward Johns, and Andrew J Davison. 2019. End-to-end multi-task learning with attention. In *Proceedings of the IEEE/CVF conference on computer vision and pattern recognition*, pages 1871–1880.

Xiaodong Liu, Jianfeng Gao, Xiaodong He, Li Deng, Kevin Duh, and Ye-Yi Wang. 2015. Representation learning using multi-task deep neural networks for semantic classification and information retrieval.

Ilya Loshchilov and Frank Hutter. 2017. Decoupled weight decay regularization. *arXiv preprint arXiv:1711.05101*.

Stephanie Lukin and Marilyn Walker. 2013. Really? Well. Apparently Bootstrapping Improves the Performance of Sarcasm and Nastiness Classifiers for Online Dialogue. In *Proceedings of the Workshop on Language in Social Media*, pages 3–40, Atlanta. Association for Computational Linguistics.

Stephanie M. Lukin, Pranav Anand, Marilyn Walker, and Steve Whittaker. 2017. Argument Strength is in the Eye of the Beholder: Audience Effects in Persuasion.

Amita Misra, Brian Ecker, and Marilyn A. Walker. 2016. Measuring the Similarity of Sentential Arguments in Dialog. In *Proceedings of the SIGDIAL 2016 Conference*, pages 276–287, Los Angeles. Association for Computational Linguistics.

Amita Misra and Marilyn Walker. 2013. Topic Independent Identification of Agreement and Disagreement in Social Media Dialogue. In *Annual Meeting of the Special Interest Group on Discourse and Dialogue*, pages 41–50, Metz, France. Association for Computational Linguistics.

Gaku Morio, Hiroaki Ozaki, Terufumi Morishita, and Kohsuke Yanai. 2022. End-to-End Argument Mining with Cross-Corpora Multi-Task Learning. 10:639–658.

Shereen Oraby, Vrindavan Harrison, Lena Reed, Ernesto Hernandez, Ellen Riloff, and Marilyn Walker. 2016. Creating and Characterizing a Diverse Corpus of Sarcasm in Dialogue. In *Proceedings of the SIGDIAL 2016 Conference*, arXiv:1709.05404, Los Angeles. Association for Computational Linguistics.

Shereen Oraby, Lena Reed, Ryan Compton, Ellen Riloff, Marilyn Walker, and Steve Whittaker. 2015. And That's A Fact: Distinguishing Factual and Emotional Argumentation in Online Dialogue. In *Proceedings of the 2nd Workshop on Argumentation Mining*, Denver.

Shereen Oraby, Lena Reed, Ryan Compton, Ellen Riloff, Marilyn Walker, and Steve Whittaker. 2017. And that's a fact: Distinguishing factual and emotional argumentation in online dialogue. *arXiv preprint arXiv:1709.05295*.

Alec Radford, Jeffrey Wu, Rewon Child, David Luan, Dario Amodei, Ilya Sutskever, et al. 2019. Language models are unsupervised multitask learners. *OpenAI blog*, 1(8):9.

Hannah Rashkin, Eunsol Choi, Jin Yea Jang, Svitlana Volkova, and Yejin Choi. 2017. Truth of Varying Shades: Analyzing Language in Fake News and Political Fact-Checking. In *Proceedings of the 2017 Conference on Empirical Methods in Natural Language Processing*, pages 2931–2937, Copenhagen. Association for Computational Linguistics.

Sara Rosenthal and Kathy McKeown. 2015. I Couldn't Agree More: The Role of Conversational Structure in Agreement and Disagreement Detection in Online Discussions. In *Proceedings of the 16th Annual Meeting of the Special Interest Group on Discourse and Dialogue*, pages 168–177, Prague. Association for Computational Linguistics.

Benjamin Schiller, Johannes Daxenberger, and Iryna Gurevych. Stance detection benchmark: How robust is your stance detection? *KI-Künstliche Intelligenz*, pages 1–13.

Claudia Schulz, Steffen Eger, Johannes Daxenberger, Tobias Kahse, and Iryna Gurevych. 2018. Multi-task learning for argumentation mining in low-resource settings. In *Proceedings of the 2018 Conference of the North American Chapter of the Association for Computational Linguistics: Human Language Technologies, Volume 2 (Short Papers)*, pages 35–41.

Emily Sheng, Kai-Wei Chang, Premkumar Natarajan, and Nanyun Peng. 2020. " nice try, kiddo": Investigating ad hominems in dialogue responses. *arXiv preprint arXiv:2010.12820*.

Connor Shorten, Taghi M. Khoshgoftaar, and Borko Furht. 2021. Text Data Augmentation for Deep Learning. *Journal of Big Data*, 8(1):101.

Christian Stab and Iryna Gurevych. 2014. Identifying Argumentative Discourse Structures in Persuasive Essays. In *Proceedings of the 2014 Conference on Empirical Methods in Natural Language Processing (EMNLP)*, pages 46–56, Doha. Association for Computational Linguistics.

Christian Stab and Iryna Gurevych. 2017. Recognizing insufficiently supported arguments in argumentative essays. In *Proceedings of the 15th Conference of the European Chapter of the Association for Computational Linguistics: Volume 1, Long Papers*, pages 980–990.

Reid Swanson, Brian Ecker, and Marilyn Walker. 2015. Argument Mining: Extracting Arguments from Online Dialogue. In *Proceedings of the 16th Annual Meeting of the Special Interest Group on Discourse and Dialogue*, pages 217–226, Prague. Association for Computational Linguistics.

Hugo Touvron, Louis Martin, Kevin Stone, Peter Albert, Amjad Almahairi, Yasmine Babaei, Nikolay Bashlykov, Soumya Batra, Prajjwal Bhargava, Shruti Bhosale, Dan Bikel, Lukas Blecher, Cristian Canton Ferrer, Moya Chen, Guillem Cucurull, David Esiobu, Jude Fernandes, Jeremy Fu, Wenyin Fu, Brian Fuller, Cynthia Gao, Vedanuj Goswami, Naman Goyal, Anthony Hartshorn, Saghar Hosseini, Rui Hou, Hakan Inan, Marcin Kardas, Viktor Kerkez, Madian Khabsa, Isabel Kloumann, Artem Korenev, Punit Singh Koura, Marie-Anne Lachaux, Thibaut Lavril, Jenya Lee, Diana Liskovich, Yinghai Lu, Yuning Mao, Xavier Martinet, Todor Mihaylov, Pushkar Mishra, Igor Molybog, Yixin Nie, Andrew Poulton, Jeremy Reizenstein, Rashi Rungta, Kalyan Saladi, Alan Schelten, Ruan Silva, Eric Michael Smith, Ranjan Subramanian, Xiaoqing Ellen Tan, Binh Tang, Ross Taylor, Adina Williams, Jian Xiang Kuan, Puxin Xu, Zheng Yan, Iliyan Zarov, Yuchen Zhang, Angela Fan, Melanie Kambadur, Sharan Narang, Aurelien Rodriguez, Robert Stojnic, Sergey Edunov, and Thomas Scialom. 2023. Llama 2: Open Foundation and Fine-Tuned Chat Models.

Iulia Turc, Ming-Wei Chang, Kenton Lee, and Kristina Toutanova. 2019. Well-read students learn better: On the importance of pre-training compact models. *arXiv preprint arXiv:1908.08962v2*.

Laurens Van der Maaten and Geoffrey Hinton. 2008. Visualizing data using t-sne. *Journal of machine learning research*, 9(11).

Henning Wachsmuth, Nona Naderi, Ivan Habernal, Yufang Hou, Graeme Hirst, Iryna Gurevych, and Benno Stein. 2017a. Argumentation quality assessment: Theory vs. practice. In *Proceedings of the 55th Annual Meeting of the Association for Computational Linguistics (Volume 2: Short Papers)*, pages 250–255.

Henning Wachsmuth, Nona Naderi, Yufang Hou, Yonatan Bilu, Vinodkumar Prabhakaran, Tim Alberdingk Thijm, Graeme Hirst, and Benno Stein. 2017b. Computational argumentation quality assessment in natural language. In *Proceedings of the 15th Conference of the European Chapter of the Association for Computational Linguistics: Volume 1, Long Papers*, pages 176–187.

Marilyn A. Walker, Pranav Anand, Jean E. Fox Tree, Rob Abbott, and Joseph King. 2012. A Corpus for Research on Deliberation and Debate. In *Proceedings of the Eighth International Conference on Language Resources and Evaluation*, pages 812–817, Istanbul.

Vern R. Walker, Krishnan Pillaipakkamnatt, Alexandra M. Davidson, Marysa Linares, and Domenick J. Pesce. 2019. Automatic Classification of Rhetorical Roles for Sentences: Comparing Rule-Based Scripts with Machine Learning. In *Proceedings of the Third Workshop on Automated Semantic Analysis of Information in Legal Text*, Montréal.

Lu Wang and Claire Cardie. 2014. Improving Agreement and Disagreement Identification in Online Discussions with A Socially-Tuned Sentiment Lexicon. In *Proceedings of the 5th Workshop on Computational Approaches to Subjectivity, Sentiment and Social Media Analysis*, pages 97–106, Baltimore. Association for Computational Linguistics.

Zhanpeng Zhang, Ping Luo, Chen Change Loy, and Xiaoou Tang. 2014. Facial landmark detection by deep multi-task learning. In *Computer Vision–ECCV 2014: 13th European Conference, Zurich, Switzerland, September 6-12, 2014, Proceedings, Part VI 13*, pages 94–108. Springer.

Xiangyun Zhao, Haoxiang Li, Xiaohui Shen, Xiaodan Liang, and Ying Wu. 2018. A modulation module for multi-task learning with applications in image retrieval. In *Proceedings of the European Conference on Computer Vision (ECCV)*, pages 401–416.

A Additional Results

In this appendix, we compare the performance of our multi-task model with alternative designs and configurations for multi-task learning, in terms of model architecture, network size, and the base encoder.

A.1 Model Architecture

Table 5 compares the performance of our multi-task model—which incorporates branched task-type and task-specific modules—with a standard "shared-trunk" alternative, which consists of only a small BERT encoder followed by a sigmoid activation layer. This comparison shows the utility of our model architecture. Our multi-task model outperforms the shared-trunk model on all but two tasks, where the F1 metric is within 1 percentage point of that of the shared-trunk model. This performance gain comes at a negligible memory cost and a small increase in computation time (Figure 5).

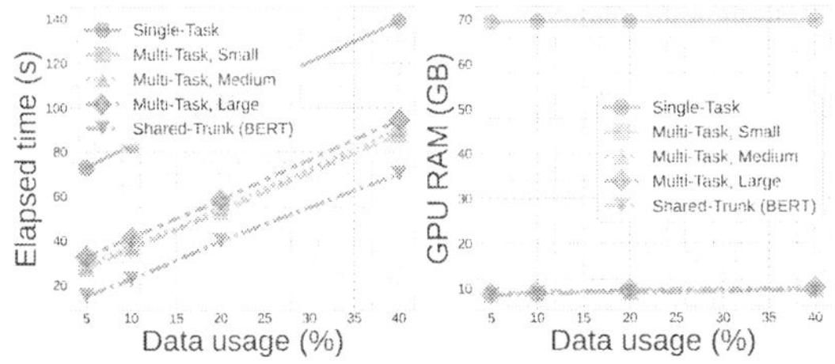

Figure 5: Computational efficiency for the single-task model as well as multi-task models with three different sizes of layers following the small BERT embedding. The small model contains 17024, medium 272384, and large 438784 trainable parameters in addition to the base encoder.

A.2 Network Size

We also compare the performance of the small multi-task model we presented in the main text with alternative networks that preserve the same architectural design but increase the sizes of the layers, from 17024 to 272384 and 438784 trainable parameters, following the base encoder. This comparison shows that the superiority in performance, due to the task-type and task-specific modules, is consistent across various network sizes and is not simply due to adding more trainable parameters on top of the shared trunk (Table 5). Moreover, Figure 5 further confirms that the layers following the BERT encoder are responsible only for a negligible increase in usage of computational resources, as multiplying the combined size of those layers by 16 (Multi-Task, Medium) and 32 (Multi-Task, Large) does not result in a substantial increase in elapsed time for training or peak GPU memory usage.

A.3 Alternative Embedding Models

In addition to comparing our model with other multi-task models, we also compare it to other base encoders. In particular, we deploy base ALBERT (Lan et al., 2019) and small ELECTRA (Clark et al., 2020), replacing the small BERT encoder with each of these other base encoders in our multi-task model. Although small BERT achieves the best average performance across different tasks, as the results in Table 6 suggest, using ELECTRA yields an average F1 score within 2 percentage points of that of small BERT, while ALBERT shows more variability across tasks with a lower average F1 score.

Task	Shared Trunk (BERT)	Multi-Task (17,024)	Multi-Task (272,384)	Multi-Task (438,784)
Propaganda	45.16	61.74	62.62	61.64
Disagree/Agree	37.96	71.38	62.07	66.74
Emotion/Fact	55.00	63.93	64.46	66.61
Attacking/Respectful	52.52	68.07	68.37	68.83
Nasty/Nice	55.62	73.69	73.04	73.38
Personal/Audience	66.51	65.69	70.17	65.24
Defeater/Undercutter	54.50	55.65	51.61	54.14
Negotiate/Attack	58.71	64.81	63.78	64.72
Questioning/Asserting	61.69	63.23	60.12	60.55
Argument Quality	79.34	79.17	68.36	81.28
Average	56.70	66.73	64.46	66.33

Table 5: Weighted F1 scores across shared layer sizes (with small BERT as base encoder). Number of trainable parameters in parentheses, not including base encoder.

Task	BERT	BERT (frozen)	ELECTRA	ALBERT	Llama 2	GPT 3
Propaganda	61.74	49.32	62.8	53.3	50.5	51.7
Disagree/Agree	71.38	62.1	59.4	69.2	65.8	68.9
Emotion/Fact	63.93	64.54	65.4	21.9	63.7	66.6
Attacking/Respectful	68.07	53.58	67.4	58.6	57.9	63.7
Nasty/Nice	73.69	52.28	71.5	61.1	59.4	66.4
Personal/Audience	65.69	10.36	68.5	64.1	59.4	65.8
Defeater/Undercutter	55.65	38.13	53.1	49.8	31.9	44.3
Negotiate/Attack	64.81	62.77	63.8	56.7	59.0	66.0
Questioning/Asserting	63.23	42.52	58.5	58.7	57.1	57.5
Argument Quality	79.17	0.76	81.2	90.0	62.5	51.4
Average	66.73	43.64	65.16	58.34	56.72	60.23

Table 6: Weighted multi-task F1 scores across base encoders and embedding models.

Computational Modelling of Undercuts in Real-world Arguments

Yuxiao Ye
Tsinghua University
Beijing, China
yeyuxiao@mails.tsinghua.edu.cn

Simone Teufel
University of Cambridge
Cambridge, UK
sht25@cl.cam.ac.uk

Abstract

Argument Mining (AM) is the task of automatically analysing arguments, such that the unstructured information contained in them is converted into structured representations. Undercut is a unique structure in arguments, as it challenges the relationship between a premise and a claim, unlike direct attacks which challenge the claim or the premise itself. Undercut is also an important counterargument device as it often reflects the value of arguers. However, undercuts have not received the attention in the filed of AM they should have — there is neither much corpus data about undercuts, nor an existing AM model that can automatically recognise them. In this paper, we present a real-world dataset of arguments with explicitly annotated undercuts, and the first computational model that is able to recognise them. The dataset consists of 400 arguments, containing 326 undercuts. On this dataset, our approach beats a strong baseline in undercut recognition, with $F_1 = 38.8\%$, which is comparable to the performance on recognising direct attacks. We also conduct experiments on a benchmark dataset containing no undercuts, and prove that our approach is as good as the state of the art in terms of recognising the overall structure of arguments. Our work pioneers the systematic analysis and computational modelling of undercuts in real-world arguments, setting a foundation for future research in the role of undercuts in the dynamics of argumentation.

1 Introduction

Social media allows people to express divergent opinions on the same subject and to reach many more people than was possible in earlier times. However, the ubiquity of the internet and social media also has some negative consequences. One of these is the growing polarisation between individuals holding different beliefs and opinions. It is thus increasingly important to promote productive communication and understanding among people with opposing perspectives. This is where Argument Mining (AM) comes into play. AM aims to automatically identify and extract arguments from natural language texts (Peldszus and Stede, 2013; Green et al., 2014). It can convert unstructured textual information into structured argument data, which not only identifies the argumentative text segments in the text but also the relations between them (Prakken and Vreeswijk, 2002; Lawrence and Reed, 2020).

A critical aspect of AM is recognising and understanding various argumentative structures, including undercuts. An undercut challenges the relationship between a premise and a claim (Pollock, 1987), unlike direct attacks that challenge the claim or the premise itself. Due to its complex structure, it is difficult to annotate undercuts or to computationally model them. There exist some AM datasets with annotation of undercuts (Peldszus and Stede, 2015a; Visser et al., 2020), but they are often limited in the size, the quality of source text, or the annotation scheme. To our best knowledge, there is no existing AM models that can automatically recognise undercuts.

To addresses this gap, in this paper we present a novel dataset of real-world arguments from Quora[1], a popular question-answering platform. Our dataset consists of 400 arguments, including 326 explicitly annotated undercuts, making it the largest AM dataset with such annotations to date. We also develop the first computational approach capable of recognising undercuts, proposing an innovative undercut-inclusive dependency representation and a GNN-based neural dependency parser.

Our work contributes to the field of AM in several ways. Firstly, we provide a comprehensive dataset with detailed annotations of undercuts, offering a valuable resource for future research. Secondly, our undercut-inclusive representation allows

[1] https://www.quora.com

Proceedings of the 11th Workshop on Argument Mining, pages 59–68
August 15, 2024 ©2024 Association for Computational Linguistics

existing neural dependency parsers to process undercuts effectively, preserving their unique status within argument structures. Lastly, our experimental results demonstrate that our GNN-based parser outperforms existing biaffine parsers in recognising undercuts and maintains state-of-the-art performance in the general AM task.

2 Related Work

Our work is closely related to existing approaches to AM, and the studies on undercuts in the field of AM.

2.1 AM Approaches

There are two kinds of approaches to AM in general, pipelined and end-to-end. Pipelined approaches break down AM into several subtasks and process them sequentially, such as in Persing and Ng (2016), Mayer et al. (2020), and Ruiz-Dolz et al. (2021). End-to-end approaches to argument mining allow for the prediction of the full argument structure with a single model, and have been gaining popularity due to their advantages over pipelined approaches, including avoiding error propagation and eliminating the need for designing different models for different subtasks (Ye and Teufel, 2021).

The tree or graph structure of arguments enables some end-to-end approaches to formulate argument mining as a dependency parsing problem. For example, Morio et al. (2020) use bidirectional LSTMs (BiLSTMs) (He et al., 2016) to encode argument components, and a biaffine dependency parser (Dozat and Manning, 2018) to classify components and their relations. Bao et al. (2021) propose a neural transition-based model to predict the dependency structure of arguments. These approaches all assume that the input text is already segmented.

In contrast, Eger et al. (2017) and Ye and Teufel (2021) take raw text as input in their end-to-end approaches based on dependency parsing. Ye and Teufel (2021) report better results than those by Eger et al. (2017), crediting the improvement to their token-level dependency representation of argument and the biaffine dependency parser they use. Our approach is based on the work by Ye and Teufel (2021), except that ours can computationally model undercuts.

2.2 Studies on Undercuts

Undercuts play a critical role in challenging the soundness or validity of an argument. They have been well defined in various theoretical argumentation models, such as Pollock's argumentation model (Pollock, 1987) and Besnard and Hunter's argumentation model (Besnard and Hunter, 2009).

In the field of AM, some datasets based on the Argument Interchange Format (Chesnevar et al., 2006) may include undercuts, for example, the QT30 corpus by Hautli-Janisz et al. (2022). However, their inclusion of undercuts is incidental and will form a small part of the overall dataset.

The Microtext dataset (Peldszus and Stede, 2015a) is one of the few AM datasets that contain explicitly annotated undercuts. The source text was produced in a highly controlled text generation experiment. The size of this dataset is small (7,846 tokens in total), each document only containing about five segments. Also, its creators do not categorise these undercuts or provide any automatic method to recognise them in their follow-up experiments. Mim et al. (2022) present some ideas that touch upon the phenomenon of undercuts in their dataset, although they do not explicitly mention undercuts when doing so. But nobody has studied which kinds of undercut strategies exist, nor is there large corpus data about them available. In contrast, to the best of our knowledge, the QuoraAM dataset we present is the biggest AM dataset that contains annotation of undercuts. We provide a taxonomy of undercuts after manually examining the annotation of our dataset, along with its distribution in our dataset. Moreover, we propose the first approach to computationally modelling undercuts.

3 The QuoraAM Dataset

We collected 400 arguments from Quora, and named this dataset as the QuoraAM dataset.

Compared to user-generated content on other online discussion platforms such as ChangeMyView, Kialo, idebate.org, and Twitter, arguments on Quora are more in line with our research interest. On Quora, users can present detailed and well-reasoned points of view in their answers to a question. As a result, each answer on Quora can be seen as containing a stand-alone cogently structured complete argument, often supplemented with explanations and supporting evidence. Platforms including ChangeMyView, Kialo and idebate.org are specifically designed for interactive debates and

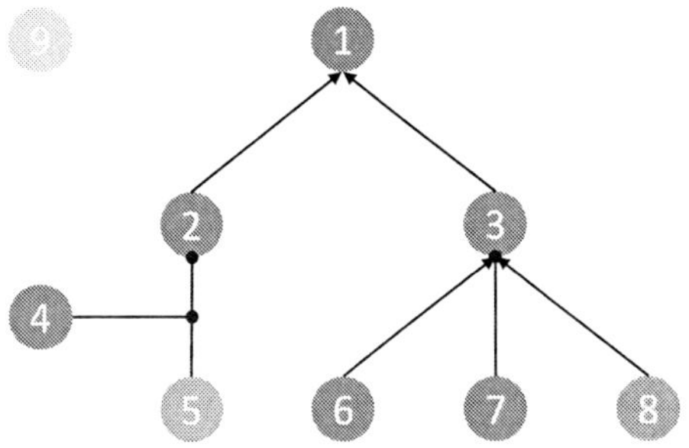

Figure 1: An example argument graph using our annotation scheme. Nodes in different colours represent components of different categories. Edges represent relations: arrow-head = SUPPORT, circle-head = ATTACK.

discussions, with a focus on the process of changing one's mind through constructive conversations. Each post on such platforms may only contain an incomplete argument, and intertextual referencing is frequent among posts, making the analysis of such posts more difficult. Twitter, unlike those previous platforms, is a more open and informal platform, where arguments can take on a more combative tone. As a result, arguments there may not always be rational and often lack the depth and nuance seen on the other platforms. Additionally, due to Twitter's character limit, arguments in tweets tend to be very short, with structures that may be too simplistic to warrant a detailed analysis. Therefore, we chose Quora over other online discussion platforms.

We first manually pre-segmented the QuoraAM dataset, and then trained two annotators to annotate this dataset using our annotation scheme. This dataset will be used for our experiments in this paper. To the best of our knowledge, this is the biggest argument mining dataset that contains explicit annotation of undercuts.

3.1 Annotation Scheme

Our scheme is illustrated in Figure 1. It includes four argument component categories and two argument relation types.

The unit of annotation for components is a segment that can be part of a sentence, a sentence or a sequence of sentences. We define four component categories in our annotation scheme, including **PROPOSITION**, **STAKE**, **ANECDOTE**, and **ANALOGY**. These categories are decided based on our manual observation of arguments on Quora and the argumentation schemes by Walton et al. (2008).

Our scheme only has two relation categories, namely **SUPPORT** (*e.g.* component 2 supporting component 1) and **ATTACK** (*e.g.* component 7 attacking component 3). In our scheme, the representation of undercuts does not rely on relation labels, but on the target of an attacking relation: if the target is a relation, an undercut occurs (*e.g.* component 4 undercutting the relation between component 5 and component 2); otherwise it is just a typical direct SUPPORT.

Component 9 in Figure 1 is a STAKE, and is a stand-alone component, In our scheme, STAKEs are always stand alone components, which do not hold any relation to other components or relations.

3.2 Dataset Creation

In order to collect 400 answers from Quora, we first selected the first 20 topics in the topic catalogue on Kialo[2] (*e.g.* "Politics", "Society", and "Technology"). Under each topic, we identified the top five popular questions, resulting in 100 candidate questions (5 questions per topic). These Kialo questions were then used to search for corresponding questions on Quora.

In the second step, we aimed to select one relevant question on Quora for each topic. We used the full string of each Kialo question as a query on Quora. Suitable questions were those relevant to the Kialo query and with at least 50 answers. If no suitable question was found, we refined our search using key terms from the Kialo question. If we still could not find a suitable Quora question, we proceeded to the next Kialo question. This process yielded 20 selected Quora questions.

In the third step, we chose 20 answers for each selected Quora question. A qualified answers must: 1) directly address the topic; 2) contain at least 30% argumentative material; and 3) be between 60 and 800 wordpieces after being tokenised by the BERT WordPiece tokeniser (Wolf et al., 2020).

Using this data collection method, we selected 400 (20×20) answers that cover various topics such as politics, environment, education, and equality. Since arguments on Quora happen in a question-answering context, each answer was appended to its corresponding question, forming a "document" for our dataset.

We manually segmented the raw text in the QuoraAM dataset and trained two annotators to apply our annotation scheme. The two annotators first

[2]https://www.kialo.com. We turned to Kialo for topic selection because Quora does not provide such a catalogue.

annotated the same 60 documents for the annotation study. The remaining 340 documents were randomly split into two equal subsets. Each subset was assigned to one annotator for annotation. The annotation process took approximately 80 hours per annotator. To compile the final collection of 400 annotated documents, we randomly selected one of the doubly annotated documents from the first step and combined it with the 340 documents from the second step.

Inter-annotator agreement was measured using Krippendorff's alpha (Krippendorff, 2018) for component classification and graph similarity measures (Kirschner et al., 2015; Putra et al., 2022) for relation identification. For component classification, the score of Krippendorff's alpha is $\alpha = 0.78$ ($N = 7,883, n = 2, k = 5$). According to the interpretation scale in Krippendorff (2018), this score is acceptable for "drawing tentative conclusions" ($\alpha \geq 0.67$), and is close to the threshold ($\alpha \geq 0.80$) for being considered "reliable". For relation identification, the graph similarity scores are: $\text{Kirschner}^{\text{mean}} = 0.69$, $\text{Kirschner}^{\text{f}} = 0.67$, $\text{MAR}^{\text{link}} = 0.64$, $\text{MAR}^{\text{path}} = 0.54$, and $\text{MAR}^{\text{dSet}} = 0.84$.

3.3 Dataset Statistics

Table 1 shows the statistics of the QuoraAM dataset. The dataset contains a total of 118,573 tokens, which is much larger than the Microtext dataset (7,846 tokens). There are over 7,800 segments in the dataset, with approximately 56% being argumentative. The QuoraAM dataset as distributed is randomly divided into three subsets: 280 documents for training, 40 for development, and 80 for testing.

Table 2 shows the distribution of components and relations. The dataset includes over 4,000 PROPOSITIONS, around 200 ANALOGIES, 79 ANECDOTES, and 28 STAKES. Due to the small number of STAKES, we merged them with ANECDOTES in our experiments in Section 5, though the original categories are preserved in the dataset for future research.

	All	Per document
Token	118,573	296.4
Segment	7,883	19.7
Component	4,381	11.0
Sentence	6,398	16.0
Paragraph	2,826	7.1

Table 1: Statistics of the QuoraAM dataset.

		All	Per doc
Component	PROPOSITION	4,075 (51.7%)	10.2
	STAKE	28 (0.4%)	0.1
	ANECDOTE	79 (1.0%)	0.2
	ANALOGY	199 (2.5%)	0.5
	Total	4,381	11.0
	Non-arg	3,502 (44.4%)	8.8
Relation	SUPPORT	2,752 (69.8%)	6.9
	ATTACK	1,190 (30.2%)	3.0
	Normal attack	864 (72.6%)	2.2
	Undercut	326 (27.4%)	0.8
	Total	3,942	9.9

Table 2: Component and relation distribution of the QuoraAM dataset.

In terms of relations, the QuoraAM dataset includes 2,752 instances of SUPPORT and 1,190 instances of ATTACK. There are 326 undercuts in the dataset, which constitutes approximately 27% of all ATTACKs. This result confirms the prevalence of undercuts in Quora arguments.

3.4 Categories of Undercuts

We manually examined all undercuts in the QuoraAM dataset, classifying them into three categories:

- **Rejection**: Rejecting the relation by denying the relevance between the source component and the target component.
- **Low importance**: Questioning the importance of the relation, or providing more important reasons.
- **Alternative option**: Stating that the current solution is not the only option, or providing alternative options. This kind of undercuts often appears in arguments about policies.

Figure 2 shows the distribution of undercuts in the QuoraAM dataset. "Low importance" (41%) is the most frequent, followed by "Alternative option" (36%), "Rejection" (15%), and others (8%). This indicates that Quora authors prefer less direct methods of undercutting relations, often pointing out weaknesses or suggesting alternatives rather than outright rejection.

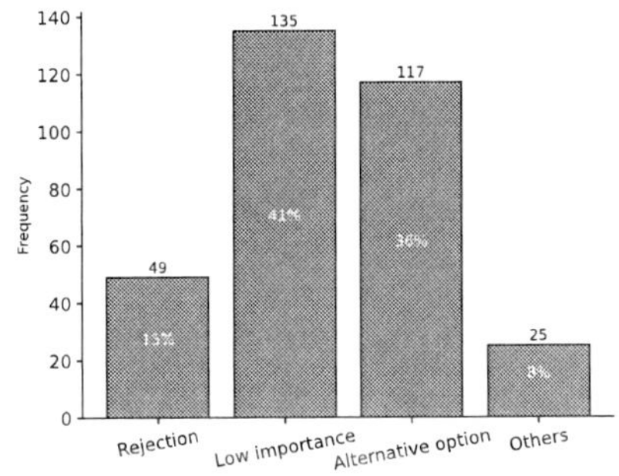

Figure 2: Distribution of undercuts in the QuoraAM dataset.

4 Computational Modelling of Undercuts

Through a redesign of an existing dependency representation of arguments by Ye and Teufel (2021), we are able to directly use existing neural dependency parsers to computationally model undercuts. We also apply a modified GNN-based dependency parser for improved performance.

4.1 Undercut-inclusive Dependency Representation

Following Ye and Teufel (2021), we also frame AM as a dependency parsing task. They propose a token-level dependency representation for arguments in order to approach argument mining in an end-to-end fashion. However, their dependency representation cannot be used for arguments containing undercuts, as undercuts involve relations between a component and a relation, and a relation cannot be a dependent or a head in typical dependency representations. Therefore, we designed an undercut-inclusive dependency representation for arguments (shown in Figure 3) to allow existing neural parsers to process undercuts directly. It is a modification of the undercut-exclusive representation by Ye and Teufel (2021). This figure uses the category labels in the Persuasive Essays dataset (Stab and Gurevych, 2017) to be consistent with the figure in Ye and Teufel (2021). New features of our undercut-inclusive representation are as follows:

- A relation node (shown as dashed-line nodes in Figure 3) for each token in the argument is added. Each relation node is indexed with the token number of its corresponding token, followed by a prime. The relation nodes are meant to represent relations. This is very different from the undercut-exclusive representation, where relations are represented by edges.
- The relation node (*e.g.* relation node $7'$) of the last token (token 7) in a component is always the head of that token, and represents the relation from that component to its target, or the other way around. The edge label between the last token in a component and its corresponding relation node is written as (*segment_label*, REL), where REL means "relation". For example, the label of the edge between token 7 and relation node $7'$ is (P, REL).
- If the relation is a SUPPORT or a direct ATTACK, the relation node's outgoing edge points to the last token in the source component. Its incoming edge comes from the last token of the target component. For example, the fact that "it killed much marine life" (tokens 3-7) supports "tourism has threatened nature" (tokens 9-12) is expressed by the incoming edge of relation node $7'$ from token 12, and the outgoing edge of relation node $7'$ to node 7.
- If the relation is an undercut, the relation node's outgoing edge points to the last token in the undercutting component. The incoming edge comes from another relation node, rather than the last token in a component. For example, the fact that tokens 14-15 undercuts the relation between tokens 3-7 and tokens 9-12 is expressed by the incoming edge of relation node $15'$ from relation node $7'$, and the outgoing edge of relation node $15'$ to node 15.

This design treats all relations as nodes, enabling undercuts to be modelled as relations between nodes while preserving their unique status. In this way, existing neural dependency parsers are able to process undercuts directly.

4.2 GNN-based Neural Dependency Parser

We modified the GNN-based dependency parser proposed by Ji et al. (2019), which uses Graph Attention Networks (GANs) (Veličković et al., 2017) to model higher-order dependencies. Compared to the biaffine parser used by Ye and Teufel (2021), we expect our GNN-based parser to capture global argument structure and higher-order dependencies more effectively.

The mathematical description of our GNN-based parser is as follows:

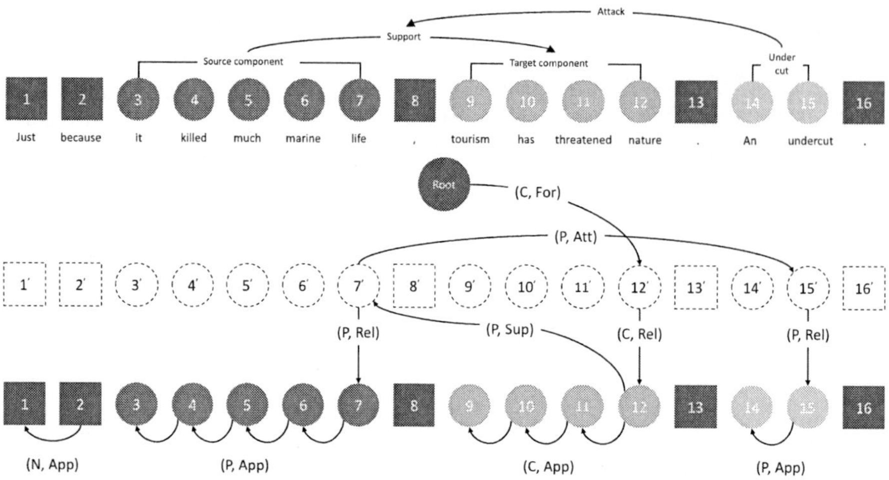

Figure 3: The structure of an example argument with a pseudo undercutting component (written as "An undercut"), and its undercut-inclusive dependency representation. C = CLAIM, P = PREMISE, Sup = SUPPORT, N = non-argumentative, App = append, Rel = relation.

$$r_S = \text{BERT}(s_1 s_2 ... s_n) \tag{1}$$

$$r_{ROOT} = \text{FFN}^{\text{ROOT}}(\text{mean}(r_S), \text{axis}=0) \tag{2}$$

$$R = [r_S; r_{ROOT}], \text{axis}=0 \tag{3}$$

$$H^{\text{e\_h}}, H^{\text{l\_h}}, H^{\text{e\_d}}, H^{\text{l\_d}} = \text{FFN}(R) \tag{4}$$

$$H_{\text{r}}^{\text{e\_h}}, H_{\text{r}}^{\text{l\_h}}, H_{\text{r}}^{\text{e\_d}}, H_{\text{r}}^{\text{l\_d}} = \begin{cases} \text{FFN}^{\text{rel\_node}}(R) & \text{if undercut\_inclusive} \\ \emptyset & \text{if undercut\_exclusive} \end{cases} \tag{5}$$

$$\begin{aligned} H_{\text{G}}^{\text{e\_h}}, H_{\text{G}}^{\text{l\_h}}, H_{\text{G}}^{\text{e\_d}}, H_{\text{G}}^{\text{l\_d}} = \text{GNN}_{\text{layer}=2}(\\ ([H^{\text{e\_h}}; H^{\text{l\_h}}], \text{axis}=1), ([H^{\text{e\_d}}; H^{\text{l\_d}}], \text{axis}=1), \\ ([H_{\text{r}}^{\text{e\_h}}; H_{\text{r}}^{\text{l\_h}}], \text{axis}=1), ([H_{\text{r}}^{\text{e\_d}}; H_{\text{r}}^{\text{l\_d}}], \text{axis}=1) \\ ) \end{aligned} \tag{6}$$

$$\text{Biaff}(x, y) = x^{\top}\text{U}y + \text{W}(x \oplus y) + b \tag{7}$$

$$sc^{\text{edge}} = \text{Biaff}^{\text{edge}}(H_{\text{G}}^{\text{e\_h}}, H_{\text{G}}^{\text{e\_d}}) \tag{8}$$

$$sc^{\text{label}} = \text{Biaff}^{\text{label}}(H_{\text{G}}^{\text{l\_h}}, H_{\text{G}}^{\text{l\_d}}) \tag{9}$$

$$y_{i,j}^{'\text{edge}} = \{sc_{i,j}^{\text{edge}} \geq 0\} \tag{10}$$

$$y_{i,j}^{'\text{label}} = \arg\max\ sc_{i,j}^{\text{label}} \tag{11}$$

We calculate four representations for all tokens $(H^{\text{e\_h}}, H^{\text{l\_h}}, H^{\text{e\_d}}, H^{\text{l\_d}})$ in Equations 1-4. Relation nodes' representations $(H_{\text{r}}^{\text{e\_h}}, H_{\text{r}}^{\text{l\_h}}, H_{\text{r}}^{\text{e\_d}}, H_{\text{r}}^{\text{l\_d}})$ are produced in Equation 5 when necessary.

In Equation 6, the eight representations above are fed into a two-layer GNN encoder, forming a fully connected graph. The head representation and the dependant representation of each node are concatenated to form a general representation. The general representation of each node is then aggregated and updated through the GNN layers. A detailed explanation can be found in Ji et al. (2019).

The GNN-encoded representations are then used for edge and label prediction, as described in Equations 7-11.

The final loss is calculated in the same way as that in Ji et al. (2019).

5 Experiments

We conducted two experiments in order to test:

- **Experiment 1** – the effectiveness of our undercut-inclusive representation and GNN-based parser on undercut recognition;
- **Experiment 2** – the impact of our undercut-inclusive representation on arguments without undercuts.

Results from these experiments can also be used to test the effectiveness of our GNN-based parser on AM in general.

5.1 Datasets

In Experiment 1, we used our QuoraAM dataset, processing each document as a data point to capture argument relations spanning paragraphs. This is because relations in the QuoraAM dataset are more likely to span across paragraphs, rather than operating within individual paragraphs, as paragraph breaks are often not used consistently in this dataset. We merged all instances of STAKE and ANECDOTE in the QuoraAM dataset to form a new category called STAKE+ANECDOTE, as discussed in Section 3.3.

In Experiment 2, we used the Persuasive Essays dataset, which is a benchmark constructed by Stab and Gurevych (2017). This dataset is also used in Ye and Teufel (2021). It comprises 402 persuasive essays randomly selected from an online forum, with 322 essays used for training and 80 essays for testing. Considering that most relations hold within paragraphs in this dataset, each paragraph was processed as a separate argument, aligning with Ye and Teufel (2021).

In both experiments, we performed the same post-processing steps as Ye and Teufel (2021).

5.2 Systems

In Experiment 1, since no existing approaches model undercuts computationally, we built a new baseline model *Biaff_exc_r*, using the biaffine parser in Ye and Teufel (2021) with their undercut-exclusive representation. We simulate Peldszus and Stede (2015b)'s approach by transforming all undercuts into direct ATTACKs during training. During inference, we randomly convert all predicted direct ATTACKs to undercuts in proportion to the ratio of undercuts to overall ATTACKs in the original QuoraAM dataset.

In Experiment 2, we selected two baseline models: *Biaff_exc* (the *BiPAM* model in Ye and Teufel (2021)), the biaffine parser in Ye and Teufel (2021) with their undercut-exclusive representation; and *GNN_exc*, our GNN-based parser with the undercut-exclusive representation in Ye and Teufel (2021).

We implemented two models in the two experiments to compare with the baselines: *Biaff_inc*, the biaffine parser with our undercut-inclusive representation; and *GNN_inc*, our GNN-based parser with our undercut-inclusive representation.

6 Results and Discussion

Table 3 shows the F_1 scores for component and relation identification in Experiment 1. Table 4 shows the results for Experiment 2. We used permutation tests from Ye and Teufel (2021) to test the significance of our results.

In Experiment 1, for undercut recognition, both models significantly outperform the baseline (*i.e.* *Biaff_exc_r*) by a large margin. *Biaff_inc* outperforms the baseline by 15.8% ($Biaff\_inc = 21.6\%$, $baseline = 5.8\%$, $p < 0.01$), which suggests that our undercut-inclusive representation can significantly improve undercut recognition compared to the undercut-inclusive representation by Ye and Teufel (2021). The increase is 33.0% for *GNN_inc* ($GNN\_inc = 38.8\%$, $baseline = 5.8\%, p < 0.01$). The performance on undercut recognition of *GNN_inc* is comparable to that on recognising direct ATTACKs ($Undercut = 38.8\%$, $DirectAttack = 40.3\%$). This suggests that undercuts, despite their intricate nature, are structures that can be effectively recognised using our approach. It also shows that the GNN-based parser is better than the biaffine parser at recognising undercuts: *GNN_inc* significantly outperforms *Biaff_inc* by 17.2% ($GNN\_inc = 38.8\%$, $Biaff\_inc = 21.6\%, p < 0.01$).

The results from two experiments suggest that the GNN-based parser is more efficient than the biaffine parser. In Experiment 1, *GNN_inc* significantly outperforms Biaff_inc by 3.8% for component identification ($GNN\_inc = 66.2\%$, $Biaff\_inc = 62.4\%$, $p < 0.01$) and 4.1% for relation identification ($GNN\_inc = 45.8\%$, $Biaff\_inc = 41.7\%, p < 0.01$); in Experiment 2, *GNN_inc* significantly outperforms Biaff_inc by 1.0% for component identification ($GNN\_inc =$

	Biaff_exc_r	Biaff_inc	GNN_inc
Component	62.4	62.4	66.2
Relation	35.2	41.7	45.8
SUPPORT	45.2	45.1	48.0
ATTACK	11.7	33.8	39.9
Direct ATTACK	14.0	38.4	40.3
Undercut	5.8	21.6	38.8

Table 3: F_1 scores for models on the QuoraAM dataset in Experiment 1.

Model	Component	Relation
Biaff_exc	72.9	45.9
Biaff_inc	72.8	45.9
GNN_exc	73.8	49.4
GNN_inc	73.8	49.4

Table 4: F_1 scores for models on the Persuasive Essays dataset in Experiment 2.

73.8%, $Biaff\_inc = 72.8\%, p < 0.01$) and 3.5% for relation identification ($GNN\_inc = 49.4\%$, $Biaff\_inc = 45.9\%, p < 0.01$).

Regarding the comparison between the undercut-exclusive and the undercut-inclusive representations in Experiment 2, the results reveals no significant difference in performance. Both representations yield similar F_1 scores for component and relation identification, which implies that our undercut-inclusive representation can also be used for arguments containing no undercuts, without performance compromise. This result suggests the flexibility of our undercut-inclusive representation.

6.1 Recognising undercuts: biaffine parser *vs.* GNN-based parser

To understand the disparity between the biaffine parser and the GNN-based parser in recognising undercuts, we compared the errors made by both parsers, so that we can discern which parts of an undercut are most error-prone for the GNN-based parser.

Figure 4 shows the structure of an undercut with its dependency representation. Nodes 1-3 are components, with nodes 1' and 2' as their corresponding relation nodes. An undercut has three elements: an undercutting component (*e.g.* node 1 in Figure 4), its target relation ("node 2 $\Leftarrow$ node 2' $\Leftarrow$ node 3"), and the link between them ("node 1' $\Leftarrow$ node 2'"). Errors can occur in recognising any single element or a combination of them. We focused on three error types illustrated in Figure 4: type I (errors in recognising the undercutting component); type II (errors in recognising the target relation); and type III (errors only in recognising the link between them). Please note that type III only include the cases where the link is incorrectly predicted but the undercutting component and the target relation are correctly predicted.

We performed an error analysis by counting the

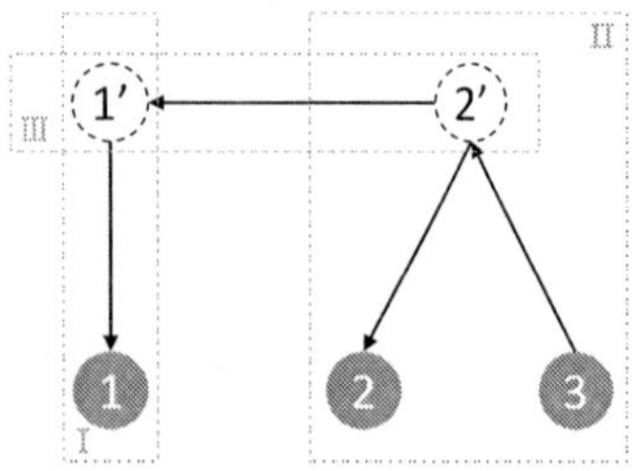

Figure 4: The dependency representation of an undercut, and three types of error in undercut recognition.

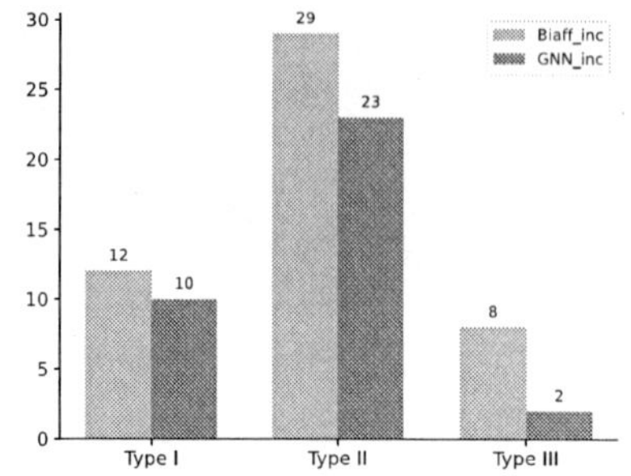

Figure 5: Distribution of three types of error in undercut recognition.

errors made by our models. Figure 5 shows the error distribution among all undercuts (N=58) in the test set. Due to the small sample size, we refrain from testing the statistical significance of the results in this figure, and instead interpret the numbers only qualitatively. According to Figure 5, *Biaff_inc* produces relatively 20% more type I errors and 26% more type II errors than *GNN_inc*. For type III errors, the difference becomes much bigger, which is 300%. This pattern suggests that the GNN-based parser recognises all three elements of an undercut more effectively, especially the link between the undercutting component and the target relation.

Regarding the disparity in link recognition between the GNN-based parser and the biaffine parser, we hypothesise that the GNN-parser's advantage in identifying higher-order dependencies is crucial. Figure 6 illustrates the number of hops required for different relation representations: (a) in the undercut-exclusive representation, a direct ATTACK requires one hop; (b) in the undercut-inclusive representation, a direct ATTACK requires two hops; (c) in the undercut-inclusive representation, an undercut requires three hops.

A direct ATTACK is a 1-hop relation in the undercut-exclusive representation, but becomes a 2-hop relation in the undercut-inclusive representation. Despite this, performance on the Persuasive Essays dataset shows no significant loss, imply-

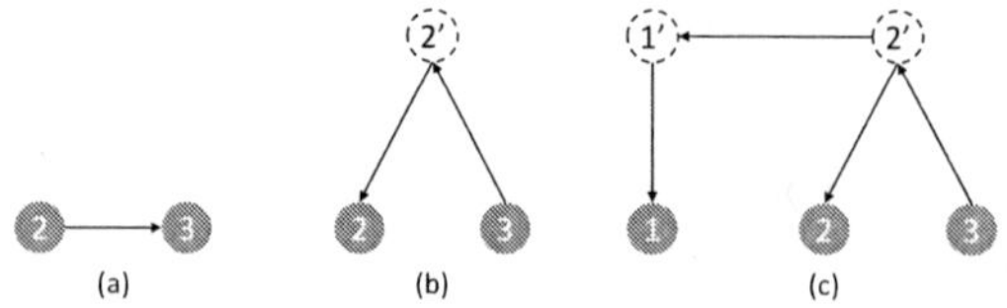

Figure 6: Illustration of the number of hops required for different relation representations.

ing neither parser suffers from the transition from 1-hop to 2-hop relations.

However, when comparing direct ATTACKs and undercuts in the undercut-inclusive representation (2-hop *vs.* 3-hop relations), both models show weaker performance for undercuts. According to Table 3, the F_1 score of *Biaff_inc* for undercuts lags by 16.8% compared to direct ATTACKs, while for *GNN_inc* the difference is only 1.5%. This suggests the GNN-based parser handles the increase from two to three hops better than the biaffine parser, supporting our earlier prediction that the GNN-based parser excels at capturing higher-order dependencies.

7 Conclusion

In this study, we addressed a critical gap in AM by focusing on the computational recognition of undercuts, a complex yet essential structure in arguments. Existing AM research has largely overlooked undercuts, primarily due to the lack of annotated datasets and effective computational models.

To tackle this, we introduced a novel dataset sourced from Quora. This dataset, is the largest that contains undercuts, providing a valuable resource for future AM research. We also developed the first computational approach capable of recognising undercuts, featuring an undercut-inclusive dependency representation and a GNN-based neural dependency parser.

Our experiments indicated that our undercut-inclusive representation can be effectively used for undercut recognition, and it does not compromise performance on datasets without undercuts, showcasing its flexibility and robustness. The results also demonstrated that the GNN-based parser is effective in general AM as well as in recognising undercuts. The GNN-based parser's ability to capture higher-order dependencies was evident, showing a notable advantage in accurately identifying the intricate structures of undercuts.

References

Jianzhu Bao, Chuang Fan, Jipeng Wu, Yixue Dang, Jiachen Du, and Ruifeng Xu. 2021. A neural transition-based model for argumentation mining. In *Proceedings of the 59th Annual Meeting of the Association for Computational Linguistics and the 11th International Joint Conference on Natural Language Processing (Volume 1: Long Papers)*, pages 6354–6364.

Philippe Besnard and Anthony Hunter. 2009. Argumentation based on classical logic. *Argumentation in artificial intelligence*, pages 133–152.

Carlos Chesnevar, Sanjay Modgil, Iyad Rahwan, Chris Reed, Guillermo Simari, Matthew South, Gerard Vreeswijk, Steven Willmott, et al. 2006. Towards an argument interchange format. *The knowledge engineering review*, 21(4):293–316.

Timothy Dozat and Christopher D Manning. 2018. Simpler but more accurate semantic dependency parsing. In *Proceedings of the 56th Annual Meeting of the Association for Computational Linguistics (Volume 2: Short Papers)*, pages 484–490.

Steffen Eger, Johannes Daxenberger, and Iryna Gurevych. 2017. Neural end-to-end learning for computational argumentation mining. In *Proceedings of the 55th Annual Meeting of the Association for Computational Linguistics (Volume 1: Long Papers)*, pages 11–22.

Nancy Green, Kevin D Ashley, Diane Litman, Chris Reed, and Vern Walker. 2014. Proceedings of the first workshop on argumentation mining. In *Proceedings of the First Workshop on Argumentation Mining*.

Annette Hautli-Janisz, Zlata Kikteva, Wassiliki Siskou, Kamila Gorska, Ray Becker, and Chris Reed. 2022. Qt30: A corpus of argument and conflict in broadcast debate. In *Proceedings of the 13th Language Resources and Evaluation Conference*, pages 3291–3300. European Language Resources Association (ELRA).

Kaiming He, Xiangyu Zhang, Shaoqing Ren, and Jian Sun. 2016. Deep residual learning for image recognition. In *Proceedings of the IEEE conference on computer vision and pattern recognition*, pages 770–778.

Tao Ji, Yuanbin Wu, and Man Lan. 2019. Graph-based dependency parsing with graph neural networks. In *Proceedings of the 57th Annual Meeting of the Association for Computational Linguistics*, pages 2475–2485.

Christian Kirschner, Judith Eckle-Kohler, and Iryna Gurevych. 2015. Linking the thoughts: Analysis of argumentation structures in scientific publications. In *Proceedings of the 2nd Workshop on Argumentation Mining*, pages 1–11.

Klaus Krippendorff. 2018. *Content analysis: An introduction to its methodology*. Sage publications.

John Lawrence and Chris Reed. 2020. Argument mining: A survey. *Computational Linguistics*, 45(4):765–818.

Tobias Mayer, Elena Cabrio, and Serena Villata. 2020. Transformer-based argument mining for healthcare applications. In *ECAI 2020*, pages 2108–2115. IOS Press.

Farjana Sultana Mim, Naoya Inoue, Shoichi Naito, Keshav Singh, and Kentaro Inui. 2022. Lpattack: A feasible annotation scheme for capturing logic pattern of attacks in arguments. In *Proceedings of the Thirteenth Language Resources and Evaluation Conference*, pages 2446–2459.

Gaku Morio, Hiroaki Ozaki, Terufumi Morishita, Yuta Koreeda, and Kohsuke Yanai. 2020. Towards better non-tree argument mining: Proposition-level biaffine parsing with task-specific parameterization. In *Proceedings of the 58th Annual Meeting of the Association for Computational Linguistics*, pages 3259–3266.

Andreas Peldszus and Manfred Stede. 2013. From argument diagrams to argumentation mining in texts: A survey. *International Journal of Cognitive Informatics and Natural Intelligence (IJCINI)*, 7(1):1–31.

Andreas Peldszus and Manfred Stede. 2015a. An annotated corpus of argumentative microtexts. In *Argumentation and Reasoned Action: Proceedings of the 1st European Conference on Argumentation, Lisbon*, volume 2, pages 801–815.

Andreas Peldszus and Manfred Stede. 2015b. Joint prediction in mst-style discourse parsing for argumentation mining. In *Proceedings of the 2015 Conference on Empirical Methods in Natural Language Processing*, pages 938–948.

Isaac Persing and Vincent Ng. 2016. End-to-end argumentation mining in student essays. In *Proceedings of the 2016 Conference of the North American Chapter of the Association for Computational Linguistics: Human Language Technologies*, pages 1384–1394.

John L Pollock. 1987. Defeasible reasoning. *Cognitive science*, 11(4):481–518.

Henry Prakken and Gerard Vreeswijk. 2002. Logics for defeasible argumentation. *Handbook of philosophical logic*, pages 219–318.

Jan Wira Gotama Putra, Simone Teufel, and Takenobu Tokunaga. 2022. Annotating argumentative structure in english-as-a-foreign-language learner essays. *Natural Language Engineering*, 28(6):797–823.

Ramon Ruiz-Dolz, Jose Alemany, Stella M Heras Barberá, and Ana García-Fornes. 2021. Transformer-based models for automatic identification of argument relations: a cross-domain evaluation. *IEEE Intelligent Systems*, 36(6):62–70.

Christian Stab and Iryna Gurevych. 2017. Parsing argumentation structures in persuasive essays. *Computational Linguistics*, 43(3):619–659.

Petar Veličković, Guillem Cucurull, Arantxa Casanova, Adriana Romero, Pietro Lio, and Yoshua Bengio. 2017. Graph attention networks. *arXiv preprint arXiv:1710.10903*.

Jacky Visser, Barbara Konat, Rory Duthie, Marcin Koszowy, Katarzyna Budzynska, and Chris Reed. 2020. Argumentation in the 2016 us presidential elections: annotated corpora of television debates and social media reaction. *Language Resources and Evaluation*, 54(1):123–154.

Douglas Walton, Christopher Reed, and Fabrizio Macagno. 2008. *Argumentation schemes*. Cambridge University Press.

Thomas Wolf, Lysandre Debut, Victor Sanh, Julien Chaumond, Clement Delangue, Anthony Moi, Pierric Cistac, Tim Rault, Rémi Louf, Morgan Funtowicz, Joe Davison, Sam Shleifer, Patrick von Platen, Clara Ma, Yacine Jernite, Julien Plu, Canwen Xu, Teven Le Scao, Sylvain Gugger, Mariama Drame, Quentin Lhoest, and Alexander M. Rush. 2020. Transformers: State-of-the-art natural language processing. In *Proceedings of the 2020 Conference on Empirical Methods in Natural Language Processing: System Demonstrations*, pages 38–45, Online. Association for Computational Linguistics.

Yuxiao Ye and Simone Teufel. 2021. End-to-end argument mining as biaffine dependency parsing. In *Proceedings of the 16th Conference of the European Chapter of the Association for Computational Linguistics: Main Volume*, pages 669–678.

MAMKit: A Comprehensive Multimodal Argument Mining Toolkit

Eleonora Mancini and **Federico Ruggeri** and **Stefano Colamonaco**
Andrea Zecca and **Samuele Marro** and **Paolo Torroni**
DISI, University of Bologna, Bologna, Italy
{e.mancini, federico.ruggeri6}@unibo.it

Abstract

Multimodal Argument Mining (MAM) is a recent area of research aiming to extend argument analysis and improve discourse understanding by incorporating multiple modalities. Initial results confirm the importance of paralinguistic cues in this field. However, the research community still lacks a comprehensive platform where results can be easily reproduced, and methods and models can be stored, compared, and tested against a variety of benchmarks. To address these challenges, we propose MAMKit, an open, publicly available, PyTorch toolkit that consolidates datasets and models, providing a standardized platform for experimentation. MAMKit also includes some new baselines, designed to stimulate research on text and audio encoding and fusion for MAM tasks. Our initial results with MAMKit indicate that advancements in MAM require novel annotation processes to encompass auditory cues effectively.

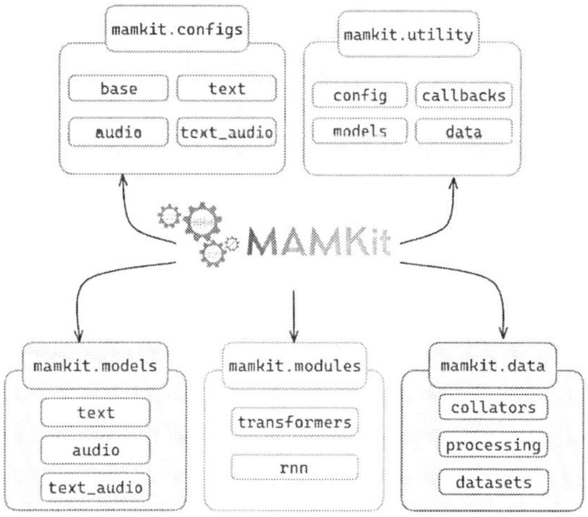

Figure 1: Overall architecture of MAMKit.

1 Introduction

Recent studies in argumentation analysis highlight the importance of including paralinguistic features in argumentative discourse analysis across various domains, including advertisements, news coverage, and legal analytics (Kišiček, 2014; Groarke and Kišiček, 2018). Similar considerations have been made for fake news detection (Ivanov et al., 2023). For these reasons, Multimodal Argument Mining (MAM) recently emerged as an extension of Argument Mining, aiming to validate these propositions empirically and gain a more comprehensive understanding of argumentative discourse by integrating multiple modalities. MAM is a growing research field. The tasks addressed so far include argument detection, argument component classification, relation classification, and fallacy classification (Lippi and Torroni, 2016a; Mestre et al., 2021a; Mancini et al., 2022; Mestre et al., 2023; Mancini et al., 2024). However, despite these encouraging results, and similarly to what happens in other domains (Li et al., 2023; Helwe et al., 2022), the lack of standardized tools is hampering progress since MAM researchers struggle to access and evaluate models and datasets. For one thing, MAM resources are often hosted across various sites and repositories, each employing its own distinct methods for loading and reconstructing datasets and models. As a consequence, a fair model comparison may be problematic, which in turn limits the experimental evaluation of new models.

We then introduce a PyTorch toolkit tailored for MAM. Our toolkit, MAMKit, currently includes 4 datasets and 6 models, providing researchers with a standardized platform for experimentation and evaluation. MAMKit offers a simple interface to load, reconstruct and process existing datasets, and contribute new resources. Moreover, all models within MAMKit are implemented uniformly, facilitating seamless integration and comparison across tasks and datasets. To ensure the reproducibility and reliability of our models, all the resources and models in MAMKit have been validated against the original research papers, offering a shared interface for benchmarking and model comparison. Besides literature models, MAMKit explores and integrates advanced audio encoding and fusion methods. Indeed, previous research in MAM has largely overlooked advanced audio encoding and fusion strategies (Mancini et al., 2024), thus MAMKit intends to present an opportunity to shed light on the significance of audio and the synergistic interaction between both modalities in argument mining tasks.

2 Related Work

We overview the MAM literature and the landscape of toolkits built to address relevant AI tasks in different application domains.

2.1 Multimodal Argument Mining

Work in MAM started relatively recently, inspired by studies on the connections between arguments and emotions (Benlamine et al., 2015), with the development of a classifier for claim detection from speech in the domain of political debates, and a small dataset built for the occasion (Lippi and Torroni, 2016a). The interest in political debates motivated further research and resource development (Lawrence and Reed, 2019; Mancini et al., 2022; Mestre et al., 2023; Mancini et al., 2024). Notably, Mancini et al. (2022) and Mestre et al. (2023) introduced two distinct expansions of USED (Haddadan et al., 2019), the US presidential election corpus. Recently, Mancini et al. (2024) proposed an extension of USED-fallacy, releasing the first corpus for multimodal fallacy classification. These resources constitute the most extensive multimodal corpora for AM to date. Another domain of interest is fake news detection. There, Ivanov et al. (2023) observed enhanced classification performance across various tasks, such as the identification of check-worthy claims, through the adoption of a multimodal formulation.

The MAM systems adopted in literature so far uncovered the importance of tackling argumentative tasks from a multimodal standpoint, but they did not introduce significant architectural innovations. On the contrary, they mostly followed the standard practice of merging unimodal models using fusion techniques (Toto et al., 2021): see for instance (Mancini et al., 2022; Mestre et al., 2023; Mancini et al., 2024). However, recent advancements in Multimodal Deep Learning (MMDL) offer an opportunity for exploring new architectural solutions. Some of the new models introduced in MAMKit extend previous work (Mancini et al., 2022) with new MAM models based on state-of-the-art models for audio encoding and multimodal fusion techniques (Boulahia et al., 2021). These include Wav2Vec 2.0 (Baevski et al., 2020), HuBERT (Hsu et al., 2021) and WavLM (Chen et al., 2022) for audio encoding, as well as early, cross-modal (Tsai et al., 2019) and late fusion.

2.2 Toolkits

In recent years, there has been a growing emphasis on streamlining training, evaluation, and benchmarking processes across diverse domains of artificial intelligence (AI). Accordingly, new resources became available to address specific tasks and applications. Regarding benchmarking, LAVIS (Li et al., 2023), MMF (Singh et al., 2020), X-modaler (Li et al., 2021) and UniLM (uni, 2020) provide user-friendly interfaces for accessing datasets and for training/evaluating language-vision models.

Furthermore, several tools have been proposed for multimodalities. Notable examples are TorchMultimodal (tor, 2022) for accessing several state-of-the-art multimodal models, ViLMedic (Delbrouck et al., 2022) for vision and language in medical AI, pyannote.metrics (Bredin, 2017) and pyannote.audio (Bredin, 2023) for speaker diarization, and Muskits (Shi et al., 2022) for end-to-end music processing.

Moreover, several specialized NLP libraries and tools focus on specific tasks. They include LogiTorch (Helwe et al., 2022) for logical reasoning in natural language, TextBox 2.0 (Tang et al., 2022) for text generation using pre-trained language models, mahaNLP (Magdum et al., 2023) for Marathi NLP, DeepPavlov (Burtsev et al., 2018) for dialogue systems, TextAttack (Morris et al., 2020) and OpenAttack (Zeng et al., 2021) for adversarial attacks in NLP, LambdaKG (Xie et al., 2023) for knowledge graph embeddings, nerblackbox (Stollenwerk, 2023) for named entity recognition, NewsRecLib (Iana et al., 2023) for news recommendation, and NeuralQA (Dibia, 2020) for question answering cater to specific NLP tasks.

To the best of our knowledge, there are no such resources to support argument mining/MAM research, so MAMKit is the first toolkit in this area.

3 MAMKit

MAMKit is an open-source, publicly available[1] PyTorch toolkit designed to access and develop datasets, models, and benchmarks for MAM. It provides a flexible interface for accessing and integrating datasets, models, and preprocessing strategies through composition or custom definition. MAMKit is designed to be extendible, ensure replicability, and provide a shared interface as a common foundation for experimentation in the field. At the time of writing, MAMKit offers 4 datasets and 6 distinct model architectures, along with audio and text processing capabilities, organized in 5 main components (see Figure 1).

3.1 Description of toolkit components

Datasets The `mamkit.data` package covers dataset creation (`data.datasets`) and preprocessing (`data.preprocessing` and `data.collators`). The `data.datasets` module provides the `Loader` interface, a general-purpose wrapper for datasets, covering data downloading, task-specific data parsing, and data interfacing. Regarding the latter functionality, the module includes ad-hoc implementations for unimodal (`UnimodalDataset`) and multimodal (`MultimodalDataset`) data based on the PyTorch `Dataset` interface. The `data.processing` module provides the `Processor` interface for defining custom data processing and implements unimodal (`UnimodalProcessor`) and multimodal (`MultimodalProcessor`) processing steps. For instance, the `AudioTransformer` class implements transformer-based audio processing. Similarly to `data.processing`, the `data.collators` module is designed to address input processing at batch-level, in compliance with PyTorch `DataLoader` APIs. The module includes implementations for unimodal (`UnimodalCollator`) and multimodal (`MultimodalCollator`) input batches.

Models The `mamkit.models` package holds definitions for the supported models. It provides `models.audio`, `models.text` and `models.text_audio` modules. Each model implements the `torch.nn.Module` interface that can be extended to define the models for each input configuration.

Modules The `mamkit.modules` package handles the definition of the shared model layers such as `transformer_modules`.

[1] `https://github.com/lt-nlp-lab-unibo/mamkit`

Utility The `mamkit.utility` package contains classes and methods used by other modules. For example, the `utility.data` module contains methods for downloading data from web storages or GitHub repositories, while `utility.model` manages the overall training and evaluation lifecycles. Currently, the `MAMKitLightningModel` class and the `to_lightning_model()` method are used to wrap models as PyTorch Lightning (Falcon and The PyTorch Lightning team, 2019) models to leverage its functionalities for training and evaluation. Incorporating PyTorch Lightning in our toolkit streamlines training and evaluation with a simplified loop, standardized interface, reproducibility, performance optimizations, accelerator integration, logging capabilities, and extensive community support.

Configs The `mamkit.configs` package serves as a streamlined interface for accessing model configurations across three modalities: audio, text, and text-audio. At its core, the `config.base` module establishes two fundamental classes: `ConfigKey`, defining configuration keys, and `BaseConfig`, providing a base configuration structure. This architecture simplifies benchmarking efforts by enabling users to instantiate models via designated configuration keys. Consequently, leveraging models with exact parameter setups for benchmarking or further experimentation becomes straightforward, enhancing research reproducibility and efficiency within the toolkit.

3.2 Example Usage

MAMKit's design facilitates access to existing datasets and models and supports future development. In this section, we present several examples to illustrate common use cases.

3.2.1 Data Loading

An important feature of MAMKit is its unified and straightforward interface for data access. Several MAM datasets are included in MAMKit. Adding a new dataset to MAMKit requires defining a new subclass of `Loader`, extending it with the specific information needed to access and reconstruct the dataset. In the example that follows, a dataset is loaded using the `MMUSED` class from `mamkit.data.datasets`, which extends the `Loader` interface and implements specific functionalities for data loading and retrieval. Users can specify task and input mode (`text-only`, audio-only, or text-audio) when loading the data, with options to use default splits or load splits from previous works. The example uses splits from Mancini et al. (2022).

```
from mamkit.data.datasets import UKDebates,
↪  InputMode

loader = UKDebates(
          task_name='asd',
          input_mode=InputMode.TEXT_ONLY,
          base_data_path=base_data_path)


split_info =
↪  loader.get_splits('mancini-et-al-2022')
```

The get_splits method of the loader returns data splits in the form of a data.datasets.SplitInfo. The latter wraps split-specific data, each implementing Pytorch's Dataset interface and compliant to the specified input modality (i.e., text-only).

The Loader interface also allows users to integrate methods defining custom splits as follows:

```
from mamkit.data.datasets import SplitInfo

def custom_splits(self) -> List[SplitInfo]:
    train_df = self.data.iloc[:50]
    val_df = self.data.iloc[50:100]
    test_df = self.data.iloc[100:]
    fold_info =
    ↪  self.build_info_from_splits(train_df=...)
    return [fold_info]

loader.add_splits(method=custom_splits,
                  key='custom')

split_info = loader.get_splits('custom')
```

3.2.2 Modelling

MAMKit offers a simple method for defining custom models and leveraging models from the literature. Utilizing the same interface for both tasks aims to simplify access to existing models and establish new ones with a coherent structure. This will hopefully facilitate the spread of established models and encourage the development of new ones by maintaining consistency throughout the process. The example below illustrates that defining a custom model is straightforward. It entails creating the model within the models package, specifically by extending either the AudioOnlyModel, TextOnlyModel, or TextAudioModel classes in the models.audio, models.text, or models.text_audio modules, respectively, depending on the input modality handled by the model.

```
from mamkit.models.text import Transformer

model = Transformer(
          model_card='bert-base-uncased',
          dropout_rate=0.1, ...)
```

The following example demonstrates how to instantiate a model with a configuration found in the literature. This configuration is identified by a key, ConfigKey, containing all the defining information. The key is used to fetch the precise configuration of the model from the configs package. Subsequently, the model is retrieved from the models package and configured with the specific parameters outlined in the configuration.

```
from mamkit.configs.base import ConfigKey
from mamkit.configs.text import TransformerConfig
from mamkit.data.datasets import InputMode

config_key = ConfigKey(
             dataset='mmused',
             task_name='asd',
             input_mode=InputMode.TEXT_ONLY,
             tags={'mancini-et-al-2022'})

config = TransformerConfig.from_config(
                            key=config_key)

model = Transformer(
         model_card=config.model_card,
         dropout_rate=config.dropout_rate
         ...)
```

In both the described use cases, the model is then encapsulated into a Pytorch Lightning model, and training and evaluation are conducted by leveraging the methods provided by this wrapper.

```
from mamkit.utility.model import
↪  to_lighting_model
import lightning

model = to_lighting_model(model=model,
        num_classes=config.num_classes,
        loss_function=...,
        optimizer_class=...)

trainer = lightning.Trainer(max_epochs=100,
                            accelerator='gpu',
                            ...)
trainer.fit(model,
            train_dataloaders=train_dataloader,
            val_dataloaders=val_dataloader)
```

3.2.3 Benchmarking

The mamkit.configs package simplifies reproducing literature results in a structured manner. Upon loading the dataset, experiment-specific configurations can be easily retrieved via a configuration key. Specifically, unlike the examples reported in Section 3.2.2, where configurations refer just to a model implementation, in the below example, they encompass both data processing and model parameterization based on previous literature work.

This enables instantiating a processor using the same features processor employed in the experiment. In the example below, we adopt a configuration akin to (Mancini et al., 2022), employing a BiLSTM model with audio encoded with MFCCs features. Hence, we define a `MFCCExtractor` processor using configuration parameters. Data splits are loaded using the experiment reference key, mirroring what was shown in Section 3.2.1.

```
from mamkit.configs.audio import
↪ BiLSTMMFCCsConfig
from mamkit.configs.base import ConfigKey
from mamkit.data.datasets import UKDebates,
↪ InputMode
from mamkit.data.processing import MFCCExtractor,
↪ UnimodalProcessor
from mamkit.models.audio import BiLSTM

loader = UKDebates(task_name='asd',
         input_mode=InputMode.AUDIO_ONLY)

config = BiLSTMMFCCsConfig.from_config(
             key=ConfigKey(dataset='ukdebates',
              input_mode=InputMode.AUDIO_ONLY,
              task_name='asd',
              tags='mancini-et-al-2022'))


for split_info in loader.get_splits(
                    key='mancini-et-al-2022'):
    processor =
        UnimodalProcessor(
            features_processor=MFCCExtractor(
                mfccs=config.mfccs, ...))

    split_info.train =
    ↪ processor(split_info.train)
    ...
    model = BiLSTM(embedding_dim=
                config.embedding_dim, ...)
```

3.3 Models

MAMKit comes with 3 models from the MAM literature and 3 original models we contribute based on state-of-the-art unimodal audio encoders and fusion strategies. All models comply with the following architecture: text and audio modules for encoding individual modalities, a fusion layer to merge them, and a final classification head tailored to the downstream task of interest. Table 1 provides a summary. Illustrations of our original architectures are shown in Appendix A. We refer to the fusion strategies as follows:

- **Concatenation**: combines features (*early fusion*) or embeddings from single modality architectures (*late fusion*) from all modalities into a single vector by concatenating them;
- **Average**: merges features (*early fusion*) or embeddings from single modality architectures (*late fusion*) by simply averaging information from each modality;
- **Crossmodal Attention**: attends to interactions between multimodal sequences across distinct time steps and facilitates the transfer of streams from one modality to another.

BiLSTM (Mancini et al., 2022) The text module comprises a pre-trained GloVe (Pennington et al., 2014) embedding layer and a stack of BiLSTM layers. Similarly, the audio module is a stack of BiLSTM layers. The fusion strategy is vector concatenation. The classification head is a Multi-Layer Perceptron (MLP).

MM-BERT, MM-RoBERTa (Mancini et al., 2024) The text module comprises a trainable text embedding model and a dropout layer on top. The audio module comprises a pre-trained audio embedding model, a BiLSTM layer, and a dropout layer. The output of the text and audio modules is concatenated and fed to the classification module, defined as a stack of dense layers.

CSA (Ours) A multimodal transformer inspired by Yu et al. (2023), whereby text and audio embeddings are concatenated along the time dimension, and a self-attention layer is employed to obtain a cross-modal text and audio embedding. This embedding is averaged over time and fed to a classification head. The main issue of this architecture is the significant difference between the lengths of the audio and text sequences. Even with downscaling, the audio embeddings tend to be significantly longer (often by a factor of ~10). Consequently, audio features dominate the early stages of training, leading to underwhelming performance. To address this issue, we develop a novel transformer variant in which we reweight the attention scores of text and audio sequences for each layer. Let m be the length of the text sequence and n the length of the audio sequence, we rescale the attention scores of the text sequence by $\frac{m+n}{2m}$ and of the audio sequence by $\frac{m+n}{2n}$. This reweighting ensures that text and audio sequences have the same total weight. Figure 2 in Appendix A summarizes our Concatenation-based early fusion with Self-Attention (CSA) transformer model.

Ensemble (Ours) This architecture consists of two independent unimodal models for text and

Model	Text Encoding	Audio Encoding	Fusion
BiLSTM (Mancini et al., 2022)	GloVe + BiLSTM	(Wav2Vec2 ∨ MFCCs) + BiLSTM	Concat-Late
MM-BERT (Mancini et al., 2024)	BERT	(Wav2Vec2 ∨ HuBERT ∨ WavLM) + BiLSTM	Concat-Late
MM-RoBERTa (Mancini et al., 2024)	RoBERTa	(Wav2Vec2 ∨ HuBERT ∨ WavLM) + BiLSTM	Concat-Late
CSA (Ours)	BERT	(Wav2Vec2 ∨ HuBERT ∨ WavLM) + Transformer	Concat-Early
Ensemble (Ours)	BERT	(Wav2Vec2 ∨ HuBERT ∨ WavLM) + Transformer	Avg-Late
Mul-TA (Ours)	BERT	(Wav2Vec2 ∨ HuBERT ∨ WavLM) + Transformer	Cross

Table 1: Multimodal models available in MAMKit. For each model, we summarize its text and audio encoding modules and its fusion strategy. *Concat*: Concatenation; *Avg*: Average; *Cross*: Crossmodal Attention.

audio, respectively. A weighted average of the probability vectors of the unimodal classification heads constitutes the final prediction. The text-only model involves averaging BERT embeddings along the time dimension and feeding them to a two-layer classification head. The audio-only model follows the same architecture as the text-only model, although with a custom transformer which is trained along with the head. The main challenge is determining how to merge the outputs of the two unimodal classification heads. We compute a weighted average with weight w_e defined as follows:

$$w_e = l + (u - l) \cdot \frac{\tanh w + 1}{2} \tag{1}$$

where w is a learnable parameter in the $[l, u]$ range. Bounding ensures that the ensemble is forced to exploit the output of both classification heads, preventing a *dead neuron* situation where the ensemble focuses on a single modality only. We set $l = 0.3$ and $u = 0.7$ for learning stability. Figure 3 in Appendix A summarizes Ensemble.

Mul-TA (Ours) We propose a variant of the MulT architecture (Tsai et al., 2019): a transformer model for carrying out multimodal tasks without the need for modality alignment. The core module of MulT is the directional pairwise crossmodal attention layer, which captures interdependencies between multimodal sequences and seamlessly adjusts information flow between modalities. In practice, the cross-modal attention layer uses one modality A as the query vector and another modality B as key and value vectors. The layer is applied for each pair of input modalities. Pairs with the same B modality are combined into a unified sequence using a self-attention layer. Lastly, each unified sequence is averaged over the time dimension and concatenated. The resulting embedding vector is fed to a classification head. While MulT was developed for three modalities, totaling six (A, B) pairs, our variant uses only two, totaling two (A, B) pairs. Additionally, we replace the self-attention unification step with an average. Figure 4 in Appendix A summarizes Mul-TA, our MulT architecture variant, tailored to text and audio modality.

3.4 Data

We now provide an overview of MAM datasets currently available in MAMKit.

UKDebates (Lippi and Torroni, 2016a) The first MAM dataset. It contains transcriptions and audio sequences of three candidates for UK Prime Ministerial elections of 2015 in a two-hour debate aired by Sky News. The candidates are David Cameron, Nick Clegg, and Ed Miliband. The dataset contains 386 sentences and corresponding audio samples. Two domain experts annotated sentences as containing or not containing a claim. The inter-annotator agreement measured via Cohen's kappa (Carletta, 1996) is 0.53 (*fair to good*).

M-Arg (Mestre et al., 2021b) A multimodal dataset built around the 2020 US Presidential elections. The dataset contains transcriptions and audio sequences of four candidates and a debate moderator concerning 18 topics. The authors design a controlled crowdsourcing data annotation process whereby each crowd worker labels sentence pairs as describing support, attack, or no relation. In total, the dataset contains 4,104 sentence pairs with corresponding aligned audio samples. A high-quality subset of the M-Arg, M-Arg$_\gamma$, containing 2,443 sentence pairs with high agreement confidence $\gamma \geq 85\%$ is commonly considered for model evaluation.

MM-USED (Mancini et al., 2022) A multimodal extension of the dataset introduced in Haddadan et al. (2019). It contains presidential candidates' debate transcripts and corresponding audio recordings aired from 1960 to 2016. In Haddadan et al. (2019), annotators labeled text sentences as containing a claim, a premise, or neither of them.

Later Mancini et al. (2022) enriched the dataset with the audio modality and aligned text sentences to audio recording snippets. This dataset consists of 26,781 labeled sentences and corresponding audio samples covering 39 debates and 26 different speakers, making it the largest MAM resource to date.

MM-USED-fallacy (Mancini et al., 2024) A multimodal extension of the dataset introduced by Goffredo et al. (2022) about argumentative fallacies. In Goffredo et al. (2022), the authors consider the dataset curated by Haddadan et al. (2019), carry out an annotation process for labeling text spans as argumentative fallacies, and introduce a taxonomy for categorizing them. Mancini et al. (2024) enrich the existing dataset with the audio modality by first converting annotations to the sentence level and then aligning them to audio recording snippets. The dataset contains 1,891 sentences labeled as argumentative fallacies belonging to six distinct categories.

3.5 Tasks

The tasks currently supported by MAMKit are derived from literature (Lippi and Torroni, 2016b; Lawrence and Reed, 2019)

Argumentative Sentence Detection Given an input sentence x, the task of argumentative sentence detection (ASD) consists of determining whether x contains an argument (*arg*) or not (*not-arg*). We extend this definition to include component detection. For instance, the task of claim detection (Levy et al., 2014; Lippi and Torroni, 2015) consists of classifying x as containing a claim (*claim*) or not (*not-claim*).

Argumentative Component Classification Given an argumentative sentence x, the task of argumentative component classification (ACC) consists of classifying x as containing one or more argumentative components according to a reference argument model. Following the *claim-premise* argument model (Walton, 2009), ACC involves identifying claims (*claim*) and premises (*premise*) in x.

Argumentative Relation Classification Given a pair of argumentative sentences x_i and x_j, the task of argumentative relation classification (ARC) consists of classifying the pair (x_i, x_j) as yielding an argumentative relation $x_i \rightarrow x_j$ of *support*, *attack*, or *neither* if no argumentative relation exists.

Argumentative Fallacy Classification Given an argumentative sentence x identified as a fallacy, the task of argumentative fallacy classification (AFC) consists of categorizing x against a given taxonomy of fallacies.

4 Experiments

We employ MAMKit to provide a robust and reproducible overview of a significant share of the work published on MAM so far. In particular, we evaluate MAMKit supported models on all available tasks and datasets. We build our evaluation as follows. Regarding model evaluation, we compute macro F1-score except on UKDebates for which we report binary F1-score (Lippi and Torroni, 2016a). We carry out a repeated five-fold cross-validation routine for UKDebates and M-Arg$_\gamma$ using the same folds defined in Mancini et al. (2022). Similarly, we perform a repeated train and test routine for MM-USED on official data splits (Haddadan et al., 2019). We set the number of repetitions to three in both cases. Lastly, we perform a leave-one-out routine for MM-USED-fallacy Mancini et al. (2024). See Appendix B for additional details.

5 Results

Table 2 reports the best classification performance for each model (See Appendix C for all results).

UKDebates We observe no notable benefits in integrating the audio modality in all models, comparable to the results reported in Mancini et al. (2022). Specifically, multimodal models show equal or lesser classification performance than their text-only modules.

M-Arg$_\gamma$ Our results significantly differ from those reported in Mancini et al. (2022). In particular, Ensemble and Mul-TA, are noticeably underperforming compared to their text-only counterparts. The only exceptions are MM-BERT and CSA with slightly higher performance. Additionally, audio-only models fail to learn the task.

MM-USED We observe a small performance gap between audio-only and text-only models, suggesting that the audio modality may be a valuable indicator in both ASD and ACC tasks. However, multimodal models achieve comparable performance to their text-only counterparts, with minor improvements only for MM-BERT (+1.7), CSA (+0.9), Ensemble (+0.2) and Mul-TA (+1.3) in ASD, CSA (+1.4), and Mul-TA (+1.8) in ACC.

Model	UKDebates (ASD)	M-Arg$_\gamma$ (ARC)	MM-USED (ASD)	MM-USED (ACC)	MM-USED-fallacy (AFC)
			Text Only		
BiLSTM (T_1)	$.552_{\pm.047}$	$.120_{\pm.006}$	$.811_{\pm.004}$	$.663_{\pm.002}$	$.525_{\pm.113}$
BERT (T_2)	$.654_{\pm.003}$	$.132_{\pm.004}$	$.824_{\pm.009}$	$.679_{\pm.004}$	$.594_{\pm.122}$
RoBERTa (T_3)	$.692_{\pm.005}$	$.172_{\pm.015}$	$.839_{\pm.010}$	$.680_{\pm.001}$	$.615_{\pm.097}$
			Audio Only		
BiLSTM (A_1)	$.393_{\pm.040}$	$.024_{\pm.012}$	$.774_{\pm.008}$	$.596_{\pm.005}$	$.657_{\pm.000}$
Transformer (A_2)	$.455_{\pm.004}$	$.000_{\pm.000}$	$.771_{\pm.019}$	$.526_{\pm.004}$	$.629_{\pm.162}$
			Text Audio		
BiLSTM ($T_1 + A_1$)	$.533_{\pm.009}$	$.084_{\pm.016}$	$.815_{\pm.006}$	$.667_{\pm.000}$	$.572_{\pm.099}$
MM-BERT ($T_2 + A_1$)	$.662_{\pm.004}$	$.160_{\pm.015}$	$.841_{\pm.005}$	$.680_{\pm.004}$	$.599_{\pm.128}$
MM-RoBERTa ($T_3 + A_1$)	$.687_{\pm.010}$	$.178_{\pm.012}$	$.837_{\pm.009}$	$.678_{\pm.003}$	$.624_{\pm.074}$
CSA ($T_2 + A_2$)	$.663_{\pm.014}$	$.160_{\pm.015}$	$.833_{\pm.011}$	$.693_{\pm.001}$	$.582_{\pm.114}$
Ensemble ($T_2 + A_2$)	$.586_{\pm.015}$	$.011_{\pm.011}$	$.826_{\pm.011}$	$.681_{\pm.002}$	$.612_{\pm.134}$
Mul-TA ($T_2 + A_2$)	$.616_{\pm.019}$	$.098_{\pm.031}$	$.837_{\pm.006}$	$.697_{\pm.003}$	$.605_{\pm.110}$

Table 2: Test classification performance on MAM datasets. For each multimodal model, we report their constituting text module (T_i) and audio module (A_j).

MM-USED-fallacy In contrast to other tasks and datasets, in MM-USED-fallacy, audio-only models are the best-performing ones. The performance of text-audio models is slightly better than that of the corresponding text-only models but below that of audio-only models. Alternative fusion strategies yielded only a moderate, non-systematic improvement.

6 Conclusion

MAM is a new, exciting and largely unexplored research domain with interesting applications. We believe that, at present, an open and collaborative standardized platform for experimentation and benchmarking has the potential to build a stronger community around it, that will be able to focus on the innovations needed to push the envelope. To this end, we developed an open-source PyTorch toolkit named MAMKit. MAMKit offers several datasets, state-of-the-art models, and processing strategies. This paper introduces the platform and discusses some initial empirical results we obtained with it.

Remarkably, the advanced audio encoding and fusion techniques we introduced do not yield the performance improvement we hoped for. This result might be ascribed to weaknesses in the architectures, and motivate further research on novel encoding and fusion methods. However, the negative result might also be attributed to the fact that, in the available datasets, annotations were first made on the transcripts, and only later extended to the audio modality. As noted by Mancini et al. (2024), such a procedure does not exploit acoustic insights, hence it should be expected that the potential of MAM architectures may not be fully leveraged, until datasets become available, that natively include auditory cues in the annotation process. This issue affects all MAM datasets in MAMKit, therefore a revision of the existing annotations would be required to effectively include auditory cues.

In conclusion, further research is needed to understand audio characteristics better and devise methods to integrate them with textual annotations. That will necessitate collaboration across fields like argumentation and signal processing. MAMKit could be a valuable resource for fostering such a collaboration. In a broader perspective, MAMKit holds potential for further development and application, including its extension to additional modalities like images and video (Birdsell and Groarke, 1996). For instance, we plan to incorporate the ImageArg dataset (Liu et al., 2022), which has been developed to address argument stance classification and image persuasiveness classification tasks. The ImageArg dataset was notably extended during ImageArg-2023 (Liu et al., 2023), the first shared task in MAM, providing additional annotated samples. This dataset has been leveraged in various studies (Sharma et al., 2023; Zong et al., 2023) proposing diverse strategies for vision-language MAM, thereby presenting an opportunity for integrating new models within MAMKit. Additionally, we plan to include in MAMKit the MMClaims dataset (Cheema et al., 2022), designed for multimodal claim detection in social media.

Furthermore, we aim to improve our understanding of multimodal discourse analysis and its practical implications through further experimentation with new datasets and by exploring transfer learning techniques to enhance model generalization across diverse domains.

7 Limitations

PyTorch Dependency. Currently, the toolkit only supports PyTorch. While PyTorch is a widely used deep learning framework, this limitation may pose challenges for researchers who prefer or require other frameworks, such as TensorFlow, as well as the integration of previous work built on these frameworks.

Incomplete Dataset and Model Integration. Not all existing datasets and models for MAM research are included. For instance, the VivesDebate-Speech dataset (Ruiz-Dolz and Iranzo-Sánchez, 2023), the ImageArg dataset (Liu et al., 2022), the MMClaims dataset (Cheema et al., 2022) and models like M-ArgNet (Mestre et al., 2021b) are currently not implemented. We plan to integrate these and other resources in the future, and we encourage MAM researchers to include their resources on our platform.

Scope Limitation. At present, the toolkit focuses solely on text and audio modalities. We recognize the importance of expanding to other modalities, such as visual AM. Resources for these additional modalities will be integrated in future work.

References

2020. Large-scale self-supervised pre-training across tasks, languages, and modalities.

2022. Torchmultimodal (beta release).

Alexei Baevski, Yuhao Zhou, Abdelrahman Mohamed, and Michael Auli. 2020. wav2vec 2.0: A framework for self-supervised learning of speech representations. In *Advances in Neural Information Processing Systems*, volume 33, pages 12449–12460. Curran Associates, Inc.

M. Sahbi Benlamine, Maher Chaouachi, Serena Villata, Elena Cabrio, Claude Frasson, and Fabien Gandon. 2015. Emotions in argumentation: an empirical evaluation. In *IJCAI*, pages 156–163. AAAI Press.

David S. Birdsell and Leo Groarke. 1996. Toward a theory of visual argument. *Argumentation and advocacy*, 33(1):1.

Said Yacine Boulahia, Abdenour Amamra, Mohamed Ridha Madi, and Said Daikh. 2021. Early, intermediate and late fusion strategies for robust deep learning-based multimodal action recognition. *Machine Vision and Applications*, 32(6):121.

Hervé Bredin. 2017. pyannote.metrics: A Toolkit for Reproducible Evaluation, Diagnostic, and Error Analysis of Speaker Diarization Systems. In *Proc. Interspeech 2017*, pages 3587–3591.

Hervé Bredin. 2023. pyannote.audio 2.1 speaker diarization pipeline: principle, benchmark, and recipe. In *Proc. INTERSPEECH 2023*, pages 1983–1987.

Mikhail Burtsev, Alexander Seliverstov, Rafael Airapetyan, Mikhail Arkhipov, Dilyara Baymurzina, Nickolay Bushkov, Olga Gureenkova, Taras Khakhulin, Yuri Kuratov, Denis Kuznetsov, Alexey Litinsky, Varvara Logacheva, Alexey Lymar, Valentin Malykh, Maxim Petrov, Vadim Polulyakh, Leonid Pugachev, Alexey Sorokin, Maria Vikhreva, and Marat Zaynutdinov. 2018. DeepPavlov: Open-source library for dialogue systems. In *Proceedings of ACL 2018, System Demonstrations*, pages 122–127, Melbourne, Australia. Association for Computational Linguistics.

Jean Carletta. 1996. Assessing agreement on classification tasks: The kappa statistic. *Comput. Linguistics*, 22(2):249–254.

Gullal Singh Cheema, Sherzod Hakimov, Abdul Sittar, Eric Müller-Budack, Christian Otto, and Ralph Ewerth. 2022. MM-claims: A dataset for multimodal claim detection in social media. In *Findings of the Association for Computational Linguistics: NAACL 2022*, pages 962–979, Seattle, United States. Association for Computational Linguistics.

Sanyuan Chen, Chengyi Wang, Zhengyang Chen, Yu Wu, Shujie Liu, Zhuo Chen, Jinyu Li, Naoyuki Kanda, Takuya Yoshioka, Xiong Xiao, Jian Wu, Long Zhou, Shuo Ren, Yanmin Qian, Yao Qian, Jian Wu, Michael Zeng, Xiangzhan Yu, and Furu Wei. 2022. Wavlm: Large-scale self-supervised pre-training for full stack speech processing. *IEEE Journal of Selected Topics in Signal Processing*, 16(6):1505–1518.

Jean-benoit Delbrouck, Khaled Saab, Maya Varma, Sabri Eyuboglu, Pierre Chambon, Jared Dunnmon, Juan Zambrano, Akshay Chaudhari, and Curtis Langlotz. 2022. ViLMedic: a framework for research at the intersection of vision and language in medical AI. In *Proceedings of the 60th Annual Meeting of the Association for Computational Linguistics: System Demonstrations*, pages 23–34, Dublin, Ireland. Association for Computational Linguistics.

Victor Dibia. 2020. NeuralQA: A usable library for question answering (contextual query expansion + BERT) on large datasets. In *Proceedings of the 2020 Conference on Empirical Methods in Natural Language Processing: System Demonstrations*, pages 15–22, Online. Association for Computational Linguistics.

William Falcon and The PyTorch Lightning team. 2019. Pytorchlightning.

Pierpaolo Goffredo, Shohreh Haddadan, Vorakit Vorakitphan, Elena Cabrio, and Serena Villata. 2022. Fallacious argument classification in political debates. In *Proceedings of the Thirty-First International Joint Conference on Artificial Intelligence, IJCAI-22*, pages 4143–4149. International Joint Conferences on Artificial Intelligence Organization. Main Track.

Leo Groarke and Gabrijela Kišiček. 2018. Sound arguments: An introduction to auditory argument. In *Argumentation and inference: Proceedings of 2nd European Conference on Argumentation*, pages 177–198. London: Collage Publications.

Shohreh Haddadan, Elena Cabrio, and Serena Villata. 2019. Yes, we can! mining arguments in 50 years of US presidential campaign debates. In *Proceedings of the 57th Annual Meeting of the Association for Computational Linguistics*, pages 4684–4690, Florence, Italy. Association for Computational Linguistics.

Chadi Helwe, Chloé Clavel, and Fabian Suchanek. 2022. LogiTorch: A PyTorch-based library for logical reasoning on natural language. In *Proceedings of the 2022 Conference on Empirical Methods in Natural Language Processing: System Demonstrations*, pages 250–257, Abu Dhabi, UAE. Association for Computational Linguistics.

Wei-Ning Hsu, Benjamin Bolte, Yao-Hung Hubert Tsai, Kushal Lakhotia, Ruslan Salakhutdinov, and Abdelrahman Mohamed. 2021. Hubert: Self-supervised speech representation learning by masked prediction of hidden units. *IEEE/ACM Trans. Audio, Speech and Lang. Proc.*, 29:3451–3460.

Andreea Iana, Goran Glavaš, and Heiko Paulheim. 2023. NewsRecLib: A PyTorch-lightning library for neural news recommendation. In *Proceedings of the 2023 Conference on Empirical Methods in Natural Language Processing: System Demonstrations*, pages 296–310, Singapore. Association for Computational Linguistics.

Petar Ivanov, Ivan Koychev, Momchil Hardalov, and Preslav Nakov. 2023. Detecting check-worthy claims in political debates, speeches, and interviews using audio data. *CoRR*, abs/2306.05535.

Gabrijela Kišiček. 2014. The role of prosodic features in the analysis of multimodal argumentation. In *International Society for the Study of Argumentation (ISSA), 8th international conference on argumentation*. Rozenberg Quarterly, The Magazine.

John Lawrence and Chris Reed. 2019. Argument mining: A survey. *Computational Linguistics*, 45(4):765–818.

Ran Levy, Yonatan Bilu, Daniel Hershcovich, Ehud Aharoni, and Noam Slonim. 2014. Context dependent claim detection. In *COLING 2014, 25th International Conference on Computational Linguistics, Proceedings of the Conference: Technical Papers, August 23-29, 2014, Dublin, Ireland*, pages 1489–1500. ACL.

Dongxu Li, Junnan Li, Hung Le, Guangsen Wang, Silvio Savarese, and Steven C.H. Hoi. 2023. LAVIS: A one-stop library for language-vision intelligence. In *Proceedings of the 61st Annual Meeting of the Association for Computational Linguistics (Volume 3: System Demonstrations)*, pages 31–41, Toronto, Canada. Association for Computational Linguistics.

Yehao Li, Yingwei Pan, Jingwen Chen, Ting Yao, and Tao Mei. 2021. X-modaler: A versatile and high-performance codebase for cross-modal analytics. In *Proceedings of the 29th ACM International Conference on Multimedia*, MM '21, page 3799–3802, New York, NY, USA. Association for Computing Machinery.

Marco Lippi and Paolo Torroni. 2015. Context-independent claim detection for argument mining. In *Proceedings of the Twenty-Fourth International Joint Conference on Artificial Intelligence, IJCAI 2015, Buenos Aires, Argentina, July 25-31, 2015*, pages 185–191. AAAI Press.

Marco Lippi and Paolo Torroni. 2016a. Argument mining from speech: Detecting claims in political debates. In *Proceedings of the Thirtieth AAAI Conference on Artificial Intelligence, February 12-17, 2016, Phoenix, Arizona, USA*, pages 2979–2985. AAAI Press.

Marco Lippi and Paolo Torroni. 2016b. Argumentation mining: State of the art and emerging trends. *ACM Trans. Internet Technol.*, 16(2).

Zhexiong Liu, Mohamed Elaraby, Yang Zhong, and Diane Litman. 2023. Overview of ImageArg-2023: The first shared task in multimodal argument mining. In *Proceedings of the 10th Workshop on Argument Mining*, pages 120–132, Singapore. Association for Computational Linguistics.

Zhexiong Liu, Meiqi Guo, Yue Dai, and Diane Litman. 2022. ImageArg: A multi-modal tweet dataset for image persuasiveness mining. In *Proceedings of the 9th Workshop on Argument Mining*, pages 1–18, Online and in Gyeongju, Republic of Korea. International Conference on Computational Linguistics.

Vidula Magdum, Omkar Jayant Dhekane, Sharayu Sandeep Hiwarkhedkar, Saloni Sunil Mittal, and Raviraj Joshi. 2023. mahaNLP: A Marathi natural language processing library. In *Proceedings of the 13th International Joint Conference on Natural Language Processing and the 3rd Conference of the Asia-Pacific Chapter of the Association for Computational Linguistics: System Demonstrations*, pages 34–40, Bali, Indonesia. Association for Computational Linguistics.

Eleonora Mancini, Federico Ruggeri, Andrea Galassi, and Paolo Torroni. 2022. Multimodal argument mining: A case study in political debates. In *Proceedings of the 9th Workshop on Argument Mining*, pages 158–170, Online and in Gyeongju, Republic of Korea. International Conference on Computational Linguistics.

Eleonora Mancini, Federico Ruggeri, and Paolo Torroni. 2024. Multimodal fallacy classification in political debates. In *Proceedings of the 18th Conference of the European Chapter of the Association for Computational Linguistics (Volume 2: Short Papers)*, pages 170–178, St. Julian's, Malta. Association for Computational Linguistics.

Rafael Mestre, Stuart E. Middleton, Matt Ryan, Masood Gheasi, Timothy Norman, and Jiatong Zhu. 2023. Augmenting pre-trained language models with audio feature embedding for argumentation mining in political debates. In *Findings of the Association for Computational Linguistics: EACL 2023*, pages 274–288, Dubrovnik, Croatia. Association for Computational Linguistics.

Rafael Mestre, Razvan Milicin, Stuart Middleton, Matt Ryan, Jiatong Zhu, and Timothy J. Norman. 2021a. M-arg: Multimodal argument mining dataset for political debates with audio and transcripts. In *ArgMining@EMNLP*, pages 78–88. Association for Computational Linguistics.

Rafael Mestre, Razvan Milicin, Stuart E. Middleton, Matt Ryan, Jiatong Zhu, and Timothy J. Norman. 2021b. M-arg: Multimodal argument mining dataset for political debates with audio and transcripts. In *Proceedings of the 8th Workshop on Argument Mining*, pages 78–88, Punta Cana, Dominican Republic. Association for Computational Linguistics.

John Morris, Eli Lifland, Jin Yong Yoo, Jake Grigsby, Di Jin, and Yanjun Qi. 2020. TextAttack: A framework for adversarial attacks, data augmentation, and adversarial training in NLP. In *Proceedings of the 2020 Conference on Empirical Methods in Natural Language Processing: System Demonstrations*, pages 119–126, Online. Association for Computational Linguistics.

Jeffrey Pennington, Richard Socher, and Christopher Manning. 2014. GloVe: Global vectors for word representation. In *Proceedings of the 2014 Conference on Empirical Methods in Natural Language Processing (EMNLP)*, pages 1532–1543, Doha, Qatar. Association for Computational Linguistics.

Ramon Ruiz-Dolz and Javier Iranzo-Sánchez. 2023. VivesDebate-speech: A corpus of spoken argumentation to leverage audio features for argument mining. In *Proceedings of the 2023 Conference on Empirical Methods in Natural Language Processing*, pages 2071–2077, Singapore. Association for Computational Linguistics.

Arushi Sharma, Abhibha Gupta, and Maneesh Bilalpur. 2023. Argumentative stance prediction: An exploratory study on multimodality and few-shot learning. In *Proceedings of the 10th Workshop on Argument Mining*, pages 167–174, Singapore. Association for Computational Linguistics.

Jiatong Shi, Shuai Guo, Tao Qian, Tomoki Hayashi, Yuning Wu, Fangzheng Xu, Xuankai Chang, Huazhe Li, Peter Wu, Shinji Watanabe, and Qin Jin. 2022. Muskits: an End-to-end Music Processing Toolkit for Singing Voice Synthesis. In *Proc. Interspeech 2022*, pages 4277–4281.

Amanpreet Singh, Vedanuj Goswami, Vivek Natarajan, Yu Jiang, Xinlei Chen, Meet Shah, Marcus Rohrbach, Dhruv Batra, and Devi Parikh. 2020. Mmf: A multimodal framework for vision and language research. `https://github.com/facebookresearch/mmf`.

Felix Stollenwerk. 2023. nerblackbox: A high-level library for named entity recognition in python. In *Proceedings of the 3rd Workshop for Natural Language Processing Open Source Software (NLP-OSS 2023)*, pages 174–178, Singapore. Association for Computational Linguistics.

Tianyi Tang, Junyi Li, Zhipeng Chen, Yiwen Hu, Zhuohao Yu, Wenxun Dai, Wayne Xin Zhao, Jian-yun Nie, and Ji-rong Wen. 2022. TextBox 2.0: A text generation library with pre-trained language models. In *Proceedings of the 2022 Conference on Empirical Methods in Natural Language Processing: System Demonstrations*, pages 435–444, Abu Dhabi, UAE. Association for Computational Linguistics.

Ermal Toto, ML Tlachac, and Elke A. Rundensteiner. 2021. Audibert: A deep transfer learning multimodal classification framework for depression screening. In *Proceedings of the 30th ACM International Conference on Information & Knowledge Management*, CIKM '21, page 4145–4154, New York, NY, USA. Association for Computing Machinery.

Yao-Hung Hubert Tsai, Shaojie Bai, Paul Pu Liang, J. Zico Kolter, Louis-Philippe Morency, and Ruslan Salakhutdinov. 2019. Multimodal transformer for unaligned multimodal language sequences. In *Proceedings of the 57th Annual Meeting of the Association for Computational Linguistics*, pages 6558–6569, Florence, Italy. Association for Computational Linguistics.

Douglas Walton. 2009. *Argumentation Theory: A Very Short Introduction*, pages 1–22. Springer US, Boston, MA.

Xin Xie, Zhoubo Li, Xiaohan Wang, ZeKun Xi, and Ningyu Zhang. 2023. LambdaKG: A library for pre-trained language model-based knowledge graph embeddings. In *Proceedings of the 13th International Joint Conference on Natural Language Processing and the 3rd Conference of the Asia-Pacific Chapter of the Association for Computational Linguistics: System Demonstrations*, pages 25–33, Bali, Indonesia. Association for Computational Linguistics.

Tianshu Yu, Haoyu Gao, Ting-En Lin, Min Yang, Yuchuan Wu, Wentao Ma, Chao Wang, Fei Huang, and Yongbin Li. 2023. Speech-text pre-training for spoken dialog understanding with explicit cross-modal alignment. In *Proceedings of the 61st Annual Meeting of the Association for Computational Linguistics (Volume 1: Long Papers)*, pages 7900–7913, Toronto, Canada. Association for Computational Linguistics.

Guoyang Zeng, Fanchao Qi, Qianrui Zhou, Tingji Zhang, Zixian Ma, Bairu Hou, Yuan Zang, Zhiyuan Liu, and Maosong Sun. 2021. OpenAttack: An open-source textual adversarial attack toolkit. In *Proceedings of the 59th Annual Meeting of the Association for Computational Linguistics and the 11th International Joint Conference on Natural Language Processing: System Demonstrations*, pages 363–371, Online. Association for Computational Linguistics.

Qing Zong, Zhaowei Wang, Baixuan Xu, Tianshi Zheng, Haochen Shi, Weiqi Wang, Yangqiu Song, Ginny Wong, and Simon See. 2023. TILFA: A unified framework for text, image, and layout fusion in argument mining. In *Proceedings of the 10th Workshop on Argument Mining*, pages 139–147, Singapore. Association for Computational Linguistics.

Appendix

A Model Architectures

We provide a comprehensive visual representation of the novel model architectures presented in this work. Figures 2, 3, and 4 show the CSA, Ensemble, and Mul-TA models, respectively.

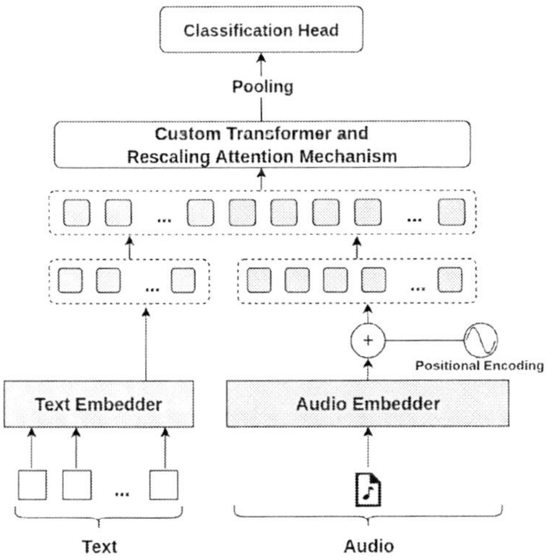

Figure 2: The CSA model architecture.

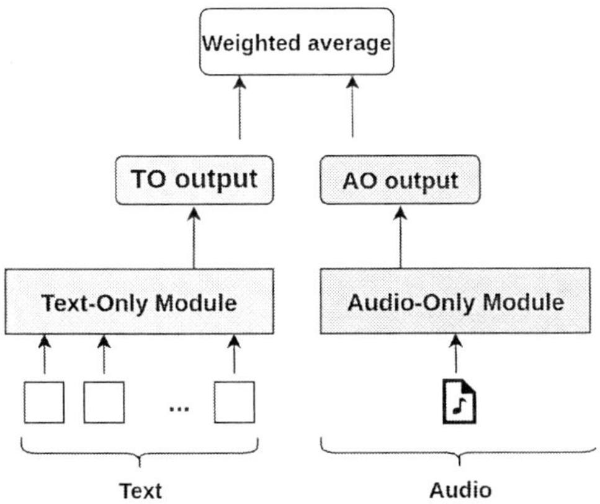

Figure 3: The Ensemble model architecture.

B Experimental Setup Details

Model Hyper-parameters Table 3 reports the main hyper-parameters used in our experiments. All model configurations can be inspected in the `mamkit.configs` package.

Training Models are trained with cross-entropy loss as standard practice for classification tasks. We additionally apply class weighting to address class imbalance in all datasets except for MM-USED ACC, where weighting is not needed. We monitor validation loss during training and load the best model checkpoint based on this metric for evaluation on validation and test splits.

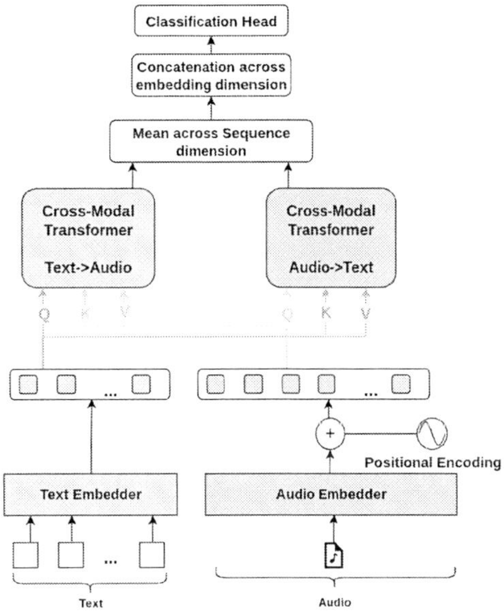

Figure 4: The Mul-TA model architecture.

General	
`optimizer`	AdamW
`batch_size`	4
`gradient accumulation steps`	3
`effective batch_size`	12
`max_epochs`	20
`early_stopping patience`	5
`early_stopping monitor`	*val_loss*
`cross-validation seeds`	42, 2024, 666
`leave-one-out seeds`	42
`train and test seeds`	42, 2024, 666

Table 3: General model hyper-parameters in our experiments.

Hardware We employ an NVIDIA 2080Ti GPU with 12 GB VRAM and an NVIDIA 3060Ti GPU with 8 GB VRAM to run our experiments. All experiments regarding a dataset are run on the same device for reproducibility and fair comparison. Furthermore, individual experiments were run on a single device.

C Additional Results

Table 4 reports results for all model combinations evaluated.

Model	UKDebates (ASD)	M-Arg$_\gamma$ (ARC)	MM-USED (ASD)	MM-USED (ACC)	MMUSED-fallacy (AFC)
			Text Only		
BiLSTM	$.552_{\pm.047}$	$.120_{\pm.006}$	$.811_{\pm.004}$	$.663_{\pm.002}$	$.525_{\pm.113}$
BERT	$.654_{\pm.003}$	$.132_{\pm.004}$	$.824_{\pm.009}$	$.679_{\pm.004}$	$.594_{\pm.122}$
RoBERTa	$.692_{\pm.005}$	$.172_{\pm.015}$	$.839_{\pm.010}$	$.680_{\pm.001}$	$.615_{\pm.097}$
			Audio Only		
BiLSTM w/ MFCCs	$.302_{\pm.047}$	$.003_{\pm.005}$	$.722_{\pm.027}$	$.527_{\pm.004}$	$\mathbf{.657}_{\pm\mathbf{.000}}$
BiLSTM w/ Wav2Vec2	$.376_{\pm.023}$	$.000_{\pm.000}$	$\mathbf{.774}_{\pm\mathbf{.008}}$	$\mathbf{.596}_{\pm\mathbf{.005}}$	$.655_{\pm.117}$
BiLSTM w/ HuBERT	$.364_{\pm.012}$	$\mathbf{.024}_{\pm\mathbf{.012}}$	$.745_{\pm.009}$	$.566_{\pm.007}$	$.638_{\pm.000}$
BiLSTM w/ WavLM	$\mathbf{.393}_{\pm\mathbf{.040}}$	$.010_{\pm.010}$	$.772_{\pm.015}$	$.583_{\pm.002}$	$.652_{\pm.000}$
Transformer w/ Wav2Vec2	$.440_{\pm.030}$	$.000_{\pm.000}$	$\mathbf{.771}_{\pm\mathbf{.019}}$	$.514_{\pm.000}$	$.567_{\pm.225}$
Transformer w/ HuBERT	$.425_{\pm.033}$	$.000_{\pm.000}$	$.765_{\pm.016}$	$.524_{\pm.004}$	$\mathbf{.629}_{\pm\mathbf{.162}}$
Transformer w/ WavLM	$\mathbf{.455}_{\pm\mathbf{.004}}$	$.000_{\pm.000}$	$.768_{\pm.005}$	$\mathbf{.526}_{\pm\mathbf{.004}}$	$.594_{\pm.217}$
			Text Audio		
BiLSTM w/ MFCCs	$.528_{\pm.039}$	$.065_{\pm.014}$	$.807_{\pm.010}$	$.662_{\pm.006}$	$\mathbf{.572}_{\pm\mathbf{.099}}$
BiLSTM w/ Wav2Vec2	$\mathbf{.533}_{\pm\mathbf{.009}}$	$.079_{\pm.014}$	$.808_{\pm.012}$	$.665_{\pm.004}$	$.505_{\pm.168}$
BiLSTM w/ HuBERT	$.409_{\pm.017}$	$.055_{\pm.020}$	$.807_{\pm.013}$	$.653_{\pm.003}$	$.456_{\pm.131}$
BiLSTM w/ WavLM	$.501_{\pm.022}$	$\mathbf{.084}_{\pm\mathbf{.016}}$	$\mathbf{.815}_{\pm\mathbf{.006}}$	$\mathbf{.667}_{\pm\mathbf{.000}}$	$.526_{\pm.174}$
MM-BERT w/ Wav2Vec2	$\mathbf{662}_{\pm\mathbf{.004}}$	$.153_{\pm.017}$	$\mathbf{841}_{\pm\mathbf{.005}}$	$.677_{\pm.003}$	$.561_{\pm.114}$
MM-BERT w/ HuBERT	$.626_{\pm.003}$	$\mathbf{.160}_{\pm\mathbf{.015}}$	$.840_{\pm.006}$	$.677_{\pm.004}$	$\mathbf{.599}_{\pm\mathbf{.128}}$
MM-BERT w/ WavLM	$.654_{\pm.019}$	$.152_{\pm.008}$	$.836_{\pm.005}$	$\mathbf{.680}_{\pm\mathbf{.004}}$	$.580_{\pm.103}$
MM-RoBERTa w/ Wav2Vec2	$.674_{\pm.009}$	$\mathbf{.178}_{\pm\mathbf{.012}}$	$.833_{\pm.006}$	$\mathbf{.678}_{\pm\mathbf{.003}}$	$.608_{\pm.126}$
MM-RoBERTa w/ HuBERT	$.624_{\pm.015}$	$.147_{\pm.004}$	$.837_{\pm.003}$	$.677_{\pm.008}$	$.576_{\pm.097}$
MM-RoBERTa w/ WavLM	$\mathbf{.687}_{\pm\mathbf{.010}}$	$.165_{\pm.018}$	$\mathbf{.837}_{\pm\mathbf{.009}}$	$\mathbf{678}_{\pm\mathbf{.003}}$	$\mathbf{.624}_{\pm\mathbf{.074}}$
CSA w/ Wav2Vec2	$\mathbf{.663}_{\pm\mathbf{.014}}$	$.137_{\pm.027}$	$.822_{\pm.002}$	$\mathbf{.693}_{\pm\mathbf{.001}}$	$.555_{\pm.118}$
CSA w/ HuBERT	$.632_{\pm.018}$	$\mathbf{.160}_{\pm\mathbf{.015}}$	$.813_{\pm.004}$	$\mathbf{.693}_{\pm\mathbf{.001}}$	$\mathbf{.582}_{\pm\mathbf{.114}}$
CSA w/ WavLM	$.655_{\pm.029}$	$.155_{\pm.030}$	$\mathbf{.833}_{\pm\mathbf{.011}}$	$.697_{\pm.001}$	$.535_{\pm.102}$
Ensemble w/ Wav2Vec2	$\mathbf{.586}_{\pm\mathbf{.015}}$	$\mathbf{.011}_{\pm\mathbf{.011}}$	$.825_{\pm.004}$	$\mathbf{.681}_{\pm\mathbf{.002}}$	$\mathbf{.612}_{\pm\mathbf{.134}}$
Ensemble w/ HuBERT	$.531_{\pm.039}$	$.010_{\pm.004}$	$.822_{\pm.007}$	$.681_{\pm.003}$	$.611_{\pm.107}$
Ensemble w/ WavLM	$.576_{\pm.006}$	$.002_{\pm.003}$	$\mathbf{.826}_{\pm\mathbf{.011}}$	$.680_{\pm.003}$	$.605_{\pm.136}$
Mul-TA w/ Wav2Vec2	$.592_{\pm.034}$	$\mathbf{.098}_{\pm\mathbf{.031}}$	$.826_{\pm.011}$	$.695_{\pm.001}$	$\mathbf{.605}_{\pm\mathbf{.110}}$
Mul-TA w/ HuBERT	$\mathbf{.616}_{\pm\mathbf{.019}}$	$.079_{\pm.053}$	$.829_{\pm.011}$	$\mathbf{.697}_{\pm\mathbf{.003}}$	$.594_{\pm.091}$
Mul-TA w/ WavLM	$.602_{\pm.017}$	$.063_{\pm.015}$	$\mathbf{.837}_{\pm\mathbf{.006}}$	$.690_{\pm.003}$	$.605_{\pm.082}$

Table 4: Test classification performance on MAM datasets. In bold, the best-performing model for each configuration.

Overview of DialAM-2024: Argument Mining in Natural Language Dialogues

Ramon Ruiz-Dolz, John Lawrence, Ella Schad and Chris Reed
Centre for Argument Technology (ARG-tech)
University of Dundee
Dundee DD1 4HN, United Kingdom
{rruizdolz001, j.lawrence, e.m.schad, c.a.reed}@dundee.ac.uk

Abstract

Argumentation is the process by which humans rationally elaborate their thoughts and opinions in written (e.g., essays) or spoken (e.g., debates) contexts. Argument Mining research, however, has been focused on either written argumentation or spoken argumentation but without considering any additional information, e.g., speech acts and intentions. In this paper, we present an overview of DialAM-2024, the first shared task in dialogical argument mining, where argumentative relations and speech illocutions are modelled together in a unified framework. The task was divided into two different sub-tasks: the identification of propositional relations and the identification of illocutionary relations. Six different teams explored different methodologies to leverage both sources of information to reconstruct argument maps containing the locutions uttered in the speeches and the argumentative propositions implicit in them. The best performing team achieved an F1-score of 67.05% in the overall evaluation of the reconstruction of complete argument maps, considering both sub-tasks included in the DialAM-2024 shared task.

1 Introduction

Argument Mining (Lawrence and Reed, 2020) investigates the automatic extraction of argument structures from natural language inputs. The nature of argumentation, however, can be very variable depending on its context, presenting significant differences between written and spoken argumentation (Hitchcock, 2009), and between monological and dialogical argumentation (O'Keefe, 1977). Research in argument mining has mainly focused on the extraction of arguments only considering argument annotations such as premises and claims (Stab et al., 2018; Reimers et al., 2019) or attacks and supports between propositions (Hou and Jochim, 2017; Ruiz-Dolz et al., 2021; Saadat-Yazdi et al., 2023), without bringing into consideration additional relevant information that could be extracted from the speeches uttered in the dialogues. This is mostly due to the lack of presence of a framework annotating dialogue information in addition to argument structures in argument mining work.

Inference Anchoring Theory (IAT) was proposed as an annotation framework for dialogue argumentation where not only the structure of arguments is captured, but also the speech acts and speaker intent is also annotated to support and contextualise argumentation in dialogues (Budzynska and Reed, 2011; Janier et al., 2014). Therefore, when approaching argument mining in dialogues, IAT represents an ideal framework to expand the standard annotations typically used in argument mining research (i.e., attacks and supports between premises and claims) integrating dialogical information to the argument mining process. Although several corpora and resources annotated with IAT such as US2016 (Visser et al., 2019), QT30 (Hautli-Janisz et al., 2022), RIP (Schad et al., 2024), or FORECAST (Górska et al., 2024) have been released in the last years[1], there is a lack of systematic research in dialogical argument mining integrating these speech features into argument mining systems.

DialAM-2024 represents the first shared task in dialogical argument mining bringing together argument and speech annotations in an attempt to systematically explore the potential benefits of combining both when developing argument mining systems to be used in transcribed argumentative dialogues. The DialAM-2024 shared task received submissions from six different teams exploring a broad set of approaches to integrate and combine argument and dialogue features for argument mining. In this paper, we describe the DialAM-2024 shared task, summarise the most important aspects

[1]All publicly available at the AIFdb: http://www.aifdb.org/search

Proceedings of the 11th Workshop on Argument Mining, pages 83–92
August 15, 2024 ©2024 Association for Computational Linguistics

of the submitted systems, and provide an in-depth analysis of the final results of the shared task. Furthermore, we perform a qualitative analysis of the output of the best performing system, pointing out the open challenges that will need to be addressed in future work.

2 DialAM-2024

2.1 Task

The DialAM-2024[2] shared task explores, for the first time, argument mining in dialogues where information from both arguments and dialogues is modelled together. For this purpose, we use IAT, a domain independent annotation framework designed for capturing argument structures anchored to locutions via illocutions. DialAM-2024, therefore, consists of two sub-tasks: the identification of propositional (argumentative) relations, and the identification of illocutionary (speech act) relations. The data used to develop and evaluate the systems submitted to the DialAM-2024 task includes annotations for both sub-tasks together, providing a direct connection between the dialogue speeches and the annotated argumentative structures. With this shared task, it is our goal to motivate the research on the relations between dialogical information and argumentative structures jointly. This way, it is our goal to take a step forward from previous sequence modelling-based approaches, only considering pairs of sentences or argumentative discourse units (ADUs) to automatically identify argument structures, where much of the relevant information to argumentation remains implicit behind the natural language.

This way, the two DialAM-2024 sub-tasks are defined as follows:

A. **Identification of Propositional Relations**. In the first task, the goal is to detect argumentative relations existing between the argumentative propositions directly extracted from the locutions uttered in the argumentative dialogues. Such relations are: Inference, Conflict, and Rephrase.

B. **Identification of Illocutionary Relations**. In the second task, the goal is to detect illocutionary relations existing between locutions uttered in the dialogue and the argumentative propositions associated with them including: Asserting, Agreeing, Arguing, Disagreeing, Challenging, Restating, Pure Questioning, Rethorical Questioning, and Assertive Questioning.

The final goal of the DialAM-2024 shared task is, therefore, to reconstruct graph-structured argument maps, containing locutions and argument propositions previously identified and segmented from argumentative dialogues.

2.2 Evaluation

We measured the macro-averaged Precision, Recall and F1-score to evaluate the performance of the submitted systems. The evaluation of the DialAM-2024 shared task was performed at two different levels: *focused* and *general*. In the *focused* evaluation setup, we only considered the related propositions/locutions in the gold standard files, ignoring all the possible combinations of non related propositions/locutions. To complement it, we also considered a *general* evluation setup, where the whole argument map was included in the evaluation. This way, a high performance in the *general* setup but low in the *focused* setup represents a pessimistic approach that leaves more nodes without any relation than it should be. For an extreme case of this first situation, see the majority baseline described below. Conversely, a high performance in the *focused* setup but low in the *general* setup represents an optimistic approach establishing more relations between propositions/locutions than actually exist.

Furthermore, the evaluation was conducted independently for the two sub-tasks included in DialAM-2024, and globally combining the scores of the two independent evaluations. We named as ARI (from argument relation identification) the evaluation of the performance on Task A: Identification of Propositional Relations, and as ILO (from illocutionary relation identification) the evaluation of the performance of the submitted systems on Task B: Identification of Illocutionary Relations. Finally, we refer to the final results combining both sub-tasks and considering the complete argument maps as the Global evaluation.

2.3 Baselines

We included two different baselines as a reference for the submitted systems to the DialAM-2024 shared task: a majority baseline that always assigns the majority class (no relation) to all the possible pairs of sequences, and a pre-trained RoBERTa-

[2]The website for this shared task can be found at the following link: `dialam.arg.tech`

large model for sequence pair classification based on (Ruiz-Dolz et al., 2021).

- MAJORITY-BL: Given that most of the possible combinations of propositions/locutions are not related at all, no relations are assigned between nodes in the argument maps for all ARI, ILO, and Global evaluations.

- ROBERTA-BL: The system consists of two RoBERTa-large (Liu et al., 2019) model architectures fine-tuned independently for both Tasks A and B, approaching the problem as a sequence pair classification problem. No interaction between argumentative and dialogue information is considered in this baseline.

3 Data

3.1 The QT30 Corpus

QT30 (Hautli-Janisz et al., 2022) is the largest individual corpus of analysed dialogical argumentation at 280,000 words, made up of thirty episodes of one of the most viewed political talk show in the UK, "Question Time"; it features topical debates where the audience members ask questions or request justifications from the panel members: people who are political or societal figures [3]. The audience members will typically be from the area in which they host that week's show, thereby also determining the kind of questions that are asked. For instance, if the show was hosted in Scotland, then there may be questions about Independence or relations between England and Scotland. These thirty episodes were broadcast in 2020 and 2021, covering national scandals and controversial debates such as Brexit, how the government handled COVID19, the subject of vaccination, as well as topics such as PartyGate (politicians in power partying during lockdowns). Question Time (QT) is moderated by a neutral third party who takes questions from the audience and prompts panel members.

The purpose of QT30 was to identify the argumentative structure within these politically relevant debates by annotating the dialogical and propositional structure, as well as identifying the relations used (support, rephrase, or attack) and the illocutionary force of contributions. The authors report inter-annotator agreement (IAA) of 0.56, using CASS (Duthie et al., 2016).

The analysis within the QT30 paper reveals interesting facets of argumentation within broadcast debate, e.g., how the use of conflicts and supports differ between roles. We use this dataset for two reasons: its size and the depth of annotation captured. The size provides us with more data with which to train models; as for depth of annotation, IAT was specifically developed to capture argumentative dialogues and, in a task where we ask participants to identify argumentative relations and illocutionary forces while incorporating additional dialogical information, is ideally suited to provide us the necessary annotation.

3.2 Annotation

IAT provides a theoretical scaffold to handle dialogue and argument structures, and the relations between them. It is used in order to represent, and to gain insight into, the arguments people make in complex dialogues. For IAT diagramming we use OVA+, an online tool developed for the analysis of arguments (Janier et al., 2014). The IAT framework and its OVA tool have been used for more than 2.5 million words of analysed argumentation.[4]

The smallest units of the IAT analysis are argumentative discourse units (ADUs), typically directly analysed as locutions. Locutions are in the text boxes on the right of the graph structure and are known as L-nodes. 'Edges' (incoming and outgoing) is the term used to describe the relations, illocutionary forces, and Default Transitions (TAs) anchored in the nodes. Propositions are on the left-hand side and are reconstructed locutions, where linguistic features like anaphora, pronouns, and deixis are resolved. IAT has three types of relations: (i) relations between locutions in a dialogue, called transitions; (ii) relations between content (propositional content of locutions); and (iii) illocutionary connections that link locutions with their content. Locutions have speakers and typically also have timestamps. The text of locutions is not reconstructed or changed in any way from the source data in contrast to the propositional content of those locutions. Locutions and propositions are connected via illocutionary connections. The guidelines used for annotation are available publicly[5].

As an example of IAT annotation, Figure 1 shows the typical structure of a QT episode: the

[3]QT30 as a corpus is publicly accessible at http://corpora.aifdb.org/qt30

[4]The OVA tool is made available at the following address: ova.arg.tech

[5]Annotation guidelines: https://www.arg.tech/index.php/annotation-guidelines/

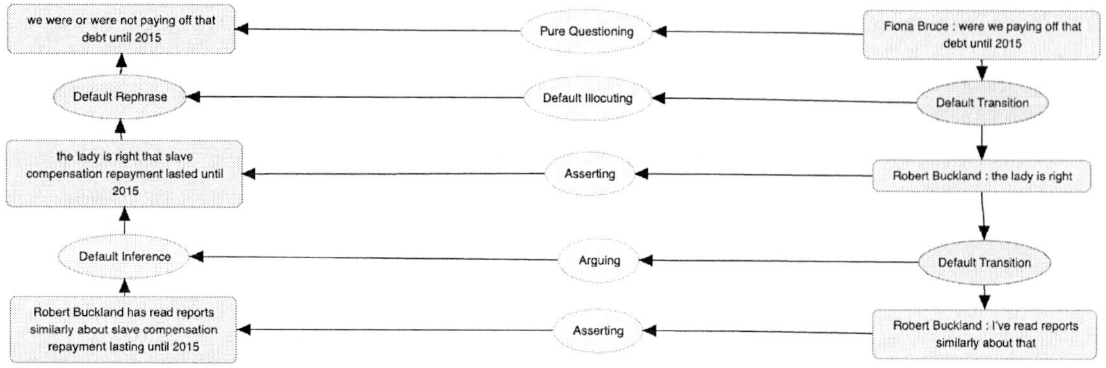

Figure 1: Example of data annotated using IAT: rectangular blue boxes indicating propositions and locutions, yellow ovals for illocutionary connections, purple ovals for discourse transitions, the green oval for inference relation, the orange oval either showing a rephrase relation or signalling the answer to a question, as is the case here.

moderator puts forward a question and a panel member replies. The Default Rephrase node is used to denote a rephrase relation, unless anchored by a "Pure Questioning" illocutionary force, as is the case here. Robert Buckland's intention of creating an argument is captured through the Default Inference. As each proposition should be understandable by itself, the second and third proposition have been reconstructed; the second with what "the lady" was right about and the third with who "I" and "that" refers to.

3.3 Training Phase

For the training phase, the participants were given the QT30 data in JSON format. We provided additional information sheets to participants on the DialAM website[6][7] about the style of annotation, as well as how to read the JSON-based format. The QT30 corpus contains 10,818 propositional relations and 32,303 illocutionary relations in 1,478 JSON files.

3.4 Evaluation Phase

For the evaluation phase, we chose eleven JSON files containing argument maps that included some challenging argument structures. This was for the purpose of evaluating how participants systems dealt with these complex cases. An example of the complex argumentation available in the data and used for evaluation would be linked, convergent, and divergent arguments.

[6]Data format details: `http://dialam.arg.tech/res/files/data-format.pdf`

[7]Annotation details: `http://dialam.arg.tech/res/files/annotation-details.pdf`

4 Submissions

Fifteen different teams registered for the DialAM-2024 shared task, of which six submitted their system outputs during the evaluation phase. All the submissions addressed the two sub-tasks of the shared task: (A) identification of propositional relations, and (B) identification of illocutionary relations. The submitted systems include a broad set of different language modelling approaches and model architectures. A summary of the submitted systems together with the references to their system description papers where the approaches are described in-depth is provided below.

4.1 System Descritpions

dfki-mlst (Binder et al., 2024) approaches the shared task as an n-ary classification problem. Their proposed method relies on three main steps: normalise the nodeset, encode the relations for both propositions and illocutions, and train a classification model. The authors submitted a fine-tuned DeBERTa-v3 model (He et al., 2021) as their classification model for the evaluation phase. In addition to DeBERTa-v3, the authors carried out an extensive comparison of different model architectures for the base classifier after the end of the evaluation phase, pointing out that DeBERTa-v1 performed better on test (although DeBERTa-v3 got better results during validation), and that combining the text data included in L and I nodes helps to improve the performance of the submitted system in both *focused* and *general* evaluation setups.

KnowComp (Wu et al., 2024) proposes a three-stage sequential inference pipeline to approach the shared task based on prompt-based fine-tuning.

The first stage is aimed at identifying direct illocutionary relations between L and I nodes. The second stage identifies argument relations between I nodes. Finally, the third stage detects indirect illocutionary relations between TA nodes and I nodes. In all the three stages, the text information included in L and I nodes is combined with a specifically curated prompt as the input to the developed models. Team KnowComp ran their experiments considering DeBERTa-base, DeBERTa-large, RoBERTa, and ALBERT (Lan et al., 2019). The best results were observed with the DeBERTa-based model architecture, which was the one selected for the final submission.

Pokemon (Zheng et al., 2024) proposes a two-stage pipeline to identify both argument relations with a two-step model filtering relations and classifying them into one of the three classes, and illocutionary relations with an eleven-class classification model covering all the possible YA nodes. The authors experiment with three different model architectures to implement the proposed pipeline, DeBERTa, RoBERTa, and LLaMa (Touvron et al., 2023). Based on the reported experimentation, their final submission consists of a DeBERTa-base combined with a RoBERTa-MNLI for the first stage (two-step) model, and a DeBERTa-large for the second stage model, meaning that RoBERTa-MNLI worked better for argument relation classification and DeBERTa-large for illocutionary relation identification.

Pungene (Chaixanien et al., 2024) approach the shared task with a pipeline system consisting of three main parts: the first part focuses on identifying illocutionary forces between locutions and propositions, the second part detects argumentative relations between propositions, and the third part identifies YA nodes between transitions and S nodes. This way, the proposed system gradually reconstructs the argument map by adding relation nodes. For the first part, the proposed system calculates BERTscore between pairs of locutions and propositions to establish the pairs, and then classifies the pair into one of the illocutionary relation classes using a fine-tuned BERT-base model. The second part of the proposed system connects argument propositions and detects the relation type between them by fine-tuning a BERT model for multi-class classification. Finally, the third part establishes the connection between transitions and S nodes by considering the natural language context of the nodes involved in the transition and the argumentative relation.

Turiya (Saha and Srihari, 2024) investigates two methods for argumentative dialogue analysis. First, by training a classification model using RoBERTa embeddings and two biaffine classifiers (Dozat and Manning, 2016). The first biaffine classifier is in charge of determining the relationship between argument propositions, between locutions and propositions, and between transitions and propositions. The second biaffine classifier is then trained to identify the remaining set of relations, the ones existing between transitions and propositions. The second explored method consists on leveraging the capabilities of generative LLMs to identify all the relations by prompting the language model with all the information extracted from the argument maps to generate an output pointing out all the potential relations between the nodes included in the map. From the reported results, it is possible to observe how in the general evaluation the LLMs perform better, but for the focused evluation combining both methods provides better results.

The sixth team, **misaka**, did not submit a system description paper.

5 Results

In order to provide an insightful analysis of the performance of the submitted systems to the DialAM-2024 shared task, we have divided the evaluation into three parts. First, the evaluation of the submitted systems when identifying propositional relations. Second, the evaluation of the submitted systems when identifying illocutionary relations. Finally, a global evaluation of the submitted systems when reconstructing argument maps looking at both, argument and discourse structures together. Furthermore, each evaluation is also done considering two different setups: by considering exclusively the related pairs of nodes in the evaluation maps (i.e., *focused*), and by considering the complete map including non-related nodes (i.e., *general*).

5.1 Propositional Relation Evaluation

The final results of the propositional relation evaluation, also known in the argument mining community as argument relation identification (ARI), have been described in Table 1.

Regarding the performance of the submitted systems on the specific aspect of identifying propositional relations, we observed that, in the *focused* setup POKEMON team was the best, while in the

Model	Rank	Precision	Recall	F1-score
POKEMON	1st	**46.26**	**32.43**	**35.89**
DFKI-MLST	2nd	43.87	24.82	30.40
ROBERTA-BL	3rd	37.10	18.42	22.80
PUNGENE	4th	30.18	17.59	20.51
KNOWCOMP	5th	23.47	5.85	9.06
MISAKA	5th	23.47	5.85	9.06
TURIYA	7th	18.95	4.21	6.65
MAJORITY-BL	8th	0	0	0
DFKI-MLST	1st	**61.96**	**53.30**	**55.33**
PUNGENE	2nd	49.21	46.32	46.22
KNOWCOMP	3rd	32.43	33.79	32.75
MISAKA	3rd	32.43	33.79	32.75
TURIYA	5th	30.81	31.52	30.75
POKEMON	6th	32.00	46.56	30.64
MAJORITY-BL	7th	28.79	30.28	29.52
ROBERTA-BL	8th	28.59	34.69	26.46

Table 1: Results of the ARI evaluation. First half reports the *focused* evaluation setup and second half the *general* setup.

Model	Rank	Precision	Recall	F1-score
ROBERTA-BL	1st	**73.10**	**72.55**	**72.09**
PUNGENE	2nd	71.18	69.23	69.95
DFKI-MLST	3rd	69.12	66.25	66.10
POKEMON	4th	54.15	49.87	51.39
KNOWCOMP	5th	48.44	41.27	44.33
MISAKA	5th	48.44	41.27	44.33
TURIYA	7th	43.81	26.09	30.41
MAJORITY-BL	8th	0	0	0
PUNGENE	1st	81.99	**80.79**	**81.17**
KNOWCOMP	2nd	**82.35**	76.26	78.90
MISAKA	2nd	**82.35**	76.26	78.90
DFKI-MLST	4th	81.08	79.25	78.78
POKEMON	5th	56.41	64.57	59.36
TURIYA	6th	51.37	57.05	53.31
ROBERTA-BL	7th	39.11	62.07	45.75
MAJORITY-BL	8th	34.71	35.90	35.29

Table 2: Results of the ILO evaluation. First half reports the *focused* evaluation setup and second half the *general* setup.

general setup DFKI-MLST outperformed the others. From the ARI results, it is also possible to observe that systems performed much better in the *general* setup than in the *focused* setup, meaning that most of them estimated that more argument propositions are not related than related, which was not the case. Furthermore, this part of the shared task was also the most challenging one, achieving significantly lower performance scores than in the illocutionary relation identification task.

5.2 Illocutionary Relation Evaluation

The final results of the illocutionary relation evaluation (ILO) are summarised in Table 2.

It is interesting to observe how, in the *focused* setup, the RoBERTa-large baseline performed the best, but in the *general* setup was one of the worst systems. This is mostly due to the fact that this baseline does not correctly model the non-related pairs of sequences. Due to this, and the high class imbalance where assertions represent the majority of illocutionary relations, the model obtains good results when only looking at the set of related nodes but performs poorly when considering the complete argument maps, being not the best option for illocutionary relation identification. The best submission in this sub-task was PUNGENE, providing consistent strong results in both *focused* and *general* evaluation setups, followed by DFKI-MLST. KNOWCOMP and MISAKA performed well in the *general* setup, but their performance significantly dropped in the *focused* evaluation, contrary to the baseline. This means that these systems modelled better the non-related locution-proposition pairs, but missed a lot of the existing illocutionary relations.

5.3 Global Results

Model	Rank	Precision	Recall	F1-score
DFKI-MLST	1st	**56.50**	**45.53**	**48.25**
ROBERTA-BL	2nd	55.1	45.49	47.45
PUNGENE	3rd	50.68	43.41	45.23
POKEMON	4th	50.20	41.15	43.64
KNOWCOMP	5th	35.95	23.56	26.70
MISAKA	5th	35.95	23.56	26.70
TURIYA	7th	31.38	15.15	18.53
MAJORITY-BL	8th	0	0	0
DFKI-MLST	1st	**71.52**	**66.28**	**67.05**
PUNGENE	2nd	65.60	63.55	63.70
KNOWCOMP	3rd	57.39	55.03	55.82
MISAKA	3rd	57.39	55.03	55.82
POKEMON	5th	44.20	55.57	45.00
TURIYA	6th	41.09	44.29	42.03
ROBERTA-BL	7th	33.85	48.38	36.10
MAJORITY-BL	8th	31.75	33.09	32.40

Table 3: Results of the Global evaluation. First half reports the *focused* evaluation setup and second half the *general* setup.

The global results of the DialAM-2024 shared task were calculated by aggregating the performance of the systems in tasks A and B. The final results can be observed in Table 3.

The best overall system was the one submitted by team DFKI-MLST, with 48.25 and 67.05 F1-scores

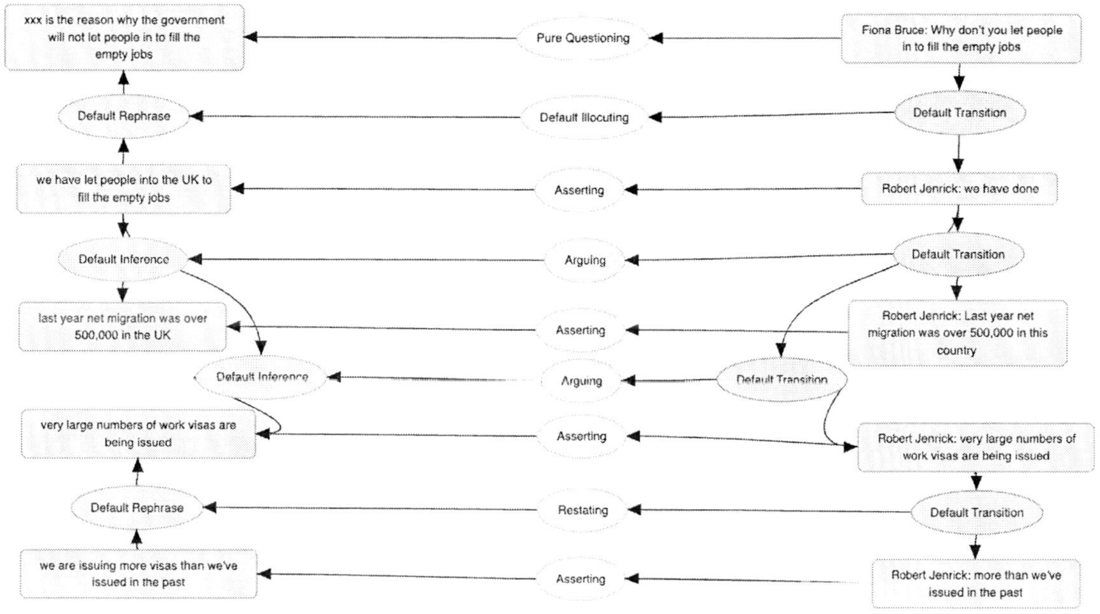

Figure 2: The gold map number 6 that correctly shows a divergent argument, with "we have let people into the UK to fill the empty jobs" as the premise to two conclusions.

in the *focused* and *general* setups respectively. This represents an improvement of 0.8% against the RoBERTa-large baseline and 3.02% against the best competitor in the *focused* evaluation, and an improvement of 3.35% against the best competitor, PUNGENE, in the general evaluation setup. Again, the RoBERTa baseline performed overall well in the focused setup, but was one of the worst systems in the *general* evaluation, only better than the majority baseline. This means that the systems submitted by the other teams, although they did not beat the RoBERTa-large baseline in the *focused* setup, will be better options for argument mining in dialogues reconstructing argument maps due to their significantly better results in the *general* evaluation.

6 Qualitative Analysis

To expand the findings observed in the analysis of the results based on the performance scores achieved by the participants, we carried out a qualitative analysis looking at the content of the submitted argument maps leading us to interesting observations. For that purpose, we compared the maps generated by the submitted systems with the eleven gold standard maps included in our test set focusing on specific aspects that influenced the performance of the systems including conflict relations or more complex argument structures such as convergent (i.e., Figure 3), divergent (i.e., Figure 2), and linked arguments (i.e., Figure 3).

In general, we observed that the submitted argument mining systems had problems recognising conflict relations, failing to identify most of them, and assigning conflicts between non-conflicting propositions. We also observed, in line with the previously reported results that, teams DFKI-MLST and PUNGENE were the ones that produced the most similar outputs compared to the gold standard maps. It was also interesting to observe how, the maps produced by team POKEMON's system contained a significantly larger amount of relations compared to the rest. This is the reason of their higher scores in the *focused* evaluation with a significant drop of performance in the *general* setup.

Although both systems had some problems detecting more complex argument structures, we observed that DFKI-MLST did a better job than PUNGENE on these ones, identifying more convergent, divergent, and linked arguments. In the case of convergent and divergent arguments, the directionality of the relations is fundamental, making the identification of inference relations more challenging. For example, in the test map number 3, DFKI-MLST identified correctly the inference relations, but failed to correctly place the one making the argument divergent. On the other hand, PUNGENE had a rephrase instead of an inference, and the

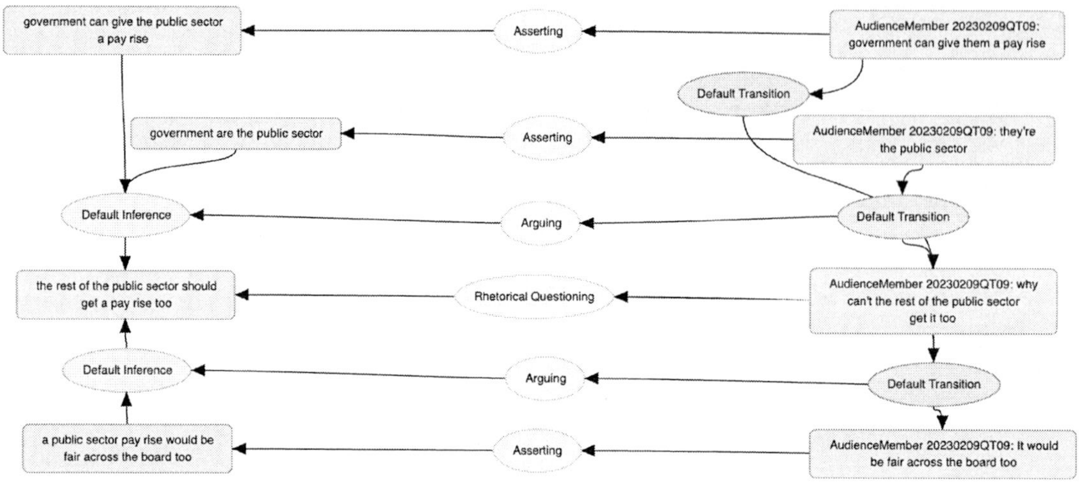

Figure 3: The gold map number 5 that correctly shows a convergent argument, with "the rest of the public sector should get a pay rise too" as the conclusion to two premises, where one of the supporting premises a linked argument consisting of two more premises.

assigned directionality made the argument convergent instead of divergent, a similar error was observed in the test map number 4. In the test map number 5, DFKI-MLST captures correctly the structure of the convergent argument, but fails to identify the two linked arguments. When looking at test map number 6, we observed again that both DFKI-MLST and PUNGENE had problems modelling the correct direction of the inference relations, identifying a convergent argument instead of the divergent one existing in the map, as seen within Figures 2 and 4.

With respect to linked arguments, team DFKI-MLST identified them in the test maps 7, 8, and 10, but represented them as convergent arguments instead of linked. A linked argument is represented by a unique inference relation including multiple premises rather than multiple inference relations between the premises and the claim, which would make it a convergent argument. We found, probably due to the implementation of the submitted systems, that this specific case was never considered as an output. In the test map number 10, we included a long linked argument, which consisted of six premises linked together in a unique inference relation towards the claim of the argument. Although the linked relation was not correctly represented (it was modelled as a convergent argument instead), it is interesting that DFKI-MLST correctly identified the six premises supporting the claim in this very particular case.

Finally, we also observed that in the evaluation set, none of the submitted systems was able to capture reported speech connecting locution nodes with illocutionary relations.

7 Conclusion

This paper presents DialAM-2024: the first shared task in dialogical argument mining. From the final results, we have been able to observe how the submitted systems that performed better in the DialAM-2024 shared task either addressed both tasks at the same time (modelling argumentative and dialogical features altogether), or first focused on task B and then task A, showing that considering speech acts and dialogical structures helped to improve the performance in the overall reconstruction of argument maps. Furthermore, from our qualitative analysis of the best submissions, we observed that there is still room for improvement in this area, specifically regarding the complex argument structures of convergent, divergent, and linked arguments, where not only the type of relation (i.e., inference) but also its directionality is of utmost important. It was also interesting to observe how, although the illocutionary relations were modelled with a reasonable success, specific cases such as reported speech represented a challenge for the systems submitted to the task.

Therefore, with the DialAM-2024 shared task, it is possible to observe the complexity of argument mining from a new dimension, pointing future work towards a more complete modelling of argumentation, including illocutionary forces and complex

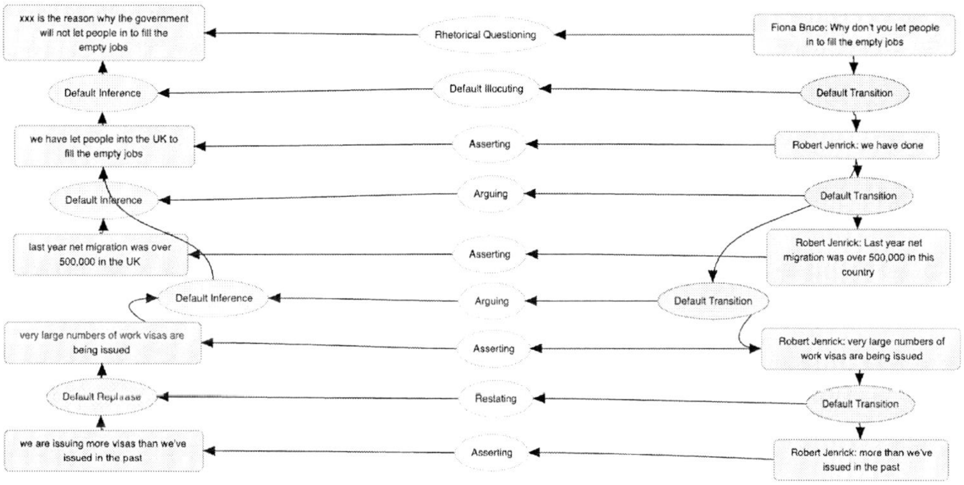

Figure 4: Pungene's model incorrectly identifying a convergent argument with "we have let people into the UK to fill the empty jobs" as the conclusion.

argument structures.

Acknowledgements

This research is supported in part by: Volkswagen Stiftung under grant Az. 98 543; the 'AI for Citizen Intelligence Coaching against Disinformation (TITAN)' project, funded by the EU Horizon 2020 research and innovation programme under grant agreement 101070658, and by UK Research and innovation under the UK governments Horizon funding guarantee grant numbers 10040483 and 10055990; the Swiss National Science Foundation under grant 10001FM_200857; and by the Office of the Director of National Intelligence (ODNI), Intelligence Advanced Research Projects Activity (IARPA), via Contract 2022-22072200004. The views and conclusions contained herein are those of the authors and should not be interpreted as necessarily representing the official policies, either expressed or implied, of ODNI, IARPA, or the U.S. Government. The U.S. Government is authorized to reproduce and distribute reprints for governmental purposes notwithstanding any copyright annotation therein.

References

Arne Binder, Tatiana Anikina, Leonhard Henning, and Simon Ostermann. 2024. Dfki-mlst at dialam-2024 shared task: System description. In *Proceedings of the 11th Workshop on Argument Mining*, Thailand. Association for Computational Linguistics.

Katarzyna Budzynska and Chris Reed. 2011. Whence inference. *University of Dundee Technical Report*.

Sirawut Chaixanien, Eugene Choi, Shaden Shaar, and Claire Cardie. 2024. Pungene at dialam-2024: Identification of propositional and illocutionary relations. In *Proceedings of the 11th Workshop on Argument Mining*, Thailand. Association for Computational Linguistics.

Timothy Dozat and Christopher D Manning. 2016. Deep biaffine attention for neural dependency parsing. In *International Conference on Learning Representations*.

R. Duthie, J. Lawrence, K Budzynska, and C. Reed. 2016. The cass technique for evaluating the performance of argument mining. In *Proceedings of the Third Workshop on Argumentation Mining*, Berlin. Association for Computational Linguistics.

Kamila Górska, John Lawrence, and Chris Reed. 2024. Forecast2023: A forecast and reasoning corpus of argumentation structures. In *Proceedings of the 2024 Joint International Conference on Computational Linguistics, Language Resources and Evaluation (LREC-COLING 2024)*, pages 7395–7405.

Annette Hautli-Janisz, Zlata Kikteva, Wassiliki Siskou, Kamila Gorska, Ray Becker, and Chris Reed. 2022. QT30: A corpus of argument and conflict in broadcast debate. In *Proceedings of the Thirteenth Language Resources and Evaluation Conference*, pages 3291–3300, Marseille, France. European Language Resources Association.

Pengcheng He, Jianfeng Gao, and Weizhu Chen. 2021. Debertav3: Improving deberta using electra-style pretraining with gradient-disentangled embedding sharing. *arXiv preprint arXiv:2111.09543*.

David Hitchcock. 2009. The culture of spoken arguments. In *Proceedings of the 8th OSSA Conference*.

Yufang Hou and Charles Jochim. 2017. Argument relation classification using a joint inference model.

In *Proceedings of the 4th Workshop on Argument Mining*, pages 60–66.

M. Janier, J. Lawrence, and C Reed. 2014. OVA+: An argument analysis interface. In *Proceedings of the Fifth International Conference on Computational Models of Argument (COMMA 2014)*, pages 463–464, Pitlochry. IOS Press.

Zhenzhong Lan, Mingda Chen, Sebastian Goodman, Kevin Gimpel, Piyush Sharma, and Radu Soricut. 2019. Albert: A lite bert for self-supervised learning of language representations. *arXiv preprint arXiv:1909.11942*.

John Lawrence and Chris Reed. 2020. Argument mining: A survey. *Computational Linguistics*, 45(4):765–818.

Yinhan Liu, Myle Ott, Naman Goyal, Jingfei Du, Mandar Joshi, Danqi Chen, Omer Levy, Mike Lewis, Luke Zettlemoyer, and Veselin Stoyanov. 2019. Roberta: A robustly optimized bert pretraining approach. *arXiv preprint arXiv:1907.11692*.

Daniel J O'Keefe. 1977. Two concepts of argument. *The Journal of the American Forensic Association*, 13(3):121–128.

Nils Reimers, Benjamin Schiller, Tilman Beck, Johannes Daxenberger, Christian Stab, and Iryna Gurevych. 2019. Classification and clustering of arguments with contextualized word embeddings. In *Proceedings of the 57th Annual Meeting of the Association for Computational Linguistics*, pages 567–578.

Ramon Ruiz-Dolz, Jose Alemany, Stella M Heras Barberá, and Ana García-Fornes. 2021. Transformer-based models for automatic identification of argument relations: A cross-domain evaluation. *IEEE Intelligent Systems*, 36(6):62–70.

Ameer Saadat-Yazdi, Jeff Z Pan, and Nadin Kökciyan. 2023. Uncovering implicit inferences for improved relational argument mining. In *Proceedings of the 17th Conference of the European Chapter of the Association for Computational Linguistics*, pages 2484–2495.

Sougata Saha and Rohini Srihari. 2024. Turiya at dialam-2024: Inference anchoring theory based llm parsers. In *Proceedings of the 11th Workshop on Argument Mining*, Thailand. Association for Computational Linguistics.

Ella Schad, Jacky Visser, and Chris Reed. 2024. The rip corpus of collaborative hypothesis-making. In *Proceedings of the 2024 Joint International Conference on Computational Linguistics, Language Resources and Evaluation (LREC-COLING 2024)*, pages 16047–16057.

Christian Stab, Tristan Miller, Benjamin Schiller, Pranav Rai, and Iryna Gurevych. 2018. Cross-topic argument mining from heterogeneous sources. In *Proceedings of the 2018 Conference on Empirical Methods in Natural Language Processing*, pages 3664–3674.

Hugo Touvron, Thibaut Lavril, Gautier Izacard, Xavier Martinet, Marie-Anne Lachaux, Timothée Lacroix, Baptiste Rozière, Naman Goyal, Eric Hambro, Faisal Azhar, et al. 2023. Llama: Open and efficient foundation language models. *arXiv preprint arXiv:2302.13971*.

Jacky Visser, John Lawrence, Jean Wagemans, and Chris Reed. 2019. An annotated corpus of argument schemes in us election debates. In *Proceedings of the 9th Conference of the International Society for the Study of Argumentation (ISSA), 3-6 July 2018*, pages 1101–1111.

Yuetong Wu, Yukai Zhou, Baixuan Xu, Weiqi Wang, and Yangqiu Song. 2024. Knowcomp at dialam-2024: Fine-tuning pre-trained language models for dialogical argument mining with inference anchoring theory. In *Proceedings of the 11th Workshop on Argument Mining*, Thailand. Association for Computational Linguistics.

Zihao Zheng, Zhaowei Wang, Qing Zong, and Yangqiu Song. 2024. Knowcomp pokemon team at dialam-2024: A two-stage pipeline for detecting relations in dialogue argument mining. In *Proceedings of the 11th Workshop on Argument Mining*, Thailand. Association for Computational Linguistics.

DFKI-MLST at DialAM-2024 Shared Task: System Description

Arne Binder* **Tatiana Anikina*** **Leonhard Hennig** **Simon Ostermann**
German Research Center for Artificial Intelligence (DFKI)
{*arne.binder, tatiana.anikina, leonhard.hennig, simon.ostermann*}@*dfki.de*

Abstract

This paper presents the `dfki-mlst` submission for the DialAM shared task (Ruiz-Dolz et al., 2024) on identification of argumentative and illocutionary relations in dialogue. Our model achieves the best results in the global setting: 48.25 F1 at the focused level when looking only at the related arguments/locutions and 67.05 F1 at the general level when evaluating the complete argument maps. We describe our implementation of the data pre-processing pipeline, relation encoding and classification, evaluating 11 different base models and performing experiments with, e.g., node text combination and data augmentation. Our source code is publicly available.[1]

1 Introduction

DialAM 2024 (Ruiz-Dolz et al., 2024) is the first shared task in dialogue argument mining. It uses the Inference Anchoring Theory (IAT) framework (Budzynska et al., 2014) as data schema. IAT describes argument structure as graphs of propositions that are derived from the argumentative discourse units (ADUs; the basic units of argumentative analysis). The shared task focuses on the detection and classification of the relations that (1) argumentatively link these propositions with each other (ARI) and that (2) anchor them in the corresponding ADUs (ILO).

The DialAM dataset is based on the QT30 corpus (Hautli-Janisz et al., 2022), which is a collection of 30 episodes of the show Question Time by the BBC. The dataset includes transcriptions of dialogues between a moderator and several panelists and audience members annotated according to the IAT. Figure 1 visualizes the structure of the data. In simplified terms, IAT models argumentation information as a bipartite graph.[2] One side

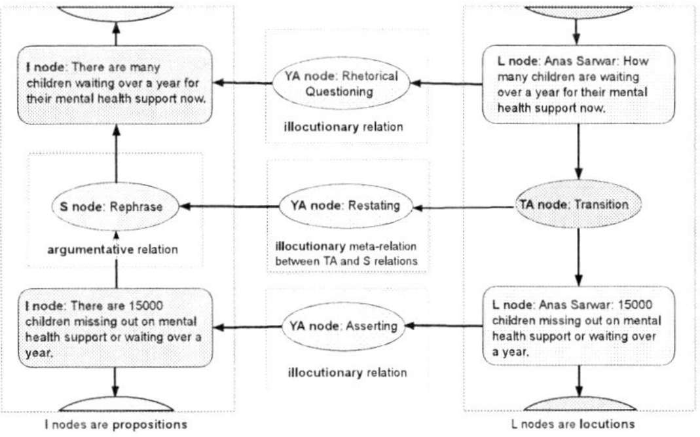

Figure 1: Extract of an example DialAM data point. Argumentative structure (left side; `I` and `S` nodes) is anchored in the dialogue structure (right side; `L` and `TA`) by illocutionary relations (middle; `YA` nodes) that are based on speech acts. The DialAM 2024 shared task requires identification as well as classification of (1) `S` node relations (ARI) and (2) `YA` node relations (ILO).

consists of the ADUs as they occur in the original text, called **locution (`L`)** nodes, and **transition (`TA`)** nodes that link them in the direction of the dialog flow. The other side consists of **information (`I`)** nodes which encode the propositions derived from the locutions and the **argumentative relation (`S`)** nodes (e.g., `Inference`, `Conflict`, or `Rephrase`) that connect them in the direction of argumentative reference. Finally, `I` and `S` nodes are anchored by **illocutionary relation (`YA`)** nodes in `L` and `TA` nodes, respectively, i.e. they encode from which `L` and `TA` nodes they are derived. The relation nodes connect to their arguments via two distinct roles: `incoming` (edges point towards the relation node) and `outgoing` (edges point away from it). The shared task data are organized in nodesets where each nodeset is a collection of annotated nodes and edges in Argument Interchange Format (Rahwan and Reed, 2009) extracted from an episode.

DialAM poses some unique challenges because it requires three different types of relations to be extracted (see Figure 1): argumentative relations

*Equal contribution.
[1]github.com/ArneBinder/dialam-2024-shared-task
[2]There are several exclusions to this, e.g., reported speech.

Proceedings of the 11th Workshop on Argument Mining, pages 93–102
August 15, 2024

between propositions (**S nodes; subtask 1**), illocutionary relations modeling speech acts (**YA:L-to-I nodes; subtask 2.1**) and, relations between argumentative relations and dialogue turn transitions (**YA:TA-to-S nodes; subtask 2.2**). Note that all relations have at least one incoming and outgoing edge, but argumentative relations (S nodes) such as Inference may have more than one incoming edge. Thus, subtask 1 is an instance of n-ary relation extraction. Furthermore, YA:TA-to-S relations link TA and S nodes which are both relation nodes, so this is a meta-relation. Both aspects circumvent usual relation extraction approaches that assume binary relations connecting spans over text. There are 25 relation labels in total with a very imbalanced distribution (see Appendix A and E.2).

Previous approaches to dialogue argument mining, such as Ruiz-Dolz et al. (2021), have shown that Transformer-based models work well on the argument relation identification task, with RoBERTa (Liu et al., 2019) significantly outperforming BERT (Devlin et al., 2019), XLNet (Yang et al., 2019), DistilBERT (Sanh et al., 2019) and ALBERT (Lan et al., 2020). They have found that in many cases misclassified relations were due to the lack of context or multiple valid interpretations of a relation. However, Ruiz-Dolz et al. (2021) address a simpler task compared to the DialAM setup because they classify only propositional relations while DialAM involves n-ary relations between different types of nodes (propositions, locutions and meta-relations).

Our contributions are as follows: (1) we introduce a unified approach towards dialogue argument mining based on n-ary relation classification and train a single model that can handle all three types of relations to get the most out of the data, (2) our dfki-mlst submission achieves the best scores in the global setting of the shared task, and (3) we conduct a comparative analysis of different types of base models, explore data augmentation, weighted loss and node text combination.

2 System Architecture

We handle all three subtasks by framing them as n-ary relation classification. Let $r^A = \{(l, a)|l \in L, a \in A\}$ be a n-ary relation with L the set of possible argument roles and A the set of possible relation arguments such as the set $S_t = \{(i, j, l)\}$ of labeled spans over a text t with i and j start and end indices with respect to t and l the label. We define n-ary relation classification as assigning a class $c \in C$ to r where C is the set of possible classes. In the following we explain how we construct relations r^{S_t}, i.e. sets of argument-role – text-span pairs over a single text, and the relation classes c from the individual relation nodes. In detail, we describe how we normalize the data (2.1), encode each task data as n-ary relations (2.2), and, finally, how we implement the relation classification (2.3).

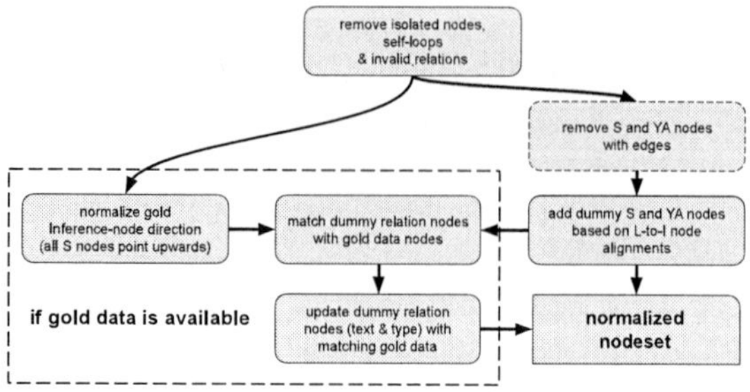

Figure 2: Nodeset normalization. Dashed boxes indicate steps that are only relevant for model training.

2.1 Nodeset Normalization

To encode the data as relations, we use some heuristics to construct a full nodeset from the provided nodes (L, I, and TA). This will include already all edges, but we assign a dummy NONE label to all relation nodes that we add. We achieve this by exploiting the following observations.

First, each I node is usually anchored by exactly one L node. Since the I node text is derived from the corresponding L node, their text contents are very similar. We use this to find an alignment of L and I nodes by computing their textual similarity using longest common substring and calculate a pairwise assignment. This alignment allows us to construct the YA:L-to-I nodes.

Second, the incoming and outgoing edges of the S nodes usually mirror their counterparts at the anchoring TA node, but in reversed direction (i.e. outgoing edges of the TA nodes mirror incoming edges of the S nodes and the other way around). This allows us to construct S nodes by reversing the TA arguments and mirroring them to I nodes by following the L-I-alignment. However, there is one prominent edge case. The S nodes with label Inference may point in the opposite direction. We can normalize that by swapping the incoming and outgoing edges of all such Inference nodes in the gold data and assigning a special node label Inference-rev(ersed) to maintain the original semantics. We can determine if an Inference node needs to be swapped by looking at the direction of the anchoring TA node.[3]

Finally, we assign gold labels to all constructed relation nodes for which we find matching gold nodes by considering only the arguments and their roles.

We found several issues with the data (e.g. isolated nodes, self-loops, relations with invalid combinations of arguments) that we fix before applying the normalization steps. Also, there are valid cases that contradict the above assumptions (I nodes of reported speech may have no directly anchoring L node; I and S nodes with multiple anchors; etc.), but since they are very rare we discard such nodes. Figure 2 visualizes the full normalization pipeline.

2.2 Encoding as Relations

To encode all task relevant relation nodes as relations r^{S_t}, we first convert them to n-ary relations over locutions (L nodes) r^L and then construct a common base text t from all locutions.

We encode the `YA:L-to-I` nodes (subtask 2.1) as unary relation classification where we use the anchoring L node as single argument with its role (`outgoing`). For `YA:TA-to-S` nodes (subtask 2.2), we use the arguments of the related TA relation with their respective roles. We encode the S nodes (subtask 1) by using the L nodes that anchor their arguments, but with the S node roles. In all three cases, we use the relation node label as label, but prefix it as well as the argument roles (`incoming` and `outgoing`) with the respective task identifier (`S`, `YA:L-to-I`, or `YA:TA-to-S`).

To get a contiguous base text t, we concatenate all locutions in the direction of the dialogue flow.[4] Note that the L nodes do not form a sequence, but a directed graph. Since there are no reliable time stamps, we linearize this graph in such a way that the ordering of the nodes is preserved.[5] We use the start and end offsets of the L node texts in t to construct r^{S_t} from r^L.

Using distinct roles and a common base text allows us to use a single model to solve all subtasks.

[3]We can use the `L-I`-alignment to get all anchoring L nodes for the arguments of the S node at hand. Then, we can check if there is a TA node with these anchor nodes as arguments or with the swapped arguments.

[4]This means, that we completely ignore I node text.

[5]i.e. for all node pairs (x, y) where there is a path from x to y, x must occur before y in the linearized nodes.

2.3 Classification Model

We use a deep learning based text classification model consisting of a contextual text encoder and a one layer classification head implemented within the PyTorch-IE framework (Binder et al., 2024). First, role specific begin- and end-marker tokens are inserted into the base text for all arguments of the relation to classify. Then, the modified text is classified by the model.

We use the cross entropy loss and the Adam optimizer to train it. The source code is publicly available.[1]

3 Experiments and Results

With the relation classification approach described in Section 2 we train our model on the DialAM data. We split the original training set into training (1259 nodesets) and validation (140 nodesets) partitions and repeat the training procedure three times with different seeds. The best model is selected based on the validation set performance. Our `dfki-mlst` submission uses DeBERTa-v3[6] (He et al., 2021) as text encoder trained with a learning rate 1e-4 and a window size of 512 tokens[7] for 20 epochs on a single GPU NVIDIA H100 80GB HBM3. We evaluate our model with the official script that outputs precision, recall and F1 scores for the ARI and ILO tasks, and the GLOBAL metrics represent the combined scores. All scores are calculated at two levels: focused (only related arguments/locutions) and general (complete argument maps).

Table 1 shows the comparison of F1 scores on the gold test data between the official RoBERTa baseline, our `dfki-mlst` submission and the best-performing competitor model in each setting. Our approach shows overall strong performance in the GLOBAL setting when complete argument maps are taken into account (+0.8% F1 in GLOBAL-Focused and +3.35% in GLOBAL-General). `dfki-mlst` also outperforms other models on the ARI-General task for propositional relations (+9.11% F1).

3.1 Error Analysis

Since the nodeset normalization plays a major role in our setup, we evaluate its impact based on our validation set with 140 nodesets. To make the normalized nodesets comparable with the original data,

[6]huggingface.co/microsoft/deberta-v3-large

[7]For each relation classification pass, the window is centered at the minimal span covering all its relation arguments.

Model	ARI		ILO		GLOBAL	
	Focused	*General*	*Focused*	*General*	*Focused*	*General*
baseline	22.80	26.46	**72.09**	45.75	47.45	36.10
best-competitor	**35.89**	46.22	69.95	**81.17**	45.23	63.70
dfki-mlst (ours)	30.40	**55.33**	66.10	78.78	**48.25**	**67.05**

Table 1: F1 scores of the official baseline, best competitor model, and `dfki-mlst` (ours) per task.

we reverse all `Inference-rev` relations back as well as remove the `NONE` nodes. We observe a lower performance, i.e. higher impact, on ARI (78.61 focused F1, 93.04 general F1) when compared to ILO (83.05 focused F1, 95.61 general F1). See Table 2 in Appendix C.1 for the complete results.

We also evaluate `dfki-mlst` performance per label based on our validation set (see Figure 5 in Appendix C for statistics). Unsurprisingly, the most common `YA` node relation `Asserting` achieves the highest F1 score (99%) since this label is also well-represented in the training set (see Appendix A for label distribution). We also observe that `NONE` relation between different types of nodes can be classified reliably in most cases. We found that some classes are distinctive and easy to classify. E.g., `Pure Questioning` between `I` and `L` nodes with the support of 120, and 1.86% representation in the training data, has 81% F1. Other categories are more challenging and result in worse scores even when they have more training samples, e.g., `Default Inference` constitutes 3.85% of the training set with the support of 246 but the classifier achieves only 43% F1.

3.2 Base Model Comparison

We explore different LLMs as text encoders in our classification model and evaluate them on the released gold test data. The results show that although DeBERTa-v3 is the best-performing model on the validation set (+0.85% on GLOBAL-General and +0.5% on GLOBAL-Focused compared to the second best model DeBERTa-v1), it shows slightly worse performance than DeBERTa-v1 on the test data. Interestingly, BART (Lewis et al., 2019) demonstrates the best F1 scores in both ILO-Focused (72.28 F1) and ILO-General (83.68 F1) settings. However, its performance on the argument relation identification task is considerably worse (-7.98% F1 in Focused and -9.84 % F1 in General). Also, models such as Mistral (Jiang et al., 2023) and Llama (Touvron et al., 2023) do not achieve very good results when fine-tuned on the relation classification task (see Appendix B for the training details). We compare Mistral and Llama fine-tuning to the setting where we freeze the base model and fine-tune only the adapter weights with LoRA (Hu et al., 2022). In both cases LoRA outperforms the fine-tuned models but still underperforms DeBERTa. The results of the full analysis are shown in Tables 3 and 4 in Appendix D.

3.3 Experiments with Input Data Modification and Weighted Loss

Although our `dfki-mlst` submission uses only `L` node texts we experimented with combining both `L` and `I` node texts when encoding relations and this setup achieves the best scores in the GLOBAL setting and also improves our performance on the ILO task compared to the original submission. Further details can be found in Section E.3 in Appendix.

After nodeset cleaning and normalization we were left with only 1259 documents (compared to the original 1478). Hence, we decided to experiment with data augmentation to increase the amount of available data and train a more robust model. We modify `L` node texts using two different approaches: paraphrase-based data augmentation and token-level perturbations based on Easy Data Augmentation (EDA) (Wei and Zou, 2019). Combining EDA-augmented and original data improves F1 scores for ARI-Focused and ARI-General tasks but results in worse performance on the ILO task. More details can be found in Section E.1.

Given that the dataset has imbalanced distribution, we also experimented with weighted loss (see Section E.2) and found that with this approach we get some improvements on the ARI task but overall worse performance compared to vanilla DeBERTa.

4 Conclusion

This paper introduces the `dfki-mlst` submission that achieves the best scores in the global evaluation setting of the DialAM shared task. We describe our nodeset pre-processing pipeline and the system architecture. We also present the comparison of different base models (DeBERTa, BART, Mistral etc.) as well as our experiments with data augmentation, class distribution and node text combination. We observe that some models (e.g., DeBERTa) demonstrate better performance on the argument relation task while other models (e.g., BART) are better at detecting illocutionary relations.

Acknowledgments

We would like to thank the anonymous reviewers for their valuable feedback on our work. This work has been supported by the German Ministry of Education and Research (BMBF) as part of the project TRAILS.

References

Arne Binder, Leonhard Hennig, and Christoph Alt. 2024. Pytorch-ie: Fast and reproducible prototyping for information extraction. *Preprint*, arXiv:2406.00007.

Katarzyna Budzynska, Mathilde Janier, Chris Reed, Patrick Saint-Dizier, Manfred Stede, and Olena Yaskorska. 2014. A model for processing illocutionary structures and argumentation in debates. In *Proceedings of the Ninth International Conference on Language Resources and Evaluation, LREC 2014, Reykjavik, Iceland, May 26-31, 2014*, pages 917–924. European Language Resources Association (ELRA).

Jacob Devlin, Ming-Wei Chang, Kenton Lee, and Kristina Toutanova. 2019. BERT: pre-training of deep bidirectional transformers for language understanding. In *Proceedings of the 2019 Conference of the North American Chapter of the Association for Computational Linguistics: Human Language Technologies, NAACL-HLT 2019, Minneapolis, MN, USA, June 2-7, 2019, Volume 1 (Long and Short Papers)*, pages 4171–4186. Association for Computational Linguistics.

Annette Hautli-Janisz, Zlata Kikteva, Wassiliki Siskou, Kamila Gorska, Ray Becker, and Chris Reed. 2022. QT30: A corpus of argument and conflict in broadcast debate. In *Proceedings of the Thirteenth Language Resources and Evaluation Conference, LREC 2022, Marseille, France, 20-25 June 2022*, pages 3291–3300. European Language Resources Association.

Pengcheng He, Jianfeng Gao, and Weizhu Chen. 2021. Debertav3: Improving deberta using electra-style pretraining with gradient-disentangled embedding sharing. *Preprint*, arXiv:2111.09543.

Edward J. Hu, Yelong Shen, Phillip Wallis, Zeyuan Allen-Zhu, Yuanzhi Li, Shean Wang, Lu Wang, and Weizhu Chen. 2022. Lora: Low-rank adaptation of large language models. In *The Tenth International Conference on Learning Representations, ICLR 2022, Virtual Event, April 25-29, 2022*. OpenReview.net.

Albert Q. Jiang, Alexandre Sablayrolles, Arthur Mensch, Chris Bamford, Devendra Singh Chaplot, Diego de las Casas, Florian Bressand, Gianna Lengyel, Guillaume Lample, Lucile Saulnier, Lélio Renard Lavaud, Marie-Anne Lachaux, Pierre Stock, Teven Le Scao, Thibaut Lavril, Thomas Wang, Timothée Lacroix, and William El Sayed. 2023. Mistral 7b. *Preprint*, arXiv:2310.06825.

Zhenzhong Lan, Mingda Chen, Sebastian Goodman, Kevin Gimpel, Piyush Sharma, and Radu Soricut. 2020. ALBERT: A lite BERT for self-supervised learning of language representations. In *8th International Conference on Learning Representations, ICLR 2020, Addis Ababa, Ethiopia, April 26-30, 2020*. OpenReview.net.

Mike Lewis, Yinhan Liu, Naman Goyal, Marjan Ghazvininejad, Abdelrahman Mohamed, Omer Levy, Veselin Stoyanov, and Luke Zettlemoyer. 2019. BART: denoising sequence-to-sequence pre-training for natural language generation, translation, and comprehension. *CoRR*, abs/1910.13461.

Yinhan Liu, Myle Ott, Naman Goyal, Jingfei Du, Mandar Joshi, Danqi Chen, Omer Levy, Mike Lewis, Luke Zettlemoyer, and Veselin Stoyanov. 2019. Roberta: A robustly optimized BERT pretraining approach. *CoRR*, abs/1907.11692.

Vukosi Marivate and Tshephisho Sefara. 2019. Improving short text classification through global augmentation methods. *CoRR*, abs/1907.03752.

George A. Miller. 1995. Wordnet: A lexical database for english. *Commun. ACM*, 38(11):39–41.

Iyad Rahwan and Chris Reed. 2009. The argument interchange format. In Guillermo Ricardo Simari and Iyad Rahwan, editors, *Argumentation in Artificial Intelligence*, pages 383–402. Springer.

Ramon Ruiz-Dolz, José Alemany, Stella Heras Barberá, and Ana García-Fornes. 2021. Transformer-based models for automatic identification of argument relations: A cross-domain evaluation. *IEEE Intell. Syst.*, 36(6):62–70.

Ramon Ruiz-Dolz, John Lawrence, Ella Schad, and Chris Reed. 2024. Overview of DialAM-2024: Argument Mining in Natural Language Dialogues. In *Proceedings of the 11th Workshop on Argument Mining*, Thailand. Association for Computational Linguistics.

Victor Sanh, Lysandre Debut, Julien Chaumond, and Thomas Wolf. 2019. Distilbert, a distilled version of BERT: smaller, faster, cheaper and lighter. *CoRR*, abs/1910.01108.

Hugo Touvron, Louis Martin, Kevin Stone, Peter Albert, Amjad Almahairi, Yasmine Babaei, Nikolay Bashlykov, Soumya Batra, Prajjwal Bhargava, Shruti Bhosale, Dan Bikel, Lukas Blecher, Cristian Canton Ferrer, Moya Chen, Guillem Cucurull, David Esiobu, Jude Fernandes, Jeremy Fu, Wenyin Fu, Brian Fuller, Cynthia Gao, Vedanuj Goswami, Naman Goyal, Anthony Hartshorn, Saghar Hosseini, Rui Hou, Hakan Inan, Marcin Kardas, Viktor Kerkez, Madian Khabsa,

Isabel Kloumann, Artem Korenev, Punit Singh Koura, Marie-Anne Lachaux, Thibaut Lavril, Jenya Lee, Diana Liskovich, Yinghai Lu, Yuning Mao, Xavier Martinet, Todor Mihaylov, Pushkar Mishra, Igor Molybog, Yixin Nie, Andrew Poulton, Jeremy Reizenstein, Rashi Rungta, Kalyan Saladi, Alan Schelten, Ruan Silva, Eric Michael Smith, Ranjan Subramanian, Xiaoqing Ellen Tan, Binh Tang, Ross Taylor, Adina Williams, Jian Xiang Kuan, Puxin Xu, Zheng Yan, Iliyan Zarov, Yuchen Zhang, Angela Fan, Melanie Kambadur, Sharan Narang, Aurelien Rodriguez, Robert Stojnic, Sergey Edunov, and Thomas Scialom. 2023. Llama 2: Open foundation and fine-tuned chat models. *Preprint*, arXiv:2307.09288.

Jason W. Wei and Kai Zou. 2019. EDA: easy data augmentation techniques for boosting performance on text classification tasks. In *Proceedings of the 2019 Conference on Empirical Methods in Natural Language Processing and the 9th International Joint Conference on Natural Language Processing, EMNLP-IJCNLP 2019, Hong Kong, China, November 3-7, 2019*, pages 6381–6387. Association for Computational Linguistics.

Zhilin Yang, Zihang Dai, Yiming Yang, Jaime G. Carbonell, Ruslan Salakhutdinov, and Quoc V. Le. 2019. Xlnet: Generalized autoregressive pretraining for language understanding. In *Advances in Neural Information Processing Systems 32: Annual Conference on Neural Information Processing Systems 2019, NeurIPS 2019, December 8-14, 2019, Vancouver, BC, Canada*, pages 5754–5764.

A Relation Label Distribution

Figure 3 and 4 show the overall and per relation node type label distribution in the train data.

B Training Details for Large Models

Since LLMs such as Mistral and LLama have a large number of parameters and fine-tuning all of them would require a lot of GPU memory, we freeze the first 30 layers and fine-tune only the last two layers together with the classification head (see Mistral-30 and Llama-30 in Tables 3 and 4).

C Error Analysis

C.1 Impact of Preprocessing

Experimental results regrading the impact of the nodeset normalization measured on the validation data can be found in Table 2.

C.2 Performance per Label

Figure 5 compares the amount of support with the per label performance.

D Model Comparison

Figure 3 and 4 show the focused as well as the general metric scores for all analysed models on the test data.

E Additional Experiments

E.1 Data Augmentation Experiments

Our experiments with data augmentation do not modify the original relations and nodeset structure, we change only the `L` node text by either paraphrasing it with a T5-based model trained on Chat-GPT paraphrases[8] or using an Easy Data Augmentation (EDA) (Wei and Zou, 2019) approach based on `textaugment` (Marivate and Sefara, 2019). In case of EDA we randomly choose whether to replace a token with a synonym from WordNet (Miller, 1995), delete it, add a new token, or swap one token with another. Ideally, such changes introduce surface perturbations without changing the original meaning, therefore annotations remain the same. E.g., for the original `L` node text *"Claire Fox: that will show how virtuous I am"* we have the following paraphrase-based augmentation: *"Claire Fox: My goodness will be demonstrated to others through this."* and the EDA-based augmentation: *"Claire Fox: appearance that will show how virtuous I am"*.

Tables 3 and 4 in Appendix D show the results for the augmented models in the lower section of each table. In case of DeBERTa-v1$_{+paraphr_data}$ we fine-tune DeBERTa-v1 model on the paraphrased data and then continue fine-tuning on the original DialAM training set. DeBERTa-v3$_{+EDA_sequential}$ follows the same strategy but instead of using paraphrased text it applies token-level perturbations (EDA). Note that we changed our base model from DeBERTa-v1 to DeBERTa-v3 in the latest experiments since it gave us the best scores on the validation set. Finally, DeBERTa-v3$_{+EDA_combined}$ simply extends the dataset by combining both original and augmented documents. The results show that among these three strategies combining the data brings some improvement compared to vanilla DeBERTa-v3 on ARI-Focused (+3.76% F1), GLOBAL-Focused (+1.23% F1), ARI-General (+1.53% F1) and GLOBAL-General (+0.36% F1) tasks but leads to worse scores on ILO-Focused (-1.3% F1) and ILO-General (-0.83% F1).

E.2 Experiments with Class Distribution

As shown in Appendix A (Figures 3, 4a, 4b, 4c), DialAM training data has an imbalanced class distribution with 12 labels representing less than 1% of all the data. Especially `YA` relations connecting locutions with propositions (see Figure 4c) have very imbalanced distribution. E.g., `Asserting` appears in more than 90% of `S` node annotations, while labels such as `Restating`, `Arguing` and `Agreeing` all together make up less than 1%, which poses a challenge for the classifier. Therefore, we test whether using a weighted loss adjusted with regards to label distribution or restricting classification only to more frequent classes (with at least 10 samples per label) can help mitigate this issue. In the experiments with weighted loss we (1) collect statistics from the training set on label distribution and (2) compute each class weight as follows: $w_c = \frac{|D|}{|D_c| \cdot |C|}$ with D the set of all samples (relation-class-pairs), $D_c = \{(r, c) \in D\}$ and C the set of all labels, and then (3) restrict the range of weight values by using 1 as the lower and 20 as the upper bound to avoid over-penalizing classifier on the truly rare classes.

The evaluation results in Tables 3 and 4 demonstrate that training with weighted loss improves the

[8]huggingface.co/humarin/chatgpt_paraphraser_on_T5_base

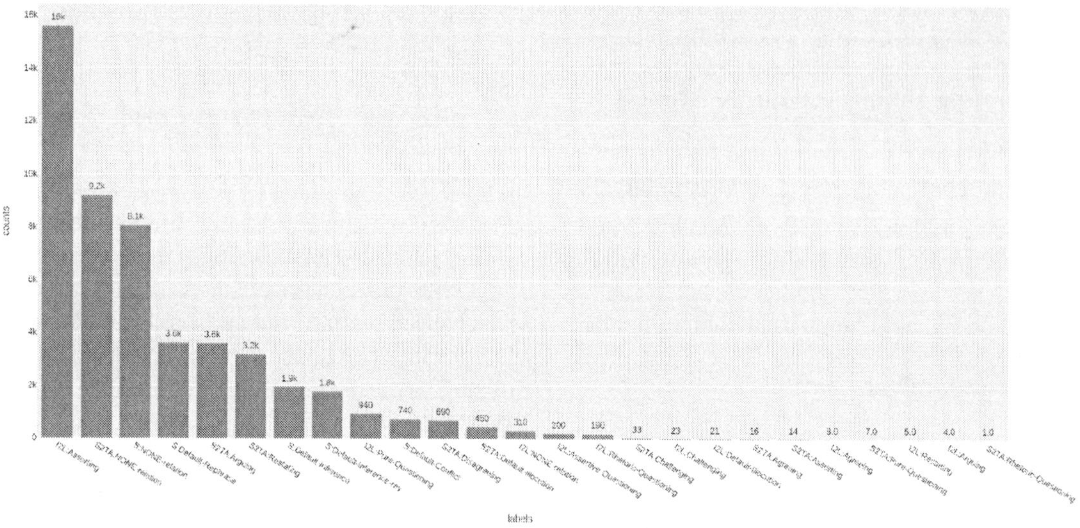

Figure 3: Overall label distribution in the DialAM training set.

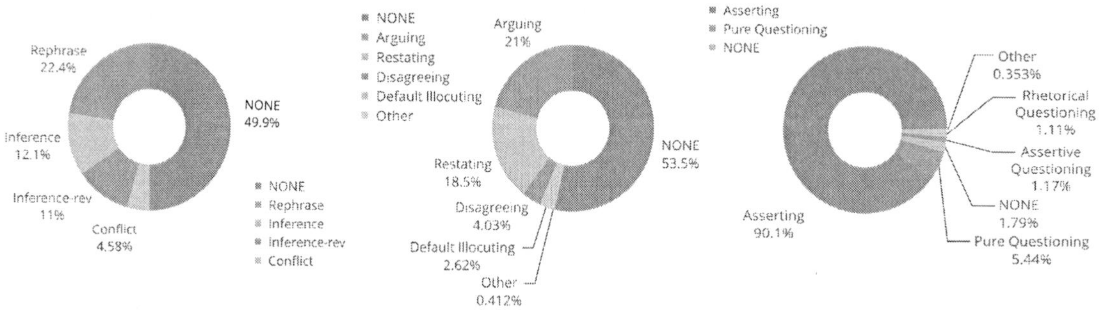

(a) S relations between I nodes. (b) YA relations between TA and S nodes. (c) YA relations between L and I nodes.

Figure 4: Label distribution for different types of relations: S nodes for argumentative relations and YA nodes for illocutionary ones.

	Model	ARI Prec	ARI Rec	ARI F1	ILO Prec	ILO Rec	ILO F1	GLOBAL Prec	GLOBAL Rec	GLOBAL F1
Focused	preprocessing only	82.85	76.60	78.61	84.17	82.27	83.05	83.51	79.44	80.83
	full pipeline	49.02	31.74	36.33	71.75	69.82	70.35	60.39	50.78	53.34
	full pipeline, normalized	59.17	41.44	46.22	85.24	84.87	84.71	72.31	63.93	65.99
General	preprocessing only	97.12	91.18	93.04	96.71	94.86	95.61	96.92	93.02	94.33
	full pipeline	66.43	58.91	60.06	86.23	84.71	85.11	76.33	71.81	72.59
	full pipeline, normalized	68.40	64.61	64.55	89.16	89.30	89.02	78.76	77.20	76.95

Table 2: Impact of nodeset normalization on the performance, evaluated on the validation data. The values for `full pipeline` are the scores of our model (dfki-mlst). `preprocessing only` values are computed by first normalizing the data as described in section 2.1, then reverting `Inference-rev` relations back as well as removing NONE relation nodes to make the normalized nodesets comparable with the original data and, finally, calculating the metrics with the official evaluation script. Values for `full pipeline, normalized` are the ones of `full pipeline` divided by `preprocessing only`.

Model	ARI-Focused			ILO-Focused			GLOBAL-Focused		
	Prec	*Rec*	*F*1	*Prec*	*Rec*	*F*1	*Prec*	*Rec*	*F*1
baseline$_{RoBERTa}$	37.10	18.42	22.80	73.10	72.55	**72.09**	55.10	45.49	47.45
best-competitor	46.26	32.43	**35.89**	71.18	69.23	69.95	50.68	43.41	45.23
dfki-mlst$_{DeBERTa\text{-}v3}$	43.87	24.82	30.40	69.12	66.25	66.10	56.50	45.53	**48.25**
DeBERTa-v1	50.98	27.98	**33.82**	66.04	64.32	64.63	58.51	46.15	**49.22**
RoBERTa	48.11	20.45	26.62	63.64	60.66	61.24	55.88	40.55	43.93
RemBERT	41.02	18.35	24.20	62.33	59.49	60.20	51.67	38.92	42.20
ELECTRA	37.46	14.65	20.25	68.76	67.54	67.37	53.11	41.10	43.81
BART	34.09	18.14	22.41	73.50	72.12	**72.28**	53.80	45.13	47.34
XLNet	36.75	19.90	24.04	60.63	58.89	58.22	48.69	39.39	41.13
Mistral-30	33.40	16.50	19.66	67.91	69.08	68.02	50.66	42.79	43.84
Llama-30	21.75	13.25	14.28	60.68	60.10	59.61	41.22	36.67	36.95
Mistral-LoRA	33.62	18.90	23.08	68.36	64.89	65.55	50.99	41.89	44.31
Llama-LoRA	39.07	16.56	22.08	64.68	62.40	63.16	51.88	39.48	42.62
DeBERTa-v1$_{+l_and_i_node_text}$	44.32	23.39	29.24	75.17	73.51	**74.10**	59.75	48.45	**51.67**
DeBERTa-v1$_{+freq_classes}$	48.04	24.44	30.37	68.09	64.24	64.81	58.06	44.34	47.59
DeBERTa-v1$_{+weighted_loss}$	47.35	28.98	**34.22**	59.48	59.75	58.85	53.41	44.37	46.53
DeBERTa-v1$_{+paraphr_data}$	43.99	22.03	27.69	68.35	66.01	66.31	56.17	44.02	47.00
DeBERTa-v3$_{+EDA_sequential}$	48.08	25.26	30.66	65.72	62.21	62.71	56.90	43.73	46.69
DeBERTa-v3$_{+EDA_combined}$	47.73	29.11	34.16	65.92	64.53	64.80	56.83	46.82	49.48

Table 3: Focused scores represent the performance on the existing relations in the gold standard maps (excluding non related propositions). The scores were computed with the official evaluation script using the gold test data.

Model	ARI-General			ILO-General			GLOBAL-General		
	Prec	*Rec*	*F*1	*Prec*	*Rec*	*F*1	*Prec*	*Rec*	*F*1
baseline$_{RoBERTa}$	28.59	34.69	26.46	39.11	62.07	45.75	33.85	48.38	36.10
best-competitor	49.21	46.32	46.22	81.99	80.79	**81.17**	65.60	63.55	63.70
dfki-mlst$_{DeBERTa\text{-}v3}$	61.96	53.30	**55.33**	81.08	79.25	78.78	71.52	66.28	**67.05**
DeBERTa-v1	64.05	57.14	**57.93**	79.04	78.19	78.12	71.55	67.66	**68.03**
RoBERTa	64.86	49.55	52.73	76.83	75.05	75.17	70.84	62.30	63.95
RemBERT	54.79	46.00	47.56	75.92	74.28	74.49	65.36	60.14	61.02
ELECTRA	46.18	39.37	41.41	81.23	81.07	80.53	63.70	60.22	60.97
BART	49.78	44.3	45.49	84.22	83.97	**83.68**	67.00	64.13	64.59
XLNet	55.51	48.28	48.80	73.88	72.93	72.05	64.69	60.61	60.42
Mistral-30	47.20	43.14	42.33	82.15	83.91	82.62	64.68	63.52	62.48
Llama-30	39.59	38.38	37.10	74.93	75.01	74.22	57.26	56.70	55.66
Mistral-LoRA	54.41	47.06	49.03	82.07	79.78	79.99	68.24	63.42	64.51
Llama-LoRA	51.72	42.95	44.89	77.03	75.55	75.99	64.38	59.25	60.44
DeBERTa-v1$_{+l_and_i_node_text}$	57.52	50.39	52.33	86.57	85.17	**85.65**	72.05	67.78	**68.99**
DeBERTa-v1$_{+freq_classes}$	65.05	52.71	55.66	80.38	77.62	77.80	72.72	65.17	66.73
DeBERTa-v1$_{+weighted_loss}$	63.81	55.97	**58.20**	73.81	74.73	73.65	68.81	65.35	65.93
DeBERTa-v1$_{+paraphr_data}$	58.42	49.66	51.36	80.44	79.30	79.16	69.43	64.48	65.26
DeBERTa-v3$_{+EDA_sequential}$	62.53	52.97	54.88	78.31	75.79	75.92	70.42	64.38	65.40
DeBERTa-v3$_{+EDA_combined}$	60.21	56.75	56.86	78.50	78.12	77.95	69.36	67.44	67.41

Table 4: General scores consider complete argument maps including non related nodes. The scores were computed with the official evaluation script using the gold test data.

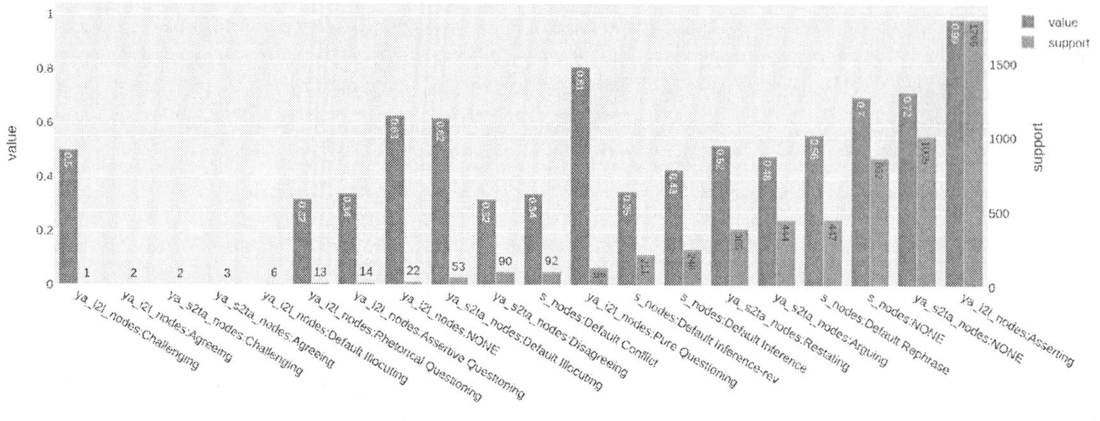

Figure 5: Performance of dfki-mlst with DeBERTa-v3 on the fixed validation set (140 documents). Blue bars indicate F1 scores while red bars correspond to the support set (how many items per class are available).

scores on the ARI task (for both Focused and General), however, this approach leads to a drop in performance for illocutionary relation identification. Furthermore, using only samples from more frequent classes results in overall worse performance which shows that having even few examples of rare labels is beneficial for the classifier.

E.3 Experiments with Combined Node Text

Since I and L nodes represent arguments and dialogue turns, they have slightly different texts. I node text often includes more details "summarizing" the content as an argument, while L node text represents an unedited dialogue turn. dfki-mlst uses only the L node texts to encode the relations because this type of text is more similar to the data used for pre-training of the base model (DeBERTa) but we also test the setting that combines both texts of the aligned L and I nodes separated by the *"Argument:"* token that indicates the transition. As shown in Tables 3 and 4, this approach results in the best performance on illocution identification and achieves overall best scores in GLOBAL, outperforming the version that uses only L node texts by 3.4% F1 in Focused and 1.9% F1 in General for DeBERTa-v3 and showing a similar trend for DeBERTa-v1. However, it under-performs on the argument relation identification task compared to the dfki-mlst submission.

KnowComp at DialAM-2024: Fine-tuning Pre-trained Language Models for Dialogical Argument Mining with Inference Anchoring Theory

Yuetong Wu*, **Yukai Zhou***, **Baixuan Xu**, **Weiqi Wang**, **Yangqiu Song**
Department of Computer Science and Engineering, HKUST, Hong Kong SAR, China
{ywufe, yzhoueg, bxuan}@connect.ust.hk

Abstract

In this paper, we present our framework for DialAM-2024 Task A: Identification of Propositional Relations and Task B: Identification of Illocutionary Relations. The goal of Task A is to detect argumentative relations between propositions in an argumentative dialogue (Inference, Conflict, Rephrase), while Task B while Task B aims to detect illocutionary relations between locutions and argumentative propositions in a dialogue, e.g.,, Asserting, Agreeing, Arguing, Disagreeing. Noticing the definition of the relations are strict and professional under the context of IAT framework, we meticulously curate prompts which not only incorporate formal definition of the relations, but also exhibit the subtle differences between them. The PTLMs are then fine-tuned on the human-designed prompts to enhance its discrimination capability in classifying different theoretical relations by learning from the human instruction and the ground truth samples. After extensive experiments, a fine-tuned DeBERTa-v3-base model exhibits the best performance among all PTLMs with an F1 score of 78.90% on Task B. It is worth noticing that our framework ranks #2 in the ILO - General official leaderboard.

1 Introduction

Dialogical argument mining is an emerging field that aims to bridge the gap between the analysis of argumentation and dialogue (Budzynska et al., 2014b; Ruiz-Dolz et al., 2024; Kawarada et al., 2024). Traditional argument mining approaches have often focused on opinion mining within monological texts (Lawrence and Reed, 2019; Arumugam, 2022) or document form contents (Ruosch et al., 2022; Sazid and Mercer, 2022; Khondoker and Yousuf, 2022). However, real-world argumentation frequently occurs in dialogical contexts, where multiple participants engage in a dynamic exchange of viewpoints (Feger and Dietze, 2024; Lai et al., 2024; Alsinet et al., 2022). This complexity necessitates a more holistic approach that considers both the argumentative structures and the dialogical interactions.

*Equal Contributions

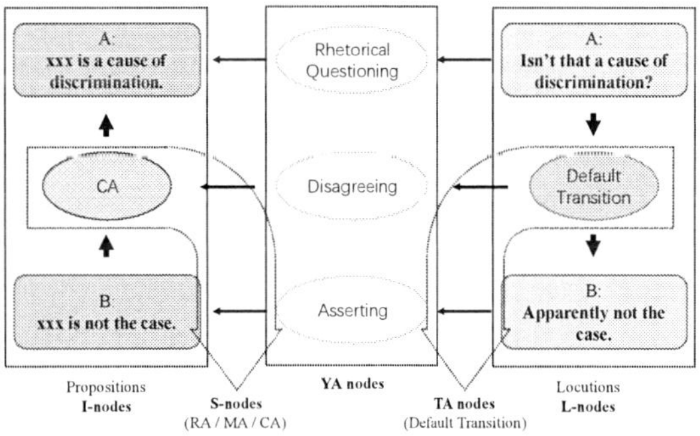

Figure 1: Inference Anchoring dialogical map example.

Apart from the dialogical information extraction paradigms explored by previous works (Dutta et al., 2022; Mestre et al., 2021), A generic modelling formalism for extracting dialogical information is the Inference Anchoring Theory (IAT) introduced by Budzynska and Reed (2011). It offers a systematic approach to decomposing text speech into distinct units (ADUs), while also anchoring and categorising logical inferences between propositions and locutions. As such, IAT provides a comprehensive methodology for analyzing the maneuvers of dialogues within a given theoretical framework, thus building an explicit scaffolding for language models to handle semantics analysis tasks (Budzynska et al., 2014a).

Based on this theory, DialAM-2024 workshop (Ruiz-Dolz et al., 2024) introduces the first shared task in dialogical argument mining, aimed at modeling argumentation and dialogue information together within a domain-independent framework. The proposed tasks of DialAM-2024 involves classification of the three-way argumentative relations between locutions and corresponding propositions,

Proceedings of the 11th Workshop on Argument Mining, pages 103–109
August 15, 2024 ©2024 Association for Computational Linguistics

detection of relevant dialogical components and completion of the inference anchoring map.

Due to the in-context learning ability of LLMs on unconventional tasks with demonstrated examples (Sun et al., 2023), our initial attempt was to use Large Language Models (LLMs) as the classifier for illocutionary relations (Chan et al., 2024; Wang et al., 2023b,a, 2024a,b; Wang and Song, 2024). A combination of zero-shot and few-shot (Brown et al., 2020) prompts integrated with Chain-of-thought (Wei et al., 2022) were tested. However, we observed that popular LLMs, such as gpt3.5-turbo (OpenAI, 2023), fail to show significant understanding of the task and yield relatively low performance after exhaustive experiment.

Notably, recent developments in Pre-Trained Language Models (PTLMs) on text classification tasks (Howard and Ruder, 2018) have empowered us to build our system the other way round. After the compilation of paired ADUs of propositions and locutions nodes embedded in a meticulously designed textual prompt, we fine-tuned our PTLMs on the reconstituted dataset as that of a traditional text classification task (Wang et al., 2023c; Peng et al., 2024; Yan et al., 2024). Using this method, we were able to achieve relatively high accuracy in the identification of illocutionary relations. The classification results of Task B were then used as textual information to assist the identification of propositional relations.

An extensive ablation study was also conducted to test the effectiveness and generalizability of our proposed system. A maximal F1 score of 78.90% and precision of 82.35% on Task B was achieved using a fine-tuned DeBERTa-v3-base model (Howard and Ruder, 2018). It is also noted that DeBERTa-v3-large underperforms its base version, with a precision difference of -0.2%. The proposed explanation is that the model already converges on the given dataset, provided the base version parameters. Several other PTLMs, including RoBERTa (Liu et al., 2019) and ALBERT (Lan et al., 2020) are also trialed using identical prompt design, which yield results inferior to DeBERTa-v3.

However, fine-tuned PTLMs converges inconsistently for Task A, with a recall of only 33.79%. We suspect that besides text from adjacent propositions and locutions, the system will need more in-context information (e.g., a dialogue 2-3 nodes away) to assist the process of relation identification according to recent works on reasoning under contexts (Dong et al., 2024; Zhang et al., 2024; Li et al., 2024).

As such, our proposed system provides valuable insight for dialogical argument mining using PTLMs on a IAT layout, and future works should be more focused on the revamp of methodology in in-context training information extraction. Our code and results are publicaly available at Arwenwutietie/DialAM-2024

2 Problem Definition

In this section, we would introduce the dataset format and elaborate on the formal definition of the shared task in DialAM-2024.

2.1 Dataset Description

In the DialAM-2024 dataset, all input texts are categorized into two primary types: locutions (L-nodes) and propositions (I-nodes). Locutions represent the original sentence segments within a complete dialogue, typically featuring speakers and timestamps. Conversely, propositions are reconstructed locutions, where linguistic elements such as anaphora, pronouns, and deixis have been resolved. These two text types are then structured into a navigable graph based on IAT, with corresponding L-nodes and I-nodes connected by three distinct relation types: (i) relations between locutions in a dialogue, known as transitions (TA-nodes); (ii) relations between propositions and locutions (YA-nodes); and (iii) illocutionary connections that link locutions with their semantic content (S-nodes).

We use QT30 corpus (Hautli-Janisz et al., 2022) as our dataset. QT30 is a collection of 30 episodes of Question Time aired between June 2020 and November 2021, with a total of more than 29 hours of transcribed broadcast material and comprising 19,842 locutions by more than 400 participants. The QT30 dataset contains 10,818 propositional relations that include Default Inferences, Default Conflicts, and Default Rephrases, and 32,303 illocutionary relations divided into Asserting, Agreeing, Arguing, Disagreeing, Restating, Questioning, and Default Illocuting.

2.2 Task Definition

The DialAM-2024 challenge comprises two distinct sub-tasks. Task A aims to detect the argumentative relations that exist between the propositions identified and segmented within the argumentative dialogue. More specifically, the objective is to use two connected I-nodes to predict the S-nodes between them. Task B, on the other hand, seeks to

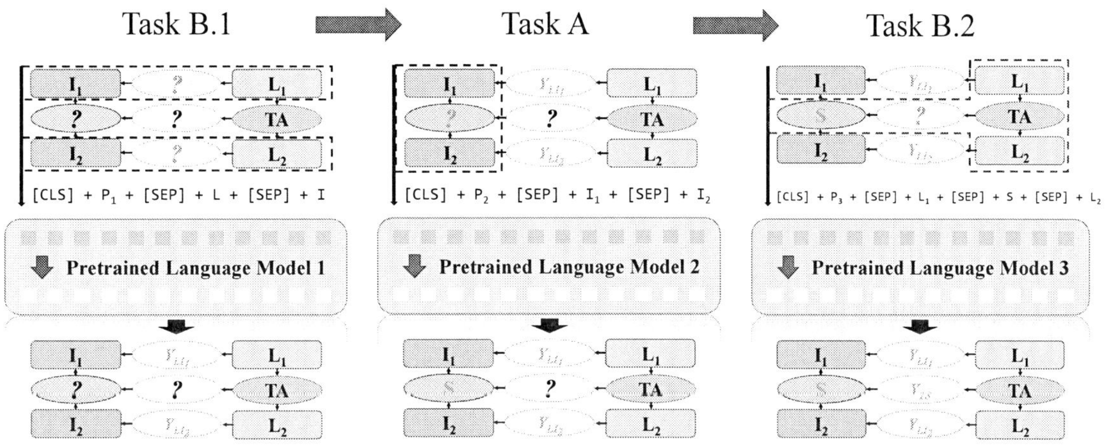

Figure 2: PTLM pipeline for DialAM-2024 dialogical argument mining tasks. Three PTLMs are fine-tuned in sequence to cope with Task B.1, Task A and Task B.2 respectively. The IAT map structure is optimally utilized for propositional & illocutionary relation classification.

identify the illocutionary relations that exist between the locutions uttered in the dialogue and the argumentative propositions associated with them. In other words, given a set of locutions (L-nodes) and propositions (I-nodes), the goal is to uncover the Illocutionary connections (YA-nodes) that link them.

To allow us to establish a clear and formal framework for analyzing the relationships. Formally, let us denote two coherent locutions as L_1 and L_2, their corresponding propositions as I_1 and I_2, the intermediate TA-nodes between L_1 and L_2 as T, the YA-nodes connecting L_1 and I_1 as Y_{LI_1}, the YA-nodes connecting L_2 and I_2 as Y_{LI_2}, the intermediary S-nodes between I_1 and I_2 as S, and the YA-nodes connecting T and S as Y_{TS}. We denote LLMs as F and the curated prompt as P_1, P_2 respectively for Task A and Task B. By these notations, the Task A and Task B could be reformatted formally as:

$$\textbf{Task A: } S = \max_i F(S_i | I_1, I_2, P_1);$$

$$\textbf{Task B: } Y_{LI_1} = \max_i F(Y_{LI_i} | I_1, L_1, P_2),$$

where S_i and Y_{LI_1} denote the output of PTLMs.

3 System Overview

In this section, we will introduce our proposed system. Our method conducts sequential inferences where we predict Y_{LI_1}, Y_{LI_2} and S in the first stage, then infer Y_{TS} with the predicted S in the previous stage.

3.1 Prompt Design

With the rapid advancement exhibited in prompt engineering technique (Chang et al., 2024; Qiao et al., 2023; Xu et al., 2024) it has been pointed out that prompting makes better use of the pre-trained data of PTLMs, allowing the model to perform better on fewer training examples, which can be helpful when classifying classes with smaller examples in this task. Being aware of this, since this text classification task is highly specified and targeted, we meticulously curated descriptive prompting for both sub-tasks. The prompt is then aggregated with given texts as the inputs for large model. Predefined special tokens like [SEP], [CLS] and [EOS] are also added to the final input texts to assist the model to understand the relationship between the different parts of the input. Totally, three different prompts have been used for Task A and B: P_1 (prompt used to predict Y_{LI_1} and Y_{LI_2}), P_2 (prompt used to predict S) and P_3 (prompt used to predict Y_{TS}).

3.2 Sequential inference and model training

Recently, decomposing complex problems into several simple one has become a fashion in LLM reasoning field (Bueno et al., 2024; Besta et al., 2024). Following this trend, in this project, the training of PTLMs is divided into three sequential stages, as shown in figure 2.

3.2.1 Stage 1: Direct Illocutionary Relation Detection (Task B.1)

In Stage 1, we instruct the model to predict Y_{LI_1} and Y_{LI_2} separately, since the illocutionary rela-

Model/Epoch	1-epoch			2-epoch		
	Y_{LI_1}+Y_{LI_2}	Y_{TS}	S	Y_{LI_1}+Y_{LI_2}	Y_{TS}	S
$DeBERTa_{base}$	0.9423	0.6137	0.5198	0.9450	0.6486	0.5676
$DeBERTa_{large}$	0.9428	0.6056	0.513	0.9359	0.6322	0.5681
RoBERTa	0.901	0.5481	0.4388	0.9234	0.5745	0.4503
ALBERT	0.8906	0.5364	0.4637	0.8906	0.5891	0.498
ChatGPT	0.72	-	-	0.72	-	-

Table 1: The experiment result for three stage inference. The result is evaluated on the validation set manually seperated by the author to demonstrate the model performance comparison.

tions between L-nodes (L_1 and L_2) and I-nodes (I_1 and I_2) is more intuitive and requires less information to classify. The raw textual prompt used is $('[CLS]' + P_1 +' [SEP]' + L_1 +' [SEP]' + I_1)$ and $('[CLS]' + P_1 +' [SEP]' + L_2 +' [SEP]' + I_2)$.

3.2.2 Stage 2: Propositional Relation Detection (Task A)

Then, in Stage 2 we subsequently classify S-nodes with textual prompt $('[CLS]' + P_2 +' [SEP]' + I_1 +' [SEP]' + I_2)$.

3.2.3 Stage 3: Indirect Illocutionary Relation Detection (Task B.2)

Finally, motivated by our observation that S and Y_{TS} are highly related, we incorporate the information yield through the previous two stages. Specifically, we leverage L_1, L_2 and the already predicted S for the prediction of Y_{TS}. The prompt we used is $('[CLS]' + P_3 +' [SEP]' + L_1 +' [SEP]' + S +' [SEP]' + L_2 +' [SEP]')$.

3.2.4 Training Objective

All models are trained with cross-entropy loss. Denote each input as x_i, its token length as $|x_i|$. Our models are denoted by p, and thus $p(x_i)$ represents the prediction made by the corresponding node, with $q(x_i)$ as its true label.

$$L(x_i, q) = -\sum_{i=1}^{|x|} p(x_i) \log(q(x_i)) \quad (1)$$

4 Experimental Setup

We followed a standard approach to partition our input data into training and validation sets. Please refer to Appendix C for more details.

5 Results and Analysis

In this section, we demonstrate our experiment results and conduct analysis on the issue we encountered through the experiments.

Our overall result is shown in Table 1. From the data we can observe that both DeBERTa-base and DeBERTa-large can achieve a relatively high accuracy on the prediction of Y_{LI_1}+Y_{LI_2}, Y_{TS} and S. However, ChatGPT's results were clearly not satisfactory, and it achieved the lowest accuracy rate on all 3 tasks. The reason could be that this text classification task is highly specialized and targeted where related resources rarely occur in ChatGPT's training data. Consequently, ChatGPT would fall short in relevant reasoning tasks. In the classification of Y_{LI_1}+Y_{LI_2}, we realize that the most numerous type in Y_{LI_1}+Y_{LI_2}, Asserting, accounts for 90% of the total number of Y_{LI_1}+Y_{LI_2}. We suspect that this may affect the final performance of the model, making it more inclined to split a new Y_{LI_1}orY_{LI_2}node into the Asserting class. Based on this, we tried to reduce the number of Asserting classes in the training set to train a more comprehensive model. However, the final results demonstrated that this actually led to a decrease in the overall accuracy. This implies that the model is scarcely affected by the imbalance of the dataset.

Further experiments indicate that the accuracy of S-node classification is greatly affected by the size of the training set. According to our observation, when 60% of the data is sampled for training, the accuracy on the test set reaches the highest (65.73%), and when all data is used for training, the accuracy decreases to 56.76%. We suspect that this may be due to model's overfitting to the training data.

6 Conclusion

In this paper, we present our system for the DialAM-2024 dialogical argument mining task, focusing on the identification of propositional and illocutionary relations within dialogues. By leveraging the IAT framework, we developed a methodology that integrates human-defined prompts to stimulate PTLMs' reasoning. Our approach features commendable results in the identification of illocutionary relations with concise preprocessing procedures, as evidenced by our high F1 score and precision in Task B. Despite the notable success in Task B, our system encountered challenges in Task A, particularly in achieving consistent recall rates. This indicates that additional context beyond adjacent propositions and locutions may be necessary for enhancing the identification of argumentative relations. Our findings contribute valuable insights into the application of PTLMs in dialogical argument mining. The results underscore the importance of designing effective prompts and highlight the need for ongoing methodological advancements to fully harness the capabilities of PTLMs in complex argumentation analysis tasks.

Ethics Consideration

The authors believe that this paper does not yield additional ethics concerns. All models and datasets accessed are freely accessible for research purposes.

References

Teresa Alsinet, Josep Argelich, Ramón Béjar, Daniel Gibert, and Jordi Planes. 2022. Argumentation reasoning with graph isomorphism networks for reddit conversation analysis. *Int. J. Comput. Intell. Syst.*, 15(1):86.

S. S. Arumugam. 2022. Development of argument based opinion mining model with sentimental data analysis from twitter content. *Concurr. Comput. Pract. Exp.*, 34(15).

Maciej Besta, Florim Memedi, Zhenyu Zhang, Robert Gerstenberger, Nils Blach, Piotr Nyczyk, Marcin Copik, Grzegorz Kwasniewski, Jürgen Müller, Lukas Gianinazzi, Ales Kubicek, Hubert Niewiadomski, Onur Mutlu, and Torsten Hoefler. 2024. Topologies of reasoning: Demystifying chains, trees, and graphs of thoughts. *CoRR*, abs/2401.14295.

Tom Brown, Benjamin F Mann, Nick Ryder, Melanie Subbiah, Jared Kaplan, Prafulla Dhariwal, Arvind Neelakantan, Pranav Shyam, Girish Sastry, Amanda Askell, Sandhini Agarwal, Ariel Herbert-Voss, Gretchen Krueger, Thomas Henighan, Rewon Child, Aditya Ramesh, Daniel M Ziegler, Jeffrey C.S. Wu, Clemens Winter, Christopher Hesse, Mark I-Cheng Chen, Eric J Sigler, Mateusz Litwin, Scott Gray, Benjamin Chess, Jack A Clark, Christopher Berner, Samuel McCandlish, Alec Radford, Ilya Sutskever, and Dario Amodei. 2020. Language models are few-shot learners. *arXiv (Cornell University)*.

Kasia Budzynska, Mathilde Janier, Chris Reed, Patrick Saint-Dizier, Manfred Stede, and Olena Yakorska. 2014a. A model for processing illocutionary structures and argumentation in debates.

Katarzyna Budzynska, Mathilde Janier, Juyeon Kang, Chris Reed, Patrick Saint-Dizier, Manfred Stede, and Olena Yaskorska. 2014b. Towards argument mining from dialogue. *HAL (Le Centre pour la Communication Scientifique Directe)*.

Katarzyna Budzynska and Chris Reed. 2011. Speech acts of argumentation: Inference anchors and peripheral cues in dialogue.

Mirelle Bueno, Roberto de Alencar Lotufo, and Rodrigo Nogueira. 2024. Lissard: Long and simple sequential reasoning datasets. *CoRR*, abs/2402.07859.

Chunkit Chan, Jiayang Cheng, Weiqi Wang, Yuxin Jiang, Tianqing Fang, Xin Liu, and Yangqiu Song. 2024. Exploring the potential of chatgpt on sentence level relations: A focus on temporal, causal, and discourse relations. In *Findings of the Association for Computational Linguistics: EACL 2024, St. Julian's, Malta, March 17-22, 2024*, pages 684–721. Association for Computational Linguistics.

Kaiyan Chang, Songcheng Xu, Chenglong Wang, Yingfeng Luo, Tong Xiao, and Jingbo Zhu. 2024. Efficient prompting methods for large language models: A survey. *CoRR*, abs/2404.01077.

Qingxiu Dong, Lei Li, Damai Dai, Ce Zheng, Jingyuan Ma, Rui Li, Heming Xia, Jingjing Xu, Zhiyong Wu, Baobao Chang, Xu Sun, Lei Li, and Zhifang Sui. 2024. A survey on in-context learning.

Subhabrata Dutta, Jeevesh Juneja, Dipankar Das, and Tanmoy Chakraborty. 2022. Can unsupervised knowledge transfer from social discussions help argument mining? In *Proceedings of the 60th Annual Meeting of the Association for Computational Linguistics (Volume 1: Long Papers), ACL 2022, Dublin, Ireland, May 22-27, 2022*, pages 7774–7786. Association for Computational Linguistics.

Marc Feger and Stefan Dietze. 2024. TACO - twitter arguments from conversations. In *Proceedings of the 2024 Joint International Conference on Computational Linguistics, Language Resources and Evaluation, LREC/COLING 2024, 20-25 May, 2024, Torino, Italy*, pages 15522–15529. ELRA and ICCL.

Annette Hautli-Janisz, Zlata Kikteva, Wassiliki Siskou, Kamila Gorska, Ray Becker, and Chris Reed. 2022. Qt30: A corpus of argument and conflict in broadcast debate.

Jeremy Howard and Sebastian Ruder. 2018. Universal language model fine-tuning for text classification. *Proceedings of the 56th Annual Meeting of the Association for Computational Linguistics (Volume 1: Long Papers)*.

Masayuki Kawarada, Tsutomu Hirao, Wataru Uchida, and Masaaki Nagata. 2024. Argument mining as a text-to-text generation task. In *Proceedings of the 18th Conference of the European Chapter of the Association for Computational Linguistics, EACL 2024 - Volume 1: Long Papers, St. Julian's, Malta, March 17-22, 2024*, pages 2002–2014. Association for Computational Linguistics.

Md Yasin Arafat Khondoker and Mohammad Abu Yousuf. 2022. Argument mining on clinical trial abstracts on lung cancer patients. In *TCCE*, pages 49–60.

Viet Dac Lai, Duy Ngoc Pham, Jonathan Steinberg, Jamie Mikeska, and Thien Huu Nguyen. 2024. CAMAL: A novel dataset for multi-label conversational argument move analysis. In *Proceedings of the 2024 Joint International Conference on Computational Linguistics, Language Resources and Evaluation, LREC/COLING 2024, 20-25 May, 2024, Torino, Italy*, pages 2673–2682. ELRA and ICCL.

Zhenzhong Lan, Mingda Chen, Sebastian Goodman, Kevin Gimpel, Piyush Sharma, and Radu Soricut. 2020. Albert: A lite bert for self-supervised learning of language representations. *arXiv:1909.11942 [cs]*.

John Lawrence and Chris Reed. 2019. Argument mining: A survey. *Computational Linguistics*, 45:1–55.

Yun Li, Zhe Liu, Hang Chen, and Lina Yao. 2024. Context-based and diversity-driven specificity in compositional zero-shot learning. *CoRR*, abs/2402.17251.

Yinhan Liu, Myle Ott, Naman Goyal, Jingfei Du, Mandar Joshi, Danqi Chen, Omer Levy, Mike Lewis, Luke Zettlemoyer, and Veselin Stoyanov. 2019. Roberta: A robustly optimized bert pretraining approach.

Rafael Mestre, Razvan Milicin, Stuart Middleton, Matt Ryan, Jiatong Zhu, and Timothy J. Norman. 2021. M-arg: Multimodal argument mining dataset for political debates with audio and transcripts. In *Proceedings of the 8th Workshop on Argument Mining, ArgMining@EMNLP 2021, Punta Cana, Dominican Republic, November 10-11, 2021*, pages 78–88. Association for Computational Linguistics.

OpenAI. 2023. Gpt-3.5 turbo.

Yinbin Peng, Wei Wu, Jiansi Ren, and Xiang Yu. 2024. Novel GCN model using dense connection and attention mechanism for text classification. *Neural Process. Lett.*, 56(2):144.

Shuofei Qiao, Yixin Ou, Ningyu Zhang, Xiang Chen, Yunzhi Yao, Shumin Deng, Chuanqi Tan, Fei Huang, and Huajun Chen. 2023. Reasoning with language model prompting: A survey. In *Proceedings of the 61st Annual Meeting of the Association for Computational Linguistics (Volume 1: Long Papers), ACL 2023, Toronto, Canada, July 9-14, 2023*, pages 5368–5393. Association for Computational Linguistics.

Ramon Ruiz-Dolz, Chr-Jr Chiu, Chung-Chi Chen, Noriko Kando, and Hsin-Hsi Chen. 2024. Learning strategies for robust argument mining: An analysis of variations in language and domain. In *Proceedings of the 2024 Joint International Conference on Computational Linguistics, Language Resources and Evaluation, LREC/COLING 2024, 20-25 May, 2024, Torino, Italy*, pages 10286–10292. ELRA and ICCL.

Ramon Ruiz-Dolz, John Lawrence, Schad Schad, and Chris Reed. 2024. Overview of DialAM-2024: Argument Mining in Natural Language Dialogues. In *Proceedings of the 11th Workshop on Argument Mining*, Thailand.

Florian Ruosch, Cristina Sarasua, and Abraham Bernstein. 2022. BAM: benchmarking argument mining on scientific documents. In *Proceedings of the Workshop on Scientific Document Understanding co-located with 36th AAAI Conference on Artificial Inteligence, SDU@AAAI 2022, Virtual Event, March 1, 2022*, volume 3164 of *CEUR Workshop Proceedings*. CEUR-WS.org.

Muhammad Tawsif Sazid and Robert E. Mercer. 2022. A unified representation and a decoupled deep learning architecture for argumentation mining of students' persuasive essays. In *Proceedings of the 9th Workshop on Argument Mining, ArgMining@COLING 2022, Online and in Gyeongju, Republic of Korea, October 12 - 17, 2022*, pages 74–83. International Conference on Computational Linguistics.

Xiaofei Sun, Xiaoya Li, Jiwei Li, Fei Wu, Shangwei Guo, Tianwei Zhang, and Guoyin Wang. 2023. Text classification via large language models.

Weiqi Wang, Tianqing Fang, Wenxuan Ding, Baixuan Xu, Xin Liu, Yangqiu Song, and Antoine Bosselut. 2023a. CAR: conceptualization-augmented reasoner for zero-shot commonsense question answering. In *Findings of the Association for Computational Linguistics: EMNLP 2023, Singapore, December 6-10, 2023*, pages 13520–13545. Association for Computational Linguistics.

Weiqi Wang, Tianqing Fang, Chunyang Li, Haochen Shi, Wenxuan Ding, Baixuan Xu, Zhaowei Wang, Jiaxin Bai, Xin Liu, Jiayang Cheng, Chunkit Chan, and Yangqiu Song. 2024a. CANDLE: iterative conceptualization and instantiation distillation from large language models for commonsense reasoning. In *Proceedings of the 62nd Annual Meeting of the Association for Computational Linguistics (Volume 1: Long Papers), ACL 2024, Bangkok, Thailand, August 11-16, 2024*. Association for Computational Linguistics.

Weiqi Wang, Tianqing Fang, Haochen Shi, Baixuan Xu, Wenxuan Ding, Liyu Zhang, Wei Fan, Jiaxin Bai, Haoran Li, Xin Liu, et al. 2024b. On the role of entity and event level conceptualization in generalizable reasoning: A survey of tasks, methods, applications, and future directions. *arXiv preprint arXiv:2406.10885*.

Weiqi Wang, Tianqing Fang, Baixuan Xu, Chun Yi Louis Bo, Yangqiu Song, and Lei Chen. 2023b. CAT: A contextualized conceptualization and instantiation framework for commonsense reasoning. In *Proceedings of the 61st Annual Meeting of the Association for Computational Linguistics (Volume 1: Long Papers), ACL 2023, Toronto, Canada, July 9-14, 2023*, pages 13111–13140. Association for Computational Linguistics.

Weiqi Wang and Yangqiu Song. 2024. Mars: Benchmarking the metaphysical reasoning abilities of language models with a multi-task evaluation dataset. *arXiv preprint arXiv:2406.02106*.

Weiqi Wang, Baixuan Xu, Tianqing Fang, Lirong Zhang, and Yangqiu Song. 2023c. Knowcomp at semeval-2023 task 7: Fine-tuning pre-trained language models for clinical trial entailment identification. In *Proceedings of the The 17th International Workshop on Semantic Evaluation, SemEval@ACL 2023, Toronto, Canada, 13-14 July 2023*, pages 1–9. Association for Computational Linguistics.

Jason Zhanshun Wei, Xuezhi Wang, Dale Schuurmans, Maarten Bosma, Ed H Chi, Quoc V Le, and Denny Zhou. 2022. Chain-of-thought prompting elicits reasoning in large language models.

Baixuan Xu, Weiqi Wang, Haochen Shi, Wenxuan Ding, Huihao Jing, Tianqing Fang, Jiaxin Bai, Long Chen, and Yangqiu Song. 2024. Mind: Multimodal shopping intention distillation from large vision-language models for e-commerce purchase understanding.

Xueming Yan, Han Huang, Yaochu Jin, Liang Chen, Zhanning Liang, and Zhifeng Hao. 2024. Neural architecture search via multi-hashing embedding and graph tensor networks for multilingual text classification. *IEEE Trans. Emerg. Top. Comput. Intell.*, 8(1):350–363.

Kaiyi Zhang, Ang Lv, Yuhan Chen, Hansen Ha, Tao Xu, and Rui Yan. 2024. Batch-icl: Effective, efficient, and order-agnostic in-context learning. *CoRR*, abs/2401.06469.

A Inference Anchoring Theory Glossary

Refer to *A Quick Start Guide to Inference Anchoring Theory (IAT)* and *Inference Anchoring Theory* for details.

B Prompt design

P1="Illocutionary relations include 0:Asserting, 1:Pure Questioning, 2:Challenging, 3:Assertive Questioning, 4:Rhetorical Questioning, 5:Agreeing, 6:Default Illocuting, 7:Arguing, 8:Restating, 9:Disagreeing.The illocutionary relation between the two sentences is [mask].".

P2="Illocutionary relations include 0:Default Inference, 1:Default Rephrase, 2:Default Conflict.The illocutionary relation between the two sentences is [mask].".

P3="Illocutionary relations include 0:Asserting, 1:Pure Questioning, 2:Challenging, 3:Assertive Questioning, 4:Rhetorical Questioning", 5:"Agreeing", 6:"Default Illocuting", 7:"Arguing", 8:"Restating", 9:"Disagreeing".The illocutionary relation between the two sentences is [mask].".

C Experiment Setup

We allocated 80% of the data to the training set, while the remaining 20% was assigned to the validation set. Prior to training, the datasets were tokenized and then fed into language models for fine-tuning. The learning rate was set to 2e-5, and the model underwent training for 2 epochs. To update the model's parameters, we employed the AdamW optimizer.

During the evaluation phase, we assessed the model's performance on the validation using accuracy as the metric. This metric takes the model's predictions and the ground-truth label as input and returns the portion of the correct predications. Every epoch, we printed out the achieved accuracy. To ensure optimal model performance, we conducted experiments with various input sizes and epochs, aiming to strike a balance between underfitting and overfitting.

To support our computations, we leveraged a single NVIDIA RTX A6000 card as our computational infrastructure. The best checkpoint, determined by our experiments, was utilized to generate the submitted maps.

KnowComp Pokemon Team at DialAM-2024: A Two-Stage Pipeline for Detecting Relations in Dialogical Argument Mining

Zihao Zheng[1], **Zhaowei Wang**[2], **Qing Zong**[2], **Yangqiu Song**[2],
[1]Harbin Institute of Technology(Shenzhen), Guangdong, China
[2]Department of Computer Science and Engineering, HKUST, Hong Kong SAR, China
{melfeszheng, zongqing0068}@gmail.com, {zwanggy, yqsong}@cse.ust.hk

Abstract

Dialogical Argument Mining (**DialAM**) is an important branch of Argument Mining (**AM**). DialAM-2024 is a shared task focusing on dialogical argument mining, which requires us to identify argumentative relations and illocutionary relations among proposition nodes and locution nodes. To accomplish this, we propose a two-stage pipeline[1], which includes the Two-Step S-Node Prediction Model in Stage 1 and the YA-Node Prediction Model in Stage 2. We also augment the training data in both stages and introduce context in Stage 2. We successfully completed the task and achieved good results. Our team **KnowComp Pokemon** ranked **1*st*** in the ARI Focused score and **4*th*** in the Global Focused score.

1 Introduction

Dialogues contain a wealth of information about arguments and their relationships, but the structure and content of dialogues are casual, which poses challenges for extracting argument structures. To handle it, Budzynska et al. (2014) provides a method for analyzing dialogue and argument structures, as well as the relations between them, using Inference Anchoring Theory (IAT) (Budzynska and Reed, 2011). In dialogues, the content of the discussions serves as locution nodes, while their propositional content serves as proposition nodes. Among these nodes, three types of relation nodes are used for connection: argumentative relations between propositions, illocutionary relations between locutions and propositions, and transitional relations between locutions. This method helps extract argument structures from dialogues, enabling further argument mining and analysis. By employing this approach, Hautli-Janisz et al. (2022) has introduced QT30, an English corpus of meticulously analyzed dialogical argumentation. This corpus encompasses the argumentative structure derived from 30 debates from the BBC television program Question Time.

The DialAM task in ACL2024 (Ruiz-Dolz et al., 2024) is the first shared task focused on dialogical argument mining. It consists of two tasks. The first task is to identify Propositional Relations, aiming to detect argumentative relations between the identified and segmented propositions in the argumentative dialogue. The second task is the Identification of Illocutionary Relations, which aims to detect the illocutionary relations between the locutions uttered in the dialogue and the argumentative propositions associated with them.

To address the two tasks proposed by DialAM-2024, we introduce a two-stage pipeline. Based on initial locutions and propositional contents, we utilize data augmentation by adding data that does not fit any relation in the relation set to increase the gap between data within and outside the relation set. Thus, we can predict the relationships between propositional contents using our proposed two-step S-node prediction model to address the first task. Building upon this, we further tackle the task of identifying illocutionary relations by bringing context to prediction and employing a multi-classification YA-node prediction model. Adopting this method, our team **Pokemon** ranked **1*st*** in the ARI Focused score and **4*th*** in the Global Focused score.

Our paper is structured as follows: Section 2 presents related work on argument mining. Section 3 describes the details of our proposed method, a two-stage pipeline. Section 4 outlines the experiments we conducted, including the models and methods used in each stage, as well as the overall pipeline experiments. Section 5 makes a conclusion and provides further discussion.

[1]Codes are avilable at https://github.com/HKUST-KnowComp/KnowComp-DialAM2024-ACL2024

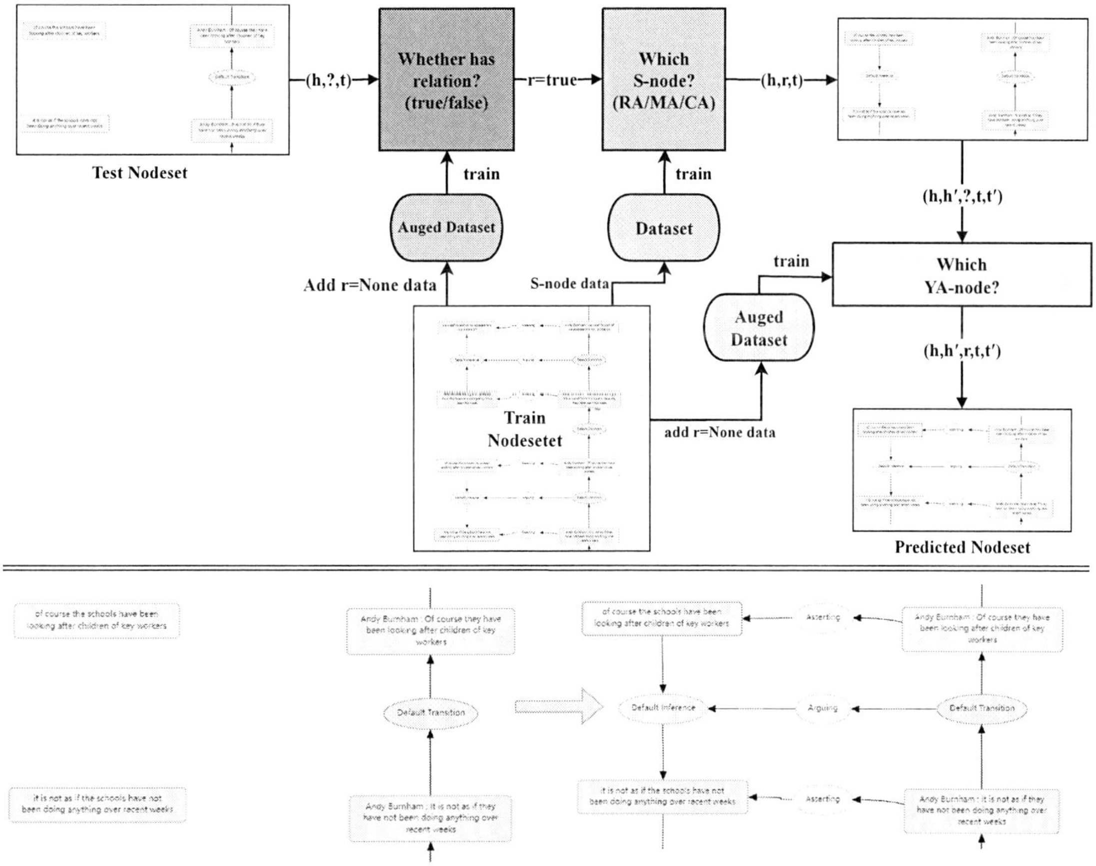

Figure 1: The 2-stage Pipeline.

2 Related Work

Argument Mining: Argument Mining involves the automatic extraction and analysis of arguments from various sources, such as texts, debates, and social media discussions (Stab and Gurevych, 2014; Habernal and Gurevych, 2017; Carlile et al., 2018; Lawrence and Reed, 2019). Some recent works study the stance and persuasiveness of the arguments in multi-modal data like tweets on Twitter (Liu et al., 2022; Zong et al., 2023b). Other works focus on dialogical argumentation, exploring how arguments are put forward, supported, and attacked through dialogue (Haddadan et al., 2019; Visser et al., 2020). QT30 corpus (Hautli-Janisz et al., 2022), which is built on Inference Anchoring Theory (IAT) (Budzynska and Reed, 2011), a prominent framework in manual argument analysis, is the largest dialogical argumentation corpus in English.

3 Method

We have developed a pipeline (Fig. 1) to address the challenge of dialogical argument mining. This pipeline consists of two stages designed to address the task of identifying propositional relations and illocutionary relations, respectively.

3.1 Two-Step S-node Prediction Model

Our primary objective in the first stage is to detect argumentative relations between propositions (I-node). According to QT30 (Hautli-Janisz et al., 2022), This kind of relation (S-node) consists of Inference (RA-node), Rephrase (MA-node), and Conflict (CA-node). However, it is worth noting that not all I-node pairs have relations. Consequently, an initial determination should be made regarding the presence of a relation between two given I-nodes, followed by a secondary prediction of the specific scheme of the relation. This binary step-wise approach forms the foundation of our two-step prediction model.

Inspired by the approach proposed by Parikh et al. (2016), we adopt a similar representation using pairs to denote our problems. Specifically, for any two distinct I-nodes denoted as h and t, wherein h represents the head node and t the tail node, the task is to predict the relation r between h and t given the tuple (h, t) and subsequently deriving the final triple (h, r, t).

The first step of determining relation existence is framed as a binary classification task, given the pair (h, t), with the relation set $R = \{true, false\}$. The principle of cross-entropy loss shapes the loss function of the model.

Similarly, the second step of ascertaining the specific relation between the I-nodes is structured as a ternary classification task, with the relation set $R = \{RA, CA, MA\}$.

3.2 YA-node Prediction Model

The illocutionary relations (YA-node) include (11 distinct types in total): 1) Asserting, Challenging, Pure Questioning, Assertive Questioning, Rhetorical Questioning between I-nodes and L-nodes, 2) Arguing, Disagreeing, Default Illocuting, Restating between TA-nodes and S-nodes, and 3) Agreeing, Challenging, Disagreeing between TA-nodes and I-nodes (Hautli-Janisz et al., 2022). The relationship between L-node and I-node is relatively direct, indicating an illocutionary relation between locutions and their propositional content. However, for the occasion where YA-nodes are connected to TA-nodes or S-nodes, since TA-nodes and S-nodes themselves do not have much meaning when considered alone, we take the context into account, that is, considering two L-nodes connected by TA-nodes and two or more I-nodes connected by S-nodes.

Our task still remains to predict the relation r between the given head node h and tail node t. Additionally, the head and tail nodes may be followed by their respective contexts h' and t'.

This is also a multi-classification task to predict the illocutionary relation r given (h, h', t, t'). The relation set $R = \{r_0, r_1, r_2, ..., r_{11}\}$, where r_0 indicates there's no illocutionary relation between the node pairs. The model's loss function is cross-entropy loss.

3.3 Data Augmentation

While we have discussed the pipeline of our framework in the above two sections (i.e., Section 3.1 and Section 3.2), we also introduced data augmentation techniques to further improve the performance of fine-tuned models in our framework.

Within the training dataset of the first step of the first stage, I-node pairs already connected by S-nodes are categorized as $r = true$. It becomes imperative to introduce $r = false$ data manually. To this end, a set number of I-node pairs without S-node connections are randomly selected to represent the training data for $r = false$. Specifically, in each nodeset within our training set, we randomly select some node pairs from all possible I-node pairs. These selected I-node pairs must satisfy the condition that there is no S-node connecting them. We think that there are no significant argumentative relations between these selected I-node pairs. Meanwhile, the training dataset for the second step is solely comprised of I-node pairs with established S-node connections, but the connections are further categorized into RA, MA, and CA.

In the training set of the YA-node prediction model of the second stage, in addition to the tuples (h, h', r_{1-11}, t, t') that already have YA-node connections as training data, a certain number of tuples (h, h', r_0, t, t') need to be extracted from node pairs that do not have YA node connections, artificially created as training data with $r = r_0$, i.e., $r = None$.

4 Experiments

4.1 Setup

The baseline models we employed include DeBERTa-base (He et al., 2021), DeBERTa-large, DeBERTa-MNLI, RoBERTa-MNLI (Liu et al., 2019). We also tried LLaMa-3-8B (AI@Meta, 2024) with LoRa (Hu et al., 2022).

The learning rate during training is 1e-5, the weight decay is 0.01, and fp16 is enabled during the training process. When utilizing Lora, the parameter r is set to 64, and alpha is set to 16. Due to time constraints, the testing of other LoRa parameters was not completed.

Our dataset comprises a total of 1,478 nodesets. We randomly selected 78 nodesets as the evaluation set, leaving the remaining 1,400 nodesets for the training set. A more detailed data description is in appendix D.

4.2 Experimental Results of S-node Prediction

First, we artificially generated a certain amount of $r = false$ data in this step and evaluated the impact of this additional data volume. Therefore, we performed experiments by controlling the ratio

Model	General Metrics			Focused Metrics		
	precision	recall	f1	precision	recall	f1
RoBERTa-MNLI	0.114	0.369	0.046	0.494	0.533	0.488
DeBERTa-large	0.099	0.376	0.050	0.511	0.548	0.503
LLaMa-3-8B-LoRa	0.100	0.289	0.018	0.261	0.432	0.315
DeBERTa-large	0.351	0.443	0.322	0.351	0.266	0.282
RoBERTa-MNLI	0.317	0.470	0.306	0.449	0.334	0.355

Table 1: Experiments on different methods of the first stage of S-node prediction. The two models in the lower part of the table are the 2nd-step models, while the four models in the upper part are four-label classification models.

Model	General Metrics			Focused Metrics		
	precision	recall	f1	precision	recall	f1
DeBERTa-large	0.746	0.862	0.784	0.757	0.760	0.753
RoBERTa-MNLI	0.650	0.772	0.691	0.834	0.842	0.834
DeBERTa-MNLI	0.627	0.744	0.667	0.823	0.830	0.823

Table 2: Experiments on the second stage of YA-node prediction.

Type	General Metrics			Focused Metrics		
	precision	recall	f1	precision	recall	f1
ARI	0.463	0.324	0.359	0.320	0.466	0.306
ILO	0.542	0.499	0.514	0.564	0.646	0.594

Table 3: The result of our submitted system

of the amount of $r = false$ data to the amount of $r = true$ data to observe the results.

Moreover, we experimented with a four-label direct classification model and compared the results with those of the two-step model we ultimately employed.

The results of the first experiment are shown in the appendix A. Based on the experimental results, the 1:1 data ratio produced the best outcome. We believe that the 1st-step model only needs to determine whether a relationship exists without considering factors such as the distribution of various relationships that the 2nd-step model should concern. Therefore, the 1:1 data ratio makes it easier for the model to distinguish the differences between $r = true$ and $r = false$ data.

The results of the second experiment are shown in Table 1. Our two-step model framework uses the *DeBERTa-base-1* model, which had the best performance in the first experiment, as the 1st-step model. It can be observed that the models trained directly for four-class classification achieve higher focused scores but have very low general scores. On the other hand, our two-step model achieves a significant improvement in general scores at the expense of sacrificing some focused scores. Overall, the two-step method yields better results.

4.3 Experimental Results of Y-node Prediction

We tested the performance of different models in Stage 2. In the experiments of this stage, we trained 12-label classification models. In addition to the training data for the 11 labels extracted from the nodesets, inspired by the experiments in the previous stage, we also included an equal amount of $r = None$ data in training.

The experimental results are shown in Table 2. Most of the models had higher Focused scores than General scores. Among them, DeBERTa-large received the highest General score, whereas RoBERTa-MNLI achieved the highest Focused score.

4.4 Experimental Results of the Pipelines

The composition of the pipeline submitted by us in DialAM-2024 is as follows: DeBERTa-base + RoBERTa-MNLI as the first stage model, and DeBERTa-large as the second stage model. The result is shown in Table 3. Our pipeline achieved first place in the ARI Focused score and fourth place in the Global Focused score.

We also modified the models in stage 1 and stage 2 and tested these different pipelines on the test dataset, which was finally released by DialAM-2024. The results are presented in appendix C, and we found that we have achieved a much higher score, with the ILO-focused scores surpassing 0.87.

5 Conclusion

We propose a two-stage pipeline that predicts argumentative relations and illocutionary relations based on the initial locutions and propositions. This method utilizes data augmentation to optimize the training data and employs a two-step model to predict the relations, incorporating contextual information during prediction. Ultimately, our method achieves good performance in the DialAM24 shared task.

However, due to time constraints and limited computational resources, there are still many aspects of our method that have not been fully optimized. For example, we could appropriately incorporate additional information in locutions to assist the prediction process. It is also worth exploring the possibility of first determining the correspondence between locutions and propositions before predicting the remaining relations. These areas can be further explored and researched.

Limitations

In this paper, we design a pipeline that utilizes knowledge of language models, like T5 and DeBERTa, to solve this argument mining problem. For LLMs, we only tested Llama3 (8B) (AI@Meta, 2024) by fine-tuning a small fraction of parameters. For future works, we can try more LLMs, like Llama2 (Touvron et al., 2023) and Mistral (Jiang et al., 2023) with more sizes (e.g., 13B, 70B). Meanwhile, we can augment our argument-mining pipeline with various external knowledge, including commonsense knowledge (Sap et al., 2019; Do et al., 2024; Deng et al., 2023; Wang et al., 2024a; Wu et al., 2023) event-centric knowledge (Wang et al., 2022, 2023; Fang et al., 2024; Wang et al., 2024c,b; Fan et al., 2023) and factual knowledge (Choi et al., 2023). More importantly, we can also add more modalities like images for relation detection in dialogical argument mining (Zong et al., 2023a; Shen et al., 2024).

Acknowledgement

The authors of this paper were supported by the NSFC Fund (U20B2053) from the NSFC of China, the RIF (R6020-19 and R6021-20), and the GRF (16211520 and 16205322) from RGC of Hong Kong. This paper was also supported by the Tencent AI Lab Rhino-bird Focused Research Program. We also thank the UGC Research Matching Grants (RMGS20EG01-D, RMGS20CR11, RMGS20CR12, RMGS20EG19, RMGS20EG21, RMGS23CR05, RMGS23EG08).

References

AI@Meta. 2024. Llama 3 model card.

Katarzyna Budzynska, Mathilde Janier, Juyeon Kang, Chris Reed, Patrick Saint-Dizier, Manfred Stede, and Olena Yaskorska-Shah. 2014. Towards argument mining from dialogue. *Frontiers in Artificial Intelligence and Applications*, 266:185–196.

Katarzyna Budzynska and Chris Reed. 2011. Speech acts of argumentation: inference anchors and peripheral cues in dialogue. In *Proceedings of the 10th AAAI Conference on Computational Models of Natural Argument*, AAAIWS'11-10, page 3–10. AAAI Press.

Winston Carlile, Nishant Gurrapadi, Zixuan Ke, and Vincent Ng. 2018. Give me more feedback: Annotating argument persuasiveness and related attributes in student essays. In *Proceedings of the 56th Annual Meeting of the Association for Computational Linguistics (Volume 1: Long Papers)*, pages 621–631, Melbourne, Australia. Association for Computational Linguistics.

Sehyun Choi, Tianqing Fang, Zhaowei Wang, and Yangqiu Song. 2023. Kcts: Knowledge-constrained tree search decoding with token-level hallucination detection. In *Proceedings of the 2023 Conference on Empirical Methods in Natural Language Processing*, pages 14035–14053.

Zheye Deng, Weiqi Wang, Zhaowei Wang, Xin Liu, and Yangqiu Song. 2023. Gold: A global and local-aware denoising framework for commonsense knowledge graph noise detection. In *Findings of the Association for Computational Linguistics: EMNLP 2023*, pages 3591–3608.

Quyet V Do, Tianqing Fang, Shizhe Diao, Zhaowei Wang, and Yangqiu Song. 2024. Constraintchecker: A plugin for large language models to reason on commonsense knowledge bases. *arXiv preprint arXiv:2401.14003*.

Wei Fan, Weijia Zhang, Weiqi Wang, Yangqiu Song, and Hao Liu. 2023. Chain-of-choice hierarchical policy learning for conversational recommendation. *arXiv preprint arXiv:2310.17922*.

Tianqing Fang, Zhaowei Wang, Wenxuan Zhou, Hongming Zhang, Yangqiu Song, and Muhao Chen. 2024. Getting sick after seeing a doctor? diagnosing and mitigating knowledge conflicts in event temporal reasoning. In *Findings of the Association for Computational Linguistics: NAACL 2024*, pages 3846–3868.

Ivan Habernal and Iryna Gurevych. 2017. Argumentation mining in user-generated web discourse. *Computational Linguistics*, 43(1):125–179.

Shohreh Haddadan, Elena Cabrio, and Serena Villata. 2019. Yes, we can! mining arguments in 50 years of US presidential campaign debates. In *Proceedings of the 57th Conference of the Association for Computational Linguistics, ACL 2019, Florence, Italy, July 28- August 2, 2019, Volume 1: Long Papers*, pages 4684–4690. Association for Computational Linguistics.

Annette Hautli-Janisz, Zlata Kikteva, Wassiliki Siskou, Kamila Gorska, Ray Becker, and Chris Reed. 2022. QT30: A corpus of argument and conflict in broadcast debate. In *Proceedings of the Thirteenth Language Resources and Evaluation Conference, LREC 2022, Marseille, France, 20-25 June 2022*, pages 3291–3300. European Language Resources Association.

Pengcheng He, Jianfeng Gao, and Weizhu Chen. 2021. Debertav3: Improving deberta using electra-style pretraining with gradient-disentangled embedding sharing. *Preprint*, arXiv:2111.09543.

Edward J Hu, Yelong Shen, Phillip Wallis, Zeyuan Allen-Zhu, Yuanzhi Li, Shean Wang, Lu Wang, and Weizhu Chen. 2022. LoRA: Low-rank adaptation of large language models. In *International Conference on Learning Representations*.

Albert Q Jiang, Alexandre Sablayrolles, Arthur Mensch, Chris Bamford, Devendra Singh Chaplot, Diego de las Casas, Florian Bressand, Gianna Lengyel, Guillaume Lample, Lucile Saulnier, et al. 2023. Mistral 7b. *arXiv preprint arXiv:2310.06825*.

John Lawrence and Chris Reed. 2019. Argument mining: A survey. *Computational Linguistics*, 45(4):765–818.

Yinhan Liu, Myle Ott, Naman Goyal, Jingfei Du, Mandar Joshi, Danqi Chen, Omer Levy, Mike Lewis, Luke Zettlemoyer, and Veselin Stoyanov. 2019. Roberta: A robustly optimized bert pretraining approach. *arXiv preprint arXiv:1907.11692*.

Zhexiong Liu, Meiqi Guo, Yue Dai, and Diane Litman. 2022. ImageArg: A multi-modal tweet dataset for image persuasiveness mining. In *Proceedings of the 9th Workshop on Argument Mining*, pages 1–18, Online and in Gyeongju, Republic of Korea. International Conference on Computational Linguistics.

Ankur Parikh, Oscar Täckström, Dipanjan Das, and Jakob Uszkoreit. 2016. A decomposable attention model for natural language inference. In *Proceedings of the 2016 Conference on Empirical Methods in Natural Language Processing*, pages 2249–2255, Austin, Texas. Association for Computational Linguistics.

Ramon Ruiz-Dolz, John Lawrence, Ella Schad, and Chris Reed. 2024. Overview of DialAM-2024: Argument Mining in Natural Language Dialogues. In *Proceedings of the 11th Workshop on Argument Mining*, Thailand. Association for Computational Linguistics.

Maarten Sap, Ronan Le Bras, Emily Allaway, Chandra Bhagavatula, Nicholas Lourie, Hannah Rashkin, Brendan Roof, Noah A Smith, and Yejin Choi. 2019. Atomic: An atlas of machine commonsense for if-then reasoning. In *Proceedings of the AAAI conference on artificial intelligence*, volume 33, pages 3027–3035.

Xiangqing Shen, Yurun Song, Siwei Wu, and Rui Xia. 2024. Vcd: Knowledge base guided visual commonsense discovery in images. *arXiv preprint arXiv:2402.17213*.

Christian Stab and Iryna Gurevych. 2014. Annotating argument components and relations in persuasive essays. In *Proceedings of COLING 2014, the 25th International Conference on Computational Linguistics: Technical Papers*, pages 1501–1510, Dublin, Ireland. Dublin City University and Association for Computational Linguistics.

Hugo Touvron, Louis Martin, Kevin Stone, Peter Albert, Amjad Almahairi, Yasmine Babaei, Nikolay Bashlykov, Soumya Batra, Prajjwal Bhargava, Shruti Bhosale, Dan Bikel, Lukas Blecher, Cristian Canton Ferrer, Moya Chen, Guillem Cucurull, David Esiobu, Jude Fernandes, Jeremy Fu, Wenyin Fu, Brian Fuller, Cynthia Gao, Vedanuj Goswami, Naman Goyal, Anthony Hartshorn, Saghar Hosseini, Rui Hou, Hakan Inan, Marcin Kardas, Viktor Kerkez, Madian Khabsa, Isabel Kloumann, Artem Korenev, Punit Singh Koura, Marie-Anne Lachaux, Thibaut Lavril, Jenya Lee, Diana Liskovich, Yinghai Lu, Yuning Mao, Xavier Martinet, Todor Mihaylov, Pushkar Mishra, Igor Molybog, Yixin Nie, Andrew Poulton, Jeremy Reizenstein, Rashi Rungta, Kalyan Saladi, Alan Schelten, Ruan Silva, Eric Michael Smith, Ranjan Subramanian, Xiaoqing Ellen Tan, Binh Tang, Ross Taylor, Adina Williams, Jian Xiang Kuan, Puxin Xu, Zheng Yan, Iliyan Zarov, Yuchen Zhang, Angela Fan, Melanie Kambadur, Sharan Narang, Aurelien Rodriguez, Robert Stojnic, Sergey Edunov, and Thomas Scialom. 2023. Llama 2: Open foundation and fine-tuned chat models. *Preprint*, arXiv:2307.09288.

Jacky Visser, Barbara Konat, Rory Duthie, Marcin Koszowy, Katarzyna Budzynska, and Chris Reed. 2020. Argumentation in the 2016 US presidential elections: annotated corpora of television debates and social media reaction. *Lang. Resour. Evaluation*, 54(1):123–154.

Weiqi Wang, Tianqing Fang, Chunyang Li, Haochen Shi, Wenxuan Ding, Baixuan Xu, Zhaowei Wang, Jiaxin Bai, Xin Liu, Jiayang Cheng, et al. 2024a.

Candle: iterative conceptualization and instantiation distillation from large language models for commonsense reasoning. *arXiv preprint arXiv:2401.07286*.

Zhaowei Wang, Quyet V Do, Hongming Zhang, Jiayao Zhang, Weiqi Wang, Tianqing Fang, Yangqiu Song, Ginny Y Wong, and Simon See. 2023. Cola: contextualized commonsense causal reasoning from the causal inference perspective. *arXiv preprint arXiv:2305.05191*.

Zhaowei Wang, Wei Fan, Qing Zong, Hongming Zhang, Sehyun Choi, Tianqing Fang, Xin Liu, Yangqiu Song, Ginny Y Wong, and Simon See. 2024b. Absinstruct: Eliciting abstraction ability from llms through explanation tuning with plausibility estimation. *arXiv preprint arXiv:2402.10646*.

Zhaowei Wang, Haochen Shi, Weiqi Wang, Tianqing Fang, Hongming Zhang, Sehyun Choi, Xin Liu, and Yangqiu Song. 2024c. Abspyramid: Benchmarking the abstraction ability of language models with a unified entailment graph. In *Findings of the Association for Computational Linguistics: NAACL 2024*, pages 3991–4010.

Zhaowei Wang, Hongming Zhang, Tianqing Fang, Yangqiu Song, Ginny Wong, and Simon See. 2022. Subeventwriter: Iterative sub-event sequence generation with coherence controller. In *Proceedings of the 2022 Conference on Empirical Methods in Natural Language Processing*, pages 1590–1604.

Siwei Wu, Xiangqing Shen, and Rui Xia. 2023. Commonsense knowledge graph completion via contrastive pretraining and node clustering. In *Findings of the Association for Computational Linguistics: ACL 2023*, pages 13977–13989.

Qing Zong, Zhaowei Wang, Baixuan Xu, Tianshi Zheng, Haochen Shi, Weiqi Wang, Yangqiu Song, Ginny Wong, and Simon See. 2023a. Tilfa: A unified framework for text, image, and layout fusion in argument mining. In *Proceedings of the 10th Workshop on Argument Mining*, pages 139–147.

Qing Zong, Zhaowei Wang, Baixuan Xu, Tianshi Zheng, Haochen Shi, Weiqi Wang, Yangqiu Song, Ginny Y. Wong, and Simon See. 2023b. TILFA: A unified framework for text, image, and layout fusion in argument mining. In *Proceedings of the 10th Workshop on Argument Mining, ArgMining 2023, Singapore, December 7, 2023*, pages 139–147. Association for Computational Linguistics.

A Experiments on different data ratios

We conducted experiments using DeBERTa models, with the numbers following the model name indicating the data ratio, i.e., the ratio between the amounts of $r = false$ and $r = true$ data. The results are showin in Table 4.

B Full Experiments of Y-node Prediction

The results are showin in Table 5. Except for the *LLaMa-3-8B* model trained with LoRa, which performed significantly worse, the other models achieved high scores. We speculate that *LLaMa-3-8B* model may not be well-suited for this multi-classification task compared to these smaller models specifically designed for this. Most of the models had higher Focused scores than General scores. Among them, DeBERTa-large received the highest General score, whereas RoBERTa-MNLI achieved the highest Focused score.

C Experiments of the pipelines

We modified the model in the second step of stage 1, as well as the model in stage 2, and tested the performance of these different pipelines. The results are shown in the Table 6.

To our surprise, the second pipeline, DeBERTa-base + RoBERTa-MNLI + RoBERTa-MNLI, which performed slightly worse on the evaluation set, obtained the highest score in the test set. Its ILO score was significantly higher than the score of the pipeline we submitted.

We speculate that this might be because our evaluation set consisted of only 78 randomly selected nodesets from the training dataset, which could have significant differences in data distribution and relationship distribution compared to the final test set. As a result, the pipeline that performed best on the validation set may have had poorer performance on the test set, while some pipelines that performed slightly worse on the validation set happened to achieve better scores on the test set.

D Additional Data Description

Our dataset comprises a total of 1,478 nodesets. We randomly selected 78 nodesets as the evaluation set, leaving the remaining 1,400 nodesets for the training set.

The training set contains 5,365 RA data samples, 1,181 CA data samples, 5,596 MA data samples, and 32,626 YA data samples. In the evaluation set, there are 268 RA data samples, 59 CA data samples, 279 MA data samples, and 1,631 YA data samples.

The selected 78 nodesets are: 'nodeset18321', 'nodeset21402', 'nodeset21463', 'nodeset23939', 'nodeset18455', 'nodeset19912', 'nodeset23828', 'nodeset21575', 'nodeset17918', 'nodeset23771', 'nodeset21041', 'nodeset18846', 'nodeset18850', 'nodeset23887', 'nodeset18775', 'nodeset21044', 'nodeset18877', 'nodeset23794', 'nodeset23512', 'nodeset25524', 'nodeset21390', 'nodeset23605', 'nodeset23769', 'nodeset23526', 'nodeset17938', 'nodeset19911', 'nodeset20342', 'nodeset21438', 'nodeset18311', 'nodeset19159', 'nodeset19742', 'nodeset23547', 'nodeset18764', 'nodeset21384', 'nodeset21294', 'nodeset19153', 'nodeset20755', 'nodeset23869', 'nodeset17923', 'nodeset20303', 'nodeset23894', 'nodeset23715', 'nodeset23484', 'nodeset20332', 'nodeset23505', 'nodeset21577', 'nodeset21595', 'nodeset19341', 'nodeset21023', 'nodeset23746', 'nodeset20871', 'nodeset25400', 'nodeset18271', 'nodeset20343', 'nodeset21473', 'nodeset21571', 'nodeset25691', 'nodeset21452', 'nodeset18848', 'nodeset23721', 'nodeset18794', 'nodeset25522', 'nodeset25499', 'nodeset21393', 'nodeset17940', 'nodeset23876', 'nodeset23927', 'nodeset23498', 'nodeset23900', 'nodeset19095', 'nodeset20981', 'nodeset21603', 'nodeset21451', 'nodeset18266', 'nodeset25754', 'nodeset19091', 'nodeset23859', 'nodeset23834'

Model	General Metrics			Focused Metrics		
	precision	**recall**	**f1**	**precision**	**recall**	**f1**
DeBERTa-base-2	0.548	0.674	0.530	0.539	0.324	0.389
DeBERTa-base-1.5	0.550	0.672	0.536	0.506	0.290	0.358
DeBERTa-base-1	0.541	0.671	0.507	0.526	0.332	0.397

Table 4: Experiments on three different data ratios.

Model	General Metrics			Focused Metrics		
	precision	**recall**	**f1**	**precision**	**recall**	**f1**
DeBERTa-large	0.746	0.862	0.784	0.757	0.760	0.753
LLaMa-3-8B-LoRa	0.252	0.213	0.105	0.491	0.517	0.502
XLM-RoBERTa-large	0.557	0.855	0.622	0.799	0.808	0.799
DeBERTa-base	0.549	0.795	0.607	0.791	0.802	0.792
RoBERTa-MNLI	0.650	0.772	0.691	0.834	0.842	0.834
DeBERTa-MNLI	0.627	0.744	0.667	0.823	0.830	0.823

Table 5: Full Experiments on the second stage of YA-node prediction.

Model	Type	General Metrics			Focused Metrics		
		precision	**recall**	**f1**	**precision**	**recall**	**f1**
DeBERTa-base + RoBERTa-MNLI + DeBERTa-large (**submitted**)	ARI	**0.463**	0.324	**0.359**	0.320	**0.466**	**0.306**
	ILO	0.542	0.499	0.514	0.564	0.646	0.594
DeBERTa-base + RoBERTa-MNLI + RoBERTa-MNLI	ARI	0.463	0.324	0.359	0.320	0.466	0.306
	ILO	0.660	**0.796**	**0.705**	**0.873**	**0.902**	**0.883**
DeBERTa-base + DeBERTa-large + DeBERTa-large	ARI	0.366	**0.469**	0.331	**0.393**	0.261	0.285
	ILO	**0.676**	0.763	0.703	0.662	0.648	0.652

Table 6: Experiments of different pipelines.

Pungene at DialAM-2024: Identification of Propositional and Illocutionary Relations

Sirawut Chaixanien*, Eugene Choi*, Shaden Shaar, Claire Cardie,
Cornell University
{sc2343, ec727, ss2753, ctc9}@cornell.edu

Abstract

In this paper we tackle the shared task DialAM-2024 aiming to annotate dialogue based on the inference anchoring theory (IAT). The task can be split into two parts, identification of propositional relations and identification of illocutionary relations. We propose a pipelined system made up of three parts: (1) locutionary–propositions relation detection, (2) propositional relations detection, and (3) illocutionary relations identification. We fine-tune models independently for each step, and combine at the end for the final system. Our proposed system ranks second overall compared to other participants in the shared task, scoring an average f1-score on both sub-parts of 63.7.

1 Introduction

This paper is a system design paper for the DialAM-2024 task. This task involves the creation of dialogue annotations from dialogue text. Specifically, annotations in the format of a graph under the Inference Anchoring Theory (IAT) Framework. The IAT (Ruiz-Dolz et al., 2024) framework allows for dialogue argumentation annotations in a way that retains relevant information and structural data irrespective of domain.

For this task, we are provided with a dataset that contains numerous .json files where each document represents a graph under the IAT framework. The data used is the QT30 corpus (Hautli-Janisz et al., 2022), where dialogue is taken from 30 episodes of the show Question Time.

Our system is a pipeline that splits the tasks into three steps. At the first step we utilize BERTScore to produce similarity scores to find connections. Then, for each step, we fine-tune a BERT model to perform multiclass classification using information gained from previous steps as input. We fine-tune each model separately and combine it into a pipeline at the end where we create a finished graph. With regards to scoring, we were second in the General case, beating third place by 8 points. We also scored third in the Focused setting.

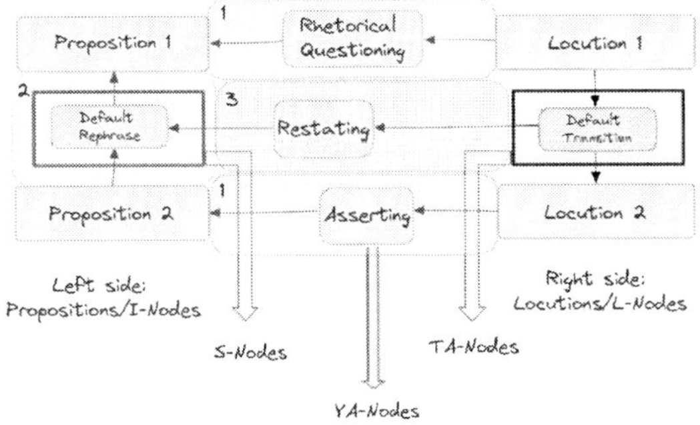

Figure 1: Example final output. The blue nodes on the left are I-nodes (propositions), the blue nodes on the right are L-nodes (locutions), the orange nodes are S-nodes (relations), the yellow nodes are YA-nodes, and the purple nodes are TA-nodes (which depict a transition from one utterance to the next). The ordering of the pipeline mentioned later is also depicted starting with green to yellow then to red as the final step.

2 Related Works and Background

2.1 Task Background

The main goal of this task is to construct a dialogue graph under the IAT format. The input of this task is an unfinished graph that contains L-nodes (Locutions), I-nodes (Propositions), and TA-nodes (Direct Transition). The L-nodes are all connected in the order they were uttered in, with a TA-node between each L-node. On the other hand, the I-nodes are unconnected with anything else.

The expected output is a fully populated graph (see Figure 1) that contains other node types. These include S-nodes which go between I-nodes, YA-nodes which go between an I- and an L-node, or between a TA- and an S-node. Unlike the given input nodes, these also have a type assigned to them.

This task is split into two subtasks. Subtask

Proceedings of the 11th Workshop on Argument Mining, pages 119–123
August 15, 2024 ©2024 Association for Computational Linguistics

A: Identification of Propositional Relations which involves the detecting argumentative relations between I-nodes and Subtask B: Identification of Illocutionary Relations which involves detecting illocutonary relations between I-nodes and L-nodes.

S-nodes can have the type of Default Inference (RA-node), Default Rephrase (MA-node), or Default Conflict (CA-node). YA-nodes can have the type of Asserting, Agreeing, Arguing, Challenging, Disagreeing, Default Illocuting, Pure Questioning, Assertive Questioning, Rhetorical Questioning, Restating, and Analysing.

2.2 Related Works

This is the first year for this shared task thus there are no prior works on it. However, many existing systems can help in finding a solution. One core system that was used in our approach is BERT (Bidirectional Encoder Representations from Transformers) (Devlin et al., 2019). This Large Language Model meets many of our requirements. Firstly, BERT is very adaptable, being able to perform well on a wide variety of tasks with some fine-tuning. Furthermore, it has been pre-trained on a large corpus allowing our approach to be able to handle information from any domain. One such byproduct of this system is BERTScore (Zhang* et al., 2020) which is also used in our approach. It is a text-generation evaluation metric that utilizes BERT's pre-trained contextual embeddings to calculate similarity scores. A similar method is ROUGE (Lin, 2004) which compares the words directly, causing it to be more easily fooled by similar surface forms as compared to BERTScore.

3 Method

To tackle the problem of populating this graph, we decided to isolate each part to create a pipeline. Rather than following the subtasks laid out, we split it into three different steps instead. The first step is to connect the I- and L-nodes and label the YA-nodes that lie between them. Secondly, as we now know the ordering of the I-nodes, we can then label the S-nodes that go between each I-node. Thirdly, we would connect the TA-nodes to the created S-nodes and label the YA-nodes that go between them. This ordering is labeled in Figure 1 as well.

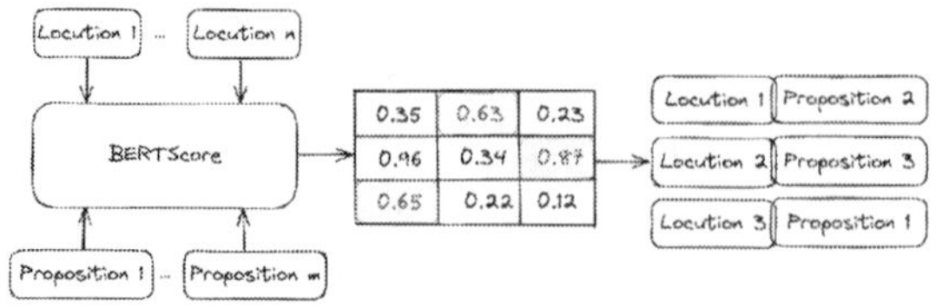

Figure 2: Each combination of locution and proposition is assigned a similarity score. The matching that maximizes the total similarity score with no overlap is chosen as the ideal matching.

3.1 Step 1: I- and L-node Connection and Classification

This step can be further split into 2 subtasks. Namely, the identification of a connection between a locution and a proposition, and the classification of the node type that connects the two.

To tackle the first subtask of identifying the connection to create a pairing, we decided to use different evaluation metrics in order to get a similarity score between propositions and locutions. For each locution, we would compare it to every proposition and select the proposition with the highest similarity score to that locution to be a pair. We calculated accuracy by taking the number of correct pairs over all the pairs in the dataset. We tried 3 different evaluation metrics: ROUGE-1, ROUGE-2, and BERTScore. Here, we found that BERTScore had the highest accuracy (97%) in identifying connections followed by ROUGE-2 (96%) and then ROUGE-1 (94%).

For a more complex approach, we also tried fine-tuning a BERT model to perform inference as to whether a locution and a proposition were connected. The data we used for this was created by going through each document in the dataset extracting each locution and proposition. We traverse through the graph to find every instance of a connection of L-node to YA-node to I-node. For each instance of this, we say that that L-node and that I-node are connected. Next, we generate every possible pair of L-node and I-node. These pairs have a label of 1 if they are connected and 0 otherwise. By doing so, we are able to create a larger dataset through negative sampling.

The results of the fine-tuned BERT not only took more time to infer but also did not perform as well as simply using BERTScore. We believe that this is because a lot of the time the proposition is just a rephrasing of the locution therefore allowing a simple technique to work fine.

As a result, we decided to use BERTScore in our final system (see Figure 2). However, rather than simply sorting by the highest similarity score and picking one by one, we used an algorithm that maximized the total similarity score by checking the total score of every possible pairing.

For the second subtask, we also decided to use a BERT model as they also perform well on classification tasks. We first decided to fine-tune a DistilBERT model (Sanh et al., 2019) to perform multiclass classification to select what type of YA-node would go between the locution and proposition pair. Due to low performance, we tried BERT-base which performed much better.

The data used for this step was just taking each example of a YA-node in between an I- and an L-node. The downside of this straightforward method is that the amount of data was quite small due to the small dataset already being a limiting factor. Furthermore, out of all the labels, "Asserting" was the most common one at 14765 samples while the rest had less than a thousand samples. Because of this class imbalance, we duplicated every other class 10 times.

To finish this step we update the graph with new nodes and edges and pass the updated graph along to the next step.

3.2 Step 2: I-node Connection and Classification

The purpose of this step is connect the I-nodes that follow one another and label the S-node that goes between them. Since all the I-nodes are connected to an L-node, this means that an ordering has already been established. Thus, the only thing we need to do is to decide whether or not two I-nodes have a connecting S-node and what the label of the S-node is. Figure 3 shows what a possible result of step 2 looks like.

This part is quite similar to step 1 where we need to decide whether there is a connection or not and then label what type of connection it is. However, unlike the first step, we already know what the pairing is (namely I-node n and I-node n+1). Therefore, instead of splitting it into two parts like the first step, we decided to do it in one go. We decide to follow a similar method of fine-tuning a BERT model to perform multiclass classification. The model would take in the two I-nodes and have the option of no connection or any one of the possible labels. The four options are: RA (Default Inference), MA (Default Rephrase), CA (Default

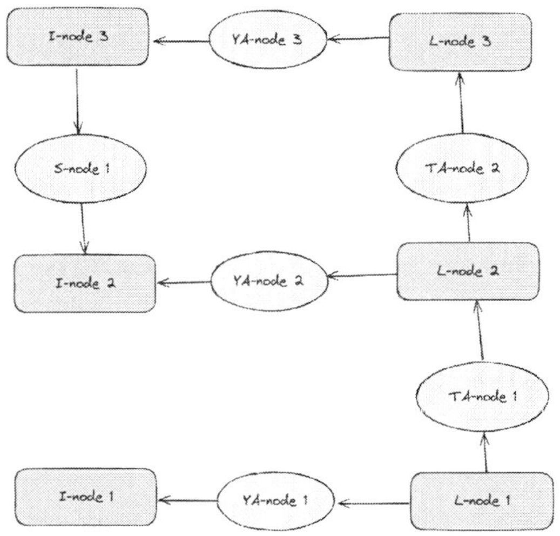

Figure 3: Possible result of the second step. Some I-nodes have an S-node between them and some don't. This image also contains the results from the first step namely the YA-nodes between the connected I- and L-nodes.

Conflict), or no connection.

The input of this model is the pair of I-nodes. We considered using other nearby nodes to provide more information, however, our results show that adding more information does not improve performance. Using only the two I-nodes gives us an F1 score of 52.5 while adding the nearby L- and YA-nodes results in a lowered F1 score of 51.6.

To fine-tune the model, the data we used was all the real connections as well as pairing up non-adjacent I-nodes. These non-adjacent sampels would be used as samples for the option of no connection. From this, RA had 5,566 samples, MA had 4,508 samples, CA had 882 samples, and no connection had 8,186 samples. Due to CA having such a low number up samples, we decided to upsample it by adding copies of the samples into the dataset. We multiplied it by 4 to give CA a total of 3,528 samples.

To finish this step, we update the graph with the new S-nodes and edges and pass the updated graph to the next step along the pipeline.

3.3 Step 3: YA-node between TA- and S-nodes Classification

The main purpose of this step is to label the YA-node that lies between every S- and TA-node in the same rank (For example S-node 1 and TA-node 2 in Figure 3). To do this, we used the same method of fine-tuning a BERT model. We took every instance of YA-nodes between S- and TA-nodes as our data. We also faced a similar problem of class imbalance which we decided to solve by upsampling the classes with fewer samples.

The input into our model was all the surrounding nodes, many of which were created in the previous steps. For example, in Figure 3, figure out the label of the YA-node between S-node 1 and TA-node 2, our inputs would be L-nodes 2 and 3, I-nodes 2 and 3, YA-nodes 2 and 3 and S-node 1. The input would be one long chunk of text that concatenated the texts of the I- and L-nodes and the labels of the YA- and S-nodes represented as an integer. The information from each node would be separated by a [SEP] token. Example input: `there's obviously some schools are going to go back on 1st June [SEP] Fiona Bruce : There's obviously some schools are going to go back on 1st June [SEP] 0 [SEP] some schools are not going to go back on the 1st June [SEP] Fiona Bruce : Some are not [SEP] 0 [SEP] 2.`

4 Experiment Details

4.1 Step 1

For the connection part, we used the Hugging Face implementation of BERTScore and our own algorithm for trying every matching. For the classification model, we used bert-base-cased. We finetuned on a GPU with a batch size of 32 and a learning rate of 5e-5 for 5 epochs.

4.2 Step 2 and 3

For the two classification models for steps 2 and 3, we used the same parameters. They both used bert-large-uncased and were fine-tuned on a CPU with a batch size of 8 and a learning rate of 2e-5 for 3 epochs.

5 Results and Analysis

The main method used to measure the success of our system is by calculating precision, recall, and macro-F1. A score will be calculated for Subtask A (ARI) and Subtask B (ILO) each as well as a global score which is the aggregate of the two. Furthermore, they will be split into two different versions: Focused and General. Focused evaluates the performance looking at only the related classes in the evaluation files only while General also includes the non-related class. This means that a high performance in the General version but low performance in the Focused versions shows a pessimistic approach (overly relies on the non-related class) while the inverse shows an optimistic approach that relates too many propositions and locutions.

Metric	F1
ARI - Focused	20.51
ARI - General	46.22
ILO - Focused	69.95
ILO - General	81.17
GLOBAL - Focused	45.23
GLOBAL - General	63.70

Table 1: F1 Score for each evaluation metric. Both Focused and General ILO are quite high. The Focused ARI has a low score while General ARI has a better score. Overall GLOBAL score, which is the aggregate of the two, is good with the General case performing better.

Another thing to note is that a big downside of our pipelined system is that it is very prone to cascading errors. This is also an additional reason as to why in step 2 we opted to use as few inputs as possible in order to prevent the cascading of errors. The only part which used a lot of the information from the previous steps was step 3. However, the added information allowed the model to get an F1 score of 96.2 which is very strong.

From Table 1 we can see that the main part that performs well is Subtask B (ILO). Both focused and general cases perform quite well indicating a good balance of predictions in every class.

6 Conclusion and Future Work

Overall our system performed quite well, especially on Subtask B which was the identification of illocutionary relations. The recurring technique that we used was fine-tuning a BERT model which proved to be quite effective. A strong point of our system is its ability to get quite similar scores among both General and Focused cases. This is likely due to our upsampling which helped with the largely imbalanced dataset. The one downside in our system seems to be the issue of cascading errors. This is reflected in the scores as we do part of Subtask B first before moving on to Subtask A and the ILO scores are much higher than our ARI scores. Moving forward we will need some way to eliminate the impact of these errors.

References

Jacob Devlin, Ming-Wei Chang, Kenton Lee, and Kristina Toutanova. 2019. BERT: Pre-training of deep bidirectional transformers for language understanding. In *Proceedings of the 2019 Conference of the North American Chapter of the Association for Computational Linguistics: Human Language Technologies, Volume 1 (Long and Short Papers)*, pages 4171–4186, Minneapolis, Minnesota. Association for Computational Linguistics.

Annette Hautli-Janisz, Zlata Kikteva, Wassiliki Siskou, Kamila Gorska, Ray Becker, and Chris Reed. 2022. QT30: A corpus of argument and conflict in broadcast debate. In *Proceedings of the Thirteenth Language Resources and Evaluation Conference*, pages 3291–3300, Marseille, France. European Language Resources Association.

Chin-Yew Lin. 2004. ROUGE: A package for automatic evaluation of summaries. In *Text Summarization Branches Out*, pages 74–81, Barcelona, Spain. Association for Computational Linguistics.

Ramon Ruiz-Dolz, John Lawrence, Ella Schad, and Chris Reed. 2024. Overview of DialAM-2024: Argument Mining in Natural Language Dialogues. In *Proceedings of the 11th Workshop on Argument Mining*, Thailand. Association for Computational Linguistics.

Victor Sanh, Lysandre Debut, Julien Chaumond, and Thomas Wolf. 2019. Distilbert, a distilled version of bert: smaller, faster, cheaper and lighter. *ArXiv*, abs/1910.01108.

Tianyi Zhang*, Varsha Kishore*, Felix Wu*, Kilian Q. Weinberger, and Yoav Artzi. 2020. Bertscore: Evaluating text generation with bert. In *International Conference on Learning Representations*.

Turiya at DialAM-2024: Inference Anchoring Theory Based LLM Parsers

Sougata Saha and Rohini Srihari
State University of New York at Buffalo
Department of Computer Science and Engineering
{sougatas, rohini}@buffalo.edu

Abstract

Representing discourse as argument graphs facilitates robust analysis. Although computational frameworks for constructing graphs from monologues exist, there is a lack of frameworks for parsing dialogue. Inference Anchoring Theory (IAT) is a theoretical framework for extracting graphical argument structures and relationships from dialogues. Here, we introduce computational models for implementing the IAT framework for parsing dialogues. We experiment with a classification-based biaffine parser and Large Language Model (LLM)-based generative methods and compare them. Our results demonstrate the utility of finetuning LLMs for constructing IAT-based argument graphs from dialogues, which is a nuanced task.

1 Introduction

Argumentation is prevalent in our daily verbal communication and represents chains of thought patterns and reasoning, making it an integral mode of persuasion (Saha et al., 2022a). Although argument mining (AM) (Stab and Gurevych, 2014a,b; Persing and Ng, 2016; Stab and Gurevych, 2017; Nguyen and Litman, 2018; Eger et al., 2017; Mirko et al., 2020; Morio et al., 2020; Lawrence and Reed, 2020; Ye and Teufel, 2021; Bao et al., 2021; Saha et al., 2022a) from monologues is well studied, formal models for parsing dialogues are lacking (Saha et al., 2022b). DialAM-2024 (Ruiz-Dolz et al., 2024) introduced the first shared task in dialogue argument mining, where argumentation and dialogue information are modeled jointly in the domain-independent IAT framework (Budzynska et al., 2014, 2016; Janier et al., 2014). The framework represents dialogues as a graph where the nodes comprise (i) Locutions (*L-nodes*)-the Argumentative Discourse Units (ADUs) from each speaker turn. (ii) Propositions (*I-nodes*)-reconstructed *L-nodes* with resolved anaphora, pronouns, and deixis, making them independently coherent. The edges comprise (i) Default Transitions (*TAs*) between *L-nodes*. (ii) *S-nodes* that connect propositions (*I-nodes*) and can be of types RA (default inference), MA (default rephrase), or CA (default conflict). (iii) *YA-nodes* that connect *L-nodes* with *I-nodes*, *TAs* with *S-nodes*, or *TAs* with *I-nodes*.

Here, we compare generative approaches against classification-based approaches for implementing the IAT framework. Since LLMs (Chang et al., 2023; Min et al., 2023; Hadi et al., 2023) attain superior results on several tasks, we test their utility in dialogical argument mining and compare them against a biaffine-parsing-based implementation (Dozat and Manning, 2016, 2018). We ask the following research questions: **(i) Can LLMs be used for parsing dialogues in the IAT framework?** We experiment with Mistral-7B-Instruct-v0.2 (Jiang et al., 2023) and present dialAM as a generative task where the *L-nodes*, *I-nodes*, and *TA-nodes* are the context of the LLM, and the task comprises determining the propositional (Task A) and illocutionary (Task B) relations. **(ii) How do LLMs compare against simpler classification-based dialogue parsers?** We compare the LLM parser against a biaffine-parsing-based parser that predicts the relationship and type between nodes.

2 Proposed Method

2.1 Classification-Based Model

As illustrated in Figure 1, the classifier is Roberta-based (Liu et al., 2019) and contains two biaffine layers, each comprising two biaffine heads, which predict the relationships and their types. Biaffine classifiers (Dozat and Manning, 2016, 2018) are generalizations of linear classifiers, which include multiplicative interactions between two vectors. The first biaffine layer determines the *S-nodes* and labels the relationships between *L - I-nodes* and *TA - I-nodes*. The second layer determines and labels relationships between the *TA* and *S-nodes*.

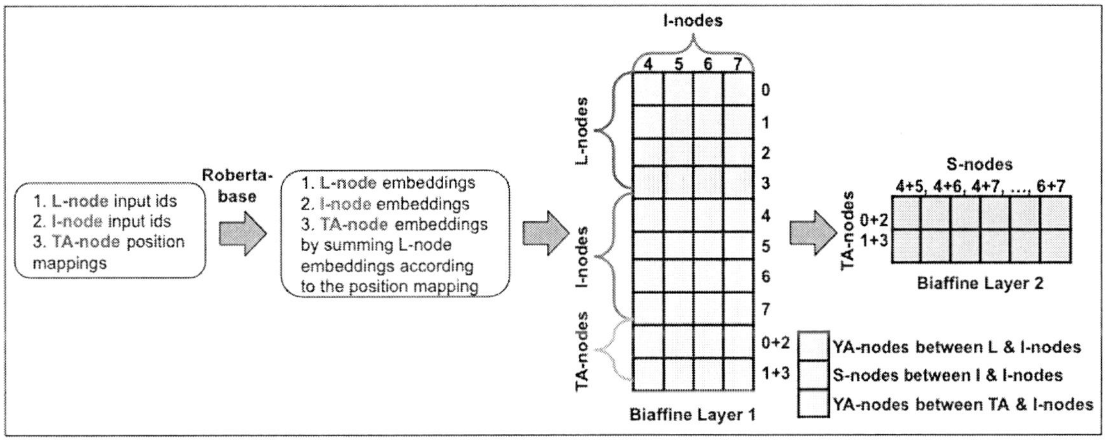

Figure 1: Architecture of the Roberta-based biaffine classifier.

The model inputs the *L*, *I-node* input ids, and the *TA-node* position mappings- A set of pairs of *L-node* indexes that form a *TA-node*. First, the parser independently encodes all *L* and *I-nodes* and then performs multi-headed attention between the embeddings (sum-pooled representation of the transformer last layer). The *TA-node* position mappings are sum-pooled to yield the *TA-node* embeddings. Then, the *L*, *I*, and *TA-node* embeddings are passed through a single-layer feed-forward neural network (FF) to generate the source representation of the biaffine heads of the first biaffine layer. The FF layer reduces the input representation from 768 dimensions to 600. Another single-layered FF computes a 600-dimensional representation of the *I-node* embeddings, and are the targets of the biaffine heads.

Since *S-node* prediction is a pre-requisite for determining relationships between the TA and *S-nodes*, two subsequent biaffine heads determine and label their relationship. We generate pairs of all possible *I-nodes*, sum-pool their embeddings, and weigh them by the predicted logits from the *S-node* relationship biaffine head. A single-layered FF computes the final 600-dimensional representation, which is the target of the biaffine heads. The source of the biaffine heads is the prior computed 600-dimensional representation of the *TA-nodes*. During inference, we only consider relationship labels with a predicted probability > 0.1 and persist the highest scored relationships such that a node is referenced only once.

2.2 Generative Model

To determine the utility of using LLMs for argument mining, we experiment with Mistral-7B-Instruct-v0.2 (Jiang et al., 2023) using two types of instructions. We pose the problem as a generation task where the model is presented with a description of the IAT annotation framework, the *L*, *I*, and *TA-nodes* and tasked to identify the *S* and *YA-nodes* sequentially. The ordering of the *L* and *I-nodes* are randomized to prevent the model from learning spurious ordering-based associations. Figures 2 and 3 illustrate Type 1 and 2 instructions with the model-generated responses. Compared to Type 1, the Type 2 instructions explicitly include all the relation labels in the response text.

2.3 Training Details

The dataset comprised 1,477 IAT annotated conversations from the QT30 corpus (Hautli-Janisz et al., 2022). We preprocess the corpus and preserve relations that strictly adhere to the IAT relationship definitions and discard others. Although training on the reduced examples might hamper performance, it eases answering the research questions- our primary objective. We randomly split the dataset into 1,327 training and 150 testing examples for our experiments. The classification-based model used Roberta-base as the base model and was trained for 15 epochs, processing 32 batches at a time, using a 5e-5 learning rate, and accumulating gradients for 16 steps. The LLM-based models were trained for two epochs using LoRA (Hu et al., 2021), a parameter-efficient fine-tuning method (Mangrulkar et al., 2022). The LoRA r and alpha were set to 16 and 32 and trained the q, v, k, o, gate, up, and down projection modules of the attention heads and the LM head using a 2.5e-5 learning rate. We use greedy decoding during inference and limit the number of new tokens to 1,000.

While evaluating the results of Type 1 and 2 in-

[INST] Below are the definitions and rules of annotating a conversation in Inference Anchoring Theory:
1. Locution nodes (L-node) denotes a speaker's turn as 'L-node id| first name last name: speech content'.
2. Proposition nodes (I-node) are reconstructed L-nodes with resolved linguistic features like anaphora, pronouns, and deixis. It is denoted as 'I-node id| proposition'.
3. LL-edges connect the L-nodes. It is denoted by 'LL-edge id: source L-node id, LL-edge label, destination L-node id'.
4. II-edges connect the I-nodes and can be either of Conflict, Inference, or Rephrase. It is denoted by 'II-edge id: source I-node id, II-edge label, destination I-node id'
5. LI-edges connect the L-nodes to the I-nodes and can be either of Asserting, Challenging, Pure Questioning, Assertive Questioning, or Rhetorical Questioning. It is denoted by 'LI-edge id: source L-node id, LI-edge label, destination I-node id'.
6. LLII-edges connect the LL-edges to the II-edges and can be either of Arguing, Disagreeing, Illocuting, or Restating. It is denoted by 'LLII-edge id: source LL-edge id, LLII-edge label, destination II-edge id'.
7. LLI-edges connect the LL-edges to the I-nodes and can be either of Agreeing, Challenging, or Disagreeing. It is denoted by 'LLI-edge id: source LL-edge id, LLI-edge label, destination I-node id'.

Task: Given the below set of L-nodes, I-nodes, and LL-edges, identify the II-edges, LI-edges, LLII-edges, and LLI-edges sequentially.
L-nodes:
571035| Steve Parish : when we look back on this, 10,000 deaths is too many
...
571061| Steve Parish : it is going to be extremely difficult

I-nodes:
571100| surely Apple and Google could come together for once
...
571078| we really could be in a terrible situation in the next two or three months

LL-edges:
571033: 571024, Transition, 571028
...
571115: 571102, Transition, 571106
[/INST]

Response:
II-edges:
II-1: 571030, Rephrase, 571026
...
II-8: 571108, Inference, 571104

LI-edges:
LI-1: 571024, Asserting, 571026
...
LI-15: 571106, Asserting, 571108

LLII-edges:
LLII-1: 571046, Restating, II-1
...
LLII-8: 571110, Arguing, II-8

LLI-edges:

Figure 2: Mistral Type 1 instruction with generated response.

structions, we observed that the model often leads to incomplete annotations. For example, for the Type 1 instructions, the model stops generating past the *S-nodes*. Similarly, for the Type 2 instructions, the model frequently does not generate all the distinct types of *YA-nodes*. Hence, we implement an iterative decoding approach by re-prompting the model with partially generated annotations until it predicts all relationship types. For the Type 1 instructions, we first pass the IAT definitions and task details (left side of Figure 2) as prompt and generate the *S-nodes* (II-nodes in Figure 2). We iteratively append the generated output (highlighted in purple) to the prompt and re-prompt the model to generate the *YA-nodes* (LI-edges in Figure 2). We follow this approach until the model identifies all types of relationships (LLII and LLI-edges in Figure 2). We follow a similar approach for Type 2 instructions by re-prompting the model incrementally with the highlighted sections in Figure 3.

2.4 Results and Observations

Although our iterative decoding approach for the generative models facilitates better annotations, they are computationally expensive. Compared to regular decoding, they are approximately 4x more expensive for the Type 1 instructions and approximately 4-15x costlier for the Type 2 instructions. Hence, we internally compare the three model variants on a random sample of 10 examples from the test set and share the results in Table 1. We use the original task evaluation script, which computes **Pr**ecision, **Re**call, and **F1** scores at *Focused* and *General* levels. *Focused* evaluates the performance of the systems by looking at the related propositions/locutions in the evaluation files only, excluding all the non-related cases. *General* looks at the whole map, including the non-related class. High performance in *General* but low in *Focused* represents over-reliability on the non-related nodes, and vice-versa for *Focused*.

		General			Focused		
Id	Model	Pr	Re	F1	Pr	Re	F1
1	Biaff	68.7	68.6	68.6	60.0	36.1	41.0
2	LLM (Type-1)	**82.4**	85.5	**83.8**	59.0	55.8	57.3
3	LLM (Type-2)	81.7	73.4	75.5	49.5	37.0	40.4
4	Biaff + LLM (Type-1)	75.2	**89.3**	80.1	**68.9**	**67.1**	**67.9**
5	Biaff + LLM (Type-2)	69.4	80.1	73.1	61.2	54.7	56.1
6	LLM (Type-1 + Type-2)	77.6	80.4	78.7	60.5	56.6	58.1
7	Biaff + LLM (Type-1 + Type-2)	68.8	83.2	73.6	67.1	65.0	65.4

Table 1: Model performance on internal test set.

We also ensemble the three model variants and report results in Table 1 (lower half). We observe the following: (i) For all model variants, the F1 scores at *General* level are higher than *Focused*,

```
[INST] Below are the definitions and rules of annotating a conversation in Inference Anchoring Theory:
1. L-nodes denotes a speaker's turn.
2. I-nodes are reconstructed L-nodes with resolved linguistic features like anaphora, pronouns, and deixis.
3. LL-edges connect the L-nodes.
4. II-edges connect the I-nodes.
5. LI-edges connect the L-nodes to the I-nodes.
6. LL-II-edges connect the LL-edges to the II-edges.
7. LL-I-edges connect the LL-edges to the I-nodes.

### Task: Given the below set of L-nodes, I-nodes, and LL-edges, identify the types of II-edges, LI-edges,
LL-II-edges, and LL-I-edges sequentially.
L-nodes:
571035| Steve Parish : when we look back on this, 10,000 deaths is too many
...
571061| Steve Parish : it is going to be extremely difficult

I-nodes:
571100| surely Apple and Google could come together for once
...
571078| we really could be in a terrible situation in the next two or three months

LL-edges:
571033: 571024, Transition, 571028
...
571115: 571102, Transition, 571106
[/INST]
```

```
### Response:
# II-edges:

Conflict:
Inference:
II-1: 571045, 571030
...
Rephrase:
II-6: 571063, 571056

# LI-edges:
Asserting:
LI-1: 571024, 571026
...
Challenging:
Pure Questioning:
Assertive Questioning:
Rhetorical Questioning:

# LL-II-edges:
Arguing:
LL-II-1: 571046, II-1
...
Disagreeing:
Illocuting:
Restating:
LL-II-6: 571066, II-6

# LL-I-edges:
Agreeing:
Challenging:
Disagreeing:
```

Figure 3: Mistral Type 2 instruction with generated response.

denoting that the models does not relate all propositions/locutions. This is expected as the models are trained on reduced relations (discussed in Section 2.3). (ii) Comparing the F1 score, the LLMs outperforms the biaffine classifier at both levels. Furthermore, the LLM trained on the Type 1 instruction outperforms the Type 2 instruction-trained model at both levels of evaluation. (iii) Ensembling the biaffine and Type 1 instruction-based LLM yields the best Precision, Recall, and F1 scores when evaluated at the *Focused* level. An ensemble comprising all three models performs the second best.

		General			Focused		
Task	Model	Pr	Re	F1	Pr	Re	F1
Task A	Majority-BL	28.8	30.3	29.5	0.0	0.0	0.0
	RoBERTa-BL	28.6	**34.7**	26.5	**37.1**	**18.4**	**22.8**
	Ours	**30.8**	31.5	**30.8**	19.0	4.2	6.7
Task B	Majority-BL	34.7	35.9	35.3	0.0	0.0	0.0
	RoBERTa-BL	39.1	**62.1**	45.8	**73.1**	**72.6**	**72.1**
	Ours	**51.4**	57.1	**53.3**	43.8	26.1	30.4
Global	Majority-BL	31.8	33.1	32.4	0.0	0.0	0.0
	RoBERTa-BL	33.9	**48.4**	36.1	**55.1**	**45.5**	**47.5**
	Ours	**41.1**	44.3	**42.0**	31.4	15.2	18.5

Table 2: Model performance on official test set.

Following our internal results, we use the ensembled biaffine and Type 1 instruction-based LLM-*Biaff + LLM (Type 1)* to parse the official test set samples and share our official test set results in Table 2. The table compares our implementation against majority-based and Roberta-based baselines for tasks A and B. It also shares global-level evaluations by looking at the complete argument maps. We observe the following: (i) Across all tasks, our implementation attains the best F1 score at the *General* level, whereas the Roberta baseline attains the best score at the *Focused* level. This observation is warranted as the *Focused* evaluates only the types of relationships prevalent in the dialogue and ignores all other classes. Our iterative decoding approach explicitly prompts the LLM to generate annotations for all relationship types, which can lead to spurious predictions by promoting recall. (ii) Similar to the baseline, our model performs Task B better than Task A.

3 Conclusion

Here, we computationally implement the theoretical IAT framework using classification and LLM-based models. We question the viability of leveraging LLMs, which are generative models, for such a nuanced task and compare them against simpler classifiers (non-generative) such as biaffine parsers. Our results indicate that posing the graph construction problem as a generative task and finetuning LLMs outperforms biaffine classifiers. Furthermore, ensembling the generative and classification-based approaches yields the best results.

References

Jianzhu Bao, Chuang Fan, Jipeng Wu, Yixue Dang, Jiachen Du, and Ruifeng Xu. 2021. A neural transition-based model for argumentation mining. In *Proceedings of the 59th Annual Meeting of the Association for Computational Linguistics and the 11th International Joint Conference on Natural Language Processing (Volume 1: Long Papers)*, pages 6354–6364, Online. Association for Computational Linguistics.

Katarzyna Budzynska, Mathilde Janier, Juyeon Kang, Chris Reed, Patrick Saint-Dizier, Manfred Stede, and Olena Yaskorska. 2014. Towards argument mining from dialogue. In *Computational Models of Argument*, pages 185–196. IOS Press.

Katarzyna Budzynska, Mathilde Janier, Chris Reed, and Patrick Saint-Dizier. 2016. Theoretical foundations for illocutionary structure parsing. *Argument & Computation*, 7(1):91–108.

Yupeng Chang, Xu Wang, Jindong Wang, Yuan Wu, Linyi Yang, Kaijie Zhu, Hao Chen, Xiaoyuan Yi, Cunxiang Wang, Yidong Wang, et al. 2023. A survey on evaluation of large language models. *ACM Transactions on Intelligent Systems and Technology*.

Timothy Dozat and Christopher D. Manning. 2016. Deep biaffine attention for neural dependency parsing. *Preprint*, arXiv:1611.01734.

Timothy Dozat and Christopher D. Manning. 2018. Simpler but more accurate semantic dependency parsing. In *Proceedings of the 56th Annual Meeting of the Association for Computational Linguistics (Volume 2: Short Papers)*, pages 484–490, Melbourne, Australia. Association for Computational Linguistics.

Steffen Eger, Johannes Daxenberger, and Iryna Gurevych. 2017. Neural end-to-end learning for computational argumentation mining. In *Proceedings of the 55th Annual Meeting of the Association for Computational Linguistics (Volume 1: Long Papers)*, pages 11–22, Vancouver, Canada. Association for Computational Linguistics.

Muhammad Usman Hadi, Rizwan Qureshi, Abbas Shah, Muhammad Irfan, Anas Zafar, Muhammad Bilal Shaikh, Naveed Akhtar, Jia Wu, Seyedali Mirjalili, et al. 2023. A survey on large language models: Applications, challenges, limitations, and practical usage. *Authorea Preprints*.

Annette Hautli-Janisz, Zlata Kikteva, Wassiliki Siskou, Kamila Gorska, Ray Becker, and Chris Reed. 2022. Qt30: A corpus of argument and conflict in broadcast debate. In *Proceedings of the 13th Language Resources and Evaluation Conference*, pages 3291–3300. European Language Resources Association (ELRA).

Edward J Hu, Yelong Shen, Phillip Wallis, Zeyuan Allen-Zhu, Yuanzhi Li, Shean Wang, Lu Wang, and Weizhu Chen. 2021. Lora: Low-rank adaptation of large language models. *arXiv preprint arXiv:2106.09685*.

Mathilde Janier, John Lawrence, and Chris Reed. 2014. Ova+: An argument analysis interface. *Frontiers in Artificial Intelligence and Applications*, 266:463–464.

Albert Q. Jiang, Alexandre Sablayrolles, Arthur Mensch, Chris Bamford, Devendra Singh Chaplot, Diego de las Casas, Florian Bressand, Gianna Lengyel, Guillaume Lample, Lucile Saulnier, Lélio Renard Lavaud, Marie-Anne Lachaux, Pierre Stock, Teven Le Scao, Thibaut Lavril, Thomas Wang, Timothée Lacroix, and William El Sayed. 2023. Mistral 7b. *Preprint*, arXiv:2310.06825.

John Lawrence and Chris Reed. 2020. Argument mining: A survey. *Computational Linguistics*, 45(4):765–818.

Yinhan Liu, Myle Ott, Naman Goyal, Jingfei Du, Mandar Joshi, Danqi Chen, Omer Levy, Mike Lewis, Luke Zettlemoyer, and Veselin Stoyanov. 2019. Roberta: A robustly optimized bert pretraining approach. *arXiv preprint arXiv:1907.11692*.

Sourab Mangrulkar, Sylvain Gugger, Lysandre Debut, Younes Belkada, Sayak Paul, and Benjamin Bossan. 2022. Peft: State-of-the-art parameter-efficient fine-tuning methods. `https://github.com/huggingface/peft`.

Bonan Min, Hayley Ross, Elior Sulem, Amir Pouran Ben Veyseh, Thien Huu Nguyen, Oscar Sainz, Eneko Agirre, Ilana Heintz, and Dan Roth. 2023. Recent advances in natural language processing via large pre-trained language models: A survey. *ACM Computing Surveys*, 56(2):1–40.

LENZ Mirko, Premtim Sahitaj, Sean Kallenberg, Christopher Coors, Lorik Dumani, Ralf Schenkel, and Ralph Bergmann. 2020. Towards an argument mining pipeline transforming texts to argument graphs. *Computational Models of Argument: Proceedings of COMMA 2020*, 326:263.

Gaku Morio, Hiroaki Ozaki, Terufumi Morishita, Yuta Koreeda, and Kohsuke Yanai. 2020. Towards better non-tree argument mining: Proposition-level biaffine parsing with task-specific parameterization. In *Proceedings of the 58th Annual Meeting of the Association for Computational Linguistics*, pages 3259–3266, Online. Association for Computational Linguistics.

Huy V. Nguyen and Diane J. Litman. 2018. Argument mining for improving the automated scoring of persuasive essays. In *AAAI*.

Isaac Persing and Vincent Ng. 2016. End-to-end argumentation mining in student essays. In *Proceedings of the 2016 Conference of the North American Chapter of the Association for Computational Linguistics: Human Language Technologies*, pages 1384–1394, San Diego, California. Association for Computational Linguistics.

Ramon Ruiz-Dolz, John Lawrence, Ella Schad, and Chris Reed. 2024. Overview of DialAM-2024: Argument Mining in Natural Language Dialogues. In *Proceedings of the 11th Workshop on Argument Mining*, Thailand. Association for Computational Linguistics.

Sougata Saha, Souvik Das, and Rohini Srihari. 2022a. EDU-AP: Elementary discourse unit based argument parser. In *Proceedings of the 23rd Annual Meeting of the Special Interest Group on Discourse and Dialogue*, pages 183–192, Edinburgh, UK. Association for Computational Linguistics.

Sougata Saha, Souvik Das, and Rohini K. Srihari. 2022b. Dialo-AP: A dependency parsing based argument parser for dialogues. In *Proceedings of the 29th International Conference on Computational Linguistics*, pages 887–901, Gyeongju, Republic of Korea. International Committee on Computational Linguistics.

Christian Stab and Iryna Gurevych. 2014a. Annotating argument components and relations in persuasive essays. In *Proceedings of COLING 2014, the 25th International Conference on Computational Linguistics: Technical Papers*, pages 1501–1510, Dublin, Ireland. Dublin City University and Association for Computational Linguistics.

Christian Stab and Iryna Gurevych. 2014b. Identifying argumentative discourse structures in persuasive essays. In *Proceedings of the 2014 Conference on Empirical Methods in Natural Language Processing (EMNLP)*, pages 46–56.

Christian Stab and Iryna Gurevych. 2017. Parsing argumentation structures in persuasive essays. *Computational Linguistics*, 43(3):619–659.

Yuxiao Ye and Simone Teufel. 2021. End-to-end argument mining as biaffine dependency parsing. In *Proceedings of the 16th Conference of the European Chapter of the Association for Computational Linguistics: Main Volume*, pages 669–678, Online. Association for Computational Linguistics.

Overview of PerpectiveArg2024
The First Shared Task on Perspective Argument Retrieval

Neele Falk[*1], **Andreas Waldis** [*2,3], **Iryna Gurevych**[2]
[1]Institute for Natural Language Processing, University of Stuttgart, Germany
[2]Ubiquitous Knowledge Processing Lab (UKP Lab)
Department of Computer Science and Hessian Center for AI (hessian.AI)
Technical University of Darmstadt
[3]Information Systems Research Lab, Lucerne University of Applied Sciences and Arts
www.ukp.tu-darmstadt.de www.hslu.ch

Abstract

Argument retrieval is the task of finding relevant arguments for a given query. While existing approaches rely solely on the semantic alignment of queries and arguments, this first shared task on perspective argument retrieval incorporates perspectives during retrieval, accounting for latent influences in argumentation. We present a novel multilingual dataset covering demographic and socio-cultural (*socio*) variables, such as age, gender, and political attitude, representing minority and majority groups in society. We distinguish between three scenarios to explore how retrieval systems consider explicitly (in both query and corpus) and implicitly (only in query) formulated perspectives. This paper provides an overview of this shared task and summarizes the results of the six submitted systems. We find substantial challenges in incorporating perspectivism, especially when aiming for personalization based solely on the text of arguments without explicitly providing *socio* profiles. Moreover, retrieval systems tend to be biased towards the majority group but partially mitigate bias for the female gender. While we bootstrap perspective argument retrieval, further research is essential to optimize retrieval systems to facilitate personalization and reduce polarization.[1]

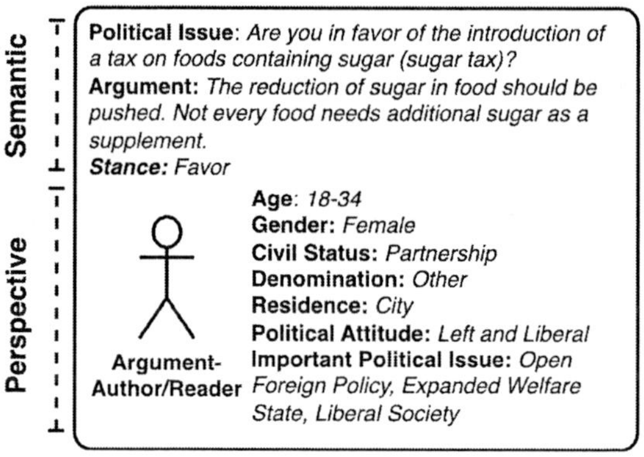

Figure 1: This example entry shows which information we consider for this shared task. First, we incorporate the *semantic* information as the text of queries and arguments. Secondly, we use the demographic and socio-cultural properties (*perspective*) of argument authors or users, including *age*, *gender*, or *political attitude*.

1 Introduction

In argument retrieval, the objective is to extract arguments that match a given query, such as a question or topic. Existing research defines the relevance and ordering of candidate arguments differently. In the simplest case, arguments are extracted based on the semantic relevance of the query. More sophisticated methods consider the quality of the arguments, suitable counterarguments (Wachsmuth et al., 2018), or arguments that answer comparative questions (Bondarenko et al., 2022). However, incorporating individual perspectives (Cabitza et al., 2023) is crucially understudied.

Addressing this research gap, we introduce the *Shared Task on Perspective Argument Retrieval* (§ 2). Incorporating the *perspective* of authors and readers (Figure 1), we aim to foster **personalization** by retrieving arguments that match individual perspectives beyond their *semantic* alignment and **reduce polarization** by enabling individuals to compare and contrast arguments from their own and other perspectives. Therefore, we present a novel multi-lingual dataset (§ 3) providing demographic and socio-cultural (*socio*) profiles of argument authors or readers for German, French, and Italian. In this context, relevant arguments are semantically aligned with a given query and match the specific *socio* variables provided in the query. We use three scenarios (Figure 2) to disentangle the effect of *perspectivism*:

- **No Perspectivism**: The vanilla argument retrieval scenario as a reference.

[*]* Equal contribution.
[1]Please find evaluation code and further information on https://github.com/Blubberli/argmin2024-perspective.

Proceedings of the 11th Workshop on Argument Mining, pages 130–149
August 15, 2024 ©2024 Association for Computational Linguistics

- **Explicit Perspectivism**: Verifying whether retrieval systems can achieve personalization regarding *socio* variables when mentioned in the query and argument corpus.

- **Implicit Perspectivism**: Assessing the solely text-based personalization abilities of retrieval systems as *socio* variables are only given in the query and we expect systems to exploit fine-grained socio-linguistic variations between authors with different profiles.

With this shared task, we aim to examine how retrieval systems can exploit the latent influence of demographic and socio-cultural profiles, such as age or political attitude, and how they are biased regarding over- or underrepresented groups (like different age groups). Current approaches in computational argumentation tend to prioritize majority groups and marginalize minority groups (Spliethöver and Wachsmuth, 2020; Holtermann et al., 2022). To fulfill these objectives, we adopt a fine-grained and comprehensive evaluation protocol and assess the performance of submitted argument retrieval systems in two tracks: **relevance** and **diversity** (§ 4). The retrieval system should provide top-k arguments that are highly relevant to the query and simultaneously diversify varying demographic and socio-cultural profiles. Therefore, we rely on prior work enforcing diversification across stances in retrieved arguments (Cherumanal et al., 2021). With this shared task and results from the six participating teams, we address the following research questions:

RQ1: Can argument retrieval systems encode socio-cultural variables? Results (§ 6) reveal substantial challenges in encoding perspectives and successfully achieving personalization. Systems struggle to capture fine-grained socio-linguistic features without explicit profile mentions. Moreover, there is a lack of suitable metrics for evaluating relevance, diversity, and fairness.

RQ2: Are argument retrieval systems biased regarding specific socio-cultural variables? While retrieval systems primarily follow the corpus bias, in-depth analysis (§ 7) shows that they balance gender bias but increase age group bias.

RQ3: How do argument retrieval systems generalize when switching the perceiving perspective from authors to readers? Perceiving perspective causes substantial performance drops (§ 6),

(1) No Perspectivsm

> **Query**: *Are you in favor of the introduction of a tax on foods containing sugar (sugar tax)?*
> **Relevant Argument:** *The reduction of sugar in food should be pushed. Not every food needs additional sugar as a supplement.*

(2) Explicit Perspectivsm

> **Query**: *Given a left political attitude, are you in favor of the introduction of a tax on foods containing sugar (sugar tax)?*
> **Relevant Argument:** *With a left political attitude, reducing sugar in food should be pushed. Not every food needs additional sugar as a supplement.*

(3) Implicit Perspectivsm

> **Query**: *Given a liberal political attitude, are you in favor of the introduction of a tax on foods containing sugar (sugar tax)?*
> **Relevant Argument:** *Eating is an individual decision. It doesn't need a nanny state.*

Figure 2: Examples of query and a relevant argument for the three scenarios: (1) no perspectivism without *socio* variables; (3) explicit perspectivism with *socio* variable in query and argument; (3) implicit perspectivism with *socio* variable only in the query.

as readers select arguments according to their political standing (attitude and important issue) but not regarding their demographic ones, like age or denomination, catholic or protestant (§ 3).

Contributions With this shared task, we establish the task of *perspective argument retrieval* and present a novel dataset covering explicitly and implicitly expressed perspectives from argument authors and readers. A comprehensive evaluation of the submitted systems underscores the challenge of this task as the system struggles to incorporate the fine-grained linguistic influence of demographic and socio-cultural variables. Further, while these systems mostly replicate the dataset bias, they partially overcome gender bias. These insights call for further research to incorporate perspectivism successfully and fairly, aiming for systems providing personalization.

2 Perspective Argument Retrieval

Argument retrieval is the task of finding top-k relevant arguments y within a corpus C for a given query q (Bondarenko et al., 2020). We formulate *perspective argument retrieval* as an expansion of argument retrieval to perspectivism (Cabitza et al., 2023) when finding best-matching arguments. By considering demographic and socio-cultural (*socio*) variables, we account for latent aspects of argumentation beyond semantic features, such as age, occupation, or political attitude. Concretely, this shared task proposes three scenarios (Figure 2) to evaluate how argument retrieval systems can account for perspectivism.

2.1 Scenario 1: No Perspectivsm

First, we test a system's ability to retrieve relevant arguments y solely using semantic features of arguments in the corpus C and the query q without any *socio* variables. This scenario represents the classical retrieval setup as reference performance.

2.2 Scenario 2: Explicit Perspectivsm

Second, we add *socio* variables to both corpus and query to test whether a retrieval system can consider *socio* variables when explicitly given, like *left political attitude*. This scenario simulates adopting the retrieval stage to specific perspectives while retaining the argument retrieval performance. For this shared task, we only consider one *socio* variable at a time to test the effect of considering them in isolation. Consequently, this scenario is computationally heavy as systems must encode the argument corpus for every considered *socio* variable in the queries. For example, when querying for a specific *socio* properties, like the age group *18-34*, the corpus must be encoded with the corresponding *socio* property of the arguments, such as the specific age group.

2.3 Scenario 3: Implicit Perspectivsm

This third scenario is similar to the second one (*explicit perspectivism*), but we only add *socio* variables to the query, like *liberal political attitude*. It is better aligned with real use cases as *socio* variables of arguments are often not given and represent true *personalization*. As a result, we aim for a retrieval system with which we can account for latent encoding of *socio* variables within arguments. Furthermore, this scenario is computationally more efficient than the *explicit* one because arguments do not need to be encoded more than once.

3 Data

In the following, we outline the data used for this shared task, involving the data source (§ 3.1), the used demographic and socio-cultural variables (§ 3.2), the composition of the argument corpus and the queries (§ 3.3).

3.1 Source

We conduct this shared task with data provided by the voting recommendation platform SmartVote[2] from the Swiss national elections of 2019 and 2023.[3] This platform provides voting suggestions based on a questionnaire that politicians and voters fill out.[4] In it, politicians can argue why they are in favor or against specific political issues. Concretely, we use these arguments formulated by politicians, the political issue addressed by one of these arguments, the stance of an argument regarding the political issue, and the *socio* variables of the politicians (authors) who formulated these arguments. We pre-process the data following (Vamvas and Sennrich, 2020) and remove arguments with less than 50 characters, including URLs, or are not formulated in German, Italian, or French. After this filtering, we compose around 41k arguments written by 3.8k unique politicians regarding 266 distinct political issues in German, Italian, and French and an average of 15.7 arguments per person. We use these arguments to form the retrieval corpus C and use the political issues as queries q, either with (*explicit & implicit perspectivism*) or without (*no perspectivism*) corresponding *socio* variables of the authors. Given a query q, we define relevant arguments as those written by politicians to address the specific political issue of q. Note that this is a binary assignment without any fine-grained relevance measure.

3.2 Demographic and Socio-Cultural Variables

We use *socio* variables of the politicians (authors) who formulated the arguments. Figure 3 provides an overview of them, including the following personal information: *gender*, *age (binned)*, *residence* (either city or countryside), *civil status*, and *denomination*. Further, SmartVote provides a *SmartMap* ranking of the politicians on a left/middle/right and conservative/liberal dimension based on answers to the full questionnaire.[5] We combine (binning) these two dimensions into a single variable *political attitude*. Finally, SmartVote indicates, with a *SmartSpider*, the *important political issues* of

[2]https://www.smartvote.ch/

[3]Data of the 2019 elections were used in previous works, like (Vamvas and Sennrich, 2020) for multi-lingual stance detection.

[4]More information about the questionnaire and scientific methodology available online.

[5]More information about the SmartMap available online.

a person based on the answered questionnaire.[6] One person can have more than one out of eight *important political issues*: open foreign policy, liberal economic, restrictive financial policy, law and order, restrictive immigration policy, extended environmental protection, expanded welfare state, and liberal society. The insights of Figure 3 show the demographic bias of politicians, such as living on the countryside, identifying as male, or being married.

3.3 Datasct Composition

We compose three versions of the dataset with distinct test sets to run three different evaluation cycles (Figure 4) covering (1) data from the 2019 election, (2) data from the 2023 election, and (3) surprise data. For every cycle, a dataset consists of distinct train, dev, and test queries (q_{train}, q_{dev}, and q_{test}) along with a corpus of arguments, $C = \{C_{train}, C_{dev}, C_{test}\}$. We include all relevant arguments for at least one query within the corresponding part of the corpus. While train q_{train} and dev queries q_{dev} remain the same, we use distinct test queries ($q_{test}^{(2019)}$, $q_{test}^{(2023)}$, and $q_{test}^{(surp.)}$) for every cycle. Subsequently, the arguments (C_{train}, C_{dev}) remain the same, but the test part of the corpus ($C_{test-2019}$, $C_{test-2023}$, and $C_{test-surp.}$) is updated with the specific arguments which are relevant for the corresponding test queries. Note that for a given q_i we expect to retrieve arguments from the full corpus C. Since every query has a German, French, and Italian version, we include a separate one for each language. However, we consider arguments for any language as relevant. For example, the German and French versions of q_i share their relevant arguments y.

Train and Dev We use 35 and 10 distinct political issues from the 2019 election as train and dev queries (q_{train}, q_{dev}) and include 21k arguments and 2k ones for dev in the corpus (C_{train}, C_{dev}).

Test Cycle-2019 During the first evaluation cycle, we use an additional 15 distinct political issues from the 2019 election as test queries ($q_{test}^{(2019)}$). The corresponding corpus ($C_{test}^{(2019)}$) consists of 6k arguments. With this test set, we evaluate the retrieval performance given the topic shift between train, dev, and test queries/arguments as they cover distinct political issues.

[6]More information about the SmartSpider available online.

Test Cycle-2023 For the second evaluation cycle, we select 62 distinct political issues from the 2023 election for testing ($q_{test}^{(2023)}$) along with 13k arguments ($C_{test}^{(2023)}$). This second cycle saturates the topic shift between train, dev, and test sets as new topics gained political relevance between 2019 and 2023, like Corona or the war in Ukraine.

Test Cycle-Surprise Finally, we conduct an annotation study to assess whether retrieval systems generalize when we change the perceiving perspectivc from authors to readers (**RQ3**). Concretely, this study covers 27 political issues and 20 arguments from the 2023 election answering these issues. We conducted this annotation study with 22 crowd workers recruited from prolific. More details about their selection, background, and payment are in Appendix § A.1. During annotation, we present the annotators with 20 arguments for every political issue and ask them to select those they intuitively perceive as relevant for answering the presented issue. Along with this selection, we collect the *socio* profile of the annotators as done by SmartVote for the authors. Based on these annotations, the test portion of the argument corpus ($D_{test}^{(sure.)}$) for this cycle consists of 540 arguments (20 arguments for every 27 political issues). Further, we use the 27 political issues and the *socio* profiles of the annotators to form the test queries ($q_{test}^{(sure.)}$). Noteworthy, we find that annotators perceive arguments as relevant when they share the *political spectrum* and *important political issues* with the authors of the arguments (see Figure 12 in Appendix § A.1).

4 Evaluation

We employ a two-folded evaluation to comprehensively measure the retrieval quality for all three scenarios. Concretely, we distinguish between **relevance** and **diversity**.

Relevance With relevance, we focus on the ability of a retrieval system to select relevant candidates given the query, for example, all arguments addressing the queried issue for the baseline scenario or arguments that additionally match specific socio-cultural properties for explicit or implicit perspectivism. Following previous work (Bondarenko et al., 2020, 2022; Thakur et al., 2021), we use the Normalized Discounted Cumulative Gain (nDCG@) and precision@ metric. Compared to precision, nDCG has the advantage of taking the position of the ranked items into account. There-

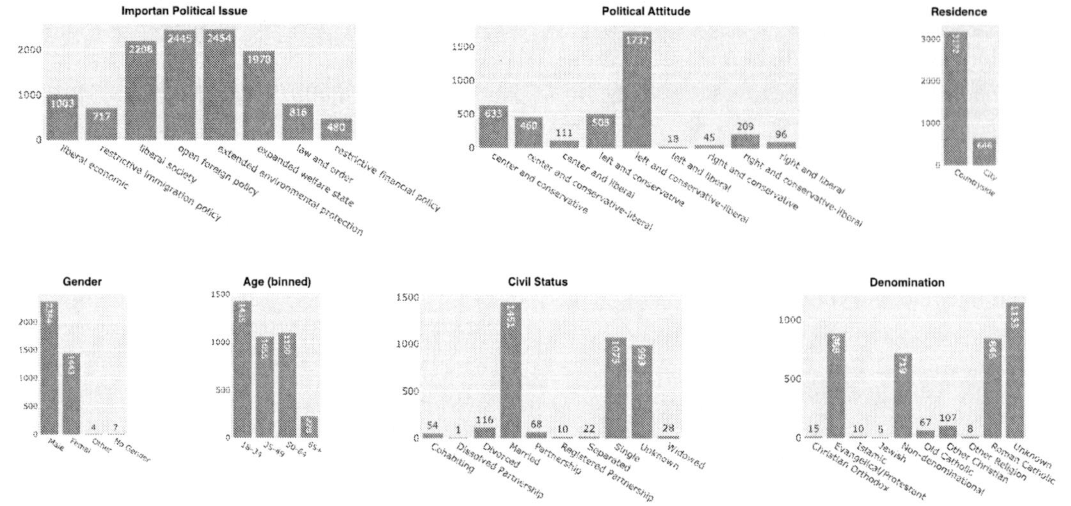

Figure 3: Distribution of the politicians' different demographic and socio-cultural variables: important political issues, political attitude, residence, gender, age (binned), civil status, and denomination. Note, that one person can have more than one important political issue.

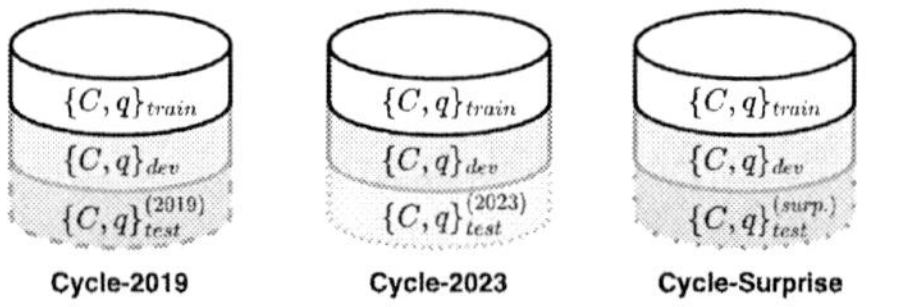

Figure 4: Overview of train, dev, and test argument corpora (C) and queries q for the three evaluation cycles dataset (*2019, 2023, surprise*)

fore, the metric places greater emphasis on higher-ranked arguments.

Diversity Using diversity, we account for the influence of perspectivism in the evaluation by measuring whether a retrieval system proposes balanced arguments regarding the stance distribution and the authors' diverse socio-cultural properties (such as gender or political attitude). Following previous studies regarding fairness in argument retrieval systems (Cherumanal et al., 2021), we calculate alpha-nDCG@ for each available property separately and average them afterwards. This metric accounts for relevance and diversity by assessing whether an item is relevant and introduces a new perspective compared to the previous one. Consider the following example: a system retrieved a list of arguments relevant to a given issue, and we aim to evaluate diversity for political attitude. The metric would prefer the arguments to be sorted like this ['liberal', 'conservative', 'left', 'conservative'] over ['conservative', 'conservative', 'liberal', 'left']. An optimal ranking ensures that all relevant perspectives for a corresponding socio-cultural variable are represented among the top-ranked arguments. Note that these conditioned properties are withheld when evaluating diversity since we condition specific socio-demographic properties in the query for explicit or implicit perspectivism (scenarios 2 and 3).

As a second metric, we look at the Normalized discounted KL-divergence, introduced as a metric of *unfairness* (Cherumanal et al., 2021). This metric evaluates the fairness of the ranking by comparing the distribution of a protected group (e.g. what is the proportion of arguments by female authors when looking at the property 'gender') in the top-k ranked items against a gold standard proportion (what is the proportion of arguments by female authors in the whole corpus?). The divergence is calculated at specified cut-off points and then averaged, with each point discounted by the logarithm of its rank, to assess how well the ranking reflects the representation of the protected group. In this case, the relevance of an argument is not considered; instead, the metric can reveal biases against specific groups. For example, it can show whether systems disproportionately favor dominant groups in the top arguments.

Final Ranking We evaluate the performance at four different values of k [4, 8, 16, 20] and calculate the average performance across these k values. This evaluation is conducted for the three scenarios across three different test sets, resulting in 9 scores for relevance and 9 for diversity. The final rank is determined by averaging these nine scores.

5 Submissions

In the following, we summarize the baseline (§ 5.1) and the submitted systems (§ 5.2). Further, we elaborate on the unique ideas incorporated by the participants.

5.1 Baseline Systems

We provide two baseline systems (`BM-25` and `SBERT`) to evaluate how simple retrieval systems perform without being optimized for any perspectivism.

Baseline `BM-25`: the BM-25 ranking algorithm ranks arguments based on lexical overlap. It is computed using tf-IDF but also accounts for document length (Robertson and Zaragoza, 2009).

Baseline `SBERT`: we use SBERT (Reimers and Gurevych, 2019) and the model `paraphrase-multilingual-mpnet-base-v2` to encode the query and the arguments from the corpus, ranking them based on cosine similarity. We encode the socio-cultural variables within the query for the perspectivist approaches. In Scenario 2, we concatenate the entire socio-cultural profile with each argument in the corpus.

5.2 Submitted Systems

This shared task received submitted systems from six teams: `twente-bms-nlp` (Zhang and Braun, 2024), `sövereign` (Günzler et al., 2024), `GESIS-DSM` (Maurer et al., 2024), `turiya` (Saha and Srihari, 2024), `xfact` (Kang et al., 2024), and `boulderNLP` (no system paper submitted). Some systems did not submit results for all three scenarios but instead focused on one or two (e.g., no perspectivism and explicit). We summarize and elaborate on the specific techniques of these systems, including embedding strategies, candidate filtering & re-ranking, using LLMs, or using auxiliary classification tasks.

Embedding queries and arguments All systems used SBERT (Reimers and Gurevych, 2019) to encode queries and arguments and retrieve an initial set of relevant arguments by calculating the cosine similarity between query and corpus embeddings. Additionally, `twente-bms-nlp` uses cross-encoding LMs to re-rank the top 50 arguments, and `turiya` fuses rankings obtained with mono- and multi-lingual embeddings, once using KNN and once cosine similiarty for ranking. Only `xfact` further fine-tunes SBERT to align the semantic representations of relevant arguments and corresponding queries. They use other arguments as negative examples and optimize the representations with multiple negative ranking losses.

Filtering out irrelevant arguments Most teams filter relevant candidates before (re)ranking: for scenario 2, they hard-filter arguments that explicitly match the socio-demographic variable in the query. `twente-bms-nlp` filters arguments that appear relevant in the training set to reduce the candidate pool arguments that likely match the political issue in test queries, as there is no overlap between train and test queries. `xfact` filter arguments that had no overlap between keywords of the query and keywords of the arguments.

Re-ranking top k arguments Some teams retrieve a larger list of relevant candidates and then adopt complex strategies to re-rank the top-k arguments due to their high weight in the evaluation. These strategies often include training a specific classifier, e.g., `turiya` trained two classifiers, one binary to assign a relevance label (0 or 1) given query and argument, and one to select the more relevant argument out of two. `sövereign` prompt an LLM to generate relevance scores given query and a list of the top 50 retrieved arguments. For perspectivism, they include instructions to determine whether the given socio-demographic property matches the arguments.

Additional use of LLMs Four out of five teams use LLMs at some point in their pipeline. Two teams (`xfact` and `GESIS-DSM`) explore the idea of 'prototypes' or 'anchors' and automatically generated arguments given a specific query. `GESIS-DSM` uses the generated arguments as a reference anchor to re-rank the relevant candidates with SBERT. For perspectivism, this generated argument should represent specific demographic properties. `xfact` utilizes LLM to generate prototypical and diverse arguments in response to a query. These generated arguments serve as centroids in a clustering process designed to identify relevant arguments within the corpus. The approach ensures that the retrieved arguments are relevant and exhibit greater diversity by creating a variety of arguments.

Additional classification tasks to identify relevant arguments Several teams train additional classifiers to enhance system performance, whether to improve the identification of relevant arguments or retrieve arguments matching specific socio-cultural variables. xfact uses stance detection as an auxiliary task to improve the system's ability to detect whether an argument matches a query. In the final stage, the classifier's confidence level is used as a cutoff radius to selectively refine the set of relevant arguments when comparing their distance to the centroids generated by the LLM. sövereign uses a logistic classifier to learn a more informed relevance score for re-ranking: the classifier incorporates cosine similarity, a demography matching score, and a topic frequency score as features. twente-bms-nlp and GESIS-DSM investigate whether classifiers can learn to predict the values for certain socio-cultural variables from the arguments. Both compared the performance of classifiers using semantic content against linguistic (style) features. twente-bms-nlp find that the classification of the different values is challenging but can improve the final results of the system using a classifier that predicts whether an issue is important for an author based on a semantic representation of the argument. GESIS-DSM finds that semantics were less predictive of differences between groups of different socio-cultural variables and instead can retrieve a better re-ranking when using several linguistic style features as predictors.

6 Results

In the following section, we discuss the results of the submitted systems focusing on **RQ1**. Additional detailed discussions regarding single scenario, evaluation cycle, and top-k are in Appendix § A.2 and § A.3.

Relevance and diversity agree but not with fairness. Table 1 shows each track's final leaderboards. Both tracks (relevance and diversity) share the same team rankings. All teams outperform the SBERT baseline when they submitted for all scenarios (xfact and boulderNLP have only submitted 6 / 3 prediction files, leading to lower scores.)

Next, we compare the metrics representing relevance (NDCG@k), diversity (αNDCG@k), and fairness (klDiv@k). Relevance and diversity are highly correlated, but diversity scores are lower than relevance, showing that no system perfectly diversifies its top-k arguments. Compared with fairness (klDiv@k), relevance and diversity are weakly correlated $\rho = 0.13$. Ideally, we expect a correlation of $\rho = -1$ as klDiv@$k = 0$ would represent a perfectly fair system and NDCG@$k = 1$ and

	Relevance		Diversity	Fairness
	ndcg@k	precision@k	αNDCG@k	klDiv@k
twente-bms-nlp	70.7	63.4	67.2	16.7
sövereign	63.2	56.1	60.1	15.9
GESIS-DSM	60.7	54.3	57.9	15.0
turiya	51.8	-	49.5	-
sbert	44.5	42.7	41.9	0.136
xfact	41.7	40.0	39.4	0.136
boulderNLP	29.2	-	27.1	-
bm25	19.5	-	18.5	-

Table 1: Final result of the shared task regarding relevance (NDCG and precision), diversity (αNDCG), and fairness (klDiv).

αNDCG@$k = 1$ indicates perfect relevance and diversity. Figure 5 confirms these patterns in more detail with results across every k, evaluation cycle, scenario, and team. Furthermorea , these insights are consistent with Cherumanal et al. (2021), which states that these metrics are not equivalent and measure different dimensions.

Considering Perspectivism is difficult. We analyze the performance differences between the three scenarios. Figure 5 and Figure 6 reveal that considering no *socio* variable (scenario one) performs the best across all test sets of the three evaluation cycles. Comparing scenarios one with two and three (considering perspectivism *explicit* or *implicit*) highlights the challenges of incorporating *socio* variables in the retrieval stage. This becomes even more apparent when comparing scenarios two and three. While considering *socio* variables in the query and corpus (scenario two) results in higher performance, it crucially requires more computing. In contrast, the more efficient approach of considering *socio* variable only in the query (scenario three) causes significant performance degradation. Thus, existing retrieval systems show crucial limitations in taking into account *perspectivism*, either *explicit* or *implicit*. Particularly, they need the signal of the *socio* variable within the query and corpus. Further analysis of the participating teams reveals that the implicit difference between arguments of distinct *socio* variables is more stylistic than semantic. **As a result, we see the need to build retrieval systems accounting for such fine-grained socio-linguistic variations to consider perspectivism accurate and efficient.**

Temporal shift reduces retrieval performance. We analyze the temporal effect when comparing results from the test sets covering the 2019 (blue) and 2023 (red) elections. Figure 6 shows that this temporal shift has a crucial effect on the retrieval

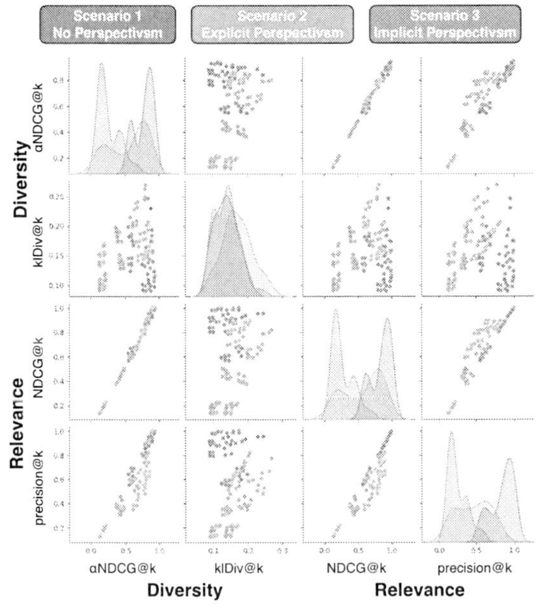

Figure 5: Performance overview regarding the four measured metrics and their relation. The color indicates the specific scenario.

performance for all three scenarios. We see this shift mainly as semantic as we consider political issues regarding freshly raised topics like Corona or the war in Ukraine.

The importance of the perceiving perspective. With the third evaluation cycle, we focus on **RQ3** and analyze how the retrieval system handles queries when the receiving perspective of the arguments changes. We see systems struggling when comparing the authors' (2019 and 2023) with the voters' perspective (surprise). Particularly for the first and second scenarios. While these results provide first insights, more extensive studies are required to cover the same demographic variance as in the 2019 and 2023 test sets. Further, this smaller corpus is also reflected in the better performance of the third test set on the third scenario (*implicit perspectivism*).

7 Analysis

In the following, we focus on **RQ2** and examine whether retrieved argument candidates are biased regarding socio-cultural groups and if submitted systems compensate for such biases. We focus on *age* and *gender*, known for which recent work found substantial bias in argumentation. Specifically, Spliethöver and Wachsmuth (2020) show that common argumentation sources (e.g. debating corpora) exhibit substantial bias regarding young ages

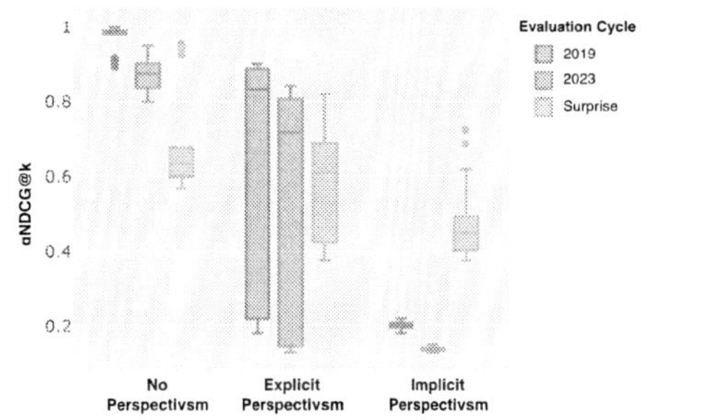

Figure 6: Performance comparison of the three evaluation cycles (color) regarding the three scenarios (x-axis) for diversity (y-axis, αNDCG@k).

and European-American males. Further, Holtermann et al. (2022) shows that fine-tuning LMs on argumentative data increases stereotypical bias, even if LMs exhibited a counter-stereotypical bias before tuning. As shown in Figure 3, our dataset is biased towards specific groups, such as male and/or young authors. We establish a random baseline by randomly sampling 20 topic-relevant arguments for every query of the implicit scenario across 10 different seeds and average the number of arguments retrieved for each group. Similarly, we average the performance metric.

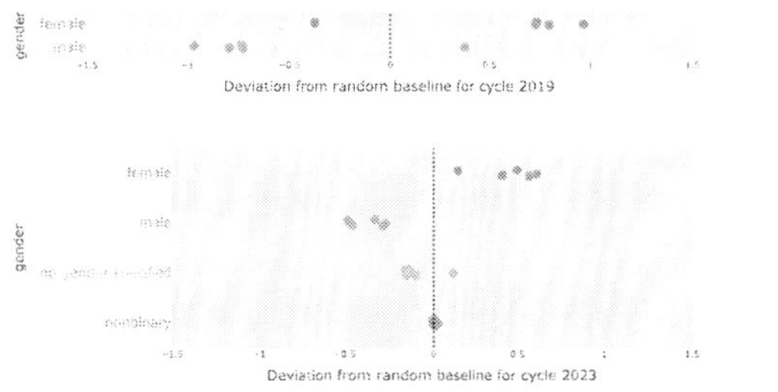

Figure 7: Extent of system deviation from random sampling representing each gender among the 20 most relevant arguments.

Systems are biased regarding majority groups. We examine the 20 most relevant arguments, count how many represent the distinct group, and compute the standard deviation for each system towards the random baseline. A negative deviation indicates that the system further reduces the representation of that group, meaning the group is less represented in the top arguments compared to its underlying distribution in the corpus. Conversely, a positive deviation indicates increased representation. In the case of a majority group, the system amplifies the bias.

Figure 7 shows the shift in representation for *gender*, comparing the 2019 and 2023 test sets.

We observe most systems (including the SBERT baseline) reducing the male bias. However, the top retrieved arguments still overrepresent male authors by a large margin, as the deviation is not more than one argument. Interestingly, one team reinforced the male bias in the 2019 dataset with a slight positive deviation. However, that system slightly outperformed the other teams in increasing the representation of other gender categories in the 2023 dataset (positive value for *no gender specified*).

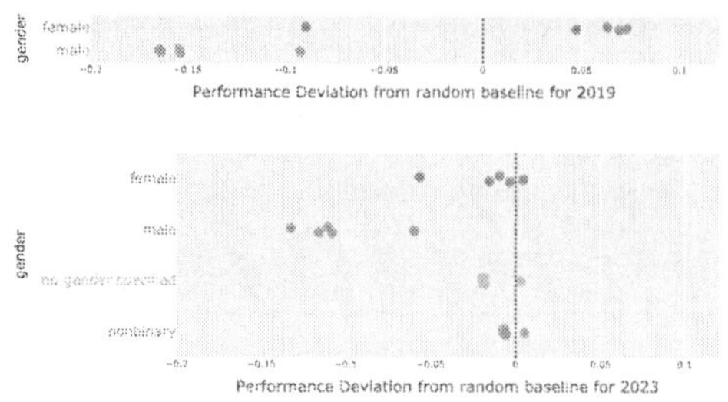

Figure 9: Extent of system deviation from random sampling in performance from the nDCG score for different gender categories.

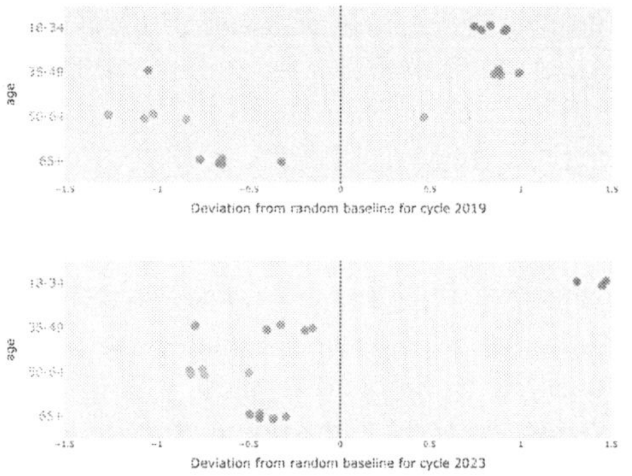

Figure 8: Extent of system deviation from random sampling representing each age group among the 20 most relevant arguments.

Figure 8 focuses on different *age* groups and shows that all systems reinforce a bias regarding young ages. This is particularly true for the 2023 dataset, where systems systematically retrieve fewer arguments written by older age groups than randomly sample arguments. This supports general findings in NLP that older age groups are underrepresented in data and models. Comparing the two middle-aged groups reveals that *35-49* is better represented than *50-64* for 2019. Since both age groups occur approximately equally frequently in the corpus, this indicates a stronger age bias, with the older group being significantly less well-represented. While these findings suggest that systems are biased toward representing the majority group, they mitigate this bias more effectively for the female gender category.

Systems partly mitigate gender but not age bias. We compute each group's deviation from the system performance to the random baseline performance. If there is no bias, the deviation for a system should be the same for each group. For *gender*, Figure 9 shows all systems reduce the bias regarding the majority group (male gender category). For nonbinary and unspecified gender, the performance pattern is similar to representation: one system shows slight bias improvement, while the others are slightly more biased than the baseline. The female group's performance improved for the 2019 dataset compared to the random baseline but not for the 2023 dataset. We assume that the SBERT model has potentially seen more topics from the 2019 election and detected sub-issue-specific differences within known topics. For example, the model could have identified specific frames used more frequently by males than females. For *age*, systems seem to agree more with the dataset distribution: younger age groups have fewer declines or even improvements (in 2023) compared to older age groups (Figure 17 in Appendix). Again, systems perform the worst on the *50-64* age group.

8 Conclusion

With the *Shared Task on Perspective Argument Retrieval*, we explore for the first time how argument retrieval systems align socio-cultural properties beyond topic relevance. Analyzing the submissions shows that semantic content alone does not distinguish between different socio-cultural groups adequately. Instead, incorporating additional classification tasks or features is crucial for accurately matching arguments to socio-cultural characteristics. The subsequent analysis shows that systems overrepresent arguments from majority groups. However, they partially mitigate these biases, such as gender bias. By publishing data reflecting authors' and readers' perspectives, this shared task represents an initial step towards advancing argument retrieval regarding perspectivism. This facilitates the investigation of personalization and polarization and addresses social bias and fairness in computational argumentation.

Acknowledgements

We thank SmartVote and Summetix for their support of this shared task. Neele Falk is supported by Bundesministerium für Bildung und Forschung (BMBF) through the project E-DELIB (Powering up e-deliberation: towards AI-supported moderation). Andreas Waldis has been funded by the Hasler Foundation Grant No. 21024.

Limitations

Geographical Limitation The underlying dataset of this shared task is solely originating from Switzerland. While it includes distinct values of Swiss society (multilingual and through political discourse), it is limited to political issues discussed in Switzerland. Furthermore, the distribution of demographic and socio-cultural variables is biased regarding the Swiss population. For example, one expects a person in Switzerland and the United States to have a different mindset while being labeled as *liberal and left*.

Societal Bias As with any usage of the language model, this work is affected by fundamental stereotypical bias injected by pre-training on past data. Even with a special focus during the analysis, this fact is one limitation that should be considered in any application.

Appropriate Evaluation In a perspective-aware retrieval system, multiple metrics are essential to evaluate the system from various aspects. The diversity metric, for instance, measures whether the top arguments cover the different values of a particular *socio* (including an argument from each age group). However, it does not consider the order in which these arguments are presented, meaning the majority group will likely always be shown as the top argument. It also does not evaluate the distribution of the remaining arguments (after all values are covered).

The fairness metric and the results for the representation analysis assess whether each group is represented in the top arguments according to its overall proportion. Nonetheless, there is a debate on whether this is fair because the majority group will be more frequently represented. An alternative approach would aim for an equal distribution of each group among the top arguments, ensuring that minority groups are as prominently represented as possible.

Ethical Considerations

Intend of Use LMs have the potential to support the formation of opinions and foster a thorough and fine-grained discourse by navigating the diversity and large size of available political statements and standpoints. While the data we use in this shared task are crucial for a comprehensive evaluation of LM's abilities regarding such supportive use cases, they have the potential for building manipulative systems. To ensure the data's supportive intent in this shared task, we will make it available solely upon request for research purposes and require concrete information about the specific usage.

Data Privacy For this shared task, we conducted an annotation study and collected personal information (demographic and socio-cultural variables) about the annotators. As part of the obtained ethical clearance, we collected the explicit consent of the annotators during participation and relied on anonymized identifiers throughout the study. Therefore, we do not have any information about the specific person beyond the collected data. Furthermore, we categorize more sensible information, like age, into different bins.

Concerning the data provided by SmartVote (including the text of the arguments and the corresponding *socio* profile of the politicians), we follow their privacy statement[7]. Specifically, the politicians agreed that all available public data on the platform could be shared anonymized.

Personalization Personalized recommendations of arguments based on one *socio* are oversimplified and reduce diversity. The presented shared task started with a simplified scenario where only one socio was presented at a time since it was the first shared task. Given the rich and diverse profiles of authors and readers available, we advocate for more research on intersectionality and a broader, more nuanced representation of users in personalization research.

As we have observed, there is a significant dataset bias with specific groups being underrepresented. Despite our efforts to incorporate diversity in the presented arguments for this shared task,

[7]Available online.

this bias heavily influences systems. We advocate for further research and development of methods to diversify recommendations effectively. We see potential in combining personalization with diversification. For instance, while users tend to prefer arguments that align with their political attitudes, a system could optimize for this preference while presenting a range of perspectives, including arguments from different genders, age groups, and educational backgrounds. This approach would ensure a more pluralistic presentation of viewpoints while still showing arguments the user perceives as convincing or relevant.

References

Alexander Bondarenko, Maik Fröbe, Meriem Beloucif, Lukas Gienapp, Yamen Ajjour, Alexander Panchenko, Chris Biemann, Benno Stein, Henning Wachsmuth, Martin Potthast, and Matthias Hagen. 2020. Overview of touché 2020: Argument retrieval: Extended abstract. In *Experimental IR Meets Multilinguality, Multimodality, and Interaction: 11th International Conference of the CLEF Association, CLEF 2020, Thessaloniki, Greece, September 22–25, 2020, Proceedings*, page 384–395, Berlin, Heidelberg. Springer-Verlag.

Alexander Bondarenko, Maik Fröbe, Johannes Kiesel, Shahbaz Syed, Timon Gurcke, Meriem Beloucif, Alexander Panchenko, Chris Biemann, Benno Stein, Henning Wachsmuth, Martin Potthast, and Matthias Hagen. 2022. Overview of touché 2022: Argument retrieval. In *Experimental IR Meets Multilinguality, Multimodality, and Interaction: 13th International Conference of the CLEF Association, CLEF 2022, Bologna, Italy, September 5–8, 2022, Proceedings*, page 311–336, Berlin, Heidelberg. Springer-Verlag.

Federico Cabitza, Andrea Campagner, and Valerio Basile. 2023. Toward a perspectivist turn in ground truthing for predictive computing. In *Thirty-Seventh AAAI Conference on Artificial Intelligence, AAAI 2023, Thirty-Fifth Conference on Innovative Applications of Artificial Intelligence, IAAI 2023, Thirteenth Symposium on Educational Advances in Artificial Intelligence, EAAI 2023, Washington, DC, USA, February 7-14, 2023*, pages 6860–6868. AAAI Press.

Sachin Pathiyan Cherumanal, Damiano Spina, Falk Scholer, and W. Bruce Croft. 2021. Evaluating fairness in argument retrieval. In *CIKM '21: The 30th ACM International Conference on Information and Knowledge Management, Virtual Event, Queensland, Australia, November 1 - 5, 2021*, pages 3363–3367. ACM.

Robert Günzler, Özge Sevgili, Steffen Remus, Chris Biemann, and Irina Nikishina. 2024. Sövereign at perpectivearg2024: Using llms with argument mining. In *Proceedings of the 11th Workshop on Argument Mining*, Bangkok. Association for Computational Linguistics.

Carolin Holtermann, Anne Lauscher, and Simone Ponzetto. 2022. Fair and argumentative language modeling for computational argumentation. In *Proceedings of the 60th Annual Meeting of the Association for Computational Linguistics (Volume 1: Long Papers)*, pages 7841–7861, Dublin, Ireland. Association for Computational Linguistics.

Wan Ju Kang, Jiyoung Han, Jaemin Jung, and James Thorne. 2024. Xfact team0331 at perpectivearg2024: Sampling from bounded clusters for diverse relevant argument retrieval. In *Proceedings of the 11th Workshop on Argument Mining*, Bangkok. Association for Computational Linguistics.

Maximilian Martin Maurer, Julia Romberg, Myrthe Reuver, Negash Desalegn Weldekiros, and Gabriella Lapesa. 2024. Gesis-dsm at perpectivearg2024: A matter of style? socio-cultural differences in argumentation. In *Proceedings of the 11th Workshop on Argument Mining*, Bangkok. Association for Computational Linguistics.

Nils Reimers and Iryna Gurevych. 2019. Sentence-BERT: Sentence embeddings using Siamese BERT-networks. In *Proceedings of the 2019 Conference on Empirical Methods in Natural Language Processing and the 9th International Joint Conference on Natural Language Processing (EMNLP-IJCNLP)*, pages 3982–3992, Hong Kong, China. Association for Computational Linguistics.

Stephen E. Robertson and Hugo Zaragoza. 2009. The probabilistic relevance framework: BM25 and beyond. *Found. Trends Inf. Retr.*, 3(4):333–389.

Sougata Saha and Rohini Srihari. 2024. Turiya at perpectivearg2024: A multilingual argument retriever and reranker. In *Proceedings of the 11th Workshop on Argument Mining*, Bangkok. Association for Computational Linguistics.

Maximilian Spliethöver and Henning Wachsmuth. 2020. Argument from old man's view: Assessing social bias in argumentation. In *Proceedings of the 7th Workshop on Argument Mining*, pages 76–87, Online. Association for Computational Linguistics.

Nandan Thakur, Nils Reimers, Andreas Rücklé, Abhishek Srivastava, and Iryna Gurevych. 2021. BEIR: A heterogeneous benchmark for zero-shot evaluation of information retrieval models. In *Proceedings of the Neural Information Processing Systems Track on Datasets and Benchmarks 1, NeurIPS Datasets and Benchmarks 2021, December 2021, virtual.*

Jannis Vamvas and Rico Sennrich. 2020. X -stance: A multilingual multi-target dataset for stance detection. In *Proceedings of the 5th Swiss Text Analytics Conference and the 16th Conference on Natural Language Processing, SwissText/KONVENS 2020, Zurich, Switzerland, June 23-25, 2020 [online only]*, volume 2624 of *CEUR Workshop Proceedings*. CEUR-WS.org.

Henning Wachsmuth, Shahbaz Syed, and Benno Stein. 2018. Retrieval of the best counterargument without prior topic knowledge. In *Proceedings of the 56th Annual Meeting of the Association for Computational Linguistics (Volume 1: Long Papers)*, pages 241–251, Melbourne, Australia. Association for Computational Linguistics.

Leixin Zhang and Daniel Braun. 2024. Twente-bms-nlp at perspectivearg 2024: Combining bi-encoder and cross-encoder for argument retrieval. In *Proceedings of the 11th Workshop on Argument Mining*, Bangkok. Association for Computational Linguistics.

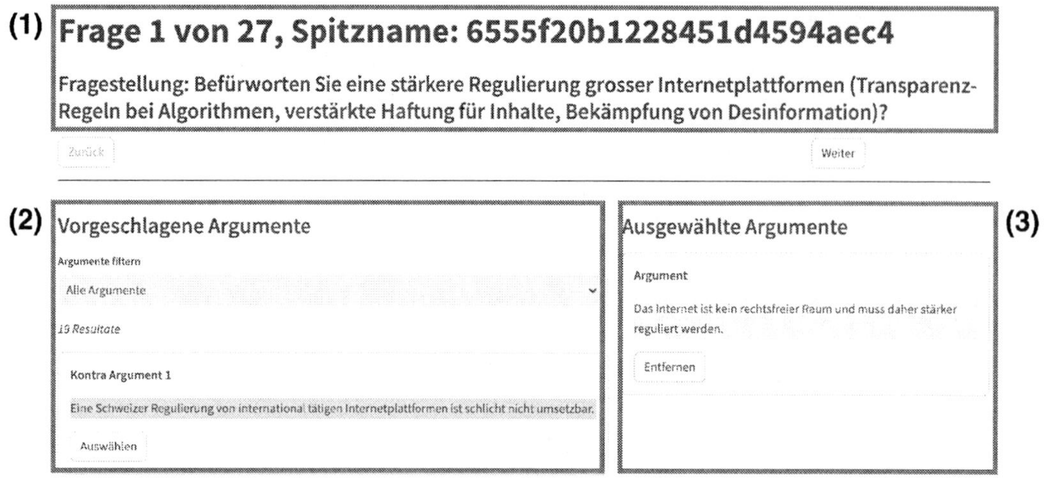

Figure 10: Screenshot of the annotation UI. It presents the annotator with the specific political question (1), 20 arguments addressing this question and allows to select the intuitively relevant ones (2), and list the already selected arguments (3).

A Appendix

A.1 Details of the Annotation Study

Within the conducted annotation study, 22 annotators were asked to select intuitively relevant arguments for 27 political questions. Specifically, we conduct a two-staged study. First, collect the *socio* variables from the annotators themselves using a survey to collect *gender*, *age*, *civil status*, and *denomination*. Note, we remove *residence* as a minority of the people were willing to share where they live. Additionally, we collect their *political attitude* and *important political issues* using the same SmartVote questionnaire as filled out by the politicians. Secondly, we present 20 arguments for every 27 political questions and let the annotators choose those that intuitively address the given question from their perspective.

Annotation Interface We show an overview of the annotation UI in Figure 10. This interface presents the annotators one political question at a time, along with 20 arguments addressing this question from different perspectives. Afterward, we ask the annotators to select which of the present arguments is intuitively relevant to them. Selected arguments will be listed on the right and can also be deleted later on.

Ethical Considerations As we collected demographic and socio-cultural data of the annotators, we collected the explicit consent of the annotators during the study. We inform them that we only collect categorized data, like the binned age, and that they can ask to delete it. This procedure has been approved by the ethical board of TU Darmstadt. However, during preliminary discussion, it was decided that full ethical approval is unnecessary.

Payment We recruit the annotators on prolific and pay them an hourly rate of 25 Swiss francs. While there is no minimum wage in Switzerland, this salary is above the minimum.

***Socio* Variable of the Annotators** We show in Figure 11 the demographic and socio-cultural variables of the 22 annotators. However, the distribution is similar to the politicians' distribution (§ 3) but on a much smaller scale. As a result, distinct values of a single variable are not covered. For example, we cover only four out of nine distinct political spectra. Further, we analyze in Figure 12 the agreement (personalization) of the annotator's perspectives with those of the authors whose arguments the annotator selects. We found that annotators highly match with the authors' perspective regarding *political spectrum* and *important political issue*, and moderately *age* and *gender*.

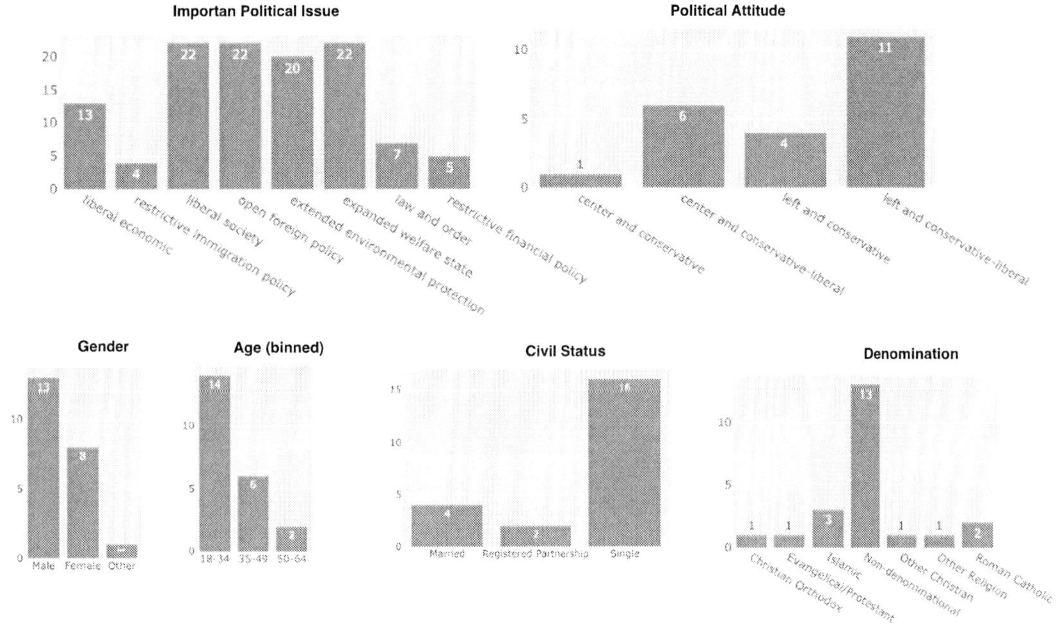

Figure 11: Distribution of the annotators' different demographic and socio-cultural variables: important political issues, political attitude, gender, age (binned), civil status, and denomination. Note, that one person can have more than one important political issue.

2019			2023			user study		
team	**rel**	**div**	**team**	**rel**	**div**	**team**	**rel**	**div**
sövereign	99.9	9.22	twente-bms-nlp	93.6	87.0	twente-bms-nlp	94.4	88.0
GESIS-DSM	98.7	91.6	sougata	92.0	85.5	sougata	76.1	71.2
sbert_baseline	98.6	91.6	sövereign	89.5	82.7	boulderNLP	75.7	70.3
boulderNLP	98.6	91.3	boulderNLP	88.5	82.2	sövereign	63.7	59.5
twente-bms-nlp	97.9	91.0	sbert_baseline	85.5	79.3	sbert_baseline	63.7	59.3
sougata	97.9	90.5	GESIS-DSM	85.5	79.3	GESIS-DSM	62.8	59.2
team031	90.4	84.4	team031	80.6	75.3	team031	59.2	55.0
bm25_baseline	65.1	62.9	bm25_baseline	73.7	69.0	bm25_baseline	36.8	34.2

Table 2: Scenario 1: No Perspectivsm

A.2 Detailed Results of Shared Tasks

Table 2, Table 3, and Table 4 show the detailed leaderboards for scenarios one, two, and three. When looking at the detailed results (per dataset and per scenario), we find that no solution fits all: sometimes a team achieves a better score on one dataset (e.g., team sövereign outperforms the other teams on the dataset of the 2019 election, but not on the 2023 / user study dataset). This can be attributed to the fact that the LLM re-ranking is less effective at ranking arguments it has not seen before, whereas the 2019 data may have been included in its training data in some form. The perspectivism scenarios are significantly more challenging than retrieving relevant arguments per topic (no perspectivism), particularly when the perspective is only implicitly encoded in the argument. This gap in performance highlights the need for further research on this issue, as perspectivist argument retrieval appears to be a particularly difficult problem. However, it is encouraging that most teams can outperform the baseline on these scenarios by a substantial margin. Their approaches to handling perspectivism are moving in the right direction.

A.3 Results regarding different top-k

We analyze how the number of retrieved candidate arguments affects the performance. From Figure 13, the performance decreases with a higher k for the first scenario (*no perspectivism*) for the baseline and the

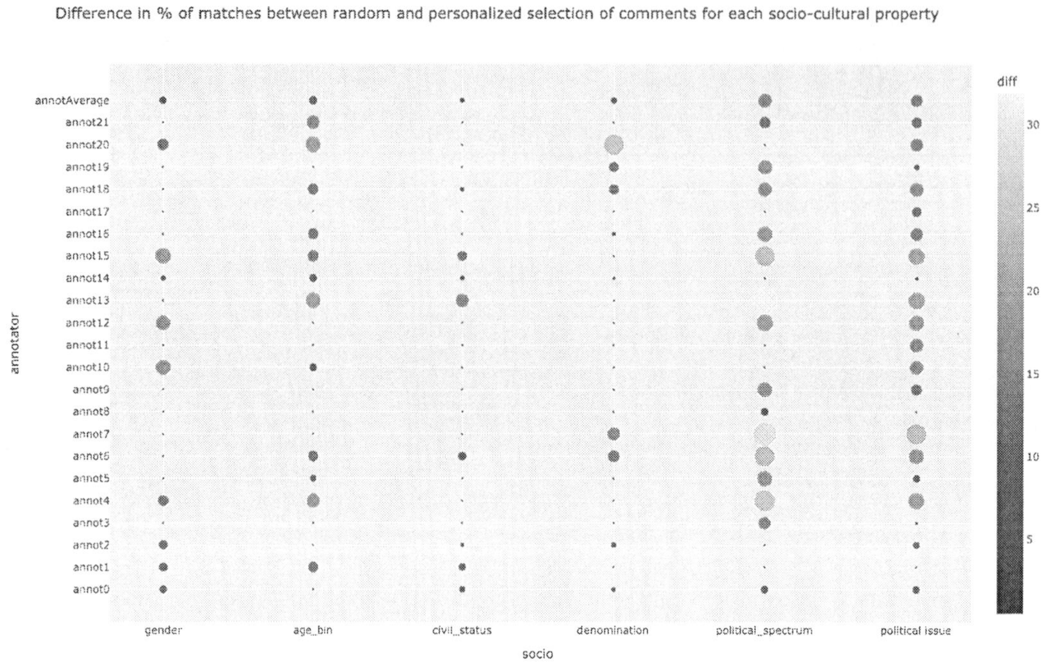

Figure 12: Amount of personalization per demographic and socio-cultural variable in the user study: percentage indicates the difference in matched arguments for a specific property when a user selects relevant arguments versus a random sample of relevant arguments.

2019			2023			user study		
team	**rel**	**div**	**team**	**rel**	**div**	**team**	**rel**	**div**
twente-bms-nlp	89.5	85.2	sövereign	82.3	79.4	twente-bms-nlp	79.8	79.3
sövereign	87.8	84.4	twente-bms-nlp	79.8	77.1	sövereign	67.3	67.5
GESIS-DSM	83.5	80.7	GESIS-DSM	72.2	70.1	sougata	648	65.9
sougata	68.4	66.5	sougata	67.4	66.3	GESIS-DSM	61.6	62.9
sbert_baseline	22.2	20.8	sbert_baseline	14.8	14.2	team031	41.3	40.1
team031	18.1	17.2	team031	13.2	12.5	sbert_baseline	40.6	40.0

Table 3: Scenario 2: Explicit Perspectivsm

2019			2023			user study		
team	**rel**	**div**	**team**	**rel**	**div**	**team**	**rel**	**div**
sövereign	21.3	19.9	twente-bms-nlp	14.9	14.3	twente-bms-nlp	65.5	63.6
twente-bms-nlp	20.3	19.0	sövereign	13.9	13.2	GESIS-DSM	471	45.4
sbert_baseline	20.2	18.9	GESIS-DSM	13.9	13.2	sövereign	43.6	42.5
GESIS-DSM	20.2	18.9	sbert_baseline	13.6	13.1	team031	41.3	40.1
team031	18.1	17.2	team031	13.2	12.5	sbert_baseline	40.9	39.7

Table 4: Scenario 3: Implicit Perspectivsm

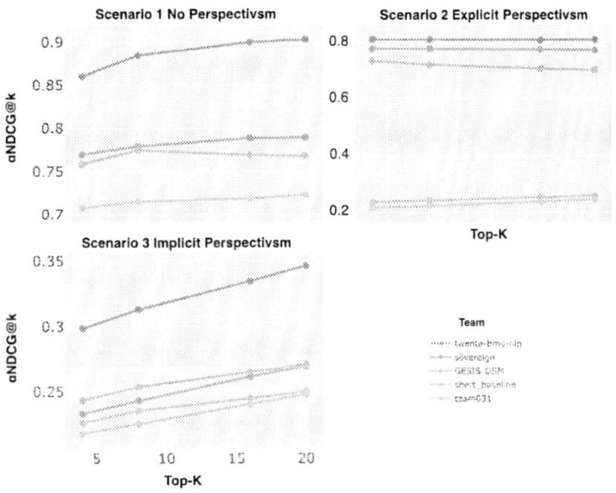

Figure 13: Overview of the per team performance regarding diversity (y-axis, αNDCG@k) regarding top4, top8, top16, and top20 retrieved candidates for the three scenarios.

submissions. Interestingly, this effect is less pronounced for the second scenario (*explicit perspectivism*) and reversed for the third one (*implicit perspectivism*). Specifically, three teams (`twente-bms-nlp`, `sövereign`, and `team031`) show more improvements with higher k than the other teams. These patterns indicate that their filtering or argument re-ranking methods work better on higher k.

A.4 Analysis of bias in representation and performance

Figure 14 shows the representation bias of the different systems in representing different **political orientations**. We can observe a shift from 2019 to 2023 in representing the center/conservative group (over- then underrepresented), which can be accounted for the shift in topics. In both years we can observe that the data bias for left and conservative is reinforced, for left and conservative-liberal its reduced in 2019 but reinforced in 2023.

Figure 18 shows that some systems reduce and some reinforce the bias for left-(conservative/liberal) political orientation as the performance increases or decreases for those groups compared to the baseline.

Figure 15 shows a lot of diversity in teams when looking at the representation of **important political issues** compared to the other socio-cultural properties which can be accounted to the strong semantic influence they have on the text, i.e. it is likely that an important political issue is expressed in the framing of the argument. This is especially the case for the election of 2019, since this data was used for training the systems, and some classifiers were used to predict which issues were important for an author of a certain argument. Some teams retrieve more arguments for law and order, liberal society, or open foreign policy, while others retrieve significantly fewer than the baseline for those issues. This only partially impacts the results (Figure 19), e.g., for law and order, all systems underperform, and over-representing open foreign policy does not increase the performance of all systems on that issue.

For **residence** we find significant differences between the elections: systems are split between reinforcing or reducing the bias of arguments by authors from countryside in 2019, in 2023 all systems reduce that bias (Figure 16). This weakly impacts performance, slightly mitigating the countryside bias for a few systems in 2019 and gaining small improvements for arguments from authors from the city in 2023.

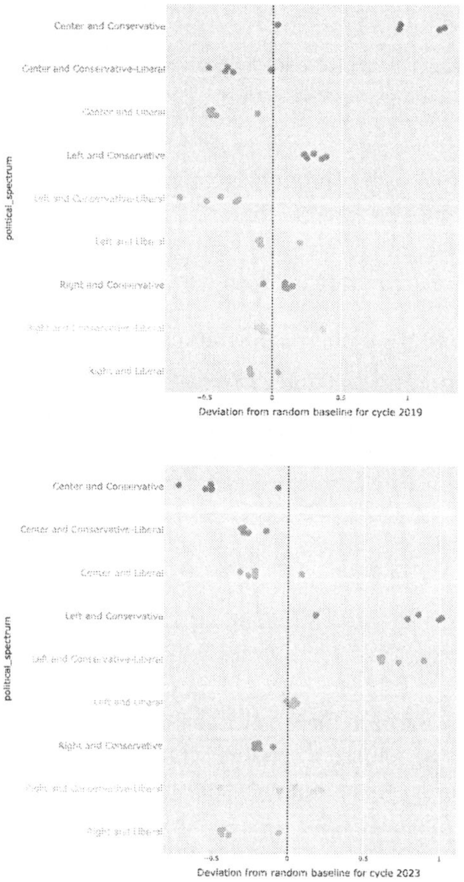

Figure 14: Extent of system deviation from random sampling representing each political spectrum among the 20 most relevant arguments.

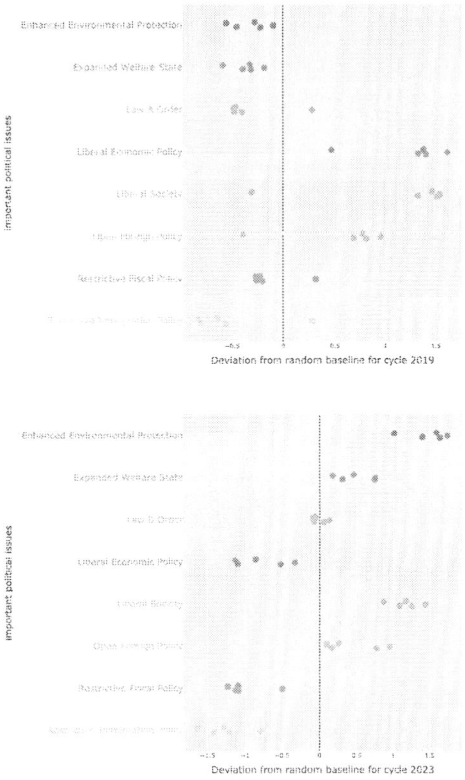

Figure 15: Extent of system deviation from random sampling representing each important political issue among the 20 most relevant arguments.

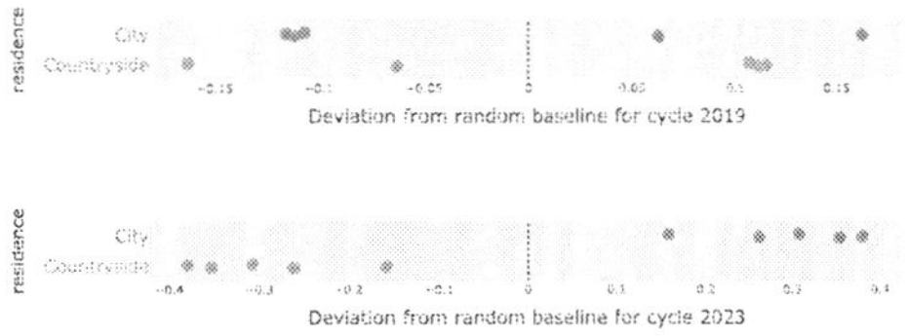

Figure 16: Extent of system deviation from random sampling representing each important residence group among the 20 most relevant arguments.

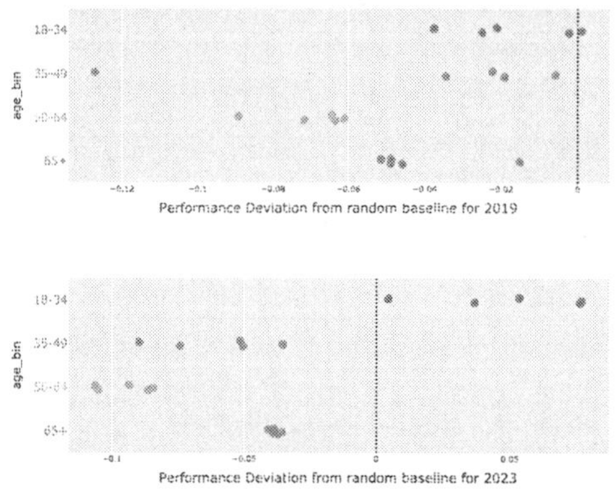

Figure 17: Extent of system deviation from random sampling in performance from the nDCG score for different age groups.

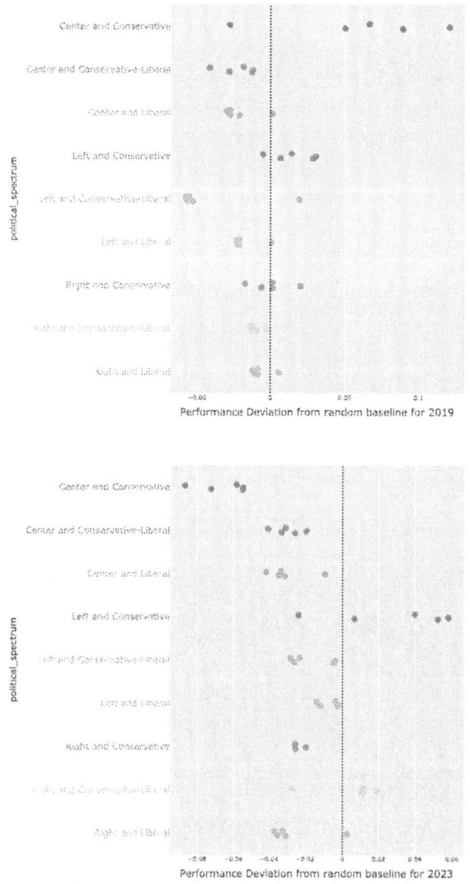

Figure 18: Extent of system deviation from random sampling in performance from the nDCG score for different groups of political spectrum.

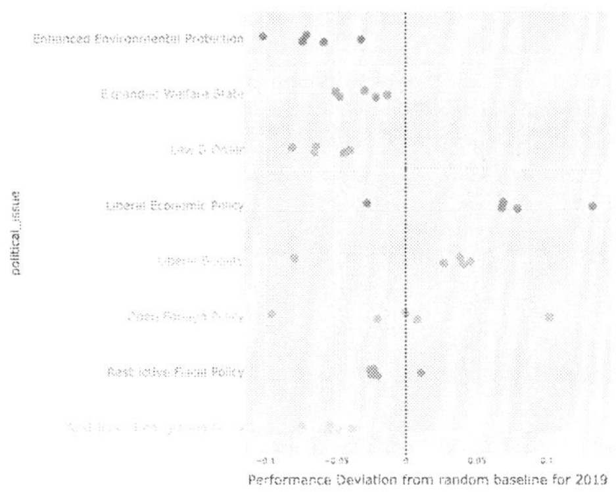

Figure 19: Extent of system deviation from random sampling in performance from the nDCG score for different groups of political spectrum.

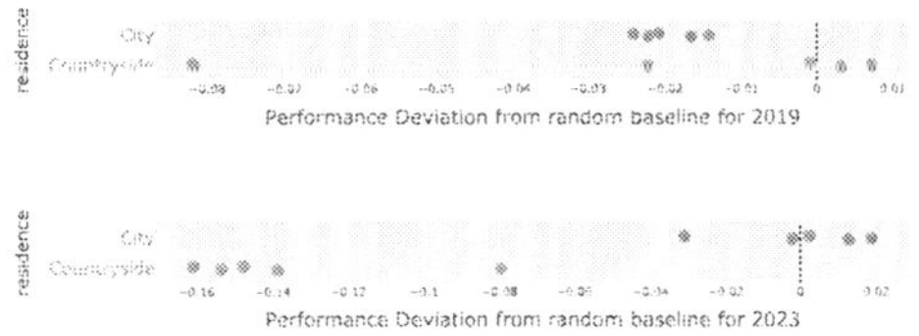

Figure 20: Extent of system deviation from random sampling in performance from the nDCG score for residence.

Sövereign at PerpectiveArg2024: Using LLMs with Argument Mining

Robert Günzler, Özge Sevgili*, **Steffen Remus, Chris Biemann, Irina Nikishina***

Universität Hamburg
Germany

Abstract

This paper presents the *Sövereign* submission for the shared task on perspective argument retrieval for the Argument Mining Workshop 2024 (Falk et al., 2024). To address the challenge, we apply open-access Large Language Models (Mistral-8x7b) in a zero-shot fashion for re-ranking and explicit similarity scoring. Additionally, we combine different features in an ensemble setup using logistic regression. Our system ranks second in the competition for all test set rounds on average for the logistic regression approach using LLM similarity scores as a feature. We also make the code publicly available[1].

1 Introduction

Although the World Wide Web is full of content, search engines nowadays still lack support for extracting information regarding argument retrieval (Bondarenko et al., 2022). Argument retrieval addresses the issue of retrieving relevant arguments from a corpus based on a specific query (Falk et al., 2024). Further issues arise for particular perspectives, i.e., an argument might only be relevant in a special situation with certain restrictions. The shared task on "Perspective Argument Retrieval" (Falk et al., 2024), investigates these challenges by including sociocultural properties/factors (e.g. political interests, occupation, age, and gender) in a multilingual setup (see Figure 1 for illustration). The data includes documents in German, French, and Italian.

Motivated by the abilities of large language models (LLMs; cf. Zhao et al., 2023), we investigate methods to leverage them for this task. We consider two approaches: implicitly re-ranking the argument candidates, and explicitly computing relevance scores for candidate arguments. First, we use the cosine similarity of Sentence BERT (Reimers and Gurevych (2019) between the encoded arguments and the query to retrieve the nearest neighbors (arguments) as candidates similar to the baseline approach by Falk et al. (2024). Note that the given arguments also contain topic labels and socio-cultural factors (e.g. in Scenario 2, Section 3), which we also benefit from. We then supply the query and the retrieved candidates to an LLM and ask it to re-rank the arguments. In our second method, the LLM is asked to produce a score for a given query-argument pair. We further train a logistic regression classifier using several initial similarity scores as features and use the computed feature weights in an ensemble fashion to compute a final relevance score.

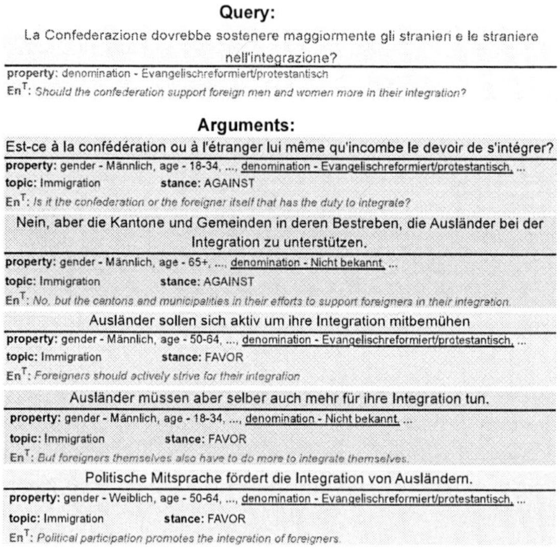

Figure 1: Cross-lingual perspective argument mining: relevant arguments are marked in green, and irrelevant arguments are marked in red or orange. In the orange one, demographic properties match, yet the texts are not relevant. The English translations (using Google Translate[2]) for the query and the arguments are denoted as En^T.

*Equal contribution.

[1] https://github.com/uhh-lt/sovereign-perspectiveArg24

[2] https://translate.google.com

Proceedings of the 11th Workshop on Argument Mining, pages 150–158
August 15, 2024 ©2024 Association for Computational Linguistics

Our LLM scoring based method shows improved performance for Scenario 1 and 2, while the LLM re-ranking performs competitively in Scenario 3, on the development set. Therefore, we submit the results obtained with the logistic regression using the LLM scoring as the final solution to the competition. The name of our team in the leaderboard of the organizers is ***"Sövereign"***.

The contributions of this paper are as follows:

- We investigate the ability of LLMs in argument mining with socio-cultural factors, experimenting with two approaches in a zero-shot setup: ranking by LLM directly and predicting relevance scores using LLM.

- We present a runner-up model, ranked as the second-best system, in the shared task in 2024.

2 Related Work

In this section, we briefly describe the existing studies that we take into consideration while developing our proposed approach.

Argument Retrieval
Apart from the current Perspective Argument Mining shared task (Falk et al., 2024), there exists a series of scientific events and shared tasks on computational argumentation and causality which named Touché (Bondarenko et al., 2022, 2023). Traditionally, the shared task is related to the specific topics, e.g., Retrieval for Comparatives / Controversy (Bondarenko et al., 2022, 2023), Image Retrieval (Bondarenko et al., 2022, 2023), etc. For a detailed overview of the Argument Mining field, we refer the reader to the papers by Lawrence and Reed (2019) and Bondarenko et al. (2023).

LLMs for Ranking
According to Qin et al. (2023), LLMs in zero-shot ranking tasks can be categorized into pointwise, listwise, pairwise, and setwise. Our approach applies the listwise method by Sun et al. (2023). The authors propose RankGPT, a generative LLM (here ChatGPT and GPT-4) for passage relevance ranking in information retrieval (IR) settings. Despite the fear of data contamination, they eventually concluded, that properly instructed LLMs can deliver competitive performance compared to supervised IR methods and can rank unknown knowledge.

3 Task Description

In this shared task, the goal is to retrieve multilingual arguments gathered from the voting recommendation platform[3]. For a description of the dataset, we refer to Falk et al. (2024). The key challenge here is to consider socio-cultural factors during retrieval. For the shared task 2024 we submit systems for all the three competition scenarios:

- **Scenario 1:** Default retrieval ranks argument candidates from a given corpus for a specific query ignoring any social-cultural attributes.

- **Scenario 2:** Explicit perspectivism adds socio-cultural information to the query and the arguments, which limits relevant arguments that match the corresponding socio-cultural factors.

- **Scenario 3:** Implicit perspectivism adds socio-cultural information only to the query, while it is not provided for the arguments.

For each evaluation round, the data consists of a set of queries and a set of candidates/arguments. The set of queries includes the query text, and for Scenarios 2 and 3 it also contains an explicitly given socio-cultural/demographic attribute. The set of candidates contains the argument text, a "stance" parameter ("favor" or "against"), and a "topic" parameter. The retrieval performance is measured using: *a)* relevance: **NDCG@k** and **Pr@k** (precision @ k), and *b)* diversity: α**NDCG@k** and **klDiv@k** (Kullback-Leibler Divergence @ k), where k is the rank of retrieved arguments.

4 Methodology

In this section, we present two approaches for the argument mining task. The first method applies the LLM directly to rank the arguments, the second integrates LLM scores as a feature for a logistic regression model. In the next subsection, we introduce scores utilized in both approaches.

4.1 Feature Scores

In both approaches, the LLM re-ranking and the logistic regression re-ranking, we employ three different scores. We describe each score in details below. In the LLM re-ranking approach presented in Section 4.2 below, scores are summed up and

[3] https://www.smartvote.ch/

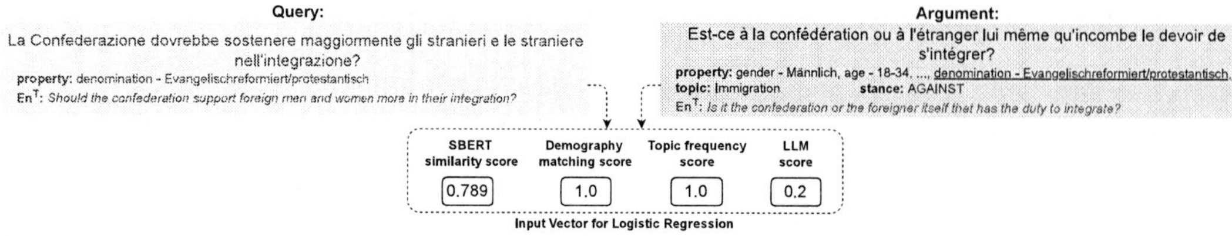

Figure 2: Inputs to the logistic regression for an example query-argument pair with scores of SBERT similarity, demography matching (1.0 in this example as they are matching), topic frequency (1.0, since for this example all 50 arguments have the same topic), and the score predicted by LLM.

the arguments are re-ranked accordingly before being sent to the LLM for re-ranking. We use each score as a feature to train a logistic regression classifier which then produces the final relevance score (Section 4.3). We demonstrate an example input for logistic regression in Figure 2 for better understanding of each score.

SBERT Cosine Similarity Score We encode queries and arguments using SBERT and utilize the cosine similarity of their embeddings to rank arguments given a query. This strategy replicates the baseline approach by the organizers.

Demography Matching Score For Scenario 2, the explicitly given socio-cultural attributes allow hard filtering of the arguments that do not match the socio-cultural attributes of the query. We assign a score of 1 to all arguments that match the given socio-cultural attribute parameter and a score of 0 to all other arguments.

Topic Frequency Score We predict the relevance of each topic to a query as the frequency of that topic among the 50 highest-ranked arguments based on SBERT cosine similarity. For each query-argument pair we use only the relevance of the given topic to the query.

4.2 LLM Ranking

As the first approach, we prompt the LLM with the current query and a list of the 50 highest-ranked arguments based on our SBERT scores. For Scenarios 1 and 3, these scores are the sum of the similarities and the topic scores, and for Scenario 2 they include the scores based on socio-cultural attributes, as well. We then ask the model to return an ordered list of the arguments based on their relevance to the query. The template prompt that we use is presented in Appendix A in Example 1.

Despite producing the machine-readable lists, the LLM output barely includes all 50 argument IDs submitted as input. We interpret all missing IDs as irrelevant to the query and rank them lower at the end of the list.

For Scenario 3, the model re-ranks the arguments according to the socio-cultural attribute from the query and the implicit socio-cultural backgrounds for each argument in Appendix A in Example 2.

4.3 LLM as Score Predictor

For the second approach, we provide the LLM with a list of the 50 highest-ranked arguments (based on the summed feature scores of SBERT, cf. Section 4.1) and prompting it to assign a relevance score between 0 and 1 for each candidate. The prompt for Scenarios 1 and 2 is presented in Appendix A in Example 3.

The expected result is supposed to render a Python dictionary, where keys are sentence IDs, and values are the assigned relevance scores. This approach is also limited by omitting argument IDs in the LLM output. In such cases, we score the missed argument IDs as 0.

For Scenario 3, we all ask the model to predict the relevance score between the given socio-cultural attribute from the query and the implicit socio-cultural backgrounds for each argument with the prompt present in Appendix A in Example 4.

4.4 Ensemble Learning

The previously computed scores are aggregated as features for a logistic regression classifier. More specifically, the feature set is comprised of the LLM relevance score, SBERT cosine similarity between query and argument, the topic frequency score, and the demography matching score based on socio-cultural attributes, as shown in Figure 2. We train a logistic regression classifier for each scenario separately; the goal is to predict whether an argument is relevant to a query or not (label 0 or 1). To train the model, we use the top-100 (Scenario 2) or top-500 (Scenarios 1 and 3) highest-ranked candidate

Rank	Team	Relevance		Diversity	
		Mean Rank	Mean NDCG	Mean Rank	Mean αNDCG@k
1	twente-bms-nlp (top-1)	1.33	0.707	1.67	0.672
2	**Sövereign (top-2)**	**2.22**	**0.632**	**2.22**	**0.601**
5	sbert_baseline	5.0	0.445	5.0	0.419
8	bm25_baseline	7.67	0.195	8.00	0.185

Table 1: Average results on all test sets and scenarios. We present the results for the baseline and the model that presented better performance for comparison.

arguments for each query from the training set.

The resulting weights from the logistic regression are presented in Table 2 in Appendix A. We interpret those scores as importance weights to rebalance the individual features of the candidate arguments. We additionally normalize them to sum up to 1. The weighted sum of the features is then used for re-ranking previously retrieved arguments.

5 Experimental Setup

We use the `Mixtral-8x7B-Instruct-v0.1`[4] LLM model by `mistralai`[5] with the default parameters using `HuggingChat`[6]. This model comes with a lenient license and offers a good balance between performance and model size[7]. By using the `HuggingChat` framework, we explicitly make the model exchangeable, and we expect increased performance by using larger models. We refrain from the model fine-tuning and apply it as a zero-shot.

Regarding SBERT, we use the pre-trained model `paraphrase-multilingual-mpnet-base-v2`[8], likewise the baseline from the organizers (Falk et al., 2024). We trained the logistic regression classifier using the `scikit-learn`[9] framework on the training dataset with the default parameters.

To choose the solution for the final evaluation round, we test our approaches on the development set and submit the test set ranking using the best-performing algorithm.

Scenario 1: Default Argument Retrieval Here, SBERT is already a very strong baseline. Logistic regression achieves better scores for **NDCG**, **Pr**, and α**NDCG** and $k > 4$ (cf. Table 4, in Appendix). Thus, for Scenario 1 we submit the results achieved with logistic regression.

Scenario 2: Explicit Perspectivism Results are shown in Appendix Table 3. LLM re-ranking performs well as compared to the SBERT baseline, however, the logistic regression ensemble achieves the best scores. For this scenario, we also submit the results achieved with logistic regression.

Scenario 3: Implicit Perspectivism In this scenario, both approaches perform almost on par; the LLM re-ranking methods perform better than other approaches, as shown in Table 5 in the Appendix. However, we still decided to submit the logistic regression approach, as we consider learned weights to be more fair for the unseen data.

6 Results on the Test Sets

In this section, we present the test results of our approach from logistic regression. These results are evaluated and shared by task organizers. Table 1 presents the average results for all scenarios and test rounds. Additionally, we show the average results of our approaches across different test rounds and scenarios in Tables 6, 7 and 8 in Appendix A. We achieve competitive results for all scenarios on test set 1 and test set 2, however, our predictions for test set 3 fall short of first place quite significantly. In Scenario 1 test 3 "Sövereign" underperforms even the SBERT baseline. We believe this happens because of the topic scores, included in the final logistic regression. If the SBERT baseline predicts relevant arguments that match the expected topic, this will improve the results by increasing the final scores for those arguments, that match the expected topic. Otherwise, this will impair the results by increasing the final scores for the arguments that do not match the topic. For test set 1 (Precision@20 $= 0.978$)

[4]https://huggingface.co/mistralai/Mixtral-8x7B-Instruct-v0.1
[5]https://mistral.ai/
[6]We use HuggingChat version v0.8.4: https://huggingface.co/chat/
[7]Measured by personal experience.
[8]https://huggingface.co/sentence-transformers/paraphrase-multilingual-mpnet-base-v2
[9]https://scikit-learn.org

and test set 2 (Precision@20 = 0.824) the topic scores are predominantly valuable, hence our results are significantly higher than the baseline. On test set 3 (Precision@20 = 0.565) the topic scores are deceptive for a significant amount of queries: the usage of this feature puts the irrelevant arguments higher. The reason for the difference across different test sets needs to be further investigated.

7 Conclusion

We present *Sövereign*, an LLM re-ranking approach for perspective argument retrieval. We show an investigation of two LLM utilizations, *a*) implicit re-ranking, and *b*) explicit relevance scoring. The explicit relevance scoring methods achieve better scores for explicit perspectivism when used in an ensemble with other similarity features, i.e., SBERT, topic, and socio-cultural (if applicable). In Scenario 3, implicit perspectivism, LLM re-ranking performs better than the LLM scoring. We believe this might be due to the formulations of the prompts in Scenario 3: ranking prompt emphasizes socio-cultural property, directly. In future work, we would like to explore more utilization methods of LLMs in this task, e.g., trying different prompts. The data additionally contains "stance" attributes, which we omitted to use for our submission, but might be an important feature. We also plan to try other LLM models and improve the results for test set 3 by classifying the topic from the query and matching it with the topics from the arguments.

Limitations

Nowadays, dozens of large pre-trained generative models exist and we report results only on `mistralai/Mixtral-8x7B-Instruct-v0.1`. It might be that some other foundation models could further push the results, however, our main goal was to investigate the ability of LLMs to re-rank arguments given socio-cultural factors.

As we use HuggingChat API[10], it could produce every time different responses, which might slightly affect the results if reproducing the approach from scratch. However, we have saved the model output used for the final score submission, therefore, they can be used to reproduce the results.

References

Alexander Bondarenko, Maik Fröbe, Johannes Kiesel, Ferdinand Schlatt, Valentin Barriere, Brian Ravenet, Léo Hemamou, Simon Luck, Jan Heinrich Reimer, Benno Stein, Martin Potthast, and Matthias Hagen. 2023. Overview of Touché 2023: Argument and Causal Retrieval. In *Experimental IR Meets Multilinguality, Multimodality, and Interaction. 14th International Conference of the CLEF Association (CLEF 2023)*, Lecture Notes in Computer Science, Berlin Heidelberg New York. Springer.

Alexander Bondarenko, Maik Fröbe, Johannes Kiesel, Shahbaz Syed, Timon Gurcke, Meriem Beloucif, Alexander Panchenko, Chris Biemann, Benno Stein, Henning Wachsmuth, Martin Potthast, and Matthias Hagen. 2022. Overview of touché 2022: Argument retrieval. In *Experimental IR Meets Multilinguality, Multimodality, and Interaction*, pages 311–336, Cham. Springer International Publishing.

Neele Falk, Andreas Waldis, and Iryna Gurevych. 2024. Overview of PerpectiveArg2024: The First Shared Task on Perspective Argument Retrieval. In *Proceedings of the 11th Workshop on Argument Mining*, Bangkok. Association for Computational Linguistics.

John Lawrence and Chris Reed. 2019. Argument mining: A survey. *Computational Linguistics*, 45(4):765–818.

Zhen Qin, Rolf Jagerman, Kai Hui, Honglei Zhuang, Junru Wu, Jiaming Shen, Tianqi Liu, Jialu Liu, Donald Metzler, Xuanhui Wang, and Michael Bendersky. 2023. Large language models are effective text rankers with pairwise ranking prompting. *CoRR*, abs/2306.17563.

Nils Reimers and Iryna Gurevych. 2019. Sentence-BERT: Sentence embeddings using Siamese BERT-networks. In *Proceedings of the 2019 Conference on Empirical Methods in Natural Language Processing and the 9th International Joint Conference on Natural Language Processing (EMNLP-IJCNLP)*, pages 3982–3992, Hong Kong, China. Association for Computational Linguistics.

Weiwei Sun, Lingyong Yan, Xinyu Ma, Shuaiqiang Wang, Pengjie Ren, Zhumin Chen, Dawei Yin, and Zhaochun Ren. 2023. Is chatgpt good at search? investigating large language models as re-ranking agents. *Preprint*, arXiv:2304.09542.

Wayne Xin Zhao, Kun Zhou, Junyi Li, Tianyi Tang, Xiaolei Wang, Yupeng Hou, Yingqian Min, Beichen Zhang, Junjie Zhang, Zican Dong, Yifan Du, Chen Yang, Yushuo Chen, Zhipeng Chen, Jinhao Jiang, Ruiyang Ren, Yifan Li, Xinyu Tang, Zikang Liu, Peiyu Liu, Jian-Yun Nie, and Ji-Rong Wen. 2023. A survey of large language models. *Preprint*, arXiv:2303.18223.

[10]`https://huggingface.co/chat/`

A Appendix

Here is the template prompt for the Scenario 1 or 2 performed with the LLM re-ranking:

(1)
```
<<SYS>>Answer with a python list containing all ranked argument ids<</SYS>>
[INST]The following are passages related to question <query text>
[/INST]

[0] <1st argument text>
...
[49] <50th argument text>

[INST]Rank these passages based on their relevance to the question.[/INST]
```

Here is the template prompt for the Scenario 3 performed with the LLM re-ranking:

(2)
```
<<SYS>>Answer with a python list containing all ranked argument ids<</SYS>>
[INST]The task is to rank arguments, if they fit the sociocultural property: <query demographic property>.[/INST]

[0] <1st argument text>
...
[49] <50th argument text>

[INST]Rank these passages based on their relevance to the sociocultural property.[/INST]
```

Here is the template prompt for Scenario 1 or 2 performed with similarity scores as a feature for Logistic Regression:

(3)
```
<<SYS>>Answer with a python dictionary containing a score between 0 and 1 for each argument id<</SYS>>
[INST]Given the question <query text> and a list of arguments with IDs. The task is to rank the arguments according to the question. The higher the score the more relevant it is to the question[/INST]

[0] <1st argument text>
...
[49] <50th argument text>

[INST]Return a python dict with every single argument id and the scores only! No text!!! e.g. 1: 0.9, 2: 0.3[/INST]
```

Here is the template prompt for Scenario 3 performed with similarity scores as a feature for Logistic Regression:

(4)
```
<<SYS>>Answer with a python dictionary containing a score between 0 and 1 for each argument id<</SYS>>
[INST]The task is to rank arguments, if they fit the sociocultural property: <query demographic property>[/INST]

[0] <1st argument text>
...
[49] <50th argument text>

[INST]Return a python dict with all argument IDs between 0 and 49 and a score between 0 if the argument does not fit the demographic and 1 if it fits very well.[/INST]
```

Scenario	SBERT similarity	Topic Frequency	Demographic Matching	LLM relevance
1	0.771	0.037	-	0.191
2	0.407	0.064	0.479	0.049
3	0.467	0.287	-	0.246

Table 2: Normalized Logistic Regression weights for the features calculated on the train set.

k	Method	Relevance		Diversity	
		NDCG@k	Pr@k	αNDCG@k	klDiv@k
4	SBERT baseline	0.180	0.182	0.167	**0.151**
	LLM reranking	0.772	0.732	0.724	0.205
	LogReg	**0.866**	**0.796**	**0.812**	0.206
8	SBERT baseline	0.181	0.181	0.169	**0.136**
	LLM reranking	0.752	0.666	0.719	0.192
	LogReg	**0.853**	**0.723**	**0.813**	0.193
16	SBERT baseline	0.180	0.178	0.172	**0.107**
	LLM reranking	0.740	0.590	0.718	0.165
	LogReg	**0.844**	**0.641**	**0.817**	0.167
20	SBERT baseline	0.180	0.176	0.172	**0.099**
	LLM reranking	0.735	0.563	0.716	0.157
	LogReg	**0.840**	**0.612**	**0.817**	0.160

Table 3: Results for Scenario 2 on the development set.

k	Method	Relevance		Diversity	
		NDCG@k	Pr@k	αNDCG@k	klDiv@k
4	SBERT baseline	**0.968**	**0.975**	**0.878**	**0.151**
	LLM reranking	0.962	0.967	0.865	0.164
	LogReg	0.967	**0.975**	0.873	0.162
8	SBERT baseline	0.965	0.967	0.880	**0.137**
	LLM reranking	0.973	0.979	0.881	0.151
	LogReg	**0.976**	**0.983**	**0.885**	0.149
16	SBERT baseline	0.957	0.954	0.892	**0.107**
	LLM reranking	0.966	0.967	0.896	0.124
	LogReg	**0.968**	**0.969**	**0.899**	0.121
20	SBERT baseline	0.954	0.950	0.897	**0.100**
	LLM reranking	0.963	0.962	0.901	0.116
	LogReg	**0.966**	**0.965**	**0.905**	0.114

Table 4: Results for Scenario 1 on the development set.

k	Method	Relevance		Diversity	
		NDCG@k	Pr@k	αNDCG@k	klDiv@k
4	SBERT baseline	0.187	0.188	0.172	**0.151**
	LLM reranking	**0.198**	**0.198**	**0.181**	0.157
	LogReg	0.193	0.194	0.177	0.156
8	SBERT baseline	0.191	0.193	0.177	**0.136**
	LLM reranking	**0.201**	**0.202**	**0.186**	0.144
	LogReg	0.198	0.200	0.184	0.142
16	SBERT baseline	0.198	0.199	0.186	**0.107**
	LLM reranking	**0.209**	**0.211**	**0.196**	0.118
	LogReg	0.204	0.206	0.192	0.114
20	SBERT baseline	0.200	0.201	0.189	**0.099**
	LLM reranking	**0.212**	**0.213**	**0.199**	0.111
	LogReg	0.207	0.207	0.195	0.106

Table 5: Results for Scenario 3 on the development set.

team	Relevance			Diversity		
	Rank	NDCG	Precision	Rank	αNDCG	klDiv
Test set 1						
sövereign	*1*	***0.999***	***0.999***	*1*	***0.922***	*0.143*
twente-bms-nlp	2	0.987	0.989	5	0.910	0.142
GESIS-DSM	3	0.986	0.983	2	0.916	0.124
sbert_baseline	3	0.986	0.983	3	0.916	0.125
bm25_baseline	7	0.651	0.613	8	0.629	**0.121**
Test set 2						
twente-bms-nlp	1	**0.936**	**0.930**	1	**0.870**	**0.115**
sövereign	*3*	*0.895*	*0.888*	*3*	*0.827*	*0.135*
sbert_baseline	5	0.855	0.848	5	0.793	0.118
bm25_baseline	7	0.737	0.722	8	0.690	0.122
Test set 3						
twente-bms-nlp	1	**0.944**	**0.938**	1	**0.880**	0.213
sbert_baseline	4	0.637	0.635	5	0.593	0.153
sövereign	*5*	*0.628*	*0.614*	*4*	*0.595*	*0.161*
bm25_baseline	7	0.368	0.372	8	0.342	**0.152**

Table 6: Average results for Scenario 1 on all test sets.

team	Relevance			Diversity		
	Rank	NDCG	Precision	Rank	αNDCG	klDiv
Test set 1						
twente-bms-nlp	1	**0.895**	**0.717**	1	**0.852**	0.181
sövereign	*2*	*0.878*	*0.707*	*2*	*0.844*	*0.181*
sbert_baseline	5	0.222	0.218	5	0.208	**0.139**
Test set 2						
sövereign	*1*	***0.823***	***0.623***	*1*	***0.794***	*0.166*
twente-bms-nlp	2	0.798	0.610	2	0.771	0.165
sbert_baseline	5	0.148	0.140	5	0.142	**0.124**
Test set 3						
twente-bms-nlp	1	**0.798**	**0.613**	1	**0.793**	0.256
sövereign	*2*	*0.673*	*0.504*	*2*	*0.675*	*0.221*
sbert_baseline	6	0.406	0.339	6	0.400	**0.163**

Table 7: Average results for Scenario 2 on all test sets.

team	Relevance			Diversity		
	Rank	NDCG	Precision	Rank	αNDCG	klDiv
Test set 1						
sövereign	*1*	***0.213***	***0.211***	*1*	***0.199***	*0.135*
twente-bms-nlp	2	0.203	0.202	2	0.190	**0.124**
sbert_baseline	3	0.202	0.201	4	0.189	0.125
Test set 2						
twente-bms-nlp	1	**0.149**	**0.144**	1	**0.143**	**0.121**
sövereign	*2*	*0.139*	*0.136*	*3*	*0.132*	*0.125*
sbert_baseline	4	0.136	0.129	4	0.131	0122
Test set 3						
twente-bms-nlp	1	**0.655**	**0.560**	1	**0.636**	0.189
sövereign	*3*	*0.436*	*0.365*	*3*	*0.425*	*0.160*
sbert_baseline	5	0.409	0.349	5	0.397	**0.158**

Table 8: Average results for Scenario 3 on all test sets.

Turiya at PerpectiveArg2024: A Multilingual Argument Retriever and Reranker

Sougata Saha and Rohini Srihari
State University of New York at Buffalo
Department of Computer Science and Engineering
{sougatas, rohini}@buffalo.edu

Abstract

While general argument retrieval systems have significantly matured, multilingual argument retrieval in a socio-cultural setting is an overlooked problem. Advancements in such systems are imperative to enhance the inclusivity of society. The Perspective Argument Retrieval (PAR) task addresses these aspects and acknowledges their potential latent influence on argumentation. Here, we present a multilingual retrieval system for PAR that accounts for societal diversity during retrieval. Our approach couples a retriever and a re-ranker and spans multiple languages, thus factoring in diverse socio-cultural settings. The performance of our end-to-end system on three distinct test sets testify to its robustness.

1 Introduction

Given a query, argument retrieval (Manning, 2008; Bondarenko et al., 2020, 2022) generally involves retrieving a set of k-relevant arguments from a corpus. Perspective argument retrieval (PAR) (Falk et al., 2024) is an expansion and concerns factoring in the socio-cultural factors during retrieval. Apart from the semantic features, it considers aspects such as persona, attitude, demographics, etc, during retrieval. Such systems are imperative to expanding the reach of argumentation technologies (Besnard and Hunter, 2008; Van Eemeren et al., 2015) among diverse socio-cultural groups. We tackle the following two scenarios of the PAR shared task: (i) **Baseline:** Given a query, retrieving the relevant arguments from a corpus. This scenario evaluates the general abilities of a system to retrieve relevant arguments. (ii) **Explicit:** This extends the baseline task by explicitly adding socio-cultural information to the query and the corpus and limiting the relevant candidates to arguments from authors matching the corresponding socio-cultural background. This scenario tests if a retrieval system can consider socio-cultural properties when explicitly mentioned in the query and the candidates.

The argument corpus comprises 26,335 arguments covering the 2019 Swiss Federal elections in German, French, and Italian. Each argument is enriched with eight socio-cultural properties and spans 45 political aspects. The queries are political issues and based on the x-stance dataset (Vamvas and Sennrich, 2020). The training queries span 35 political aspects, whereas the development set queries span the other 10 aspects. The final evaluation set comprises three secret test sets.

2 Proposed Method

Our implemented architecture comprises a retriever and a re-ranker. Figure 1 illustrates our architecture, which we explain in detail below.

2.1 Corpus Processing

We use *Mistral-7B-Instruct-v0.2* (Jiang et al., 2023) (henceforth referred to as Mistral) in a zero-shot setting to first translate all arguments in the corpus to English. The zero-shot prompt is *"Translate the following text to English."*. Next, we use the *multi-qa-mpnet-base-dot-v1* (Reimers and Gurevych, 2019) model to generate the English embeddings and the *paraphrase-multilingual-mpnet-base-v2* model for multilingual embeddings for each argument. We populate a graph-based vector index (Hsnwlib[1] (Malkov and Yashunin, 2018)) with the English embeddings for performing an approximate K-nearest neighbor search during retrieval. The Hsnwlib index and the multilingual embeddings comprise our retrieval argument collection.

2.2 Retriever

We represent a query using two embeddings: (i) We translate the multilingual query to English using Mistral and generate its English-translated

[1]https://github.com/nmslib/hnswlib

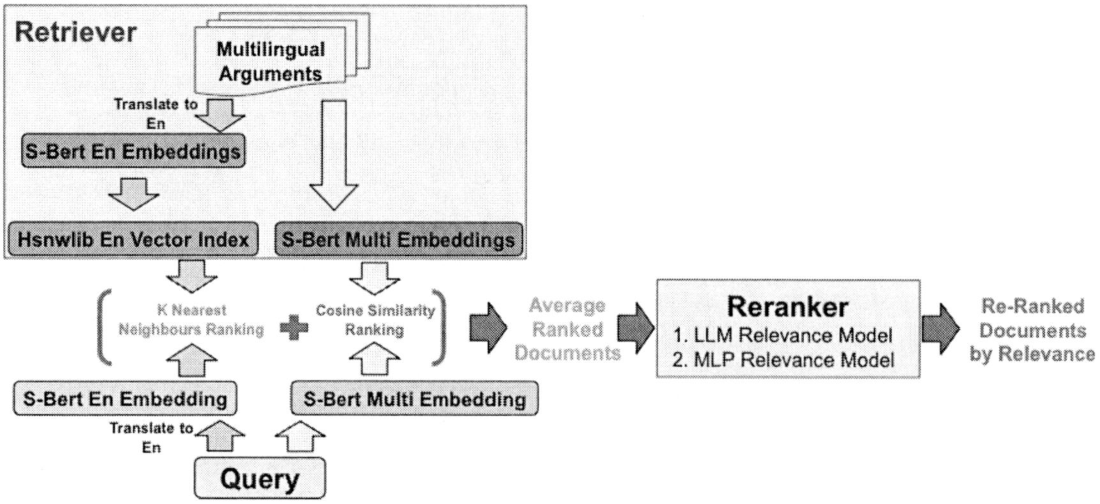

Figure 1: End-to-end architecture of the retrieval system.

embedding using the *multi-qa-mpnet-base-dot-v1* model. (ii) We generate the multilingual embedding from the original non-translated query using the *paraphrase-multilingual-mpnet-base-v2* model. Cosine similarity is computed between the query and corpus multilingual embeddings to retrieve the top 1000 most similar arguments. K-nearest neighbor (KNN) search is performed on the Hsnwlib index to retrieve the top 1000 similar arguments to the English-translated embedding. We average the two rankings and order them to yield the final top 1000 documents. The choice of averaging the multilingual embedding-based cosine similarity ranking with the translated KNN-based ranking is determined empirically. Listed in Table 1, we experimented with different combinations and chose the combination that yielded the best NDCG (Wang et al., 2013) (Normalized discounted cumulative gain) score on the development set.

Id	Combination	4	8	16	20
1	cos_multi	0.97	0.96	0.96	0.95
2	cos_en	0.98	0.96	0.95	0.95
3	knn_multi	0.94	0.93	0.91	0.90
4	knn_en	0.97	0.97	0.97	0.96
5	cos_en + cos_multi	0.97	0.98	0.98	0.98
6	knn_en + knn_multi	**1.00**	**0.99**	0.97	0.97
7	cos_multi + knn_multi	0.96	0.96	0.96	0.95
8	cos_en + knn_en	0.98	0.97	0.96	0.95
9	cos_multi + knn_en	**1.00**	**0.99**	**0.99**	**0.99**
10	cos_en + knn_multi	0.96	0.97	0.96	0.96
11	cos_en + cos_multi + knn_en	0.99	0.98	0.98	0.98
12	cos_en + cos_multi + knn_multi	0.96	0.97	0.97	0.96
13	cos_en + knn_en + knn_multi	0.99	**0.99**	0.97	0.97
14	cos_multi + knn_en + knn_multi	0.99	**0.99**	0.98	0.98
15	cos_en + cos_multi + knn_en + knn_multi	0.98	0.98	0.98	0.98

Table 1: Dev set NDCG results of different scoring combinations for the baseline scenario. Best scores highlighted in bold. cos: cosine similarity, knn: K-nearest neighbours, multi: multilingual, en: English.

2.3 Re-ranker

The re-ranker is an ensemble of a Large Language Model (LLM (Chang et al., 2023; Min et al., 2023; Hadi et al., 2023))-based and a Multi-Layered Perceptron (MLP)-based relevance model. Given a list of the 1000 retrieved documents to a query, we re-order the top 30 by persisting the ones deemed relevant to the query by both models. Below, we detail each model and our internally constructed dataset to train them.

2.3.1 Dataset Construction

We run the retriever on the training set and bucket the retrieved documents by their ranking as follows: 1-20, 21-100, 101-300, 301-700, 700-1000. For each bucket, we check if the retrieved documents are relevant and construct a balanced dataset (named *rel*) of 6,150 examples (4,815 train, 1,335 dev) comprising query and document pairs with a binary label denoting whether the document is relevant to the query. We consider the English-translated text of the query and document. Furthermore, we construct 8,795 examples (6,895 train, 1,900 dev, and named *mcq*) where, given a query and two retrieved documents, the task requires comparing the documents to determine the more relevant one. From each bucket, we randomly pair relevant and non-relevant retrieved documents. Additionally, we include two cases where random pairs of documents from the same bucket within a window of 3 are marked relevant or non-relevant to the same degree. Constructing the *rel* and *mcq* datasets using the bucketed approach helps adjust the dataset's difficulty, where examples from the lower buckets are more challenging than the higher ones.

2.3.2 MLP Re-ranker

The MLP-based relevance model is a 2-layered neural network. It inputs 768-dimensional query and document embeddings and independently encodes them to a 128-dimensional representation using a single-layered neural network, followed by a non-linear ReLU activation. The encoded representations are concatenated (now 256-dimensional) and passed through a 2-layered neural network, where the hidden layer contains 128 nodes with ReLU activation, and the final layer is a single node that denotes the relevance score (logit). We use *multi-qa-mpnet-base-dot-v1* to compute the 768-dimensional input query and document embeddings. The model is trained on the *rel* dataset in mini-batches of 32 with AdamW (Loshchilov and Hutter, 2017) optimizer, using a 1e-5 learning rate and early stopping for five epochs. It attains an F1 score of 73% on the *rel* dataset dev split.

2.3.3 LLM Re-ranker

We fine-tune Mistral-7B-Instruct-v0.2 on instructions from the *rel* and *mcq* datasets. Table 2 illustrates samples from each dataset. The model was trained for two epochs using LoRA (Hu et al., 2021), a parameter-efficient fine-tuning (Mangrulkar et al., 2022) method. The LoRA r and alpha were set to 16 and 32 and trained the q, v, k, o, gate, up, and down projection modules of the attention heads and the LM head using a 2.5e-5 learning rate. Fine-tuning LLMs on multiple tasks has shown to be fruitful. Since the *rel* dataset instructions only entail comparing query-document pairs, we include the *mcq* dataset to increase the task variety as it additionally entails comparing documents. Fine-tuning on multiple tasks (multi-task learning (Caruana, 1997; Zhang and Yang, 2021)) has proven to improve performance on the individual tasks. The fine-tuned model attains an F1 score of 79% on the *rel* dataset and an accuracy score of 51% on the *mcq* dataset dev splits.

During inference we ensemble the MLP and LLM-based re-rankers, where given a list of the 1000 retrieved documents to a query, we re-order the top 30 by persisting the ones deemed relevant to the query by both models.

Sample from the *rel* dataset
[INST] Identify using true/false if a document is relevant to a query. Query: Should the Confederation support foreigners in integration? Document: "Integration is good and important. However, it is now necessary at the cantonaland community levels." [/INST] Answer: true
Sample from the *mcq* dataset
[INST] Given a query and two retrieved documents, identify which of the following options is correct. Query: Should the Confederation support foreigners in integration? Document A: Political co-determination promotes foreigner integration. Document B: It is desirable to integrate foreigners on a political level. i. Document A is more relevant than Document B. ii. Document B is more relevant than Document A. iii. Both the documents are equally relevant to the query. iv. None of the documents are relevant to the query. [/INST] Answer: iv

Table 2: Samples of Mistral training instructions.

3 Results

We run our pipeline on the three official test sets and share the results for the baseline scenario in Table 3 and the explicit scenario in Table 4. We compare our results against BM-25-based and embedding cosine similarity-based (Sbert) baselines. For the baseline scenario (Table 3), our implementation significantly outperforms both baselines in test sets 2 and 3. Although we significantly outperform the BM-25 baseline for test set 1, the Sbert baseline attains a comparable score to our implementation. For the explicit scenario, we only persist the baseline ranked documents where the query socio-cultural features match with the document. As evident from Table 4, our implementation significantly outperforms the Sbert baseline for all test sets.

4 Conclusion

Here, we present an end-to-end retrieval and ranking system capable of retrieving multilingual arguments to user queries while factoring in the socio-cultural features. Our implementation uses the original and English-translated text and implements an ensembled retriever and re-ranker to retrieve relevant documents. Our retriever combines the semantic relatedness of embedding a similarity-based

		Ndcg				Precision			
Set	Model	4	8	16	20	4	8	16	20
1	BM25	0.72	0.67	0.62	0.60	0.68	0.64	0.58	0.55
	Sbert	**0.99**	**0.99**	**0.98**	**0.98**	**0.99**	**0.99**	**0.98**	**0.98**
	Ours	**0.99**	0.98	**0.98**	0.97	0.98	0.97	0.97	0.97
2	BM25	0.78	0.76	0.72	0.69	0.78	0.76	0.69	0.66
	Sbert	0.88	0.86	0.84	0.84	0.89	0.86	0.82	0.82
	Ours	**0.94**	**0.93**	**0.91**	**0.90**	**0.94**	**0.93**	**0.90**	**0.89**
3	BM25	0.36	0.37	0.38	0.37	0.36	0.37	0.39	0.37
	Sbert	0.67	0.68	0.61	0.59	0.69	0.69	0.59	0.56
	Ours	**0.80**	**0.80**	**0.73**	**0.70**	**0.82**	**0.81**	**0.70**	**0.67**

Table 3: Model performance on diverse test sets for the Baseline scenario.

		Ndcg				Precision			
Set	Model	4	8	16	20	4	8	16	20
1	Sbert	0.22	0.22	0.23	0.23	0.22	0.22	0.22	0.22
	Ours	**0.71**	**0.69**	**0.67**	**0.66**	**0.66**	**0.60**	**0.54**	**0.52**
2	Sbert	0.15	0.15	0.15	0.15	0.15	0.14	0.13	0.13
	Ours	**0.72**	**0.69**	**0.65**	**0.64**	**0.67**	**0.60**	**0.53**	**0.50**
3	Sbert	0.38	0.39	0.42	0.44	0.38	0.36	0.32	0.31
	Ours	**0.70**	**0.65**	**0.62**	**0.61**	**0.67**	**0.58**	**0.49**	**0.47**

Table 4: Model performance on diverse test sets for the Explicit scenario.

approach with a KNN-based approach to yield an initial retrieved ordering of documents. Our ensemble of LLM and MLP-based re-rankers re-orders the documents by their relevance to generate the final list of ordered documents for a query. Evaluations against two baselines across three distinct test sets testify to the robustness of our approach.

References

Philippe Besnard and Anthony Hunter. 2008. *Elements of argumentation*, volume 47. MIT press Cambridge.

Alexander Bondarenko, Maik Fröbe, Meriem Beloucif, Lukas Gienapp, Yamen Ajjour, Alexander Panchenko, Chris Biemann, Benno Stein, Henning Wachsmuth, Martin Potthast, et al. 2020. Overview of touché 2020: argument retrieval. In *Experimental IR Meets Multilinguality, Multimodality, and Interaction: 11th International Conference of the CLEF Association, CLEF 2020, Thessaloniki, Greece, September 22–25, 2020, Proceedings 11*, pages 384–395. Springer.

Alexander Bondarenko, Maik Fröbe, Johannes Kiesel, Shahbaz Syed, Timon Gurcke, Meriem Beloucif, Alexander Panchenko, Chris Biemann, Benno Stein, Henning Wachsmuth, et al. 2022. Overview of touché 2022: argument retrieval. In *International Conference of the Cross-Language Evaluation Forum for European Languages*, pages 311–336. Springer.

Rich Caruana. 1997. Multitask learning. *Machine learning*, 28:41–75.

Yupeng Chang, Xu Wang, Jindong Wang, Yuan Wu, Linyi Yang, Kaijie Zhu, Hao Chen, Xiaoyuan Yi, Cunxiang Wang, Yidong Wang, et al. 2023. A survey on evaluation of large language models. *ACM Transactions on Intelligent Systems and Technology*.

Neele Falk, Andreas Waldis, and Iryna Gurevych. 2024. Overview of perpectivearg2024: The first shared task on perspective argument retrieval. In *Proceedings of the 11th Workshop on Argument Mining*, Bangkok. Association for Computational Linguistics.

Muhammad Usman Hadi, Rizwan Qureshi, Abbas Shah, Muhammad Irfan, Anas Zafar, Muhammad Bilal Shaikh, Naveed Akhtar, Jia Wu, Seyedali Mirjalili, et al. 2023. A survey on large language models: Applications, challenges, limitations, and practical usage. *Authorea Preprints*.

Edward J Hu, Yelong Shen, Phillip Wallis, Zeyuan Allen-Zhu, Yuanzhi Li, Shean Wang, Lu Wang, and Weizhu Chen. 2021. Lora: Low-rank adaptation of large language models. *arXiv preprint arXiv:2106.09685*.

Albert Q. Jiang, Alexandre Sablayrolles, Arthur Mensch, Chris Bamford, Devendra Singh Chaplot, Diego de las Casas, Florian Bressand, Gianna Lengyel, Guillaume Lample, Lucile Saulnier, Lélio Renard Lavaud, Marie-Anne Lachaux, Pierre Stock, Teven Le Scao, Thibaut Lavril, Thomas Wang, Timothée Lacroix, and William El Sayed. 2023. Mistral 7b. *Preprint*, arXiv:2310.06825.

Ilya Loshchilov and Frank Hutter. 2017. Decoupled weight decay regularization. *arXiv preprint arXiv:1711.05101*.

Yu A Malkov and Dmitry A Yashunin. 2018. Efficient and robust approximate nearest neighbor search using hierarchical navigable small world graphs. *IEEE transactions on pattern analysis and machine intelligence*, 42(4):824–836.

Sourab Mangrulkar, Sylvain Gugger, Lysandre Debut, Younes Belkada, Sayak Paul, and Benjamin Bossan. 2022. Peft: State-of-the-art parameter-efficient fine-tuning methods. `https://github.com/huggingface/peft`.

Christopher D Manning. 2008. *Introduction to information retrieval*. Syngress Publishing,.

Bonan Min, Hayley Ross, Elior Sulem, Amir Pouran Ben Veyseh, Thien Huu Nguyen, Oscar Sainz, Eneko Agirre, Ilana Heintz, and Dan Roth. 2023. Recent advances in natural language processing via large pre-trained language models: A survey. *ACM Computing Surveys*, 56(2):1–40.

Nils Reimers and Iryna Gurevych. 2019. Sentence-bert: Sentence embeddings using siamese bert-networks. *arXiv preprint arXiv:1908.10084*.

Jannis Vamvas and Rico Sennrich. 2020. X-stance: A multilingual multi-target dataset for stance detection. *arXiv preprint arXiv:2003.08385*.

Frans H Van Eemeren, Frans H van Eemeren, Sally Jackson, and Scott Jacobs. 2015. Argumentation. *Reasonableness and effectiveness in argumentative discourse: Fifty contributions to the development of Pragma-dialectics*, pages 3–25.

Yining Wang, Liwei Wang, Yuanzhi Li, Di He, and Tie-Yan Liu. 2013. A theoretical analysis of ndcg type ranking measures. In *Conference on learning theory*, pages 25–54. PMLR.

Yu Zhang and Qiang Yang. 2021. A survey on multi-task learning. *IEEE Transactions on Knowledge and Data Engineering*, 34(12):5586–5609.

Twente-BMS-NLP at PerspectiveArg 2024: Combining Bi-Encoder and Cross-Encoder for Argument Retrieval

Leixin Zhang
University of Twente
l.zhang-5@utwente.nl

Daniel Braun
University of Twente
d.braun@utwente.nl

Abstract

The paper describes our system for the Perspective Argument Retrieval Shared Task. The shared task consists of three scenarios in which relevant political arguments have to be retrieved based on queries (Scenario 1). In Scenario 2 explicit socio-cultural properties are provided and in Scenario 3 implicit socio-cultural properties within the arguments have to be used. We combined a Bi-Encoder and a Cross-Encoder to retrieve relevant arguments for each query. For the third scenario, we extracted linguistic features to predict socio-demographic labels as a separate task. However, the socio-demographic match task proved challenging due to the constraints of argument lengths and genres. The described system won both tracks (relevance and diversity) of the shared task.

1 Introduction

The perspective argument retrieval shared task (Falk et al., 2024) addresses the challenge of incorporating socio-cultural factors into argument retrieval. It is based on the x-stance dataset (Vamvas and Sennrich, 2020) and includes three scenarios: baseline, explicit, and implicit. Queries in the baseline scenario are provided without socio-demographic requirements on extracted arguments. In the explicit and implicit scenarios, one socio-demographic feature is provided along with the query as an additional requirement to retrieve arguments that match the label, (e.g.{gender: male}). An extracted argument is considered a true candidate only if it is relevant to the query text and matches the socio-demographic label provided with the query in explicit and implicit scenarios.

The difference between the explicit and implicit scenarios is that in the explicit scenario, the socio-demographic information of argument authors is available in the corpus, whereas in the implicit scenario it is not. This means that in the implicit scenario, systems must predict or match the socio-demographic features in addition to determining relevance to the query.

In our system, we combine bi-encoder and cross-encoder models to retrieve relevant arguments. Additionally, we predict socio-demographic features from argument texts in the implicit scenario, using sentence embeddings, n-gram of part-of-speech (POS) tags and stop words, and token length distributions as input features. The system performed best in both tracks of the shared task, relevance and diversity.

2 Related Work

Previous studies have employed several strategies to model query and argument sentences before they can be matched subsequently: Simple statistical features like token n-grams or part-of-speech (POS) n-grams (Clement and Sharp, 2003), TF-IDF (Ramos et al., 2003), or word2vec (Sardianos et al., 2015; Jang and Kwon, 2023). Word embeddings with mean pooling or other techniques to generate sentence embeddings of fixed lengths (Devlin et al., 2018; Liu et al., 2019), sentence embedding models such as Sentence-BERT (Reimers and Gurevych, 2019) or LaBSE (Feng et al., 2020), and ensemble approaches combining models from the aforementioned categories (Zhang and Çöltekin, 2024; Reimers et al., 2019).

Sentence embedding models typically use a bi-encoder architecture, such as a Siamese Neural Network. The relevance of two sentences is often measured with the cosine similarity of their embeddings. Bi-encoders are more suitable for symmetric searches where two sentences are interchangeable (Muennighoff, 2022). Asymmetric scenarios like answering a specific question often benefit more from cross-encoder models. Thakur et al. (2020) pointed out the challenge in training bi-encoders to represent two asymmetric sentences within a shared vector space. Beyond encoder architectures,

Muennighoff (2022) proposed a method that employs decoders for sentence embeddings and semantic search.

2.1 Socio-Demographic Features

One goal of the the perspective argument retrieval shared task is to retrieve a set of diverse with regard to the socio-demographic features of the argument providers, such as age and political stances. Most works that attempt to explicitly extract such features require long texts as input. In age and gender prediction, for example, the majority of studies work with texts with 250 words or more (Peersman et al., 2011). By contrast, for the dataset in this shared task, the average length of each argument is less than 30 words (25.86 excluding punctuation tokens). Some studies also work with shorter texts: Peersman et al. (2011) analyzed chat messages averaging 12.2 tokens each and achieved an accuracy of 88.8% for age prediction. Zhang and Zhang (2010) studied blog posts averaging 15 tokens per segment, achieving an accuracy of 72.10% for gender prediction. When shorter texts are used, these are often collected from social media, which may include more personal styles such as abbreviations or emoticons. This may simplify the task compared to the dataset of the shared task, which consists of political arguments from a dedicated platform, less likely to contain such explicit clues.

3 Dataset Analysis

In the training and development datasets, we observed that the queries and candidates are structured as follows: the same query is provided in three languages: German, French, and Italian. Though as separate query entries, each language version shares the same list of candidate arguments. Options for addressing this cross-lingual setting include using or fine-tuning cross-lingual sentence embedding models or translating different languages into one.

Additionally, we noted that an argument candidate only appears under one query (or the same query of three language versions). This suggests that the dataset might have been created from an existing set of query arguments (in the X-stance dataset), with arguments randomized and compiled into a mixed arguments corpus, rather than through annotations of argument relevance for each query. This setup could pose challenges for traditional semantic search tasks: if an argument could validly answer two different queries, it is still tied to only the query with which it was originally associated, and appearing under the other query would be considered a false retrieval, even if it might be correct.

A potential strategy to address this issue is to evaluate each candidate's relevance across all queries, assigning it to only one query. However, this approach has a drawback: if an argument is incorrectly assigned to one query, it precludes the possibility of it being correctly assigned to another query. Ultimately, we adopted a hybrid strategy. For queries in the development set, we only considered candidates that had not appeared under training queries. Similarly, for each test set, we only considered candidates that had not appeared in either the training or development queries, which helps narrow down the argument pools and potentially enhance retrieval accuracy. This strategy was implemented across all test sets and scenarios. Nevertheless, we also provide unfiltered results in this paper for broader comparison with the baselines.

4 System Design

4.1 Baseline Scenario

As discussed in Section 2, previous work has shown that bi-encoders generally perform less well than cross-encoders for asymmetric retrieval tasks. However, cross-encoders have a disadvantage in terms of computing complexity. If there are M samples in the query set and N samples in the corpus, the model needs to be run $M \times N$ times, compared to $M + N$ for bi-encoders. In our system, we employed a strategy to combine both: we used a bi-encoder (`paraphrase-multilingual-mpnet-base-v2`) to retrieve the top 1000 argument candidates and then used a cross-encoder model (`ms-marco-MiniLM-L-12-v2`[1]) to re-rank the top 50. We compared both multilingual and monolingual cross-encoders and found that the monolingual model performs better. Therefore, we translate[2] the top 50 into English before using the cross-encoder.

4.2 Explicit Scenario

To extract semantically relevant arguments in the explicit scenario, we applied the same method as

[1] https://www.sbert.net/docs/pretrained-models/ce-msmarco.html

[2] We use Google translate API from the following GitHub repository to translate all queries and top-50 arguments to English: https://github.com/ssut/py-googletrans.

Factor	Algorithm	Input	Accuracy	Class num.	Prop. bounds
residence	MLP	sbert embedding	0.93	2	0.094 - 0.906
important issues	MLP	sbert embedding	0.65	8	multi-label case
gender	Ran. Forest	bigram POS/STOP	0.67	2	0.377 - 0.622
political spectrum	MLP	sbert embedding	0.52	9	0.003 - 0.455
civil status	MLP	sbert embedding	0.44	9	$6.8e^{05}$ - 0.367
age_bin	MLP	sbert embedding	0.43	4	0.054 - 0.330
denomination	MLP	sbert embedding	0.42	10	0.0004 - 0.409
education	MLP	sbert embedding	0.34	13	0.007- 0.281

Table 1: Overview of the best-performing approaches for the prediction of socio-demographic features ('Label num.' indicates the number of target labels per factor and 'Prop. bounds' shows the lower and upper bounds of label proportions).

in the baseline scenario. However, in this scenario, the retrieved arguments should not only be semantically relevant but also match the (explicitly provided) socio-demographic features of the query. While integrating these socio-demographic labels into the query and argument texts and converting the extended texts into sentence embeddings could be an option, this approach may introduce additional noise and degrade both relevance and socio-demographic matching. We instead employed exact label matching. For instance, if the query feature is `{gender: female}`, we filtered the corpus to select arguments that match this socio-demographic feature.

4.3 Implicit Scenario

In the implicit scenario, the explicitly provided socio-demographic features for the arguments should not be used. This means that, in order to perform the socio-demographic matching, the factors have to be extracted from the text. Our approach is to predict the socio-demographic labels for arguments and then use these predictions in the same way as in the explicit scenario. The training data was collected from the training query documents. We retrieved socio-demographic labels from the query requirement and assigned socio-demographic labels to their corresponding argument candidate lists, creating a pseudo-corpus for socio-demographic feature training.

Our preliminary analysis suggests that for categories like important issues or political spectrum, semantic information is crucial, hence sentence embeddings that capture meaning should be used as input. However, categories such as gender and age, are influenced more by lexical preferences as documented in previous research. Thus, apart from sentence embeddings, we also conducted feature engineering, focusing on German arguments (which comprise about 70% of our corpus). We extracted the following features:

- Token Length Distribution: We used the NLTK package to tokenize sentences and words for each argument, then calculated the token lengths and their distribution.
- POS & Stop Unigram Distribution: We converted all argument texts into part-of-speech (POS) tags for content words while retaining stop words in their original form.
- POS & Stop Bigram Distribution: bigrams from the POS and stop words sequences and computed their distribution.

We input these statistical features and sentence-bert embeddings into MLP, SVM, and random forest models and compare their performance in predicting the different socio-demographic factors.[3]

The best performance for each demographic category prediction is displayed in Table 1. While most categories achieved an accuracy below 0.7, the residence category showed the highest accuracy of 0.93. This performance can most likely be explained by the imbalanced data, with the majority label comprising 90.6% of the data and the minority 9.4%, leading the model to (correctly) predominantly predict the majority label. This issue of imbalance is also present in other socio-demographic factors. Poor accuracy in certain categories can also

[3]Due to time constraints of the shared task, not all combinations of model algorithms, input features, and demographic features were tested; however, MLP was used for all socio-demographic feature predictions.

	important issues		gender	
top-k	ndcg	precision	ndcg	precision
4	0.180	0.182	0.170	0.172
8	0.181	0.182	0.171	0.172
16	0.182	0.180	0.172	0.170
20	0.182	0.180	0.171	0.166

Table 2: Prediction results from the development set when matching socio-demographic labels for 'important issues' and 'gender' requirements respectively. We left the remaining categories uncontrolled as the baseline method.

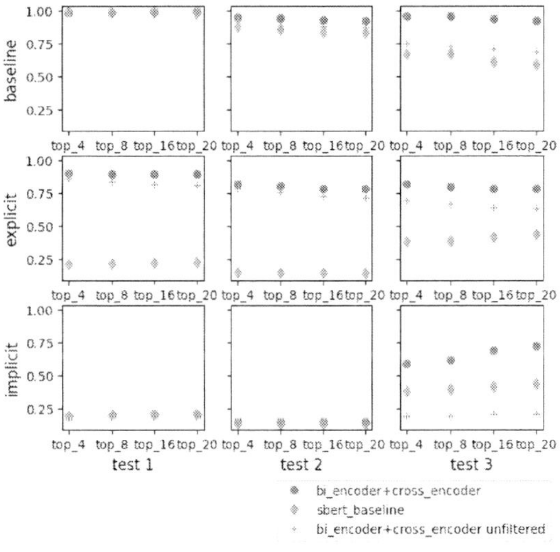

Figure 1: Relevance results (NDCG scores) for retrieved argument candidates from the top 4 to top 20 across three scenarios and three test sets.

potentially be attributed to the large number of target labels, such as in education (13 labels) and denomination (10 labels). Furthermore, labels within a demographic category are not mutually exclusive, for example, 'Rechts und Konservativ-Liberal' (right and conservative-liberal), 'Rechts und Konservativ' (right and conservative), and 'Rechts und Liberal' (right and liberal) are treated as separate labels, complicating correct assignment despite statistical indicators from the texts.

The categories 'important issues' and 'gender' predicted better than others. Moreover, the accuracy for 'important issues' is underestimated by the standard accuracy score since it is a multilabel classification (one argument may correspond to more than one important issue) with each class having a binary label as its target. Separate accuracy computations for each class revealed better results, as shown in Table 3 in the Appendix.

Our approach intends to use our predictions to filter corpus arguments and then select semantically relevant arguments from the filtered corpus. For query requirements where demographic features other than 'important issues' and 'gender', we do not apply filtering and focus only on semantic matching. Results on the development set revealed that filtering based on 'important issues' was more effective than gender filtering. Indeed, gender filtering performed worse than no filtering at all when tested with the development set. Consequently, we decided to only apply demographic filtering for 'important issues' for the final submission.

5 Results and Discussion

Figure 1 presents the comparison between our system and Sentence-BERT. The first row shows the NDCG scores of three test sets in the baseline scenario. Our system performs similarly well in Test 1 but shows a significant advantage over Sentence-BERT in Tests 2 and 3. In test 3, it also reveals that the high accuracy can largely be attributed to the filtering procedure and the narrowing down of the corpus size. For explicit scenarios (the second row in Figure 1), our system significantly outperforms Sentence-BERT by using exact demographic label matches from queries to arguments in the corpus.

For implicit scenarios (the third row in Figure 1), our system shows no difference from Sentence-BERT, except in Test 3, which is significantly better with the filtering procedure but much worse without filtering. The implicit scenario shows that the benefits of utilizing the 'important issues' classifier to filter first are not evident. The predicted important issues' might also be decoded by Sentence-BERT, and overall low precision may result from the mismatch of other demographic factors. Despite performing less well in the implicit scenario than in the other two, our results still achieved first place among all participated teams in Tests 2 and 3, and second in Test 1.

6 Conclusion

This study demonstrates the advantages of combining bi-encoder and cross-encoder models over solely using the bi-encoder (Sentence-BERT). We also found that perspective argument retrieval or inferring socio-demographic features from short arguments remains challenging, accompanied by the disadvantage of the number and quality of labels.

Moreover, longer argument texts may be necessary to decode the socio-demographic features of argument providers in the future.

References

Ross Clement and David Sharp. 2003. Ngram and bayesian classification of documents for topic and authorship. *Literary and linguistic computing*, 18(4):423–447.

Jacob Devlin, Ming-Wei Chang, Kenton Lee, and Kristina Toutanova. 2018. Bert: Pre-training of deep bidirectional transformers for language understanding. *arXiv preprint arXiv:1810.04805*.

Neele Falk, Andreas Waldis, and Iryna Gurevych. 2024. Overview of perpectivearg2024: The first shared task on perspective argument retrieval. In *Proceedings of the 11th Workshop on Argument Mining*, Bangkok. Association for Computational Linguistics.

Fangxiaoyu Feng, Yinfei Yang, Daniel Cer, Naveen Arivazhagan, and Wei Wang. 2020. Language-agnostic bert sentence embedding. *arXiv preprint arXiv:2007.01852*.

Jae-Seok Jang and Hyuk-Yoon Kwon. 2023. Question-answering pair matching based on question classification and ensemble sentence embedding. *Comput. Syst. Sci. Eng.*, 46(3):3471–3489.

Yinhan Liu, Myle Ott, Naman Goyal, Jingfei Du, Mandar Joshi, Danqi Chen, Omer Levy, Mike Lewis, Luke Zettlemoyer, and Veselin Stoyanov. 2019. Roberta: A robustly optimized bert pretraining approach. *arXiv preprint arXiv:1907.11692*.

Niklas Muennighoff. 2022. Sgpt: Gpt sentence embeddings for semantic search. *arXiv preprint arXiv:2202.08904*.

Claudia Peersman, Walter Daelemans, and Leona Van Vaerenbergh. 2011. Predicting age and gender in online social networks. In *Proceedings of the 3rd international workshop on Search and mining user-generated contents*, pages 37–44.

Juan Ramos et al. 2003. Using tf-idf to determine word relevance in document queries. In *Proceedings of the first instructional conference on machine learning*, volume 242, pages 29–48. Citeseer.

Nils Reimers and Iryna Gurevych. 2019. Sentence-bert: Sentence embeddings using siamese bert-networks. *arXiv preprint arXiv:1908.10084*.

Nils Reimers, Benjamin Schiller, Tilman Beck, Johannes Daxenberger, Christian Stab, and Iryna Gurevych. 2019. Classification and clustering of arguments with contextualized word embeddings. *arXiv preprint arXiv:1906.09821*.

Christos Sardianos, Ioannis Manousos Katakis, Georgios Petasis, and Vangelis Karkaletsis. 2015. Argument extraction from news. In *Proceedings of the 2nd Workshop on Argumentation Mining*, pages 56–66.

Nandan Thakur, Nils Reimers, Johannes Daxenberger, and Iryna Gurevych. 2020. Augmented sbert: Data augmentation method for improving bi-encoders for pairwise sentence scoring tasks. *arXiv preprint arXiv:2010.08240*.

Jannis Vamvas and Rico Sennrich. 2020. X-stance: A multilingual multi-target dataset for stance detection. In *5th SwissText & 16th KONVENS Joint Conference 2020*, page 9. CEUR-WS. org.

Cathy Zhang and Pengyu Zhang. 2010. Predicting gender from blog posts.

Leixin Zhang and Çağrı Çöltekin. 2024. Tübingen-CL at SemEval-2024 task 1: Ensemble learning for semantic relatedness estimation. In *Proceedings of the 18th International Workshop on Semantic Evaluation (SemEval-2024)*, pages 1019–1025, Mexico City, Mexico. Association for Computational Linguistics.

A Appendix

Issue	Accuracy
Restriktive Finanzpolitik	0.86
Liberale Wirtschaftspolitik	0.79
Ausgebauter Sozialstaat	0.76
Law & Order	0.75
Restriktive Migrationspolitik	0.73
Liberale Gesellschaft	0.73
Ausgebauter Umweltschutz	0.72
Offene Aussenpolitik	0.66

Table 3: Individual accuracy per class in 'important issues' (a multi-label classification problem).

GESIS-DSM at PerpectiveArg2024: A Matter of Style? Socio-Cultural Differences in Argumentation

Maximilian Martin Maurer[1], **Julia Romberg**[1], **Myrthe Reuver**[3 ♥], **Negash Desalegn Weldekiros**[1,4], and **Gabriella Lapesa**[1,2]
[1]GESIS - Leibniz Institute for the Social Sciences, [2]Heinrich-Heine University Düsseldorf
[3]Vrije Universiteit Amsterdam, [4]Technical University of Munich
[1]first.last@gesis.org, [3]myrthe.reuver@vu.nl, [4]negash.weldekiros@tum.de

Abstract

This paper describes the contribution of team GESIS-DSM to the Perspective Argument Retrieval Task, a task on retrieving socio-culturally relevant and diverse arguments for different user queries. Our experiments and analyses aim to explore the nature of the socio-cultural specialization in argument retrieval: (how) do the arguments written by different socio-cultural groups differ? We investigate the impact of content and style for the task of identifying arguments relevant to a query and a certain demographic attribute. In its different configurations, our system employs sentence embedding representations, arguments generated with Large Language Model, as well as stylistic features.

Our final method places third overall in the shared task, and, in comparison, does particularly well in the most difficult evaluation scenario, where the socio-cultural background of the argument author is implicit (i.e. has to be inferred from the text). This result indicates that socio-cultural differences in argument production may indeed be a matter of style.

1 Introduction

Argument retrieval is a well-established task in computational argumentation (Wachsmuth et al., 2017; Stab et al., 2018): given a query or question, e.g. on "should we have free trade agreements?", the task aims to retrieve **topically relevant** arguments. Topically relevant arguments can be heterogeneous, even for arguments with the same stance (for vs. against) - i.e. someone can focus on quality of the products as essential to free trade, while another may focus on international collaboration. These different perspectives in arguments can be relevant for the personalization and diversification of argument retrieval, and in online debate portals.

The *Perspective Argument Retrieval Task* (Falk et al., 2024) argues that the socio-cultural background (e.g. gender, religion) can be taken into account when selecting relevant arguments. Socio-cultural information can determine the dynamics of argumentation at different levels. For example, socio-demographics can be used to approximate the stance of an argument about a specific topic (e.g., women, pro abortion); additionally, the specific arguments used to support a stance can be a correlate of a specific socio-cultural attribute (religious being against abortion because *it is a sin*).

Differences between arguments of different socio-cultural groups have mostly been researched as differences in **argument content**, meaning the semantic differences in the arguments: which phrases, aspects, and points are mentioned. For instance, Spliethöver and Wachsmuth (2020) analyze how social groups differ in the social bias of their arguments, i.e., male users using terms that indicate a gender bias. However, previous research indicated that **argument style** may be different between socio-cultural groups as well. With argument style, we mean *how* something is said, e.g. features of form and not content like complexity of words, length of words and sentences, grammatical tenses, or pronoun usage. Such stylistic features have mostly been studied from the perspective of argument persuasiveness (El Baff et al., 2020) but also have been used to analyze socio-demographic differences in deliberation processes, i.e., women referring more to others than men in their arguments (Klinger and Russmann, 2015).

While the shared task does not address the issue of persuasiveness of the arguments directly, the intuition that "an argument I would write is one that is likely to resonate stronger with me", builds a potential bridge between socio-demographic retrieval and persuasion research (e.g., consider El Baff et al.

<♥> Contributions mostly completed during a visit funded by a GESIS Visiting Junior Researcher grant at GESIS – Leibniz Institute for the Social Sciences.

Proceedings of the 11th Workshop on Argument Mining, pages 169–181
August 15, 2024 ©2024 Association for Computational Linguistics

(2018) on empowering vs. challenging arguments). Additionally, diversity (providing arguments with different perspectives on the same query) can be employed to maximize the reception of a certain argument. Also, such a diversity of perspectives in recommendations can be beneficial, for instance for citizens in democracies (Reuver et al., 2021).

In approaching the task of argument retrieval for specific socio-cultural profiles, we can also resort to findings from other tasks, such as author profiling (Koppel et al., 2002). This task aims to predict author characteristics from user-generated text, with these characteristics often having a socio-demographic nature, (i.e., gender or age). Successful approaches use semantic content as well as style to profile authors of user-generated texts (Rangel et al., 2021; Bevendorff et al., 2023).

Our approach The perspectivist argument retrieval task raises the question of how socio-cultural groups differ in their arguments for a given query. These differences can be semantic, i.e., groups may differ in *what* they say in their arguments, or stylistic, i.e., groups may differ in *how* they formulate them. We first explore this distinction in the shared task data in Section 3. We then describe our approaches to ranking arguments according to socio-cultural specific relevance in Section 4: One is based on semantic content similarity using 'prototypical' arguments generated with a Large Language Model (LLM). The other uses stylistic features. Our final method places third overall in the shared task, and, in comparison, does particularly well in the most difficult scenario, the one in which the socio-cultural background of the argument author is implicit (i.e. has to be inferred from the text). It implements a three-step pipeline, using semantic information in a ranking step and stylistic information to classify whether arguments are relevant for a given socio-cultural group. Our results indicate that the stylistic differences in the arguments of different socio-cultural groups are more relevant to the task of retrieving relevant arguments than semantic differences in our setup. We publicly release our code for the experiments and analyses.[1]

2 Task: Data and Evaluation Scenarios

The question at the core of the task is: Can we find the arguments that members of a given socio-cultural target group would write for this query?

[1]github.com/mmmaurer/perspective_argument_retrieval

Data The task data is a multilingual dataset in three different cycles of each +/- 30,000 arguments and +/- 300 related queries (in German, Italian, and French). The provided socio-cultural information covers gender, age, place of residence, civil status, denomination, education, political spectrum, and political issues that are of importance to the authors of queries. Additionally, the stance and political topic of the argument are provided.

Details on the size and train/dev/test splits of the three cycles is provided in Table 2 in Appendix B. In the first two cycles, politicians express their stances regarding different political issues in the context of the 2019 and 2023 Swiss elections. In contrast, the third cycle consists of voters' perspectives. For this, samples of the arguments given by politicians for the 2023 election were annotated by amateur annotators. The resulting third cycle data consists of the arguments that intuitively match their perspectives. Socio-cultural profiles were collected for both politicians and voters.

Evaluation Scenarios The systems are evaluated on three scenarios: 1. Argument retrieval without consideration of socio-cultural differences (baseline). 2. Argument retrieval for a specified socio-cultural attribute. Information about any other attribute could be used to diversify the set of retrieved arguments (explicit scenario). 3. Argument retrieval for a specified socio-cultural attribute. In contrast to explicit, information about other attributes is hidden (implicit scenario). System evaluation is based on both relevance and diversity of the selected arguments (in terms of socio-cultural attributes) to promote the diversity of opinions.

3 Data Analysis: Content Or Style?

In the development of our pipeline, data analysis played a crucial role. In the following, we summarize core findings for *content* and *style*. These analyses were conducted on the cycle 1 corpus.

Semantic content differences Firstly, we assess whether there are arguments that multiple socio-cultural groups share and find that ~ 11% of the arguments appear with the same argument text for at least two different socio-cultural profiles. The same argument may, for instance, be produced by a non-religious man and a roman-catholic woman. While this is expected in a natural setting, as groups may share views and thus arguments, this raises the question of differentiation between socio-cultural groups, in particular for the implicit scenario.

Secondly, we cluster Sentence-BERT representations of arguments using the k-means algorithm and evaluate the resulting clusters against the ground-truth socio-cultural groupings, as well as stance and topic. Per socio-cultural attribute, we run one clustering with k equaling the number of groups in the attribute (e.g. for residence $k = 2$, as there are the two groups *city* and *countryside*). We find that all of the socio-cultural groups have an adjusted Rand score (Hubert and Arabie, 1985) of ≤ 0.1 with the respective clustering, indicating virtually no overlap of the clusters with the groups. Only the topic shows a relatively higher adjusted Rand score (for an overview of the results of our clustering experiments, see Appendix E). These analyses indicate that there is little semantic distinction between arguments of different socio-cultural groups, at least in the present semantic representation space.

Stylistic differences To examine stylistic differences in the arguments, we carried out exploratory linear regression analysis. We exclusively focused on the German-language share[2], which comprises about 22k of the in total 32k arguments. The socio-cultural attributes served as independent variables and stylistic features of the arguments as dependent variables. We tested a number of stylistic features, which can be divided into surface and syntactic features and are explained in detail in Table 5 in Appendix F. The seven surface features include measures of word and sentence length, long and complex words, the variety of vocabulary used, and two readability indices. The syntactic features cover part-of-speech (POS) tags, named entities, present tense tokens, imperative tense tokens, and first person writing. Each POS tag forms an extra feature, giving us a total of 21 syntactic features.

We ran one linear regression per stylistic feature to estimate the relationship between socio-cultural information and the particular stylistic feature. In particular, we looked into interactions between variables to take a step into the direction of socio-cultural profiles rather than single attributes. Due to the space limitations, we cannot discuss all features in the paper. However, the full set of regression outputs can be found in the project's GitHub repository. All details are outlined in Appendix D.

Our assumption is that if socio-cultural groups differ in style with respect to specific stylistic features, our regression models will be able to account for a significant amount of that variance (higher adjusted R^2). Models that explain the surface features show notably higher adjusted R^2 values than those for the syntactic ones (cf. Table 3 in Appendix D). We find the highest explanatory power for long words, words per sentence, and the Gunning Fog Index with adjusted R^2 of 0.1557, 0.1422, and 0.1256, respectively. This suggests that socio-cultural characteristics can explain the writing style of the arguments to at least some extent. A closer look into the individual effects and interactions within the socio-cultural attributes reveals several significant effects. For instance, liberals use significantly fewer long words than conservatives, which is even more pronounced in connection with civil status divorced (compared to conservative and single). Liberals in the center or right of the political spectrum exhibit a higher Gunning Fog Index than left-wing conservatives, hinting at the number of years of formal education a person needs to understand a text on the first reading.

While some of these effects certainly also depend on further factors like the context of an argument (i.e., stance and the topic of discussion), the findings add to our underlying hypothesis of different stylistic fingerprints.

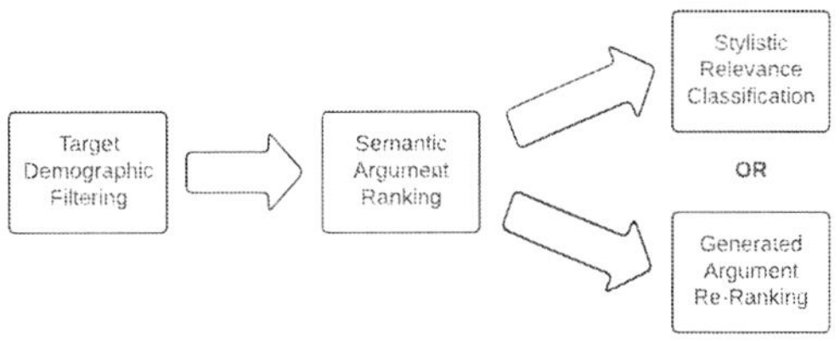

Figure 1: Illustration of our three-step pipeline.

4 System Description

As discussed in the introduction, we want to assess the impact of *content* and *style* on the perspective argument retrieval performance. We thus divide the problem into two steps covering these aspects, with an additional filtering step.[3]

Our resulting pipeline, depicted in Figure 1, consists of three steps: 1) **Target Demographic Filtering**: If arguments of a specific socio-cultural group are queried and socio-cultural information for the arguments is available, only consider the arguments from the respective socio-cultural tar-

[2]Details on the language detection are in Appendix A.

[3]All hyperparameters and implementation details of our analyses and models are given in Appendix A.

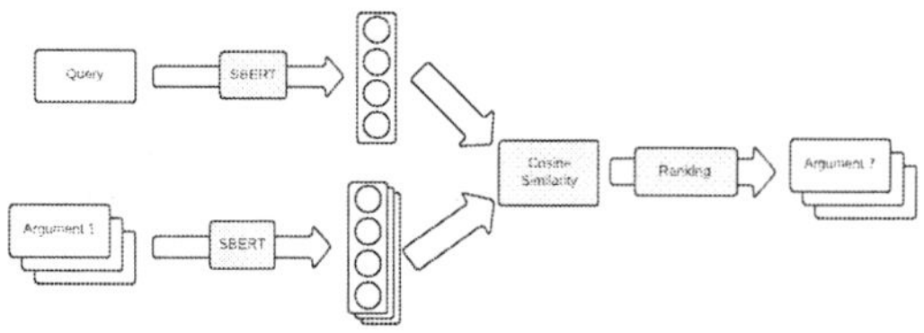

Figure 2: Semantic argument ranking step.

get group for the subsequent steps. 2) **Semantic Argument Ranking**. Find the top k arguments that are semantically closest to the query. 3) **Final Candidates Retrieval**. Option (a) **Stylistic Relevance Classification**: Select only those from the pre-selected k arguments with a stylistic *fingerprint* indicating a relevant argument given the target socio-cultural group. Option (b) **Generated Argument Re-ranking**: Per query and socio-cultural attribute, generate an argument and find the top k arguments that are semantically closest to the generated argument.

For the non-perspectivist **baseline** scenario, only step 2), semantic argument ranking, is executed. For the **explicit perspectivism** scenario, all three steps are executed. Finally, for the **implicit perspectivism** scenario, we execute solely steps 2) and 3) as no socio-cultural information is accessible.

In what follows, we detail the operationalization of these three steps.

4.1 Target Demographic Filtering

To reduce the search space in cases where only the arguments of a specific socio-cultural group are queried and the socio-cultural profiles of the authors of the arguments are known, i.e. in the *explicit perspectivist scenario*, we filter out the arguments that do not match the queried attribute.

4.2 Semantic Argument Ranking

A necessary condition for a given argument to be *relevant* for a query, both in the perspectivist and the baseline cases, is that they are semantically related, or, in other words, that the argument supports a stance towards the question stated in the query. The relevant candidate arguments for a given query should thus be selected such that their semantic similarity is as high as possible.

To operationalize this, as illustrated in Figure 2, we rely on retrieving sentence embeddings using Sentence-BERT (Reimers and Gurevych, 2019) both for the query and the arguments in a corpus and calculate the cosine similarity between the query's representation and each of the arguments' representations. Finally, the arguments are sorted according to the cosine similarity and only the top k arguments are considered.

As a backbone Sentence-BERT model, we use `paraphrase-multilingual-mpnet-base-v2`[4], a multilingual model trained on paraphrases in 50+ languages, among them the three Swiss official languages present in the dataset.

4.3 Final Candidates Retrieval

4.3.1 Stylistic Relevance Classification

A classification step to differentiate between semantically generally relevant arguments (i.e. arguments relevant to a query, regardless of socio-cultural information) and relevant arguments for a specific socio-cultural group is implemented next.

We implement a semantic selection step before the classification step and assume that the set of relevant arguments of a specific socio-cultural group given a query is a real subset of the set of relevant arguments given a query. Based on this insight, we construct positive and negative examples from the training subsets of the provided datasets: For each unique query text q, we collect the set of the overall relevant candidates $C_{q,\text{all}}$. A candidate is considered a positive example and assigned the label *relevant* for the respective socio-cultural group t if it is in the set of the relevant arguments given t and q, $C_{q,t}$. A candidate is considered a negative example and assigned the label *not relevant* if it is in $C_{q,\text{all}} \setminus C_{q,t}$. To end up with a more balanced training set, we only collect $|C_{q,t}|$ negative examples if $|C_{q,\text{all}}| \geq |C_{q,t}|$. Per example (i.e. per argument), we encode a one-hot representation of the queried socio-cultural attribute and concatenate it with surface-level stylistic features of the respective argument as input features. A full overview of the stylistic features can be found in Table 5 in Appendix F. As the majority of arguments are in German, the feature extraction assumes the language to be German. While this is sub-optimal (style may differ across languages), this serves as a first assessment of whether stylistic differences can help in this task.

For the resulting classification step of our pipeline, as visualized in Figure 3, we train a random forest classifier on the training set portion (80%) of our dataset constructed from a union of

[4]https://huggingface.co/sentence-transformers/paraphrase-multilingual-mpnet-base-v2

	Model	Election 2019			Election 2023			2023, User Study			Avg.		
		Baseline	Explicit	Implicit	Baseline	Explicit	Implicit	Baseline	Explicit	Implicit	Baseline	Explicit	Implicit
Relevance	SBERT	**0.986**	0.222	**0.202**	**0.855**	0.148	0.136	**0.637**	0.406	0.409	**0.826**	0.252	0.249
	STY	**0.986**	**0.835**	**0.202**	**0.855**	**0.722**	**0.139**	**0.637**	**0.616**	**0.471**	**0.826**	**0.724**	**0.271**
	GEN	**0.986**	0.645	0.185	**0.855**	0.597	0.127	**0.637**	0.493	0.348	**0.826**	0.578	0.220
Diversity	SBERT	**0.916**	0.208	**0.189**	**0.793**	0.142	0.131	**0.593**	0.400	0.397	**0.767**	0.250	0.239
	STY	**0.916**	**0.807**	**0.189**	**0.793**	**0.701**	**0.132**	**0.593**	**0.629**	**0.454**	**0.767**	**0.654**	**0.258**
	GEN	**0.916**	0.618	0.173	**0.793**	0.579	0.121	**0.593**	0.493	0.331	**0.767**	0.563	0.208

Table 1: Results for the Sentence-BERT baseline (SBERT), and our pipeline with the final step being stylistic relevance classification (STY) and a re-ranking step using generated arguments (GEN). We present mean results across k per test set (election 2019 and 2023, and the 2023 user study), scenario (Baseline, Explicit and Implicit perspectivism), and evaluation (relevance, measured by $nDCG$, and diversity, measured by αDCG). The best result per test set, scenario, and evaluation track is printed in bold.

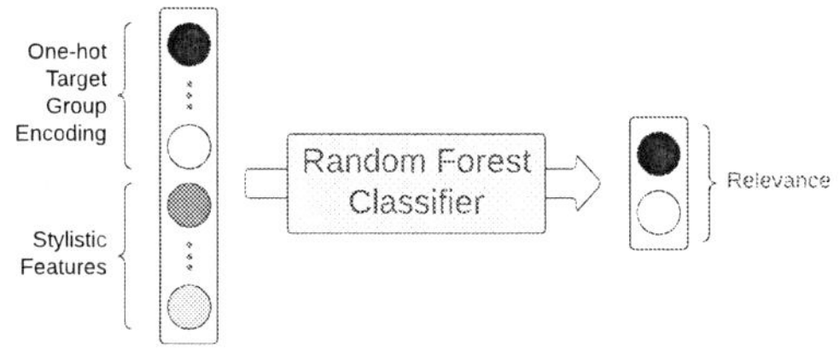

Figure 3: Stylistic relevance classification step.

the training subsets of the three datasets. The classifier achieves an $F_1 = 0.60$ for both the positive and negative classes on the held-out test set portion (20%) of our dataset. We provide a feature importance overview in Figure 6 in Appendix G.

4.3.2 Generated Argument Re-Ranking

Following the hypothesis[5] that arguments of different socio-cultural groups are differentiable by their semantic content, we implement a re-ranking step using LLM-generated arguments. We generate arguments for specific groups and queries using `occiglot-7b-eu5-instruct`[6], a `Mistral-7B-v0.1` model with continued pre-training on the five biggest languages in Europe: English, Spanish, French, German, and Italian. We generate one argument per query, which is then used to re-rank the candidates from the second step in our pipeline. Specifically, per query, we gather the Sentence-BERT representation of the generated argument and re-rank the candidates according to their cosine similarity with the generated argument. Appendix C provides more details about the generated arguments (prompts, statistics, examples, and qualitative analysis).

[5]Our initial hypothesis was that arguments differ in their semantic content across socio-cultural groups. Our downstream analysis of the semantic representation space in combination with the results did however proved our hypothesis wrong.

[6]https://huggingface.co/occiglot/occiglot-7b-eu5-instruct

5 Discussion of Results

The results of our different systems over the three test sets are displayed in Table 1. It can be seen that using stylistic relevance classification as the final step in our pipeline yields results well over the Sentence-BERT baseline across explicit scenario test sets, and for the final implicit scenario test set (Table 1: 2023, User Study).

Moreover, this approach outperforms the use of generated argument re-ranking across all perspectivist test sets. Overall, our findings show that content plays a role in pre-selecting arguments to fit the respective query, as evidenced by the comparably high baseline scenario results. For the same queries, however, socio-cultural groups appear to be less different in the content of their arguments than in their style.

6 Conclusion and Future Work

We present our approach to the Perspective Argument Retrieval Shared Task 2024. Our proposed method implements a three-step pipeline, leveraging semantic information in a ranking step and stylistic information to classify whether arguments are relevant for a given socio-cultural group. The performance of this approach, in particular for the implicit scenario, showcases the potential of including stylistic information for the task of perspectivist argument retrieval. This raises several questions for future research.

Especially with regard to the third test set, in which the perspectives of politicians and voters were flipped, we argue that investigating the reasons for differences in production and perception of arguments of different socio-cultural groups, e.g. through semantic or stylistic differences, is of interest. Consequently, how to combine this information in retrieval scenarios should be investigated.

7 Ethical Considerations and Limitations

Shared tasks have previously focused specifically on author profiling, e.g. profiling spreaders of hate speech in English and Spanish (Rangel et al., 2021) or profiling crypto influencers (Bevendorff et al., 2023), where one system contribution used LLMs and bi-encoding (Giglou et al., 2023). We acknowledge the task of authorship profiling and our approach, using stylistic features, has some established ethical harms to individuals and society at large. These harms are mostly relating to privacy and giving agency to powerful actors to track or harm individuals. However, we also found work that is meant to reduce these specific harms.

7.1 Established harms and limitations

Author profiling and related tasks on detecting user characteristics based on written content have some long-established ethical issues. Among these are concerns about privacy and revealing user identity when users write about sensitive topics (Brennan et al., 2012), and also identifying characteristics that authors may want to keep private, such as their age, gender, or religion. The perspectivist argument retrieval task is a use-case which we consider to benefit users and society: providing diverse perspectives on issues and relevant arguments, which is useful for instance for online deliberation platforms where a diversity of perspectives and interactions between different groups are important. However, this task can also be used to censor, track, or harm specific groups and individual users who write the arguments.

It is also important to be aware of legal frameworks, such as the European Unions general data protection regulation (GDPR), on datasets aimed at detecting author profiles. Rangel and Rosso (2019) have described how, for 2019 PAN shared task dataset on author profiling, all legal limitations have been followed. They also state that their interpretation of GDPR Article 22 means profiling is illegal, though with an exception for non-commercial purposes and scientific research.

7.2 Approaches to protect users from harm

The ethical and legal issues with author profiling have triggered several approaches aimed at **preventing** authorship profiling for harmful contexts. One such set of tasks is known as *adversarial stylometry* (Brennan et al., 2012) (not to be confused with adversarial learning). This set of tasks is specifically aimed at preventing user profiling based on style. For instance, in the subtask of **authorship obfuscation** the idea is to re-write the texts to such an extent that stylometric features cannot distinguish different authors or author groups anymore while leaving semantic coherence of the text intact. Successful and robust approaches across multiple models and datasets, such as by Emmery et al. (2021), use an approach of lexical substitution: changing content words strongly related to certain labels.

Other works have also looked into ethical versions of profiling tasks. For instance, Allein et al. (2023) have looked into fake news detection without author profiling: with the assumption that similar users may share similar fake news articles, they use a latent representation of a group of authors and a fake news article, without ever providing the model with direct user profile information.

Acknowledgements

Myrthe Reuver's contributions were funded by a Visiting Junior Researcher grant from GESIS – Leibniz Institute for the Social Sciences, and also the *Rethinking News Algorithms* project (grant nr 406.D1.19.073) by the Netherlands Organization of Scientific Research (NWO).

Thanks to Neele Falk, whose scripts for feature extraction[7] provided a starting point for the stylistic features.

References

Hirotogu Akaike. 1998. *Information Theory and an Extension of the Maximum Likelihood Principle*, pages 199–213. Springer New York, New York, NY.

Liesbeth Allein, Marie-Francine Moens, and Domenico Perrotta. 2023. Preventing profiling for ethical fake news detection. *Information Processing & Management*, 60(2):103206.

Ryan Bakker and Sara Hobolt. 2013. Measuring Party Positions. In *Political Choice Matters: Explaining the Strength of Class and Religious Cleavages in Cross-National Perspective*. Oxford University Press.

Janek Bevendorff, Ian Borrego-Obrador, Mara Chinea-Ríos, Marc Franco-Salvador, Maik Fröbe, Annina Heini, Krzysztof Kredens, Maximilian Mayerl, Piotr Pęzik, Martin Potthast, et al. 2023. Overview of pan 2023: Authorship verification, multi-author writing style analysis, profiling cryptocurrency influencers,

[7] https://github.com/Blubberli/featureExtraction

and trigger detection: Condensed lab overview. In *International Conference of the Cross-Language Evaluation Forum for European Languages*, pages 459–481. Springer.

Michael Brennan, Sadia Afroz, and Rachel Greenstadt. 2012. Adversarial stylometry: Circumventing authorship recognition to preserve privacy and anonymity. *ACM Transactions on Information and System Security (TISSEC)*, 15(3):1–22.

Roxanne El Baff, Henning Wachsmuth, Khalid Al-Khatib, and Benno Stein. 2018. Challenge or empower: Revisiting argumentation quality in a news editorial corpus. In *Proceedings of the 22nd Conference on Computational Natural Language Learning*, pages 454–464, Brussels, Belgium. Association for Computational Linguistics.

Roxanne El Baff, Henning Wachsmuth, Khalid Al Khatib, and Benno Stein. 2020. Analyzing the Persuasive Effect of Style in News Editorial Argumentation. In *Proceedings of the 58th Annual Meeting of the Association for Computational Linguistics*, pages 3154–3160, Online. Association for Computational Linguistics.

Chris Emmery, Ákos Kádár, and Grzegorz Chrupała. 2021. Adversarial stylometry in the wild: Transferable lexical substitution attacks on author profiling. In *Proceedings of the 16th Conference of the European Chapter of the Association for Computational Linguistics: Main Volume*, pages 2388–2402.

Neele Falk, Andreas Waldis, and Iryna Gurevych. 2024. Overview of PerpectiveArg2024: The First Shared Task on Perspective Argument Retrieval. In *Proceedings of the 11th Workshop on Argument Mining*, Bangkok. Association for Computational Linguistics.

Hamed Babaei Giglou, Mostafa Rahgouy, Jennifer D'Souza, Milad Molazadeh, Hadi Bayrami Asl Tekanlou Oskuee, and Cheryl D Seals. 2023. Leveraging large language models with multiple loss learners for few-shot author profiling. *Working Notes of CLEF*.

L. Hubert and P. Arabie. 1985. Comparing partitions. *Journal of Classification*, 2:193–218.

Albert Q Jiang, Alexandre Sablayrolles, Arthur Mensch, Chris Bamford, Devendra Singh Chaplot, Diego de las Casas, Florian Bressand, Gianna Lengyel, Guillaume Lample, Lucile Saulnier, et al. 2023. Mistral 7b. *arXiv preprint arXiv:2310.06825*.

Ulrike Klinger and Uta Russmann. 2015. The sociodemographics of political public deliberation: Measuring deliberative quality in different user groups. *Communications*, 40(4):471–484.

Moshe Koppel, Shlomo Argamon, and Anat Rachel Shimoni. 2002. Automatically categorizing written texts by author gender. *Literary and linguistic computing*, 17(4):401–412.

M. J. Laver and Ian Budge. 1992. *Measuring Policy Distances and Modelling Coalition Formation*, pages 15–40. Palgrave Macmillan UK, London.

Stuart Lloyd. 1982. Least squares quantization in pcm. *IEEE transactions on information theory*, 28(2):129–137.

Ines Montani, Matthew Honnibal, Adriane Boyd, Sofie Van Landeghem, and Henning Peters. 2023. explosion/spaCy: v3.7.2: Fixes for APIs and requirements.

Fabian Pedregosa, Gaël Varoquaux, Alexandre Gramfort, Vincent Michel, Bertrand Thirion, Olivier Grisel, Mathieu Blondel, Peter Prettenhofer, Ron Weiss, Vincent Dubourg, et al. 2011. Scikit-learn: Machine learning in python. *the Journal of machine Learning research*, 12:2825–2830.

Francisco Rangel, Gretel Liz de la Peña-Sarracén, María Alberta Chulvi-Ferriols, Elisabetta Fersini, and Paolo Rosso. 2021. Profiling hate speech spreaders on twitter task at pan 2021. In *Proceedings of the Working Notes of CLEF 2021, Conference and Labs of the Evaluation Forum, Bucharest, Romania, September 21st to 24th, 2021*, pages 1772–1789. CEUR.

Francisco Rangel and Paolo Rosso. 2019. On the implications of the general data protection regulation on the organisation of evaluation tasks. *Language and Law/Linguagem e Direito*, 5(2):95–117.

Nils Reimers and Iryna Gurevych. 2019. Sentence-BERT: Sentence embeddings using Siamese BERT-networks. In *Proceedings of the 2019 Conference on Empirical Methods in Natural Language Processing and the 9th International Joint Conference on Natural Language Processing (EMNLP-IJCNLP)*, pages 3982–3992, Hong Kong, China. Association for Computational Linguistics.

Myrthe Reuver, Nicolas Mattis, Marijn Sax, Suzan Verberne, Nava Tintarev, Natali Helberger, Judith Moeller, Sanne Vrijenhoek, Antske Fokkens, and Wouter van Atteveldt. 2021. Are we human, or are we users? the role of natural language processing in human-centric news recommenders that nudge users to diverse content. In *1st workshop on NLP for positive impact*, pages 47–59. Association for Computational Linguistics.

Maximilian Spliethöver and Henning Wachsmuth. 2020. Argument from old man's view: Assessing social bias in argumentation. In *Proceedings of the 7th Workshop on Argument Mining*, pages 76–87, Online. Association for Computational Linguistics.

Christian Stab, Johannes Daxenberger, Chris Stahlhut, Tristan Miller, Benjamin Schiller, Christopher Tauchmann, Steffen Eger, and Iryna Gurevych. 2018. ArgumenText: Searching for arguments in heterogeneous sources. In *Proceedings of the 2018 Conference of the North American Chapter of the Association for Computational Linguistics: Demonstrations*, pages 21–25, New Orleans, Louisiana. Association for Computational Linguistics.

Henning Wachsmuth, Martin Potthast, Khalid Al-Khatib, Yamen Ajjour, Jana Puschmann, Jiani Qu, Jonas Dorsch, Viorel Morari, Janek Bevendorff, and Benno Stein. 2017. Building an argument search engine for the web. In *Proceedings of the 4th Workshop on Argument Mining*, pages 49–59, Copenhagen, Denmark. Association for Computational Linguistics.

Thomas Wolf, Lysandre Debut, Victor Sanh, Julien Chaumond, Clement Delangue, Anthony Moi, Pierric Cistac, Tim Rault, Rémi Louf, Morgan Funtowicz, et al. 2020. Transformers: State-of-the-art natural language processing. In *Proceedings of the 2020 conference on empirical methods in natural language processing: system demonstrations*, pages 38–45.

Appendix

A Hyperparameters and Implementation Details

Our models were implemented and experiments conducted using Python 3.11 unless stated otherwise.

A.1 Data Analysis

Stylistic features Stylistic features were obtained using the *readability* (https://pypi.org/project/readability/) and *SpaCy* python packages (https://pypi.org/project/spacy/; Montani et al. 2023) .

Linear Regression To select German-language arguments, we used the *langdetect* Python package (https://pypi.org/project/langdetect/). The linear regression was implemented in R 4.4.1. We used the packages *stats*, *MASS*, and *car* for the step-wise building of the regression models and inspection of variance inflation factors.

Content clustering Clustering of our Sentence-BERT embeddings was done with the *scikit-learn* (Pedregosa et al., 2011) Python package implementation of the K-means clustering algorithm (Lloyd, 1982). We clustered for each socio-cultural variable (e.g. gender, denomination) and then also combined attributes in pairs of two to test for cluster coherence. For calculating cluster coherence, we use the Adjusted Rand score as also implemented in the *scikit-learn* Python package. Detailed clustering results can be found in Appendix E.

A.2 Base Model

Our sentence embeddings model was *paraphrase-multilingual-mpnet-base-v2* (Reimers and Gurevych, 2019), implemented through the huggingface *transformers* (Wolf et al., 2020) and *sentence_transformers* (Reimers and Gurevych, 2019) Python packages. For ranking the top documents to a query, we selected k=200 using cosine similarity.

A.3 Argument Generation Model

Our generated arguments were obtained with the *occiglot-7b-eu5-instruct* model (https://huggingface.co/occiglot), a fine-tuned Mistral-7B (Jiang et al., 2023) model, called with Huggingface's *transformers* (Wolf et al., 2020) package. The model was run on an NVIDIA A100 GPU. Prompt template details, and a short analysis of these generated arguments, are provided in Appendix C.

We memory-optimize our prompting by loading an int8-quantized version of the model. For quantization, we use the *quanto* library (https://github.com/huggingface/optimum-quanto).

A.4 Stylistic Relevance Classification

Random Forest classifier The random forest classifier for detecting socio-cultural background based on the stylistic features was implemented with the scikit-learn (Pedregosa et al., 2011) package, using its default implementation and parameters: 100 trees, splitting on gini impurity, and no max depth.

B Details of the Dataset

Cycle	Corpus	Queries					
		Baseline			Perspective		
		train	dev	test	train	dev	test
Election 2019	32,387	104	134	44	5,577	1,611	2,358
Election 2023	39,093	104	134	39	5,577	1,611	1,782
2023, User Study	28,684	104	134	26	4,737	1,371	729

Table 2: Dataset sizes for the retrieval argument corpus and for the queries, divided into train/dev/test set for the baseline and the perspective scenario. The task ran for three evaluation cycles with different evaluation data.

C Prompt Formulation & Generated Arguments

We generated arguments based on queries in the corpus with the prompt in Figure 5 and the *occiglot-*

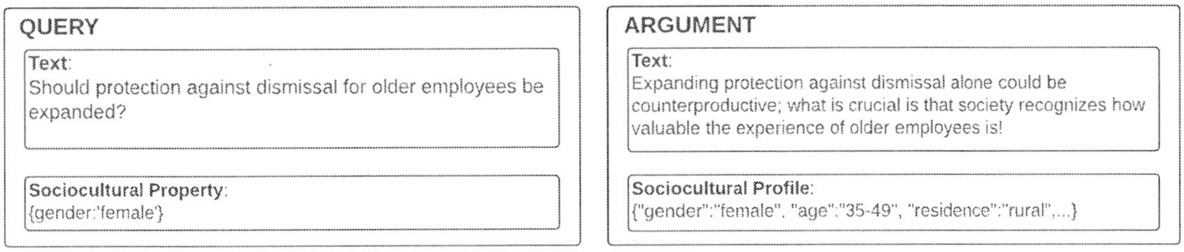

Figure 4: Example for a pair of a query and a relevant argument. Original in German, automatically translated using Google translate.

> Given the question {query}, use your knowledge of the Swiss political landscape to provide a pro argument a person whose {attribute} is {group} would produce.

Figure 5: Prompt formulation.

7b-eu5-instruct model (implementation details in Appendix A). Below we provide a short description and analysis of the arguments generated with this method.

C.1 Statistics on Generated Arguments

Across the three test sets, the model produced an argument over 90% of the time. No argument was generated for 6.2%/1.2%/1.6% of prompts, respectively). While across the three test sets, 95% of the generated arguments are truncated, i.e. they end mid-sentence, the generated arguments are on average longer than the arguments in the corpus (mean raw text length of 190 characters for the corpus vs. 267/429/297 characters generated per test set, respectively).

C.2 Qualitative Analysis of Generated Arguments

Based on a qualitative inspection, we have gathered the following observations regarding the generated arguments. In Section C.3, we provide some examples of the generated arguments (German, translated into English with DeepL) to illustrate our analysis.

First of all, we notice an (unsurprising) tendency to repeat the demographics from the prompts, and additionally to generate intersectional types. Consider for example query 20191712, where the author of the (generated) argument identifies himself as young, man, and a student. Query 20191712 illustrates also another property, shared with query 201911545: the tendency of the generated arguments to be accompanied by fully fledged, unprompted, personas, e.g. descriptions of argument 'authors' (e.g. professions and other sociodemographics).

The arguments also vary greatly in complexity and overall quality. Some arguments, i.e., 201911569 (test 2), exhibit a very low degree of justification and/or resort to very abstract principles ("The federal government should invest more in education and research because it would advance us socially"), or essentially just rephrase the stance (201911545). Others, instead, display a very articulated structure with multiple supporting premises (e.g., four, explicitly listed in 201911652 (test 2)).

In addition to the degree of justification, arguments also vary greatly in terms of the type of evidence they use to support their stance. The speaker in 201911630 (test 2), for example, resorts to reporting personal experiences. The speaker in 201911777 (test 2), instead, mentions his profession "As an entrepreneur for many years" to establish himself as an authoritative source on the topic at issue.

C.3 Selected generated arguments

Query: "Should the federal government spend more or less on development cooperation?"

201911777-test 2 (Prompt: attribute: political spectrum; value: center and conservative/liberal), "As an entrepreneur for many years, I have seen how important it is to promote international relations and engage in global cooperation. Especially in times when job creation is a major challenge, it is crucial to place a strong focus on development cooperation. This is because we can help to improve economic conditions in certain regions and thus give more people access to a livelihood."

201911781-test 2 (Prompt: attribute: political spectrum; value: right and liberal) "It is not the task of the federal government to invest financial resources in the area of development cooperation. The responsibility for development cooperation lies with the countries and economies affected by poverty and underdevelopment. The federal government has no responsibility to become active in these areas, and by increasing funding it could interfere with the sovereignty of these countries. Therefore, the federal government should invest less and not more money in development cooperation."

20191712-test 3 (Prompt: attribute: civil status; value: single) "Hello, my name is John and I'm 22 years old. I'm from Switzerland, where I'm currently studying in Zurich, and as a young man and a student at that, I firmly believe and think it's important that the federal government spends more on development cooperation, especially as we can't deny that"

Query: Should the federal government spend more or less on public transport?

201911630-test 2 (Prompt: attribute: civil status; value: married), "As a Swiss citizen who has been working for many years, I believe that the federal government needs to spend more on public transport. I am married myself and I have seen how difficult it can be to get to a meeting within a few minutes by bus. I've also seen how people can't use the train because there are too many connections that don't go to where they live. So we should spend more money and improve public transport."

201911651-test 2 (Prompt: attribute: political spectrum; value: center and conservative/liberal) "The federal government should spend more on public transport. This would improve the population's mobility options and at the same time create a more environmentally friendly way of travelling."

201911652-test 2 (Prompt: attribute: political spectrum; value: center and liberal), "I am in favour of the federal government investing more in public transport because the advantages outweigh the disadvantages. Firstly, clean air and improved quality of life are essential for citizens, and secondly, investment in public transport improves the efficiency and profitability of the transport system. Thirdly, public transport can help to unite and motivate the population towards common goals. Fourthly, investment in public transport contributes to economic development"

Query: Should the federal government spend more or less on education and research?

201911569-test 2 (Prompt: attribute: political spectrum; value: left and liberal) "Better more than less on education and research. In today's globalised society, the expansion of knowledge will not only advance us technologically, but also socially. That is why the promotion of education and research is essential."

201911571-test 2 (Prompt: attribute: political spectrum; value: center and conservative/liberal), "We should invest more money in education and research. This is the only way we can ensure that our children and grandchildren have a brilliant future. They will be the ones who have to live and work in an increasingly complex world and they need to be ready to meet these challenges, and we should also think about how we can encourage people in our communities to invest in these areas. This can be done through incentives such as tax breaks and other incentives."

201911545-test2 (Prompt: attribute: civil status; value: single), "More education and research are crucial for the progress of our society. The federal government should therefore provide more financial support in this area. We need qualified specialists and innovations to secure our prosperity.Julia, 25, ZurichJulia (25) is a young woman from Zurich with an affinity for technology and an interest in science. As a high school graduate, she dreams of doing something "meaningful" one day."

D Regression analysis

In the linear regression analysis, we include the socio-cultural attributes gender, age, residence, civil status, denomination, and political spectrum. The additionally given information about important political issues is not taken into account for now, given the large number of different profiles in this attribute.

To counter sparsity of the results, in a preprocessing step all groups in the attributes that appeared rarely (< 50) were removed. This includes "Aufgelöste Partnerschaft" and "Getrennt" in civil status, as well as "Andere Kirchen/Religionsgemeinschaften", "Christlich-orthodox", "Jüdische Gemeinschaften", and "Islamische Gemeinschaften" in denomination. Furthermore, missing value groups ("Nicht bekannt") in civil status, denomination, and education were removed. For better interpretability of levels of education, we summarized "Höhere Fachschule", "Handelsschule", and "Höhere Berufsausbildung" as "Höhere Berufsausbildung", and "Berufs-

DV	Adjusted R^2	DV	Adjusted R^2
Characters per word	0.0613	NOUN	0.0285
Words per sentence	0.1422	NUM	0.0155
Type-token ratio	0.0596	PART	0.0077
Long words	0.1557	PRON	0.0355
Complex words	0.1068	PROPN	0.0150
Flesch Reading Ease	0.0880	PUNCT	0.0412
Gunning Fog Index	0.1256	SCONJ	0.0129
ADJ	0.0165	SYM	-
ADP	0.0041	VERB	0.0232
ADV	0.0187	X	0.0022
AUX	0.0157	Named entities	0.0110
CCONJ	0.0104	Present tense	0.0123
DET	0.0121	Imperative	0.0022
INTJ	-	First person	0.0272

Table 3: Adjusted R^2 scores of the linear regression models. INTJ and SYM did not occur in the arguments and because of this, no model was built in these cases.

matura" and "Diplommittelschule" as "Berufsmatura/Diplommittelschule". Likewise, for the sake of interpretability, the given socio-cultural attribute political spectrum was divided into quasi-RILE (Laver and Budge, 1992) (an ideological scale measuring general left-to-right position; left, center, and right) and quasi-GALTAN (Bakker and Hobolt, 2013) scores (an ideological scale measuring the policy position on social issues; conservative, conservative-liberal, and liberal). The resulting dataset contains 11289 arguments.

We ran one linear regression per stylistic feature (see Table 5 for more information on the stylistic features) to estimate the relationship between socio-cultural information and the particular stylistic feature. The models were built step-wise ("forward") using the Akaike information criterion (Akaike, 1998). In particular, we looked into interactions between variables to take a step into the direction of socio-cultural profiles rather than single attributes. The formula used was *DV ~ (gender + age + residence + civil_status + denomination + education + rile + galtan)^2* where *DV* is a placeholder for any one of the dependent variables (implementation details can be found in Appendix A). Due to the large number of variables in the resulting models, it is not possible to present them in their entirety in the paper. We selected highlighted results in the paper and make the R code available in the corresponding GitHub repository.

Table 3 illustrates the explained variance of the best model selected by StepAIC for each of the 21 stylistic features. Overall, we find small adjusted R^2 scores, signaling that the socio-cultural variables we selected as predictors can explain a limited amount of the variance in our stylistic features. The fit of the models is however still highly significant and in our discussion we focus on significant effects. Looking more into detail into the models (the full set of regression outputs can be found on GitHub), we see significant effects across the different socio-cultural attributes and groups. While such effects may also be triggered by the large scale of the dataset, our findings inspire us to incorporate stylistic features into the retrieval models discussed in Section 4.

E Clustering Results

Attribute	Adjusted Rand Score
Gender	0.0009
Age	-0.0011
Denomination	0.0004
Residence	0.0007
Political Spectrum	-0.0011
Stance	0.0005
Topic	0.1947

Table 4: K-means clustering result per socio-cultural attribute, plus stance and topic.

F Stylistic Features

Table 5 describes the different stylistic features used in the linear regression analysis and the random forest classifier.

	Feature	Description
Surface Features	Characters per word	Average number of characters per word, calculated by dividing the total number of characters in a text by the total number of words. Functions as a measure of text complexity as longer words can be harder to process.
	Words per sentence	Average number of words per sentence, calculated by dividing the total number of words by the total number of sentences in a text. Functions as a measure of text complexity as longer sentences can be harder to process.
	Type-token ratio (TTR)	Indication of the diversity of vocabulary usage in a text, calculated by dividing the total number of unique words by the total number of words.
	Long words	Number of words that consist of 7 or more characters. Functions as a measure of text complexity as longer words can be harder to process.
	Complex words	Number of words that consist of 3 or more syllables. Functions as a measure of text complexity as longer words can be harder to process.
	Flesch Reading Ease	Assesses the approximate reading grade level of a text, based on average sentence length and word complexity. A higher score indicates easier readability, while lower scores indicate more difficult readability. $$\text{Flesch Reading Ease} = 206.835 - 84.6 \cdot \frac{\text{\# syllables}}{\text{\# words}} - 1.015 \cdot \frac{\text{\# words}}{\text{\# sentences}}$$
	Gunning Fog Index	Estimates the years of formal education required to understand a particular text on first reading. $$\text{Gunning Fog Index} = 0.4\left(\frac{\text{\# words}}{\text{\# sentences}} + 100 \cdot \frac{\text{\# complex words}}{\text{\# words}}\right)$$
Syntactic Features	Part-of-speech tags	Proportion of tokens tagged as a specific part-of-speech category in the text. We make use of the universal part-of-speech tagging schema and calculate a distinct score for ADJ (adjectives), ADP (adpositions), ADV (adverbs), AUX (auxiliaries), CCONJ (coordinating conjunctions), DET (determines), INTJ (interjections), NOUN (nouns), NUM (numerals), PART (particles), PRON (pronouns), PROPN (proper nouns), PUNCT (punctuations), SCONJ (subordinating conjunctions), SYM (symbols), VERB (verbs), and X (words that do not fit into the other part-of-speech categories).
	Named entities	Proportion of named entities in a text, calculated by dividing the number of named entity tokens by the total number of tokens. Functions as a measure of writing style.
	Present tense	Number of present tense verbs in a text, normalized by text length. Functions as a measure of writing style.
	Imperative	Number of imperative verb forms in a text, normalized by text length. Functions as a measure of writing style.
	First person	Number of first-person verb forms in a text, normalized by text length. Functions as a measure of writing style.

Table 5: Stylistic features and their descriptions.

G Random Forest Feature Importance

Figure 6 provides an overview of the importance of different features (stylistic, stance) in the random forest classifier.

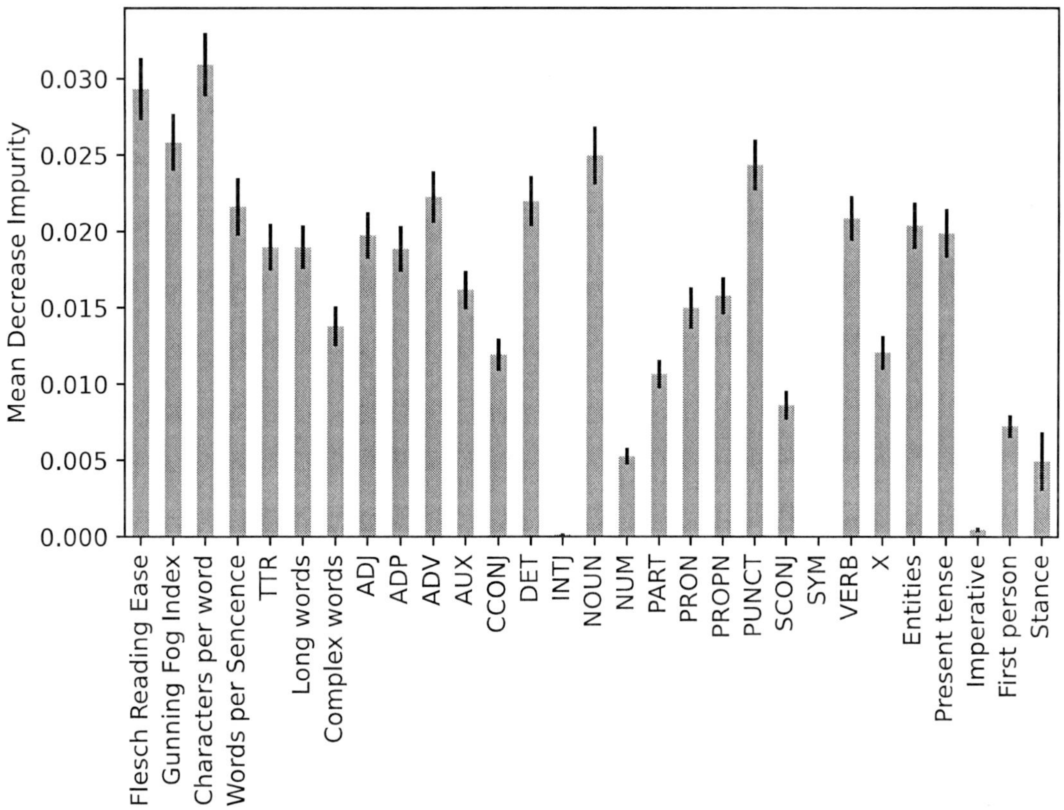

Figure 6: Random forest feature importance measured by the mean decrease impurity.

XFACT Team0331 at PerspectiveArg2024: Sampling from Bounded Clusters for Diverse Relevant Argument Retrieval

Wan Ju Kang, Jiyoung Han, Jaemin Jung, and **James Thorne**
KAIST
Republic of Korea

Abstract

This paper reports on the argument mining system submitted to the ArgMining workshop 2024 for The Perspective Argument Retrieval Shared Task (Falk et al., 2024). We combine the strengths of a smaller Sentence BERT model and a Large Language Model: the former is fine-tuned for a contrastive embedding objective and a classification objective whereas the latter is invoked to augment the query and populate the latent space with diverse relevant arguments. We conduct an ablation study on these components to find that each contributes substantially to the diversity and relevance criteria for the top-k retrieval of arguments from the given corpus.

1 Introduction

Argument retrieval remains a challenging problem in the natural language processing domain, when considered jointly with perspectives and diversity. The problem is defined as the collection of claims carrying a stance towards a query. A query may be of various topical widths ranging from an entire issue or a single statement. Arguments are a widely utilized discursive tools, and performant systems of argument recognition will prove useful in further advancing bias analyses, slant measurement (Devatine et al., 2022), content recommendation, and text generation tasks (El Baff et al., 2019). Perspectives can prove a useful clue in the argument retrieval problem but at the same time bring about an additional challenge. Especially with shorter texts, such as the ones handled in this shared task, the demographic profile of the argument author may be of use in trying to extract opinions grounded in various populations.

In this paper, we present the work conducted by our team, "XFACT team0331", for the ArgMining 2024 shared task of perspective argument retrieval. Our findings indicate feasibility of the system design across the three scenarios, helping us better understand the complexities of taking perspectives into consideration when retrieving arguments.

This shared task involves a unique challenge in terms of perspectives and socio-cultural variables. Not only are the systems required to pursue relevance to a given query, but they are also assessed in terms of the demographic profile of the argument authors.

2 Related Work

Recent years have seen rapid progress of argument retrieval along several lines of research.

Teufel et al. (1999) studied argument extraction in the scientific text domain. Later works extend the argument retrieval work to arbitrary domains and eventually the entire world wide web, such as in Rahwan et al. (2007) and similar systems discussed in the seminal text (Manning, 2008). Wachsmuth et al. (2017) designed an argument search engine involving an indexing process, which takes candidate documents over the web and indexes the assessed arguments therein into a corpus, and a retrieval process, which, upon arrival of a query, ranks and presents relevant indices of arguments. Stab et al. (2018) put together an offline component and an online component, which account for the indexing and retrieval tasks, respectively.

In the closely related problem of stance detection, Hardalov et al. (2021) proposed methods for recognizing stance across texts from multiple domains, with their design of label embeddings in the latent space that adapt to the arbitrary topic at hand. Arakelyan et al. (2023) presented a similar approach leveraging a topic-guided sampler for alleviating inherent imbalance in the data. Then, a pre-trained language model is fine-tuned against a contrastive learning objective for recognizing the in-favor and the against statements.

In news writing, Baly et al. (2018), Baly et al. (2020a), and Baly et al. (2020b) profiled media sources by measuring their bias in terms of factuality reporting and any conveyed political ideology. Ko et al. (2023) solved a five-scale political stance prediction problem by incorporating texts from various sources beyond news articles, such as Reddit posts, and employs a multi-granularity hierarchy on the texts to capture any subtleties carrying stance information. In a related work by Liu et al. (2022), a triplet loss was imposed on an anchor article with two same-story versions – one leftist and the other rightist – to train a language model to identify and distinguish ideology-informed representations between articles.

Argumentative language modeling techniques have also been studied. For instance, Jo et al. (2021) proposed counterargument generation methods assisting language models with knowledge graphs such that the natural language inference process can determine the entailment/relevance of a claim more effectively. Holtermann et al. (2022) studied a similar problem but with an additional pursuit for fairness in argument generation. For every instance deemed biased, a counter-stereotypical statement is synthesized and used in training.

3 Task

The ArgMining 2024 Shared Task for Perspective Argument Retrieval consists of the following three retrieval scenarios:

- Scenario 1 is dubbed the "baseline" scenario and is a retrieval of top-k arguments from a corpus given a query alone and no additional information on the demographic profile on either of the query or the argument side.
- Scenario 2 is the explicit perspectives scenario where a demographic property is provided in addition to the query. This property may be used explicitly to filter or process arguments from the corpus.
- Scenario 3 is the implicit perspectives scenario where a demographic property is still available on top of the query, but it may not be used explicitly on the corpus-processing step. Only latent encoded information may be used to retrieve relevant arguments.

The dataset is originally from Vamvas and Sennrich (2020), where comments in the French, German, and Italian language are organized across various political issues (queries) for the 2019 Swiss federal elections.

4 Method

We propose a novel approach to retrieve relevant and diverse arguments. Major components of our design are as follows:

- an embedding model fine-tuned for two training objectives
- a large language model instructed to generate its own arguments given the query
- a topic sampler to filter the vast majority of the corpus

The overview of the proposed system is presented in Fig. 1. An embedding model produces latent vectors of arguments and a given query. These are then spread out in the latent space, to be clustered according to the nearest generated argument. More details follow in Section 4.5.

4.1 Embedding Model

We choose the PARAPHRASE-MULTILINGUAL-MPNET-BASE-V2 sentence transformer (Reimers and Gurevych, 2019), (Reimers and Gurevych, 2020) as our embedding model, given its state-of-the-art performance and capability to handle multiple languages. We further train this embedding model on a weighted combination of two losses, with the exact weighting as a hyperparameter: a contrastive loss and a classification loss. (See Appendix A)

The training of the embedding model incorporates two desirable directions of the model enhancement: we want the model (i) to produce sufficiently different latent representations for "on-set"(relevant) and "off-set"(irrelevant) arguments and (ii) to capture any underlying connections between the query and its on-set arguments sufficiently such that, when presented with a (query, irrelevant) pair, it is successfully discarded as an outlier. For these objectives, we detail the training process below.

For objective (i), we aim to enhance the embedding model's ability to widen the gap between relevant arguments and irrelevant arguments with respect to a query. For this, the multiple negatives ranking loss (Henderson et al., 2017) was chosen, and the given corpus dataset was rearranged in triplets (q, a_p^i, a_n^j), where the query q is followed by a randomly selected relevant candidate a_p and then by a randomly selected argument not in the

RELEVANT CANDIDATES list for that query, for all i in the RELEVANT CANDIDATES list.

For objective (ii), a linear layer is appended to the embedding model to from a binary classifier between FAVOR and AGAINST, labels both available in the given corpus. The corpus is rearranged in pairs (q, a_p^i), the query and its relevant candidate for all candidates i in the query's RELEVANT CANDIDATES list. The classifier outputs a real value from 0 to 1, trained on binary cross entropy loss.

For Scenario 2, the query is concatenated with its demographic property, and each corpus argument is concatenated with its demographic profile before passing through the embedding model. For Scenario 3, only the query is augmented with the socio-cultural variables information.

4.2 Argument Generator Model

We employ several open-source large language models to leverage argument generation. PHI-3-MINI-4K-INSTRUCT and GEMMA-1.1-2B-IT have each been invoked to produce 20 relevant key arguments with respect to a query in their respective instruction prompt formats: 10 favoring it and 10 against it. The purpose of these LLM-generated arguments is twofold. One is that, since the corpus contains comments from individuals who might have a rather local view on the topic at hand, the LLM, as a generic knowledge entity can provide more diverse and holistic takes on the issue. Where necessary, we make the distinction between the natural and synthesized arguments as "corpus arguments" and "LLM-generated arguments" henceforth. These two sets are produced to form the augmented corpus. The other purpose of the LLM-generated arguments is to filter out corpus arguments that are too far from the LLM-generated arguments in the latent space. The mild assumption underneath is that, if a corpus argument is relevant enough, it must be close to at least one of the LLM-generated arguments. The exact cut-off distance criterion is described in Section 4.5

4.3 Topic Filter Model

At execution time, as a first measure, we invoke a KeyBERT (Grootendorst, 2020) instance between the query and the augmented corpus to discard a large portion of the augmented corpus as irrelevant. This is a simple filter based on latent encodings from BERT (Devlin et al., 2019), which takes a document and find sub-phrases that most closely resembles a given topic by cosine similarity. The filter proceeds to retain only the arguments whose keyword set contains any of the keywords in the query's keyword set. That is, all arguments whose $k_q \cap k_a = \emptyset$ are screened away.

4.4 Clusterer

The vector representations produced by the embedding model undergo a simple clustering process equivalent to running a K-Means for one iteration. The LLM-generated arguments serve as the initial centroids, and the corpus arguments are each assigned a group it belongs to by nearest centroid. In other words, if an argument can find a cluster it can belong in, it is considered relevant. Each cluster's member argument count is calculated and used for diversity sampling as explained in Section 4.5.

4.5 Overview

In this section, we describe how the components tie in together. In Section 4.2, corpus arguments' proximity to LLM-generated arguments was chosen as a criterion for determining the relevance. We construct this criterion as a function of the classifier confidence, as measured in the classifier's final layer value. That is, if the learned classifier from Section 4.1 can barely determine whether an argument is in favor or against some given query, then that argument should be allowed to exist in a generously larger ball from the LLM-generated arguments in the latent space. The converse also applies; a confident classifier should indicate the argument's high proximity to at least one of the LLM-generated arguments. In short, the cut-off criterion is governed by the learned classifier's decision. The actual cut-off procedure then takes an indicator function over the respective ball of r^{cutoff} around each LLM-generated argument embedding a_i, that, when evaluated as all off-ball, considers the corpus argument a_c irrelevant:

$$\prod_i \mathbb{1}(\text{dist}(a_c, a_i) > r^{\text{cutoff}}) = \begin{cases} 0, \text{ if } a_c \text{ relevant} \\ 1, \text{ otherwise} \end{cases} \quad (1)$$

The relevance cut-off criterion above doubles as a diversity sampling criterion, and we capitalize on this extension by introducing a per-a_i cut-off radius instead of a uniform radius for all the balls. Each LLM-generated argument embedding is assigned its own cut-off radius r_i^{cutoff} that is inversely proportional to its member argument count. In practice, the base cut-off radius is first calculated with the

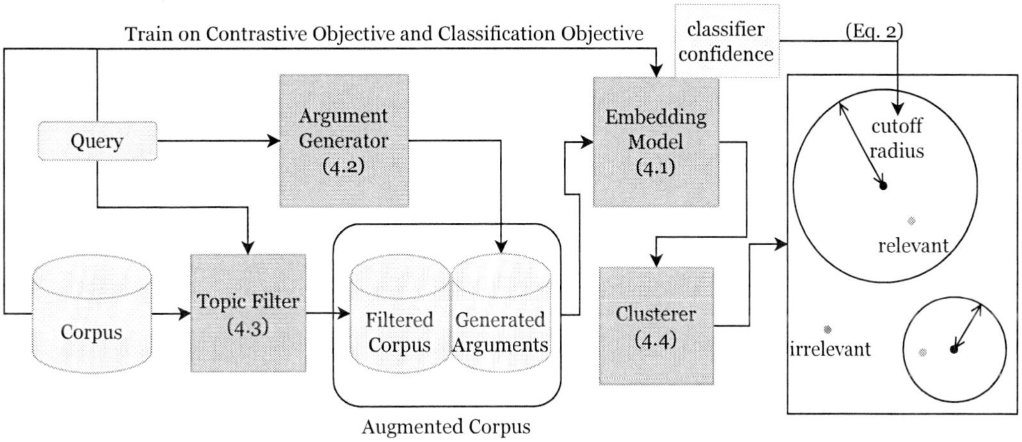

Figure 1: An overview of the proposed stance detector; sections detailing the components are in parentheses

classifier confidence and then is further adjusted by cluster member count. We re-write Equation 1 with the generalized cut-off radii. Let A_i denote the set of corpus arguments belonging to the cluster centered by the LLM-generated argument embedding a_i:

$$\prod_i \mathbb{1}(\text{dist}(a_c, a_i) > r_i^{\text{cutoff}}) = \begin{cases} 0, \text{if } a_c \text{ relevant} \\ 1, \text{otherwise,} \end{cases} \tag{2}$$

where $r_i^{\text{cutoff}} = r^{\text{cutoff}} + r_i^{\text{adjustment}}$
and $r_i^{\text{adjustment}} \propto \frac{1}{|A_i|}$

Having a cut-off radius may be advantageous over a ranking method: one that ranks the arguments by the distance from the centroid. First, ranking takes $O(n \log n)$ time whereas cut-off executes in linear time. Second, the proposed system works regardless of whether the k value is known. That is, it is flexible enough to accommodate an arbitrary downstream ranker of k unknown *a priori*.

5 Results

Our results are presented in Tables 1 and 2. All reportings are on the dev sets, averaged across the three scenarios, due to limited print space.

5.1 Ablation

5.1.1 Effects of Relevance Cut-off

We report the results of applying only the relevance cut-off radius, as in the uniform criterion in Equation 1.

Table 3 shows that the absence of the diversity sampler compromises the diversity scores of the

k	ndcg@k	precision@k
4	0.694	0.692
8	0.679	0.671
16	0.670	0.660
20	0.677	0.673

Table 1: Relevance scores averaged across the three scenarios

k	alpha_ndcg@k	kl_divergence@k
4	0.625	0.151
8	0.618	0.134
16	0.626	0.100
20	0.638	0.091

Table 2: Diversity scores averaged across the three scenarios

k	alpha_ndcg@k	kl_divergence@k
4	0.557	0.158
8	0.565	0.140
16	0.579	0.104
20	0.580	0.094

Table 3: System follows Eq. 1. (Diversity component ablated). Diversity scores averaged across the three scenarios

k	ndcg@k	precision@k
4	0.627	0.617
8	0.625	0.619
16	0.624	0.620
20	0.618	0.613

Table 4: System follows Eq. 2 with $r_i^{\text{cutoff}} = \infty$ (Relevance component removed). Relevance scores averaged across the three scenarios

system. While KL divergence was measured (ommitted for spacing) to be similar as in Table 2, alpha_ndcg@k values have dropped substantially and seemingly relies on k value alone for diversity gains, rather than on the constituent arguments of the k retrieved passages. Since demographic profile information is latently encoded in the query and arguments, the decrease in KL divergence scores indicate that the role of the diversity sampler is indeed to take into account various demographic profiles.

5.1.2 Effects of Diversity Sampling

We report the results of applying only the diversity sampler. This is done by running K-Means on the augmented corpus for a number of iterations and then sampling from the resulting clusters inversely proportionately to each cluster size.

With no relevance cut-off and only clustering and then sampling for proportionate representation, Table 4 shows that the ndcg@k and precision@k values have both fallen by 6-7%p. This supports that the relevance threshold aids in discarding certain arguments, however diverse they may be in constituting their respective cluster.

6 Conclusion

We present an argument retrieval system combining the strengths of a fine-tuned embedding model and open-source large language models. The embedding model is trained to tell apart relevant arguments from the irrelevant arguments through triplet loss signals leveraging hard negatives. At the same time, the embedding model is also exposed to in-distribution classification examples, such that it detects out-of-distribution (irrelevant) arguments and relays the anomalous finding to the relevance cut-off criterion. LLMs provide diverse anchors to which a given corpus argument may be checked against for membership, and then the member densities are utilized for diverse representation of arguments relevant to a given query.

References

Erik Arakelyan, Arnav Arora, and Isabelle Augenstein. 2023. Topic-guided sampling for data-efficient multi-domain stance detection. *arXiv preprint arXiv:2306.00765*.

Ramy Baly, Giovanni Da San Martino, James Glass, and Preslav Nakov. 2020a. We can detect your bias: Predicting the political ideology of news articles. In *Proceedings of the 2020 Conference on Empirical Methods in Natural Language Processing (EMNLP)*, pages 4982–4991.

Ramy Baly, Georgi Karadzhov, Dimitar Alexandrov, James Glass, and Preslav Nakov. 2018. Predicting factuality of reporting and bias of news media sources. *arXiv preprint arXiv:1810.01765*.

Ramy Baly, Georgi Karadzhov, Jisun An, Haewoon Kwak, Yoan Dinkov, Ahmed Ali, James Glass, and Preslav Nakov. 2020b. What was written vs. who read it: News media profiling using text analysis and social media context. *arXiv preprint arXiv:2005.04518*.

Nicolas Devatine, Philippe Muller, and Chloé Braud. 2022. Predicting political orientation in news with latent discourse structure to improve bias understanding. In *3rd Workshop on Computational Approaches to Discourse (CODI 2022)*, pages 77–85. ACL: Association for Computational Linguistics.

Jacob Devlin, Ming-Wei Chang, Kenton Lee, and Kristina Toutanova. 2019. BERT: Pre-training of deep bidirectional transformers for language understanding. In *Proceedings of the 2019 Conference of the North American Chapter of the Association for Computational Linguistics: Human Language Technologies, Volume 1 (Long and Short Papers)*, pages 4171–4186, Minneapolis, Minnesota. Association for Computational Linguistics.

Roxanne El Baff, Henning Wachsmuth, Khalid Al Khatib, Manfred Stede, and Benno Stein. 2019. Computational argumentation synthesis as a language modeling task. In *Proceedings of the 12th International Conference on Natural Language Generation*, pages 54–64, Tokyo, Japan. Association for Computational Linguistics.

Neele Falk, Andreas Waldis, and Iryna Gurevych. 2024. Overview of perpectivearg2024: The first shared task on perspective argument retrieval. In *Proceedings of the 11th Workshop on Argument Mining*, Bangkok. Association for Computational Linguistics.

Maarten Grootendorst. 2020. Keybert: Minimal keyword extraction with bert.

Momchil Hardalov, Arnav Arora, Preslav Nakov, and Isabelle Augenstein. 2021. Cross-domain label-adaptive stance detection. *arXiv preprint arXiv:2104.07467*.

Matthew Henderson, Rami Al-Rfou, Brian Strope, Yun-Hsuan Sung, László Lukács, Ruiqi Guo, Sanjiv Kumar, Balint Miklos, and Ray Kurzweil. 2017. Efficient natural language response suggestion for smart reply. *arXiv preprint arXiv:1705.00652*.

Carolin Holtermann, Anne Lauscher, and Simone Paolo Ponzetto. 2022. Fair and argumentative language modeling for computational argumentation. *arXiv preprint arXiv:2204.04026*.

Yohan Jo, Haneul Yoo, JinYeong Bak, Alice Oh, Chris Reed, and Eduard Hovy. 2021. Knowledge-enhanced evidence retrieval for counterargument generation. *arXiv preprint arXiv:2109.09057*.

Yunyong Ko, Seongeun Ryu, Soeun Han, Youngseung Jeon, Jaehoon Kim, Sohyun Park, Kyungsik Han, Hanghang Tong, and Sang-Wook Kim. 2023. Khan: knowledge-aware hierarchical attention networks for accurate political stance prediction. In *Proceedings of the ACM Web Conference 2023*, pages 1572–1583.

Yujian Liu, Xinliang Frederick Zhang, David Wegsman, Nick Beauchamp, and Lu Wang. 2022. Politics: Pretraining with same-story article comparison for ideology prediction and stance detection. *arXiv preprint arXiv:2205.00619*.

Christopher D Manning. 2008. *Introduction to information retrieval*. Syngress Publishing,.

Iyad Rahwan, Fouad Zablith, and Chris Reed. 2007. Laying the foundations for a world wide argument web. *Artificial intelligence*, 171(10-15):897–921.

Nils Reimers and Iryna Gurevych. 2019. Sentence-bert: Sentence embeddings using siamese bert-networks. In *Proceedings of the 2019 Conference on Empirical Methods in Natural Language Processing*. Association for Computational Linguistics.

Nils Reimers and Iryna Gurevych. 2020. Making monolingual sentence embeddings multilingual using knowledge distillation. In *Proceedings of the 2020 Conference on Empirical Methods in Natural Language Processing*. Association for Computational Linguistics.

Christian Stab, Johannes Daxenberger, Chris Stahlhut, Tristan Miller, Benjamin Schiller, Christopher Tauchmann, Steffen Eger, and Iryna Gurevych. 2018. Argumentext: Searching for arguments in heterogeneous sources. In *Proceedings of the 2018 conference of the North American chapter of the association for computational linguistics: demonstrations*, pages 21–25.

Simone Teufel et al. 1999. *Argumentative zoning: Information extraction from scientific text*. Ph.D. thesis, Citeseer.

Jannis Vamvas and Rico Sennrich. 2020. X-stance: A multilingual multi-target dataset for stance detection. *arXiv preprint arXiv:2003.08385*.

Henning Wachsmuth, Martin Potthast, Khalid Al Khatib, Yamen Ajjour, Jana Puschmann, Jiani Qu, Jonas Dorsch, Viorel Morari, Janek Bevendorff, and Benno Stein. 2017. Building an argument search engine for the web. In *Proceedings of the 4th Workshop on Argument Mining*, pages 49–59.

Hyperparameter	**Value**
Embedding Model, epochs	10
Embedding Model, ratio (contrastive-to-classification multi-objective relative weighting)	5
Embedding Model, batch size	64
Embedding Model, learning rate	2e-05
Embedding Model, warmup steps	10000
Embedding Model, weight decay	0.01
Clusterer, K (full system)	1
Clusterer, K (ablated (Section 5.1.2))	100

Table 5: Hyperparameters of the system

A Appendix

A.1 Table of hyperparameters

Table 5 shows our system components and its hyperparameters, where relevant.

A.2 Instruction prompt and response examples

Below is a sample from invoking a PHI-3-MINI-4K-INSTRUCT.

Prompt Sample:
Can you provide 10 arguments that favor the following statement and 10 arguments that are against it?: Faut-il renforcer la protection contre le licenciement des travailleuses et travailleurs plus âgé·e·s?

Response Sample:
Arguments in favor of strengthening protection against the dismissal of older workers:

1. Age discrimination: Strengthening protection against dismissal helps prevent age discrimination, ensuring that older workers are not unfairly targeted for layoffs. 2. Experience and knowledge: Older workers often have valuable experience and knowledge that can benefit the company, and protecting them from dismissal helps retain this expertise. 3. Economic stability: Older workers are more likely to have dependents and financial obligations, so protecting them from dismissal can help maintain economic stability for families. 4. Reduced turnover costs: Retaining older workers can reduce

turnover costs, as it is generally more expensive to hire and train new employees. 5. Diversity and inclusion: Protecting older workers from dismissal promotes diversity and inclusion in the workplace, which can lead to better decision-making and innovation. 6. Social justice: Strengthening protection against dismissal of older workers can be seen as a step towards social justice, ensuring that all workers are treated fairly regardless of age. 7. Improved morale: Protecting older workers from dismissal can improve morale and job satisfaction, as employees feel valued and secure in their positions. 8. Reduced unemployment: By protecting older workers from dismissal, the number of unemployed individuals may decrease, as they are less likely to be laid off. 9. Long-term planning: Companies that protect older workers from dismissal can benefit from long-term planning, as they can rely on the experience and knowledge of these employees. 10. Legal compliance: Strengthening protection against dismissal of older workers can help companies comply with existing labor laws and regulations.

Arguments against strengthening protection against the dismissal of older workers:

1. Merit-based decisions: Some argue that dismissals should be based on merit and performance, rather than age, and that protecting older workers from dismissal may hinder this process. 2. Job opportunities for younger workers: Critics argue that protecting older workers from dismissal may limit job opportunities for younger workers, potentially leading to higher unemployment rates among the youth. 3. Innovation and adaptability: Some believe that companies need to be able to adapt quickly to changing market conditions, and protecting older workers from dismissal may hinder this process. 4. Financial burden: Strengthening protection against dismissal of older workers may place a financial burden on companies, as they may be required to provide additional benefits or compensation. 5. Workforce flexibility: Critics argue that protecting older workers from dismissal may limit a company's ability to restructure its workforce and adapt to changing business needs. 6. Ageism concerns: Some argue that strengthening protection against dismissal of older workers may inadvertently reinforce ageism, as it may be perceived as favoring older workers over younger ones. 7. Skill gaps: Critics argue that protecting older workers from dismissal may lead to skill gaps in the workforce, as companies may be less willing to invest in training and development for older employees. 8. Competitive disadvantage: Companies that protect older workers from dismissal may be at a competitive disadvantage compared to those that can more easily restructure their workforce. 9. Employee motivation: Some argue that protecting older workers from dismissal may reduce employee motivation, as younger workers may feel that their opportunities for advancement are limited. 10. Economic efficiency: Critics argue that strengthening protection against dismissal of older workers may reduce economic efficiency, as companies may be less able to respond to market changes and adjust their workforce accordingly.

Author Index

Association for Computational Linguistics
209 N. Eighth Street
Stroudsburg, Pennsylvania 18360

CURRAN ASSOCIATES INC.
proceedings.com

ISBN 979-8-3313-0156-9